Bulimia Nervosa: Basic Research, Diagnosis and Therapy

Bulimia Nervosa: Basic Research, Diagnosis and Therapy

EDITED BY
Manfred M. Fichter

FOREWORD BY
Gerald F. M. Russell

JOHN WILEY & SONS
Chichester · New York · Brisbane · Toronto · Singapore

Original edition – BULIMIA NERVOSA Grundlagen und Behandlung
Published by Ferdinand Enke Verlag, Stuttgart

Other Wiley Editorial Offices

John Wiley & Sons, Inc., 605 Third Avenue, New York, NY 10158-0012, USA

Jacaranda Wiley Ltd, G.P.O. Box 859, Brisbane, Queensland 4001, Australia

John Wiley & Sons (Canada) Ltd, 22 Worcester Road, Rexdale, Ontario M9W 1L1, Canada

John Wiley & Sons (SEA) Pte Ltd, 37 Jalan Pemimpin 05-04, Block B, Union Industrial Building, Singapore 2057

Library of Congress Cataloging-in-Publication Data:

Bulimia nervosa. English.
Bulimia nervosa : basic research, diagnosis, and therapy / edited by Manfred M. Fichter. – English language ed.
p. cm.
Translation of: Bulimia nervosa.
Includes bibliographical references.
ISBN 0 471 92405 9
I. Bulimia nervosa. I. Fichter, Manfred M. II. Title.
[DNLM: 1. Bulimia. WM 175 B9325]
RC552.B84B8413 1990
616.85'263–dc20
DNLM/DLC
for Library of Congress 89–24973
CIP

British Library Cataloguing in Publication Data:
Bulimia nervosa.
1. Man. Bulimia
I. Fichter, Manfred M.
616.85'2

ISBN 0 471 92405 9

Typesetting by Witwell Ltd, Lord Street, Southport
Printed and bound in Great Britain by Courier International Ltd, Tiptree

Contributors

Beumont, Peter, J. V. *Department of Psychiatry, Royal Prince Alfred Hospital; and The University of Sydney, Camperdown, NSW 2006, Australia*

Blundell, John E. *Department of Psychology, University of Leeds, Leeds LS2 9JT, UK*

Bradburn, Isabel S. *Graduate Student in Clinical Psychology, University of California–Berkeley, USA*

Colon, Eduardo *Department of Psychiatry, University of Minnesota, Box 393, Mayo Memorial Building, 420 Delaware Street SE, Minneapolis, MN 55455, USA*

Cooper, Peter J. *Department of Psychiatry, University of Cambridge, Addenbrooke's Hospital, Cambridge CB2 2QQ, UK*

Elton, Martin *Psychiatrische Universitätsklinik München, Nußbaumstr. 7, 8000 München 2, FRG*

Engel, Klaus *Psychiatrisches Landeskrankenhaus, Postfach 41 03 45, 4600 Dortmund, FRG*

Fairburn, Christopher G. *University of Oxford, Department of Psychiatry, Warneford Hospital, Oxford OX3 7JX, UK*

Fichter, Manfred, M. *Klinik Roseneck, Am Roseneck 6, 8210 Prien; and Psychiatrische Klinik und Poliklinik der Universität München, Nußbaumstr. 7, 8000 München 2, FRG*

Grossman, Sebastian P. *The University of Chicago, Department of*

Behavioral Sciences, Committee on Biopsychology, Green Hall, 5848 South Univ. Ave, Chicago, Ill. 60 637, USA

Halmi, Katherine A. *Cornell University Medical College, New York Hospital – Westchester Division, 21 Bloomingdale Road, White Plains, NY 10 605, USA*

Herpertz-Dahlmann, Beate *Klinik für Kinder- und Jugendpsychiatrie, Klinikum der Phillips-Universität Marburg, Hans-Sachs-Str. 6, 3550 Marburg, FRG*

Herzog, David B. *Eating Disorders Unit, Child Psychiatry Service, Massachusetts General Hospital; and Associate Professor of Psychiatry at the Harvard Medical School, Boston, MA 02 114, USA*

von der Heydte, Sybille *Psychiatrische Universitätsklinik München, Nußbaumstr. 7, 8000 München 2, FRG*

Hill, Andrew J. *Department of Psychology, University of Leeds, Leeds LS2 9JT, UK*

Hoffmann, Romana *Aktionskreis Eß- und Magersucht, Westendstr. 39, 8000 München, FRG*

Hudson, James I. *Epidemiology Laboratory and Laboratories for Psychiatric Research, McLean Hospital, 115 Mill St, Belmont, Massachusetts 02 178; and Harvard Medical School, Boston, MA 02 114, USA*

Keller, Martin B. *Outpatient Research, Department of Psychiatry, Massachusetts General Hospital; and Associate Professor of Psychiatry at the Harvard Medical School, Boston, MA 02 114, USA*

Laessle, Reinhard G. *Max-Planck-Institut für Psychiatrie, Kraepelinstr. 10, 8000 München 40, FRG*

Lavori, Philip W. *Department of Psychiatry, Massachusetts General Hospital; and Associate Professor of Psychiatry at the Harvard Medical School, Boston, MA 02 114, USA*

Lawton, Clare L. *Department of Psychology, University of Leeds, Leeds LS2 9JT, UK*

Lennerts, Wolfgang *Department of Psychiatry, Royal Prince Alfred*

Hospital; and The University of Sydney, Camperdown, NSW 2006, Australia

Mall, Hartmut *Department of Psychosomatic Medicine, University of Ulm, Hochsträß 8, 7900 Ulm, FRG*

Meyer, Adolf-Ernst *Abt. für Psychosomatik/Psychotherapie, II. Medizinische Klinik des Universitätskrankenhauses, Eppendorf, Martinistr. 52, 2000 Hamburg, FRG*

Mitchell, James E *Department of Psychiatry, University of Minnesota, Box 393, Mayo Memorial Building, 420 Delaware Street SE, Minneapolis, MN 55455, USA*

Morley, John E. *St Louis University, School of Medicine, 1402 S. Grand, Room M-239, St Louis, Missouri 63104, USA*

Nutzinger, D. O. *Psychiatrische Universitätsklinik Wien, Währinger Gürtel 18–20, 1090 Wien, Austria*

Ott, Ingrid L. *Harvard Medical School, Boston, MA 02 114, USA*

O'Connor, M. *Department of Psychiatry, Royal Prince Alfred Hospital; and The University of Sydney, Camperdown, NSW 2006, Australia*

Pirke, Karl M. *Neuroendokrinologie, Max-Planck-Institut für Psychiatrie, Kraepelinstr. 10, 8000 München 40, FRG*

Pomeroy, Claire *Department of Psychiatry, University of Minnesota, Box 393, Mayo Memorial Building, 420 Delaware Street SE, Minneapolis, MN 55455, USA*

Pope, Harrison G. Jr *Epidemiology Laboratory and Laboratories for Psychiatric Research, McLean Hospital, 115 Mill St, Belmont, Massachusetts 02 178, USA; and Harvard Medical School, Boston, MA 02 114, USA*

Poustka, Fritz *Department for Child and Adolescent Psychiatry, University of Frankfurt, Heinrich-Hoffmann-Str. 10, 6000 Frankfurt, FRG*

Remschmidt, Helmut *Klinik für Kinder- und Jugendspsychiatrie, Klinikum der Phillips-Universität, Hans-Sachs-Str. 6, 3550 Marburg, FRG*

Robinson, Paul *Academic Department of Psychological Medicine, Kings College School of Medicine and Dentistry; and The Institute of Psychiatry, Denmark Hill, London SE5 9RS, UK*

Rogers, Peter J. *Department of Psychology, University of Leeds, Leeds LS2 9JT, UK*

Russell, Gerald F. M. *The Institute of Psychiatry, De Crespigny Park, London SE5 8AF, UK*

Steere, Jane *Department of Experimental Psychology, University of Cambridge, Downing Street, Cambridge CB2 3EB, UK*

Touyz, S. W. *Department of Psychiatry, Royal Prince Alfred Hospital; and The University of Sydney, Camperdown, NSW 2006, Australia*

Vandereycken, Walter *Department of Psychotherapy, University Psychiatric Center, Leuvensesteenweg 517, 3070 Kortenberg, Belgium*

Zwaan, M. de *Psychiatrische Universitätsklinik Wien, Währinger Gürtel 18–20, 1090 Wien, Austria*

Contents

Foreword *G. F. M. Russell* xi

Part I. Introduction

1 **Bulimia nervosa and bulimic behaviour** 3
M. M. Fichter

Part II. Diagnosis, Symptomatology and Course of Illness

2 **The diagnostic status and clinical assessment of bulimia nervosa** 17
G. F. M. Russell

3 **Assessment of the specific psychopathology of bulimia nervosa** 37
C. G. Fairburn, J. Steere and *P. J. Cooper*

4 **The Structured Interview for Anorexia and Bulimia Nervosa (SIAB): development and characteristics of a (semi-) standardized instrument** 57
M. M. Fichter, M. Elton, K. Engel, A.-E. Meyer, F. Poustka, H. Mall, and *S. von der Heydte*

5 **Medical complications in bulimia nervosa** 71
J. Mitchell, C. Pomeroy and *E. Colon*

6 **Bulimia in children and adolescents** 84
H. Remschmidt and *B. Herpertz-Dahlmann*

7 **Bulimia (nervosa) in the male** 99
M. M. Fichter and *R. Hoffmann*

8 **Affective disorders and bulimic syndromes** 112
R. G. Laessle

9 **Course and outcome of bulimia nervosa** 126
D. B. Herzog, M. B. Keller, P. W. Lavori, I. S. Bradburn and *I. L. Ott*

Part III. Biological Basis

10 **Brain mechanisms concerned with food intake and body-weight regulation** 145
S. P. Grossman

11 **Gastric control of food intake** 160
P. Robinson

12 **Perception of satiety in bulimia (nervosa)** 180
K. A. Halmi

13 **Psychopharmacology of hunger and satiety** 188
J. E. Blundell, C. L. Lawton, A. J. Hill and *P. J. Rogers*

14 **Stress as a modulator of ingestive behaviors** 208
J. E. Morley

15 **Central neurotransmitter disturbances in bulimia (nervosa)** 223
K. M. Pirke

16 **Endocrine dysfunctions in bulimia (nervosa)** 235
M. M. Fichter and *K. M. Pirke*

17 **Menstrual cycle and neuroendocrine disturbances of the gonadal axis in bulima (nervosa)** 258
K. M. Pirke

Part IV. Therapy

18 **Psychological therapies in bulimia nervosa** 273
M. M. Fichter

19 **Behavioural treatment of bulimia (nervosa)** 292
D. O. Nutzinger and *M. de Zwaan*

20 **Nutritional counselling in the treatment of bulimia** 308
P. J. V. Beumont, M. O'Connor, W. Lennerts and *S. W. Touyz*

21 **The relevance of body-image disturbances for the treatment of bulimia** 320
W. Vandereycken

22 **Psychopharmacological treatment of bulimia** 331
J. I. Hudson and *H. G. Pope Jr*

Part V. Appendices

Appendix 1 Diagnostic criteria 345

Appendix 2 Self-report instruments for the assessment of relevant symptoms in eating disorders 352

Index 357

Foreword

The English version of this book is timely and follows an earlier version in the German language. For the first time a truly international team of clinicians and scientists has been assembled to pool their knowledge about the recently discovered disorder — 'bulimia nervosa'. It is highly appropriate that this book contains several contributions emanating from the continent of Europe where important advances have been made in recent years.

The first detailed description of 'bulimia nervosa' appeared in 1979. I must bear the responsibility for applying this term to patients troubled by recurrent bouts of overeating, who are so anxious to nullify the fattening effects of food that they induce vomiting or abuse purgatives. As in patients with anorexia nervosa there is a preoccupation with eating and a morbid dread of fatness; indeed there is frequently a history of a previous episode of anorexia nervosa. On the one hand the body weight of these patients may be below, at or above the average range shown in population statistical tables. On the other hand, they struggle relentlessly to maintain their weight below a self-imposed threshold. My concern about the consequences of having described and labelled this disorder is twofold. First there is a view that 'binge eating' — a distasteful term — can spread through social contagion. Let us trust that the medical and scientific literature is not part of this contagion. Secondly, there remains much concern among writers that patients with bulimia nervosa do not make up a homogeneous diagnostic entity. This was recognised in the original description. Understandably there is a wish to delineate more sharply categories of eating disorders. Yet it is doubtful whether our level of knowledge justifies further sub-classification of bulimia nervosa, or indeed of anorexia nervosa. Both the Diagnostic and Statistical Manual of Mental Disorders (DSM3R) and the International Classification of Disease (draft of ICD10) have accepted the term 'bulimia nervosa' and there is now close agreement between the diagnostic criteria of the two classificatory systems. This is satisfying and will facilitate the comparison of research findings from different countries.

Significant progress has been made in disentangling the causes of bulimia nervosa but much remains unknown about the fundamental aetiology. It is best to consider a multidimensional approach to the understanding of bulimia nervosa, partly because no clear single causal factor has yet emerged, partly because it is likely that several interacting causes need to be present before the illness manifests itself in a given patient. It is clearly important to conduct more research into the aetiology of bulimia nervosa which is now more prevalent than anorexia nervosa. Like anorexia nervosa it is much commoner in young women than men, but the occurrence of the disorder in the male is probably under reported. It may be useful to draw attention to one specific pathogenic mechanism for bulimia nervosa which is stressed in several chapters in this book including those by M. M. Fichter and K. M. Pirke. This is the mechanism of a sub-optimal nutritional state resulting from the alternation between fasting and overeating, and from maintaining body weight at a level below an individual patient's 'healthy' or optimal level. An important part of this pathogenesis may be the patient's careful avoidance of carbohydrates while fasting, which may interfere with central nervous concentrations of serotonin.

It is not appropriate to mention any further individual contributions in this book. Suffice it is to say that the Editor has assembled a team of investigators whose research in recent years has increased our understanding of the clinical features and associated morbidity of bulimia nervosa, its causation and pathogenesis, and its treatment. The Editor merits warm congratulations for his initiative and for persuading the contributors to document concisely the accumulated knowledge on bulimia nervosa in this well-timed book. It is to be hoped that the next decade will witness further successful research. In the meantime this book will facilitate the clinician's task to treat his patients more effectively and understand better the nature of bulimia nerovsa.

Gerald F. M. Russell MD
Institute of Psychiatry, London

Part I

Introduction

1

Bulimia nervosa and bulimic behaviour

Manfred M. Fichter
University of Munich, Munich
and Klinik Roseneck, Prien

Russell (1979; see also this volume, Chapter 2) fired the starting pistol for the scientific investigation of a hitherto barely recognized syndrome, bulimia nervosa. He saw the disorder as characterized by an irresistible urge to consume large quantities of food, purging behaviour (e.g. self-induced vomiting, abuse of laxatives), and a morbid fear of fatness. The syndrome is not new. In the year AD 8 in the eighth book of the *Metamorphoses* the Roman poet Ovid described the saga of the godless transgressor Erysichton, whom the goddess Ceres punished with an insatiable hunger; she forced him to eat himself out of house and home and finally to eat himself. Syndromes similar to bulimia nervosa were given earlier names which did not become established, for example hyperorexia nervosa (Ziolko, 1967, 1976), thin–fat people (Bruch, 1973), bulimiarexia (Boskind-Lohdahl, 1976), dietary-chaos syndrome (Palmer, 1979) and bulivomia (Meyer, 1980). In past decades some cases of bulimia—for example Janet's 'Nadia' (1903) and Binswanger's 'Ellen West' (1944)—were categorized under a different diagnosis for want of an appropriate name. The existence of the syndrome as such is therefore not new. However, what is new is its relatively wide distribution, especially in young women.

The epidemiology of bulima (nervosa) has been reviewed by Fichter (1984) and recently by Gray, Ford and Kelly (1987) and Cooper, Charnock and Taylor (1987). In this volume it is reviewed by Remschmidt and Herpertz-Dahlmann. The conclusion that in Western Europe and North America 2–4 per cent of all young women between 18 and 35 years suffer from bulimia according to DSM-III criteria (American Psychiatric Association, 1980) may not be far from correct.

Figure 1.1 summarizes the scientific studies of various eating disorders from 1964 to 1985/86 based on data from two reputable German medical (MEDLARS) and psychological (PSYCHINFO) literature services. Publications on anorexia nervosa and hyperphagia increased in the middle of the seventies and those on bulimia at the beginning of the eighties. The relatively broad distribution of bulimic eating disorders, especially in young women, represents a challenge for clinicians and scientists to develop an effective therapy, and it poses further questions regarding the aetiology and reasons for the increased prevalence of this syndrome.

In this volume, internationally acknowledged experts (e.g. Russell, Fairburn) contribute to the discussion of problems of diagnosis, nosological subdivision and categorization of eating disorders and to the recognition of relevant symptoms. It is due to these European scientists that the American Psychiatric Association's new diagnostic criteria for bulimia nervosa (DSM-III-R) are narrower and more precise than the broader criteria for bulimia set by the *Diagnostic and Statistical Manual of Mental Disorders* (DSM-III) which were previously used. The criterion 'E' (persistent overconcern with body shape and weight) has been introduced and the name of the syndrome has been changed to 'bulimia nervosa'. However, the use of this name in the literature has varied: (1) Russell (1979) suggested that it be used for bulimic patients whose case histories include anorexia nervosa; (2) according to DSM-III-R criteria, patients with anorexia are explicitly excluded from the diagnosis 'bulimia nervosa'; or, in the rare cases in which both disorders are manifested, both diagnostic terms should be applied. In its diagnostic criteria, ICD 10 follows the international diagnostic scheme of WHO (1987). The following diagnostic groups are proposed: anorexia nervosa, bulimia nervosa, bulimia in persons with normal body weight; overweight in association with psychiatric disorders; vomiting associated with psychological disorders; and other less clearly defined eating disorders. Thus, in ICD 10, several categories are available for bulimic behaviour. The present volume is primarily concerned with bulimia nervosa, but also considers other bulimic syndromes which do not satisfy the narrower criteria. In view of this, we use the purely descriptive term 'bulimic syndrome'. This volume is not concerned with the more common, less severe forms of bulimic behaviour which are not clinically significant. However, the reader must bear in mind that contributions to this volume (and the literature cited in these) include examples of bulimic patients diagnosed according to broader (DSM-III) or narrower (Russell, 1979; DSM-III-R, 1987) criteria.

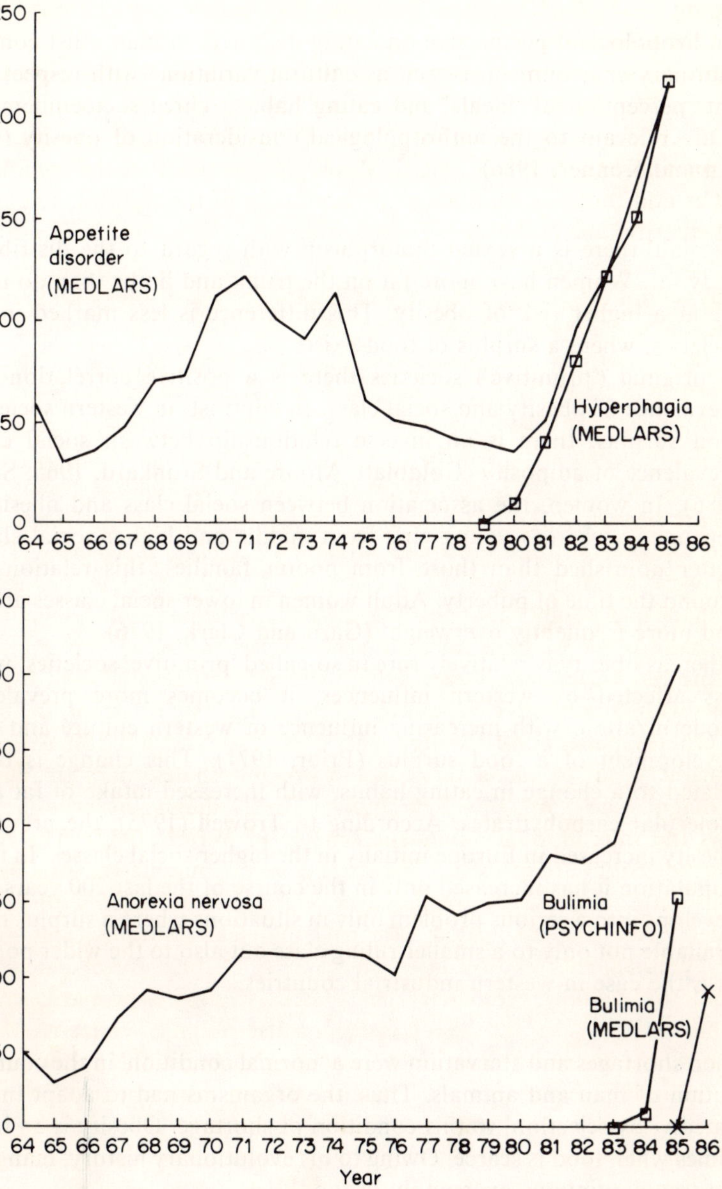

Figure 1.1. Number of publications per year from 1964 to 1985/1986 on various eating disorders from data collated by two information services for scientific literature (MEDLARS, PSYCHINFO)

Anthropological Perspectives on Eating Disorders

An anthropological perspective on eating disorders in man must consider his evolutionary environment as well as cultural variations with respect to body weight, perception of 'ideals' and eating habits. Three socioepidemiological facts are relevant to the anthropological consideration of obesity (compare Brown and Konner, 1986):

1. In 'man' there is a sexual dimorphism with regard to the distribution of body fat. Women have more fat on the trunk and limbs than do men, and are at a higher risk of obesity. This difference is less marked in western societies, where a surplus of food exists.
2. In original ('primitive') societies there is a positive correlation between prevalence of obesity and social class. In contrast, in western societies with food surplus, there is an inverse relationship between social class and prevalence of adiposity (Goldblatt, Moore and Stunkard, 1965; Stunkard, 1986). In women, the association between social class and obesity is age dependent: whereas young girls from middle and higher social classes are better nourished than those from poorer families, this relation reverses around the time of puberty. Adult women in lower social classes are heavier and more frequently overweight (Garn and Clark, 1976).
3. Whereas obesity is relatively rare in so-called 'primitive' societies, which are less affected by western influences, it becomes more prevalent with modernization, with increasing influence of western culture and with the development of a food surplus (Prior, 1971). This change is obviously related to a change in eating habits, with increased intake of fat and low-molecular carbohydrates. According to Trowell (1975), the prevalence of obesity increased in Europe initially in the higher social classes. In the wider population it has increased only in the course of the last 200 years. Obesity develops into a serious problem only in situations where a surplus of food is available not only to a smaller ruling class but also to the wider population, as is the case in western industrial countries.

Food shortages and starvation were a 'normal condition' in the course of the evolution of man and animals. Thus, the organisms had to adapt themselves repeatedly, by selection, to this condition of shortage. Obesity is an insurance for times when food is scarce. Owing to his evolutionary history, man is poorly suited to a continuous oversupply of food!

Changes in 'ideal body image' can be considered in this evolutionary context. In so-called 'primitive' cultures, accumulation of fat and obesity were desirable aims for men, and especially for women. A corpulent body conformed with prevailing aesthetic ideals and was an expression of wealth, success and influence. In this century — especially in the past three decades (Garner *et al.*, 1980) — a change has occurred in western industrial countries with regard to the aesthetically ideal body shape. From an anthropological, evolutionary and epidemiological point of view this development is understandable: had the previous ideal of a well-covered body continued, the risk of obesity and its consequent diseases would have been greater for the wider population than it is under conditions in which the 'thinness ideal' prevails. The ideal of the slim body is more strongly developed in women than in men (Fallon and Rozin, 1985). Particularly for women in western industrialized countries, sociocultural ideals regarding the criteria for an attractive body exert pressure to lose body weight and to pursue a cosmetic ideal which can no longer be medically approved.

Garner *et al.* (1980) showed that the 'thinness ideal' affects different social groups in different ways. People to whom body shape and weight are important (e.g. for professional reasons), and who are also achievement oriented (e.g. ballet dancers), run a higher than normal risk of developing eating disorders. In addition, for women in North America, the gap between desired and 'real' body weight has increased. The ideal of physical slimness for women (and increasingly for men) is so ubiquitous in our western culture that researchers have thus far seen little reason for systematic study of this allegedly obvious fact.

In western industrial countries (and increasingly also in third world countries), this slimness ideal, understandable from an anthropological and evolutionary point of view, often leads to drastic dieting and fasting which, based on medical–physiological considerations, cannot be healthy and can cause considerable disturbances in neurotransmitter functions (see Pirke, this volume, Chapter 15) and hormonal regulation (see Fichter and Pirke, this volume, Chapter 16). Changes in noradrenaline turnover due to insufficient nutrition and decrease in blood concentrations of the thyroid hormone T3 cause vegetative dysfunctions and a decrease in basal metabolism. These temporarily increase food utilization and the tendency to gain weight after periods of dieting and fasting.

The fact that it is predominantly women who are affected by bulimic and anorexic eating disorders and psychogenic overweight has given rise to feminist interpretations of eating disorders (Orbach, 1985; Wooley and Wooley, 1982; Wooley, Wooley and Dyrenforth, 1979). From this perspective, the 'thinness ideal' is viewed as a further means of oppressing women in a patriarchal society. Dieting and fasting are supposedly only an expression of this oppression. Independent of these feminist origins, this 'antidiet model' (Orbach, 1982, 1985) has been incorporated into the treatment of eating disorders (see chapters on therapy in this volume).

Obesity and Bulimia

Stunkard (1986, p. 589) reported that the 'night-eating syndrome' occurs in approximately 10 per cent of obese subjects, mainly women. This syndrome is characterized by lack of appetite in the morning and hyperphagia and sleeplessness in the evening. It is presumed to be triggered by stress, similar to the 'binge-eating' syndrome, which Stunkard found in about 5 per cent of obese subjects. Hilde Bruch (1973) has expressed the firm opinion that there are important similarities between psychologically based obesity, bulimia ('thin–fat people') and anorexia nervosa. Disturbances of body image, disturbances of proprio- and interoceptive perception, and an all-pervasive feeling of personal ineffectiveness and worthlessness are present in all three disorders. This does not exclude other reasons for under- or overweight. Although anorexia nervosa, bulimia and psychogenic obesity differ with regard to weight dimensions, they overlap quantitatively and, in psychological characteristics, show considerable similarities (see Bruch, 1973). Hudson *et al.* (unpublished manuscript) found a high prevalence rate of affective disorders in underweight and overweight bulimic patients, but not in non-bulimic overweight persons. In the future, closer collaboration between researchers who deal with obesity and those who study bulimic and anorexic eating disorders seems desirable. Biological research papers on obesity (Bray, 1986; Garrow, 1986; Björntorp, 1986), analyses of the influence of psychological variables on the development of obesity (Striegel-Moore and Rodin, 1986), and the investigation of the benefits and limitations of weight-reducing diets (Nicholas and Dwyer, 1986) can make a considerable contribution to the understanding of bulimic and anorexic eating disorders.

Aetiological Factors in the Development of Bulimic Syndromes

The 'thinness ideal' has an especially powerful adverse effect on younger persons who are searching for their identity, lack self-confidence and self-assurance, are overinfluenced by social norms, and who suppress or do not recognize their own needs and are therefore unable to express these. These persons depend to a high degree on the attention of and acknowledgement by other people. Deviation from the real or perceived 'thinness ideal' may precipitate a severe crisis in these insecure subjects and, in extreme cases, induce them to force their body into the polypemonic bed of the ruling aesthetic ideal through fasting and dieting on the one hand and through purging behaviour (e.g. vomiting, abuse of laxatives, appetite-reducing drugs, spitting out of food and the taking of diuretics and thyroid preparations) on the other. Questioning of 764 bulimic women revealed that 80 per cent were unwilling to gain, say, 5 kg in weight in order to prevent attacks of extreme hunger. They preferred to accept the disorder rather than distance themselves from the societal ideal of slimness (Fichter *et al.*, 1986).

It would be one-sided to take into account only sociocultural factors in the development of the disorder. In considering the aetiology of bulimic disorders it is important to bear in mind that the majority of women (and men) do *not* develop bulimic eating disorders. Sociocultural factors can explain the marked increase in the prevalence of bulimic and anorexic diseases. They are, however, not able to explain the high concordance rate of monozygotic twins in comparison with dizygotic twins in anorexic patients (Fichter, 1985) and in bulimic patients (Fichter, Nögel and Brunner, 1990); nor can they explain the above-mentioned fact that under the same social conditions the majority of the population do not develop bulimic or anorexic eating disorders.

Figure 1.2 shows the effects of the most important aetiological factors (biological factors, individual deficiencies, sociocultural factors and life events and chronic difficulties) on the individual. The bulimic disorder may be regarded as an attempt to solve problems of insecurity, anxiety and mood lability. This one-sided battle to achieve physical slimness and to eliminate other concerns leads, however, to a vicious circle: bulimic behaviour with reduced food intake and partial malnutrition (often in people with suboptimal individual body weight) causes vitamin and mineral deficiencies, endocrine dysfunctions, disorders of the vegetative nervous system, temporarily decreased basal metabolism and increased irritability. Physiological consequences include uncontrollable hunger and attacks of 'binge-eating' which, due to the concern to avoid weight gain, lead to anxiety, reduced self-esteem and social isolation. The fear of being too fat is fought by further dieting and fasting or by 'purging behaviour'; thus the bulimic circle is closed.

Principles for the treatment of bulimic eating disorders can be derived from this model. Occasionally, patients' will to cure themselves may suffice, so that a single-pointed approach (e.g. mere advice on eating habits, or exclusive work on dysfunctional thoughts and the maintenance of self-esteem) can lead to considerable improvement. In more severely affected bulimic patients the therapeutic approach has to proceed from several angles. Descriptions of such therapeutic approaches can be found in the chapters by Beumont *et al.*, Fichter, Hudson and Pope, Nutzinger and de Zwaan, and Vandereycken (this volume, Chapters 18–22). Diagnostic criteria and issues concerning bulimic eating disorders are dealt with in detail by Russell (this volume, Chapter 2). During the past decade, this area has undergone extensive development and revision. In this field Russell's contributions are considerable and his article gives first-hand information regarding the history and current state of the diagnosis of bulimic eating disorders.

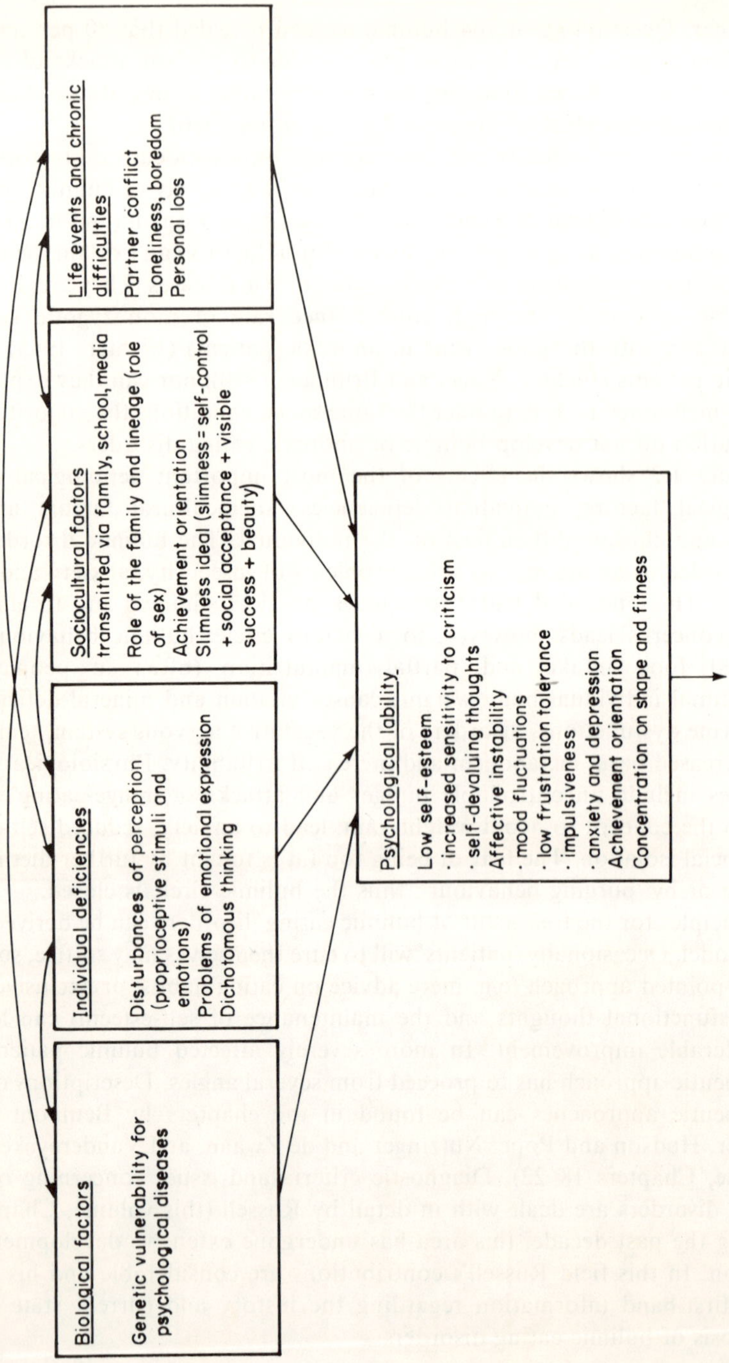

Biological factors
Genetic vulnerability for psychological diseases
Individual deficiencies
Disturbances of perception (proprioceptive stimuli and emotions)
Problems of emotional expression
Dichotomous thinking
Sociocultural factors
transmitted via family, school, media
Role of the family and lineage (role of sex)
Achievement orientation
Slimness ideal (slimness = self-control + social acceptance + visible success + beauty)
Life events and chronic difficulties
Partner conflict
Loneliness, boredom
Personal loss
Psychological lability
Low self-esteem
increased sensitivity to criticism
. self-devaluing thoughts
Affective instability
. mood fluctuations
. low frustration tolerance
. impulsiveness
. anxiety and depression
Achievement orientation
Concentration on shape and fitness

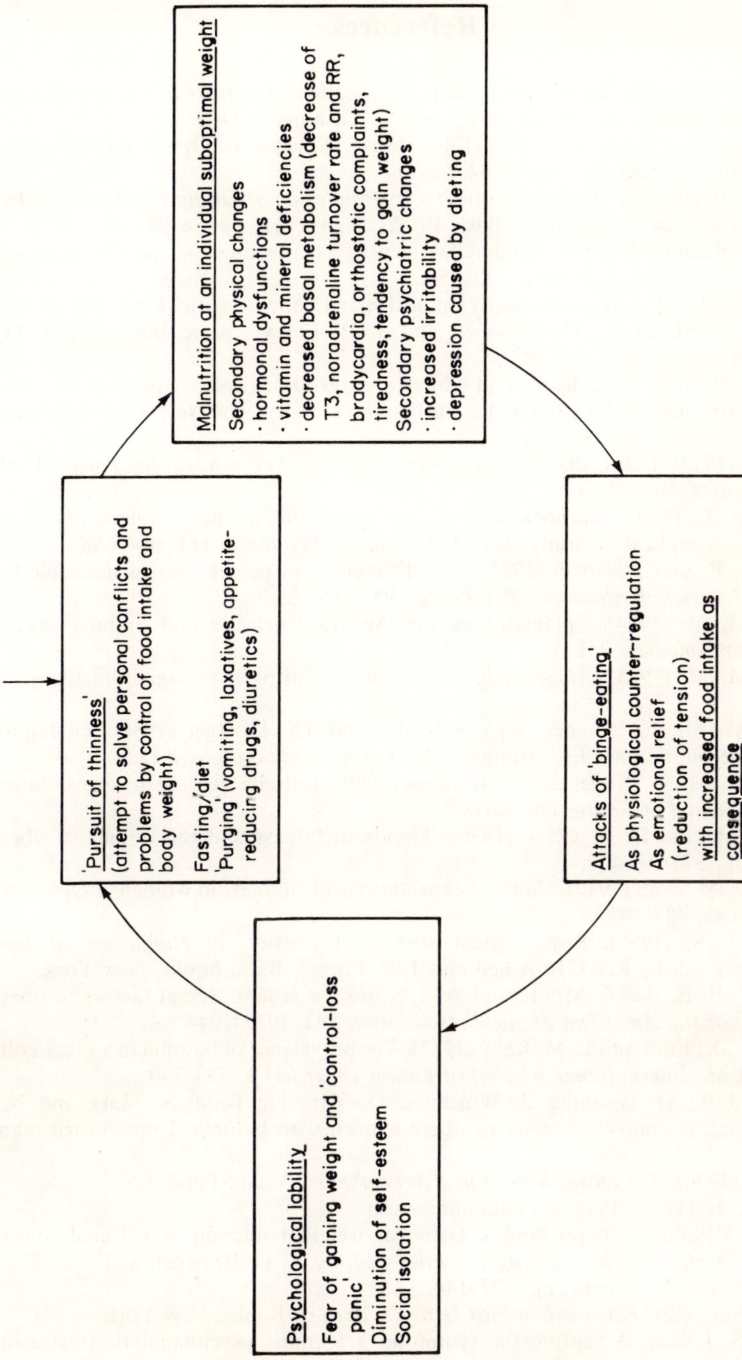

Figure 1.2. Model for the development and maintenance of bulimic eating disorders

References

American Psychiatric Association (1980). *Diagnostic and Statistical Manual of Mental Disorders — Revision (DSM-III-R).* APA, Washington DC.

Binswanger, L. (1944). Der Fall Ellen West. *Schweizer Archiv für Neurologie, Neurochirurgie und Psychiatrie* **54**, 69–117.

Björntorp, P. (1986). Fat cells and obesity. In *Handbook of Eating Disorders*, ed. by K. D. Brownell and J. P. Foreyt. Basic Books, New York, pp. 88–98.

Boskind-Lohdahl, M. (1976). Cinderella's stepsisters: a feminist perspective of anorexia nervosa and bulimia. *Signs* **2**, 342–356.

Bray, G. A. (1986). Effects of obesity on health and happiness. In *Handbook of Eating Disorders*, ed. by K. D. Brownell and J. P. Foreyt. Basic Books, New York, pp. 3–44.

Brown, P. J. and M. J. Konner (1986). An anthropological perspective on obesity. Paper presented at the Conference on Human Obesity, The New York Academy of Sciences, June.

Bruch, H. (1973). Eating disorders. *Obesity, Anorexia Nervosa and the Person Within.* Basic Books, New York.

Cooper, P. J., D. J. Charnock and M. J. Taylor (1987). The prevalence of bulimia nervosa. A replication study. *British Journal of Psychiatry* **151**, 684–686.

Fallon, A. E. and P. Rozin (1985). Sex differences in perceptions of desirable body shape. *Journal of Abnormal Psychology* **94**, 102–105.

Fichter, M. M. (1984). Epidemiologie der Anorexia nervosa und Bulimia. *Aktuelle Ernährungsmedizin* **9**, 8–13.

Fichter, M. M. (1985). *Magersucht und Bulimia.* Springer Verlag, Heidelberg, New York.

Fichter, M. M., E. Brunner, B. Wellhoener and Th. Eiberger (1986). Epidemische Zunahme bulimischer Eßstörungen. *Psychoneuroendocrinology* **12**.

Fichter, M. M., R. Nögel and E. Brunner (1990). Bulimia nervosa in twins. *International Journal of Eating Disorders.*

Garn, S. M. and D. C. Clark (1976). Trends in fatness and the origins of obesity. *Pediatrics* **57**, 443–456.

Garner, D. M. *et al.* (1980). Cultural expectations of thinness in women. *Psychological Reports* **47**, 483–491.

Garrow, J. S. (1986). Physiological aspects of obesity. In *Handbook of Eating Disorders*, ed. by K. D. Brownell and J. P. Foreyt. Basic Books, New York.

Goldblatt, P. B., M. E. Moore and A. J. Stunkard (1965). Social factors in obesity. *Journal of the American Medical Association* **192**, 1039–1044.

Gray, J. J., K. Ford and L. M. Kelly (1987). The prevalence of bulimia in a black college population. *International Journal of Eating Disorders* **6**, 733–740.

Hudson, J. I., H. G. Pope, J. Wurtman, D. Yurgelun-Todd, S. Mark and N. E. Rosenthal. A controlled study of obese women with bulimia. Unpublished manuscript.

Janet, P. (1930). *Les Obsessions et la Psychasthenie*. Alcan, Paris.

Meyer, A. E. (1980). Personal communication.

Nicholas, P. and J. Dwyer (1986). Diets for weight reduction: nutritional considerations. In *Handbook of Eating Disorders*, ed. by K. D. Brownell and J. P. Foreyt. Basic Books, New York, pp. 122–144.

Orbach, S. (1982). *Fat is a Feminist Issue II.* Berkley Books, New York.

Orbach, S. (1985). Accepting the symptom: a feminist psychoanalytic treatment of anorexia nervosa. In *Handbook of Psychotherapy for Anorexia Nervosa and*

Bulimia, ed. by D. M. Garner and P. E. Garfinkel. Guilford Press, London, New York.

Palmer, R. L. (1979). The dietary chaos syndrome: a useful new term? *British Journal of Medical Psychology* **52**, 187–190.

Prior, I. A. (1971). The price of civilization. *Nutrition Today* **6**(4), 2–11.

Russell, G. F. M. (1979). Bulimia nervosa: an ominous variant of anorexia nervosa. *Psychological Medicine* **9**, 429–448.

Striegel-Moore, R. H. and J. Rodin (1986). The influence of psychological variables in obesity. In *Handbook of Eating Disorders*, ed. by K. D. Brownell and J. P. Foreyt. Basic Books, New York, pp. 99–121.

Stunkard, A. J. (1986). Adipositas. In *Psychosomatische Medizin*, ed. by T. von Uexkull. Urban & Schwarzenberg, Munich, Vienna, Baltimore, pp. 583–599.

Trowell, H. (1975). Obesity in the western world. *Plant Foods for Man* **1**, 157–165.

Wooley, O. W., S. C. Wooley and S. R. Dyrenforth (1979). Obesity and women II. A neglected feminist topic. *Women's Studies International Quarterly* **2**, 81–92.

Wooley, O. W. and S. C. Wooley (1982). The Beverly Hills eating disorders: the mass marketing of anorexia nervosa (editorial). *International Journal of Eating Disorders* **1**, 57–69.

Ziolko, H. U. (1967). Hyperorexia-anorexia. *Hippokrates* **13**, 522–526.

Ziolko, H. U. (1976). Hyperorexia nervosa. *Psychotherapy and Medical Psychology* **26**, 10–12.

Part II

Diagnosis, Symptomatology and Course of Illness

2

The diagnostic status and clinical assessment of bulimia nervosa

Gerald F. M. Russell
The Institute of Psychiatry and the Maudsley Hospital, London

The diagnostic term 'bulimia nervosa' was introduced in the late nineteen seventies to describe a category of patients who were prone to episodes of overeating and attempted to mitigate the fattening effects of the ingested food by inducing vomiting or abusing purgatives (Russell, 1979). This new terminology was considered to be appropriate in view of the constancy and significance of this behaviour, but it was thought premature to regard the disorder as constituting a distinct syndrome. Since then much has been written on the subject of bulimia nervosa and the less clearly defined disorder of 'bulimia' or 'normal-weight bulimia'. In particular, there has been a vigorous debate about terminology, specific diagnostic criteria and the relationship of this group of disorders to anorexia nervosa (Russell, 1985a; Halmi, 1985; Fairburn and Garner, 1986). These discussions have generally been fruitful. They were followed by a welcome degree of international agreement regarding terminology and diagnostic criteria. The agreements have been embodied in the two principal systems of classification of diseases — the tenth revision of the *International Classification of Diseases* (ICD 10, World Health Organization, 1987) and the Revision of the *Diagnostic and Statistical Manual of Mental Disorders* (DSM-III-R) (American Psychiatric Association, 1987). In particular, both systems have adopted the term 'bulimia nervosa' for the more distinctive syndrome.

Nevertheless, the diagnostic status of bulimic disorders, including bulimia nervosa, remains problematic for several reasons. First, this clinical syndrome has only been recognized in recent years and a body of solid research findings has yet to be accumulated. Secondly, there is evidence to suggest that bulimia nervosa may be particularly prone to changes in its clinical form and content, representing a transformation of anorexia nervosa over recent decades in response to social and cultural forces. Such a transformation is in keeping with the historical evolution of psychiatric disorders in general under the influence of changing fashions (Hare, 1981). The neuroses in particular have for long been recognized as having a 'contemporary style' of presentation (Jaspers, 1959). Similar arguments have been brought forward to suggest that anorexia nervosa and bulimic disorders have evolved under the influence of pathoplastic causal factors, and this evolution may not yet be complete (Russell, 1985b).

In order to tackle the problems surrounding the specific delineation of bulimia nervosa and particularly its relationship to anorexia nervosa, it will be necessary to set these issues in the general context of the diagnostic exercise in psychiatry. We shall need to consider the theoretical principles underlying systems of classification of disease and psychiatric disorders in particular. Before turning to this task, however, we should carefully examine the different ways patients present themselves to clinicians and review the data pertinent to the diagnosis of bulimia nervosa. The diagnosis of an individual patient's disorder should obviously go beyond mere labelling. To be useful it should include a broad clinical appraisal so as to point the way to the optimum choice of treatment and the accurate prediction of outcome in that patient.

The Clinical Presentations of Bulimia Nervosa

By the time a patient presents herself for treatment, her symptoms may have been established for a long time, often several years. The onset and course of her illness should be reconstructed. The patient's narrative will disclose precipitating events, portray the setting for the origin of her symptoms, and reveal fluctuations in their severity in response to changing circumstances. It is important to focus on the onset of the patient's concern about her body size and shape, a concern which often begins in adolescence. The following two case histories illustrate the settings in which bulimia nervosa may develop, the clinical presentations and course according to the type and severity of the illness.

Illustrative case histories

Patient 1

This patient finally sought treatment at the age of 29, although she had halfheartedly approached doctors and therapists during the preceding six years only to neglect their advice. She linked the onset of her illness with two events. She felt that her puberty had been rather late, having experienced a growth spurt and her first menstrual period at 16. Her weight had risen to over 60 kg (133 lb), and she decided to follow a diet. She lost some weight but could not remember how much. The second event occurred at the age of 17: she became pregnant by a boyfriend she had first met while they were both schoolchildren. She decided to have an abortion which she found distressing and began to feel depressed, guilty, shameful, unattractive and lacking in self-confidence. She found that she could obtain temporary relief from her tension and unhappiness by overeating and vomiting.

The eating disturbance persisted for the following 12 years. She began each day with a resolution to avoid food as much as possible. But she usually succumbed to one or two episodes of overeating daily. At first she would eat the remnants of meals left by other members of the family, but went on to the consumption of sandwiches, one or more packets of biscuits, liquorice confectionery and chocolates. The overeating was followed by vomiting, which had become effortless: 'I just have to think about it. I don't have to put my fingers down my throat. I press my stomach and I am sick'. Her weight fluctuated over the course of years, from a minimum of 50 kg (112 lb) to 64 kg (140 lb). At an earlier age she had experienced amenorrhoea for six months. She admitted that she would feel deeply troubled if her weight were to exceed 59 kg (130 lb).

Socially she had achieved a great deal. She was a good scholar and obtained a university degree. She found work which carried managerial responsibilities. At the age of 25 she married a successful businessman and they had two young children. On the negative side, she complained of intermittent depression and irritability. She obtained little satisfaction from the sexual side of her marriage and had in part concealed the severity of her symptoms from her husband. She had occasionally drunk alcohol in excess but had recently given up drinking for fear of becoming seriously dependent on alcohol. She had left home on going to university and described a cool and distant relationship with both parents. A younger brother had unexpectedly committed suicide. The patient had succeeded in reducing her vomiting during both pregnancies from fear of harming her babies. Her motivation for seeking treatment had improved after her second pregnancy. Treatment consisted of supportive psychotherapy and conjoint interviews when the patient and her husband were encouraged to discuss whether they wanted further children. The patient frequently expressed concern about possible harm to her physical health from vomiting and requested investigations. She stopped vomiting soon after the first interview and tolerated her weight rising to 67 kg. She partly attributed her sustained improvement to the shock she experienced when her therapist expressed gloom about her chances of overcoming habitual vomiting of 12 years' duration.

This patient's case history indicates that she suffered from bulimia nervosa of moderate severity only, but which was nevertheless deeply entrenched. She tended to react to adversity with depressive symptoms and her bulimic behaviour had been precipitated by an unwanted pregnancy. During early adolescence she had developed excessive concern about her weight. Although she had lost some weight from dieting and had briefly been amenorrhoeic, this did not amount to an episode of anorexia nervosa. Her motivation to seek treatment gradually improved after a successful marriage, having two children and wishing to become a responsible mother.

Patient 2

The onset of this patient's eating disorder was at the age of 19. During the course of her nurse training she began to avoid food and within one year her weight had fallen from 54 kg (119 lb) to 35 kg (77 lb). She nevertheless completed her training and qualified as a nurse. Amenorrhoea occurred when she was 19 and has persisted since, except for two periods when she achieved a higher weight. She sought no treatment for this early phase of her illness, which was clearly one of anorexia nervosa. Bulimic behaviour commenced when the patient was 22. An attempt by her mother to stop her overeating led to a suicidal gesture when she took an overdose of antihistamines. Her eating pattern eventually settled into one of intermittent starvation alternating with eating orgies when she would consume bread, butter, potatoes or 'anything that was available'. Vomiting occurred two or three times daily after overeating or even after ordinary meals. At first it was induced by inserting her fingers down her throat, but in later years she simply drank some fluid and leaned over the toilet so that 'it all came up in one go'. She also took three to 13 purgative tablets daily (Senokot). Her exercise consisted of cycling four miles each day.

When discussing the antecedents to her illness, the patient dwelt on the strained home atmosphere during her early adolescence. Her mother had had a prolonged extramarital affair. Yet the patient was on the worst terms with her father, neither communicating with the other. After her illness had become established its reactivity to emotional disturbances was shown by sharp losses of weight in response to the breaking up of love affairs on three occasions. When she was at her lowest weights she was twice suspended from work because her efficiency was impaired. Nevertheless she only sought psychiatric care at the age of 25, when it was made a condition of probation following three offences involving the theft of food and potted plants from shops. The shoplifting occurred after her mother had threatened that if she continued to vomit she would have to leave home. It was remarkable in that she stole the goods in the knowledge that she was being observed at the time by security officers. After the last offence she was temporarily suspended from the nursing register.

The patient was referred to the Maudsley Hospital and attempts made to treat her as an outpatient, but without success. By the age of 28 her weight had dropped to 38.5 kg and she was admitted. Although superficially friendly, smiling and charming, her cooperation was limited. She controlled the interviews and denied personal difficulties which were clearly apparent. In hospital her bulimic symptoms and vomiting ceased but she became reluctant to let her weight rise to the recommended level. On reaching 44 kg she discharged herself.

With a medical recommendation she was reinstated as a nurse. She irregularly attended hospital as an outpatient and without specific treatment her weight gradually rose to 53 kg by her thirtieth birthday, its highest level for many years. She has menstruated once. Nevertheless vomiting persists at an average frequency of once daily, leading to a persistently low serum potassium (2.8–3.2 mmol/l) and an elevated serum bicarbonate (34–40 mmol/l). She obtains satisfaction from her nursing work. Socially she remains isolated without close friends. She has not shoplifted again but has acquired £400 of debts from purchases on credit cards.

In conclusion, this patient has suffered from a severe eating disorder for 10 years, evolving from classical anorexia nervosa to bulimia nervosa over the course of three years. There have been marked losses of weight at different times. Vomiting has become habitual and led to electrolyte disturbances. The course of her illness has been adversely affected by emotional upheavals such as failed love affairs. Apart from success at work, her social life remains barren and she has failed in interpersonal relationships. Her personality betrays hysterical traits which have probably contributed to the shoplifting, the accumulation of debts and the poor motivation for treatment.

Antecedents of bulimia nervosa

The disorder occurs usually in females. The age of onset of bulimic symptoms ranges from the late teens to the twenties; for example, in two reported series the mean ages of onset were 21.2 years (SD 6.5) (Russell, 1979) and 19.7 years (SD 4.2) (Fairburn and Cooper, 1984a). But there is a likelihood of earlier symptoms of an eating disturbance occurring during adolescence (at a mean age of 18.8 years (SD 6.2) in the first series).

When eliciting the patient's history, the clinician should explore aspects of her personality which indicate vulnerability to eating disorders, as well as habitual responses to conflicts and emotional upheavals. Among these antecedents, that most specific to the diagnosis of bulimia nervosa is earlier evidence, usually during adolescence, that the patient has displayed sensitivity about her appearance, her shape and her size. This sensitivity is usually expressed by the patient having attempted to follow a weight-reducing diet. Admittedly the pursuit of dieting has become very common among young women in western cultures (Nylander, 1971). It is necessary therefore to determine whether the patient's early dieting led to significant weight loss, loss of menstruation and/or the advent of emotional disturbances. This theme will be taken up again later when the consequences of a previous episode of anorexia nervosa will be examined.

Less specific to the diagnosis of bulimia nervosa is the demonstration that the patient has formerly displayed vulnerability to adverse events and conflicts by reacting with symptoms of depression, anxiety and/or irritability. Here it is pertinent to mention the findings of some family studies which suggest that affective disorders are commoner in the families of bulimic patients than in the general population (Gershon *et al.*, 1984). The tentative conclusion is that eating disorders and affective illnesses may be variants of a common underlying genetic aetiology. The evidence for an association is stronger with unipolar depression than bipolar affective disorder (Strober and Humphrey, 1987). Common examples of conflict-laden situations triggering off bulimia nervosa are the sexual conflicts of adolescence, impending marriage, uncertainty about childbearing, an unwanted pregnancy or an abortion. More general difficulties in interpersonal relationships, particularly those within the family, may also be associated with the onset of bulimic behaviour.

There is growing evidence that the family environment of patients with bulimic disorders is often adverse in its influence. This evidence has been ably reviewed by Strober and Humphrey (1987). These families have been depicted as hostile and negative on the one hand and lacking in parental nurturing and empathy on the other. The authors postulate that such a family environment may lead to a failure of coping mechanisms whereby the patient feels overwhelmed by painful emotional states. They further suggest that these vulnerabilities may lead to bulimic behaviour when additionally the patient feels under pressure to diet and maintain a low body weight. In a proportion of patients there may also be innate tendencies towards impulsivity resulting in periodic overeating, and a constitutional resistance to weight loss in view of an association between bulimia and parental obesity. Although it is premature to conclude that these family characteristics play a causative role, it is important to recognize them when present as they are likely to influence the content of the bulimic illness and its course.

Specific symptoms and behaviour in bulimia nervosa

Episodic overeating

Episodes of overeating usually alternate with periods of undereating or even abstinence. Patients volunteer that their minds are almost constantly filled with thoughts of food. Yet they will often deny that they feel true hunger; instead they describe being unable to stop eating once they have commenced. They are particularly cautious or fearful about consuming carbohydrate-containing foods. There is an all-or-none pattern to the sequence of eating. Food intake may be kept to a minimum, especially with regard to carbohydrates, but sooner or later the patient succumbs by overeating huge quantities of food, including those kinds they regard as 'forbidden'. The amounts consumed may be extraordinarily large and include bread, biscuits and chocolate, which together with ingested fluids might weigh 7 lb. Patients sometimes claim they ingest 15 000 calories at one sitting. The frequency of overeating varies greatly but ranges from less than one episode weekly to several daily. Bulimic patients generally dislike sharing any meal with relatives or friends. More particularly, the overeating is always a solitary and secretive habit. After each episode the patient will feel distressed, or alarmed, because of the prospect of gaining weight from the ingested food.

Methods of mitigating the fattening effects of food

The patient is likely to resort to habitual devices to counteract the effects of the food ingested. Self-induced vomiting is the method most commonly employed. At first she is likely to achieve her aim by inserting her fingers down her throat, thus inducing the gag reflex. If this method is used repeatedly she may develop abrasions, ulcers or calluses on her fingers or on the back of the hand, signs indicative of self-induced vomiting (Russell, 1979; Wynn and Martin, 1984; Williams, Friedman and Steiner, 1986). Often, however, the vomiting becomes progressively easier, requiring merely simple aids such as drinking a quantity of water, bending over the toilet and applying some pressure to the abdomen. Rumination is another phenomenon which may result from frequent vomiting and persist after it is controlled (Fairburn and Cooper, 1984b; Robinson, 1988).

Some patients place greater reliance on other weight-losing devices or may combine them with self-induced vomiting. Abuse of laxatives is one such method, the patient ingesting up to 20 or 30 tablets daily instead of a customary dose of one or two tablets only. Laxative preparations are unfortunately readily available in chemist's shops without prescription. Laxative abuse is, in fact, a much less effective method of reducing weight than self-induced vomiting (Lacey and Gibson, 1985). Prolonged starvation between eating orgies may be another approach adopted by some patients; or taking part in excessive exercise. Less frequently, patients may take amphetamine or other appetite suppressants, thyroid preparations or diuretics. A particularly pitiable group of patients are those who suffer from diabetes mellitus complicated by bulimia nervosa. They may utilize an effective, and most dangerous, way of achieving weight loss by neglecting their insulin requirements, thereby employing their diabetes to achieve their morbid goal of weight control (Szmukler and Russell, 1983).

The patient's psychopathology: morbid dread of fatness

It has already been indicated that bulimic patients resort to vomiting, purgation or exercise in order to counteract the dreaded effects of food, especially after a bout of overeating. This behaviour betrays the patient's deep concern about the risk of weight gain. Thus the specific psychopathology of bulimia nervosa is the same as in anorexia nervosa. The patient may also express her morbid dread of fatness directly or she may try to minimize it.

The bulimic patient's weight may not be remarkable at first sight, and it may even exceed average levels. The important point at issue, however, is that she is struggling to maintain her weight strictly below a threshold level that is self-imposed. This becomes clearer when the clinician elicits a detailed weight history. The patient will usually remember former weights with great accuracy. It is best to question her about her weight during early adolescence at the time of her menarche and to establish its highest level before the onset of disturbed eating behaviour. This range of weights provides a good guide to the weight which is constitutionally optimal for her, i.e. her 'healthy' weight. It will often transpire that the patient's current weight is less than her 'healthy' weight (e.g. by 5–7 kg); the patient's 'desired' weight will nearly always be considerably less than her 'healthy' weight (e.g. by over 7 kg). It is also necessary to assess the patient's attitudes to her previous healthy weight, her current weight and her desired weight. If she is currently weighing less than her healthy weight she should be gently asked whether she would allow herself to return to her former healthy weight. Her response will provide a measure of her dread of fatness: it is likely to range from evasiveness to distress or outraged anger. Thus it will be possible to gauge the patient's emotional investment in issues of weight control.

A similar approach has been incorporated in a structured interview by Fairburn and Cooper (1984a) which provides a method of rating the four psychopathological features they consider specific for bulimia nervosa:

(i) a morbid dread of fatness
(ii) an extreme sensitivity to weight gain
(iii) the pathological pursuit of weight loss

(iv) expressions of disparagement of various parts of her body.

The revised versions of DSM-III and ICD 10 both include the patient's morbid dread of fatness among their diagnostic criteria or guidelines.

Complications of bulimia nervosa: assessment of severity

Some of the following complications also occur in bulimia nervosa when the patient resorts to weight-losing devices such as vomiting or laxative abuse. Erosion of dental enamel is due to gastric hydrochloric acid coming in frequent contact with the teeth during repeated vomiting (Hurst, Lacey and Crisp, 1977). The daily loss of gastric contents will also give rise to low levels of plasma potassium and chloride and elevated plasma bicarbonate. These electrolyte disturbances, and especially the low potassium levels, are responsible for cardiac arrhythmias, muscular paralysis, renal impairment, urinary infection and epileptic seizures (Russell, 1979). Tetany may result from hypokalaemic alkalosis. Bulimic patients may develop bilateral painless swellings of the salivary glands. The mechanism is uncertain: it may be due to repeated ingestion of foods causing increased salivation (e.g. chocolate) or it may be due to repeated vomiting. Bulimic patients are also prone to register elevated serum salivary amylase levels (Kronvall and Theander, 1988). Abuse of laxatives over long periods may lead to injury to the myenteric plexuses of the large bowel and thus cause intractable constipation (Smith, 1968).

The severity of bulimia nervosa should not be gauged simply from the patients' own statements regarding the frequency of overeating and self-induced vomiting. Some patients exaggerate these symptoms and more objective indices are preferable. Estimates of plasma levels of potassium and other electrolytes provide a guide to the severity of self-induced vomiting before the advent of the complications listed above. Serum levels of salivary amylase are also thought to be correlated with frequency of overeating (Kronvall and Theander, 1988). The presence of abrasions on the fingers or back of the hand may reflect the use of manually induced vomiting. Amenorrhoea occurs in a proportion of bulimic patients and provides a general indication of severity, but is most often associated with weight loss.

The severity of the eating disorder should also be assessed by the extent of the psychosocial upheavals encountered by the patient. Thus her life may revolve around ritualistic eating habits and a compulsion to keep her weight below a self-imposed threshold, at the cost of her health, marriage and social adjustment.

The relationship of bulimia nervosa to anorexia nervosa

Patients with the more severe forms of bulimia nervosa often give a history of a previous episode of anorexia nervosa which may have been fully manifest or present in an attenuated form only. In the original series, 80 per cent of patients had experienced an earlier overt or cryptic form of anorexia nervosa (Russell, 1979). In two other series of patients, this percentage was much lower: 34 per cent reported by Fairburn and Cooper (1984a) and a similar percentage by Lacey (1983). These variations are probably due to differences in patterns of patient referral between treatment centres. ICD 10 allows for this variation because it states that 'there is often, but not always, a history of an earlier episode of anorexia nervosa'. We may thus identify two subgroups of bulimia nervosa, one following an episode of anorexia nervosa, the other arising *de novo*. The two disorders share a similar psychopathology, so that it is logical to enquire whether the patient experienced a full or minor form of anorexia nervosa at an earlier stage of her life. Bulimia nervosa probably includes a heterogeneous collection of eating disorders. It is likely that a greater clinical homogeneity will be obtained by grouping together patients with bulimia nervosa who have a history of a previous episode of anorexia nervosa. Admittedly the evidence for this view is not very compelling, perhaps because the required research is still at an early stage. Some support can, however, be derived from one study in which the patients with an earlier history of anorexia nervosa responded less well than the others to a programme of psychological treatments (Lacey, 1983).

When a patient is followed up from the initial phase of anorexia nervosa to that of bulimia nervosa, a number of clinical changes can often be observed. Her weight is likely to increase and her general appearance will improve. There may be a resumption of menstruation and a development of sexual interest. Consequently, fertility may be restored.

The association of bulimia nervosa with affective disorder

Depressive symptoms have been found to be associated with bulimia nervosa since its first description (Russell, 1979). This association has received support in more recent studies, and is considered to be stronger than that between anorexia nervosa and affective disorders (Vandereycken, 1987; Fairburn and Garner, 1986). The severity of depressive symptoms has been found to be similar to that in major depressive disorder (Fairburn and Cooper, 1984a). The relationship of bulimia nervosa to depressive illness may vary from one subgroup of bulimic patients to another (Vandereycken, 1987). For example, Cooper and Fairburn (1986) consider that the depression is a secondary manifestation as it usually lifts in response to psychological treatments which enhance control over eating. On the other hand, Walsh *et al.* (1985) have described patients in whom the depressive episode preceded the eating disorder, and in them an affective disorder might be viewed as 'primary'.

The presence of a personality disorder or personality trait accentuation

In many patients with bulimia nervosa, their premorbid personalities do not appear to be obviously disturbed, but they display accentuated personality traits which mould the clinical picture and the patient's behaviour and may influence prognosis. The frequency of these traits in bulimic patients has been recognized but their importance may have been underestimated (Russell, 1979). For example, in a study by Levin and Hyler (1986), the majority of the 24 bulimic patients were found to meet the criteria for one or more DSM-III personality disorders. The commonest types of personality disorders identified were described as 'histrionic' and 'borderline', followed by 'compulsive' and 'avoidant'. These authors found no relationship between abnormal personality traits and the severity of bulimic symptoms. In terms of the ICD 10 classification, the personality traits found to be most commonly accentuated are those described as 'histrionic', 'anankastic' and 'impulsive'.

Patients with bulimia nervosa who display accentuated personality traits are more likely to show disturbances of behaviour which, though not specific for the eating disorder, are recognized as associated with it. For example, shoplifting and the accumulation of debts are more likely to occur in patients with histrionic character traits. Patients with accentuated impulsiveness are liable to repeated self-injury, including the ingestion of overdoses of drugs. Others may become dependent on illicit drugs or alcohol. This last group of patients are prone to denial and dissimulation, thus accentuating therapeutic difficulties (Jones, Cheshire and Moorhouse, 1985).

It has also been suggested that patients with bulimia nervosa are frequently ambivalent about the treatment offered to them. Their motivation is particularly likely to fail when they are asked to allow their weight to rise (Russell, 1979). In another study, that of a double-blind controlled trial of d-fenfluramine in bulimia nervosa, a high proportion of the patients initially enrolled failed to enter the trial. Among those patients who did enter the study several failed to complete the drug trial, and it transpired that these patient 'drop-outs' specifically included many who had actually benefited from the active drug treatment (Russell *et al.*, 1988). The rate of 'attrition' (dropping out) from trials of psychological treatments has also been reviewed by Garner, Fairburn and Davis (1987), who conclude that attrition is a major problem in most studies.

The Clinical Formulation in the Patient with Bulimia Nervosa

The detailed and integrated clinical assessment of an individual patient is known as the clinical formulation. It goes well beyond the mere assertion that a given patient 'satisfies the diagnostic criteria of DSM-III-R (or ICD 10)'. Moreover, a research report that simply relies on this glib formula when describing the patients under study fails to convey the presence or absence of important variables. In the case of patients with bulimia nervosa, data on the severity of their illness and its possible association with a personality disorder or an affective illness should always be included.

When attempting a diagnostic formulation in a patient with bulimia nervosa, the clinician will endeavour to integrate the clinical data described in the preceding sections of this chapter. Thus he will try to blend together the various causal factors in order to achieve a multidimensional view of his patient's illness. In addition to establishing the degree to which the diagnostic criteria of bulimia nervosa are met, he will assess the following:

1. The severity of the disorder and the occurrence of complications
2. The possible association with anorexia nervosa (previous or current loss of weight)
3. The possible concurrence of an affective disorder
4. The likelihood of a personality disorder or accentuated personality traits

In order to guide treatment it is necessary to identify important clinical presentations which may coexist:

1. The presence of significant loss of weight
2. The pattern of the eating disturbance — food restriction or bulimic episodes — which may require different therapeutic approaches.

The Identity of Bulimia Nervosa as a Psychiatric Illness

When bulimia nervosa was first described in 1979 it was thought premature to consider it as constituting a distinct syndrome (Russell, 1979). Since then bulimia nervosa has become accepted as a psychiatric entity, but a great deal of discussion was needed to achieve the current level of international agreement. Bulimic disorders did not feature in the ninth edition of the *International Classification of Diseases*, published in 1987. In the third edition of the *Diagnostic and Statistical Manual of Mental Disorders*, published in 1980, 'bulimia' was allocated a place and defined according to a set of diagnostic criteria. The DSM-III description attracted several criticisms (Russell, 1985b; Fairburn and Garner, 1986). First, insufficient emphasis was given to the specific psychopathology of the disorder, namely the patient's pervasive dread of fatness. Secondly, the diagnosis of bulimia excluded patients in whom 'the bulimic episodes are due to anorexia nervosa'. This statement led to the exclusion of patients in whom the bulimic disorder supervened in the course of anorexia nervosa. Thus there was a failure to tackle the issue of the relationship between the two disorders. These criticisms and omissions have largely been met in the current systems of classification.

Current classifications of psychiatric disorders: ICD 10 and DSM-III-R

It will be seen that there is now close agreement between ICD 10 and DSM-III-R and both systems incorporate earlier and more specific diagnostic criteria

(Russell, 1979, 1985b; Fairburn and Garner, 1986). In particular, both systems adopt the same name for the disorder 'bulimia nervosa'.

The ICD 10 diagnostic guidelines are summarized in Table 2.1 and given in full in Appendix 1 at the end of the book.

The DSM-IIIR diagnostic criteria are listed in Table 2.2 and in detail also in Appendix 1.

ICD 10 proposes that an earlier episode of anorexia nervosa should be noted, thus opening up the possibility of two subgroups being recognized within bulimia nervosa — patients with and without antecedent anorexia nervosa. DSM-III-R indicates that when anorexia nervosa occurs in a person with bulimia nervosa, both diagnoses should be given. This advice is acceptable so long as it is acknowledged that the patient is suffering from one illness only, an illness which is mixed in form.

Justification for according a diagnostic status to bulimia nervosa

It is appropriate first to summarize the main principles underlying the diagnostic exercise in medical and psychiatric practice. The diagnostic assessment itself signifies the distinguishing of one disease process from another (Cooper, 1984). Its purpose is to provide the most useful summary of current medical knowledge, enabling clinicians to communicate to each other their deductions about their patients. Whenever possible, the aim is to identify an underlying morbid process, associated with a regular pattern of symptoms, presumably resulting from a specific cause or causes. It is obviously desirable that a diagnosis should lead to the best choice of treatment and an accurate prognosis.

Scadding (1967) has identified three main stages in the growth of knowledge of disease, and the nature of the diagnosis should evolve accordingly. First, a 'descriptive' diagnosis is appropriate when it becomes recognized that an illness presents with a number of symptoms or clinical signs which are regularly grouped together, thus constituting a syndrome. Secondly, a 'pathological' diagnosis becomes possible when an anomaly of structure, function or chemistry is regularly found to be associated with the disorder. (In the case of a psychiatric disorder, a characteristic psychopathology, in the sense of a pathogenesis, is also admissible under this heading.) Finally, a truly 'aetiological' diagnosis may be achieved when it is possible to identify the underlying causes (including psychological causes) of the disease.

Unfortunately, knowledge about the causation of most psychiatric disorders remains rudimentary:

> 'The setting up of an orderly and consistent table of "diagnostic entities" has long been the bugbear of psychiatry. . . . There are two major obstacles: the aetiology of many important forms of mental illnesses is not known, and the causes of every mental illness (where they are known) are multiple.' (Lewis, 1972)

Table 2.1. Diagnostic guidelines for bulimia nervosa (F 50.1; ICD 10)

1. Preoccupation with eating and episodes of overeating (large amounts rapidly)

2. The patient attempts to counteract the fattening effects of food by one or more of the following:
   Self-induced vomiting
   Purgative abuse
   Alternating starvation
   Use of drugs (appetite suppressants, thyroid or diuretics)
   Neglect of insulin treatment (in diabetics)

3. A morbid dread of fatness; the patient sets herself a weight threshold below her 'healthy' weight

4. A history of a previous episode of anorexia nervosa (often, but not always present)

Table 2.2. Diagnostic criteria for bulimia nervosa (307.51; DSM-III-R)

A. Recurrent episodes of binge-eating (rapid consumption of a large amount of food in a discrete period of time)

B. A feeling of lack of control over eating behaviour during the eating binges

C. The person regularly engages in either self-induced vomiting, use of laxatives or diuretics, strict dieting or fasting, or vigorous exercise in order to prevent weight gain

D. A minimum average of two binge-eating episodes a week for at least three months

E. Persistent overconcern with body shape and weight

The concept of a 'clinical entity' in psychiatry is thus a relative one.

How does the diagnostic status of bulimia nervosa fit into the framework outlined above? Bulimia nervosa does qualify as a syndrome in view of the consistent association of symptoms and behaviours described in this chapter and incorporated in ICD 10 and DSM-III-R (Russell, 1979; Fairburn and Cooper, 1984a). But we cannot claim any firm knowledge of the causes underlying the disorder, so that a true 'aetiological' diagnosis remains out of reach. We may, however, aspire to an intermediate level of diagnostic status — that of the 'pathological' diagnosis. There is strong evidence to indicate that the episodes of overeating are triggered by the patient's suboptimal weight, in turn due to intermittent starvation. The underlying pathogenesis probably includes physiological and cognitive mechanisms. This accords with 'set-point' theory, whereby a suboptimal weight gives rise to corrective overeating as a means of restoring body weight to a more optimal level (Keesey and Corbett, 1984). A related explanatory model recognizes that abnormal cognitive processes occur in bulimic patients. The paradoxical response of 'counter regulation' described by Herman (1978) has been demonstrated in patients with bulimia nervosa: a food load failed to reduce their hunger ratings and instead gave rise to an increased urge to eat (Robinson, Checkley and Russell, 1985). These findings provide evidence that intermittent starvation and a suboptimal body weight contribute to the pathogenesis of bulimia nervosa.

Remaining problems: bulimia nervosa vs anorexia nervosa

There remain some disagreements regarding the relationship between bulimia nervosa and anorexia nervosa. We have seen that a morbid dread of fatness constitutes an important and necessary diagnostic feature of bulimia nervosa, one which is shared with the diagnosis of anorexia nervosa. Difficulties arise when clinicians and researchers attempt to draw a sharp line of demarcation between the two disorders. While agreeing that bulimia nervosa should not be viewed as a syndrome entirely distinct from anorexia nervosa, Fairburn and Garner (1986) betrayed some ambivalence when they proposed that the diagnosis of anorexia nervosa should be restricted to patients who do not experience episodes of bulimia. They went on to say that 'weight is not relevant to the diagnosis of bulimia nervosa'. They recommended their diagnostic rules as providing a clear means of 'distinguishing between the two diagnoses'. In adopting this approach, they criticize researchers who allow the diagnosis of anorexia nervosa to 'trump' that of DSM-III bulimia. This argument can best be illustrated with a Venn diagram depicting two populations of patients (Figure 2.1). Figure 2.1a shows the position taken by Fairburn and Garner, whereby they accord precedence to the occurrence of bulimic behaviour; Figure 2.1b shows the position they criticize, whereby primacy is given to the occurrence of severe weight loss; Figure 2.1c illustrates the possibility that there may be an overlap between the populations of patients with anorexia nervosa and bulimia nervosa.

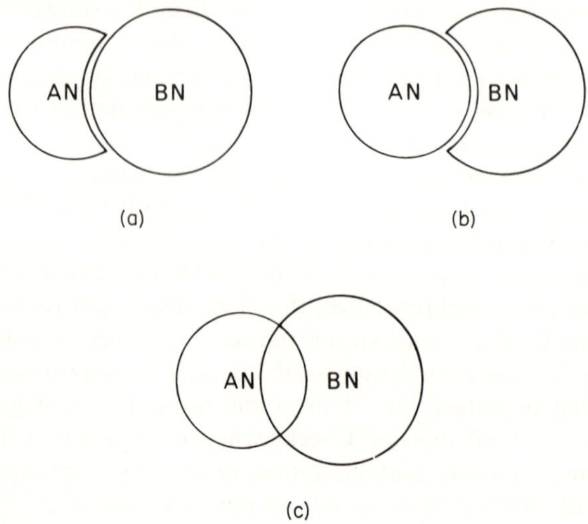

Figure 2.1. Three different ways in which the two patient populations — that with anorexia nervosa and that with bulimia nervosa — may be viewed. (a) Diagnostic primacy is given to the occurrence of bulimic behaviour, irrespective of weight loss; (b) diagnostic primacy is given to weight loss, irrespective of bulimic behaviour; (c) anorexia nervosa and bulimia nervosa overlap inextricably in a minority of patients. AN, anorexia nervosa; BN, bulimia nervosa

The overlap of diagnostic categories is so common in psychiatric practice that it merits a new look at the classification of psychiatric disorder. Classical systems of classification assume that a category can be defined by a relatively small set of features, each one of which is necessary; when these features are jointly present in an individual he becomes a member of the category. Classical systems thus require agreed definitions and homogeneous categories. Especially with psychiatric classifications, the 'typicality' of a member of the group is a critical factor: the more typical the disorder, the more reliably, simply, and accurately it can be categorized. On the other hand, any one or more of the following problems may be met with the classical approach:

(i) uncertainty regarding clear defining features for many categories
(ii) the existence of borderline cases
(iii) heterogeneity of the members of a category with respect to their features so that they may vary in typicality and ease of categorization.

Cantor *et al.* (1980) have proposed that the 'prototype' view of categorization is better suited to psychiatric diagnosis. The term 'prototype' means that the features of category membership need not always be precisely definable: they need only be correlated with category membership. Thus any given feature may not be absolutely necessary: neither may a set of features suffice for inclusion in the category. Consequently, greater reliance is placed on correlated features. The way to determine whether a given patient belongs to a diagnosis is to compute the overlap in clinical features between the patient's symptoms and the diagnostic prototype. In typical cases there will be a close fit and the diagnosis will be simple and efficient.

On the other hand, prototypes permit heterogeneity of cases within categories. When the prototypes (or syndromes) of two categories have many features in common, the diagnostician may find it difficult to distinguish between members of these two categories. This difficulty should not be interpreted as a failure to define diagnostic categories correctly, as suggested by Zigler and Phillips (1961) when faced with heterogeneous populations within the same diagnostic category. Instead:

> 'Heterogeneity of category membership, borderline cases, and imperfect inter- and intrajudge reliability can all be accepted and studied as fundamental properties of the system, rather than branded as aberrations, errors in measurement or faulty utilization of an otherwise classical scientific system'. Cantor *et al.* (1980)

This more flexible approach to psychiatric classification stresses the probabilistic nature of diagnostic categorization. It is pertinent to the problem of attempting too sharp a distinction between bulimia nervosa and anorexia nervosa. It makes more clinical sense to accept the impossibility of drawing a sharp line of demarcation between the two disorders. A substantial minority of patients present with both sets of behaviours (bulimic behaviour and weight loss). Moreover, many patients show a transition from anorexia nervosa to bulimia nervosa, and a few change in the reverse direction. When patients display severe weight loss as well as marked bulimia and self-induced vomiting, it is best to indicate that they suffer from a mixed eating disorder. This view is represented by the overlap of the two patient populations illustrated in Figure 2.1c (Russell, 1988).

Conclusion

The diagnosis of bulimia nervosa can be established readily when a patient presents with the three key sets of phenomena: episodes of overeating, behaviour aimed at mitigating the fattening effects of food, and a morbid dread of fatness. But a true clinical assessment should achieve much more than merely labelling the patient. It is necessary therefore to establish the following:

1. Antecedents which may have played a causal role. Most specific is evidence that the patient has for long been highly sensitive about her appearance and weight. Less specific are former displays of vulnerability to life events and a history of adverse family influences
2. The severity of the patient's disorder, preferably before the advent of complications or social deterioration
3. The possible previous occurrence of an episode of anorexia nervosa
4. The possible concurrence of an affective illness
5. The likelihood of abnormal personality traits.

Bulimia nervosa can now be considered to qualify as a psychiatric syndrome whose pathogenesis can be understood, in part, by the patient's persistent food avoidance and pursuit of a constitutionally suboptimal weight. There now exists close international agreement regarding the key diagnostic features of bulimia nervosa, as reflected in current classifications of psychiatric disorders — ICD 10 and DSM-III-R. There remains some disagreement about the relationship of anorexia nervosa to bulimia nervosa. In some patients it is not possible to draw a sharp diagnostic line between the two disorders; in their case it is best to concede that they suffer from a mixed form of eating disorder.

References

American Psychiatric Association (1980). *Diagnostic and Statistical Manual of Mental Disorders*, 3rd edn (DSM-III). American Psychiatric Association, Washington DC.

American Psychiatric Association (1987). *Diagnostic and Statistical Manual of Mental Disorders*, 3rd edn revised (DSM-III-R). American Psychiatric Association, Washington DC.

Cantor, N., R. de S. French, E. E. Smith and J. Mezzich (1980). Psychiatric diagnosis as prototype categorization. *Journal of Abnormal Psychology* **89**, 181–193.

Cooper, J. E. (1984). Diagnosis and the diagnostic process. In *Handbook of Psychiatry*, Vol. I, ed. by M. Shepherd and O. L. Zangwill. Cambridge University Press, Cambridge, pp. 199–209.

Cooper, P. J. and C. G. Fairburn (1986). The depressive symptoms in bulimia nervosa. *British Journal of Psychiatry* **148**, 268–274.

Fairburn, C. G. and P. J. Cooper (1984a). The clinical features of bulimia nervosa. *British Journal of Psychiatry* **144**, 238–246.

Fairburn, C. G. and P. J. Cooper (1984b). Rumination in bulimia nervosa. *British Medical Journal* **288**, 826–827.

Fairburn, C. G. and D. M. Garner (1986). The diagnosis of bulimia nervosa. *International Journal of Eating Disorders* **5**, 403–419.

Garner, D. M., C. G. Fairburn and R. Davis (1987). Cognitive-behavioural treatment of bulimia nervosa. *Behavior Modification* **11**, 398–431.

Gershon, E. S., J. L. Schreiber, J. R. Hamovit, E. D. Dibble, W. H. Kaye, J. I. Nurnberger, A. Andersen and M. H. Ebert (1984). Clinical findings in patients with anorexia nervosa and affective illness in their relatives. *American Journal of Psychiatry* **141**, 1419–1422.

Halmi, K. A. (1985). Review: classification of eating disorders. *Journal of Psychiatric Research* **19**(2/3), 113–120.

Hare, E. (1981). The two manias: a study of the evolution of the modern concept of mania. *British Journal of Psychiatry* **138**, 89–99.

Herman, C. P. (1978). Restrained eating. *Psychiatric Clinics of America* **1**, 593–607.

Hurst, P. S., J. H. Lacey and A. H. Crisp (1977). Teeth, vomiting and diet: a study of the dental characteristics of seventeen anorexia nervosa patients. *Postgraduate Medical Journal* **53**, 298–305.

Jaspers, K. (1962). *Allgemeine Psychopathologie*, 7th edn 1959 (translated by J. Hoenig and M. W. Hamilton). Manchester University Press, Manchester, pp. 732 and 742.

Jones, D. A., N. Cheshire and H. Moorhouse (1985). Anorexia nervosa, bulimia and alcoholism — association of eating disorder and alcoholism. *Journal of Psychiatric Research* **19**(2/3), 377–380.

Keesey, R. E. and S. W. Corbett (1984). Metabolic defense of the body weight set-point. In *Eating and Its Disorders*, ed. by A. J. Stunkard and A. Stellar. Research Publications: Association for Research in Nervous and Mental Disease, Vol. 62. Raven Press, New York, pp. 87–96.

Kronvall, P. and S. Theander (1988). Elevation of serum salivary amylase in bulimia nervosa. In *Eating Disorders in Adolescents and Young Adults*, ed. by D. Hardoff and E. Chigier. Freund Publishing House, Tel Aviv.

Lacey, J. H. (1983). Bulimia nervosa, binge eating, and psychogenic vomiting: a controlled treatment study and long-term outcome. *British Medical Journal* **288**, 1609–1613.

Lacey, J. H. and E. Gibson (1985). Controlling body weight by purgation and vomiting: a comparative study of bulimics. *Journal of Psychiatric Research* **19**(2/3), 337–341.

Levin, A. P. and S. E. Hyler (1986). DSM-III personality diagnosis in bulimia. *Comprehensive Psychiatry* **27**(1), 47–53.

Lewis, A. J. (1972). Classification and diagnosis in psychiatry: a historical note. In *Psychiatric Diagnosis in New York and London*, ed. by J. E. Cooper, R. E. Kendell, B. J. Gurland, L. Sharpe, J. R. M. Copeland and R. Simon. Institute of Psychiatry, Maudsley Monographs, No. 20. Oxford University Press, Oxford, pp. 1–5.

Nylander, I. (1971). The feeling of being fat and dieting in a school population: epidemiologic, interview investigation. *Acta Sociomedica Scandinavica* **3**, 17–26.

Robinson, P. H. (1988). Control of food intake in eating disorders. In *Principles and Practice of Biological Psychiatry*, ed. by T. G. Dinan. Clinical Neuroscience, London.

Robinson, P. H., S. A. Checkley and G. F. M. Russell (1985). Suppression of eating by fenfluramine in patients with bulimia nervosa. *British Journal of Psychiatry* **146**, 169–176.

Russell, G. F. M. (1979). Bulimia nervosa: an ominous variant of anorexia nervosa. *Psychological Medicine* **9**, 429–448.

Russell, G. F. M. (1985a). Bulimia revisited. *International Journal of Eating Disorders* **4**, 681–692.

Russell, G. F. M. (1985b). The changing nature of anorexia nervosa; an introduction to the conference. *Journal of Psychiatric Research* **19**(2/3), 101–109.

Russell, G. F. M. (1988). The diagnostic formulation in bulimia nervosa. In *Diagnostic Issues in Anorexia Nervosa and Bulimia Nervosa*, ed. by D. M. Garner and P. Garfinkel. Brunner/Mazel, New York, pp. 3–25.

Russell, G. F. M., S. A. Checkley, J. Feldman and I. Eisler (1988). A controlled trial of d-fenfluramine in bulimia nervosa. Supplement to *Clinical Pharmacology*, in press.

Scadding, J. G. (1967). Diagnosis: the clinician and the computor. *Lancet* **2**, 877–881.

Smith, B. (1968). Effect of irritant purgatives on the myenteric plexus in man and the mouse. *Gut* **9**, 139–143.

Strober, M. and L. L. Humphrey (1987). Familial contributions to the etiology and course of anorexia nervosa and bulimia. *Journal of Consulting and Clinical Psychology* **55**(5), 654–659.

Szmukler, G. I. and G. F. M. Russell (1983). Diabetes mellitus, anorexia nervosa and bulimia. *British Journal of Psychiatry* **142**, 305–308.

Vandereycken, W. (1987). Are anorexia nervosa and bulimia variants of affective disorders? *Acta Psychiatrica Belgica* **87**, 267–280.

Walsh, B. T., J. W. Stewart, L. Wright, G. M., Roose and A. H. Glassman (1984). Treatment of bulimia with phenelzine. *Archives of General Psychiatry* **41**, 1105–1109.

Williams, J. F., I. M. Friedman and H. Steiner (1986). Hand lesions characteristic of bulimia. *American Journal of Diseases of Childhood* **140**, 28–29.

World Health Organization (1987). *International Classification of Diseases — Tenth Revision.* Chapter V (f): Mental, behavioural and developmental disorders. Clinical descriptions and diagnostic guidelines: 1986 draft for field trials. World Health Organization, Division of Mental Health, Geneva.

Wynn, D. R. and M. J. Martin (1984). Hand lesions as a sign of bulimia. *Mayo Clinic Proceedings* **59**, 722.

Zigler, E. and L. Phillips (1961). Psychiatric diagnosis: a critique. *Journal of Abnormal and Social Psychology* **63**, 607–618.

3

Assessment of the specific psychopathology of bulimia nervosa

Christopher G. Fairburn
University of Oxford and Warneford Hospital, Oxford
Jane Steere
University of Cambridge
and
Peter J. Cooper
University of Cambridge and Addenbrooke's Hospital, Cambridge

This chapter is concerned with the assessment of the specific psychopathology of bulimia nervosa and thus will exclude consideration of the associated general psychopathology such as depression, anxiety and low self-esteem. While this associated psychopathology is important in understanding the disorder and is certainly relevant to treatment, there exist well-established and accepted instruments for its assessment. The evaluation of the physical state of patients with bulimia nervosa will also not be covered.

Any discussion of the assessment of psychopathology requires prior consideration of the purpose of the assessment. In this chapter we will be considering the assessment of bulimia nervosa from the clinician's and research worker's points of view. We will be concerned with establishing how best to elicit information which will be maximally useful in the diagnosis, description and treatment of individual patients. It should be noted that in clinical practice the assessment process is not discrete and confined to the initial few sessions with the patient, but continues throughout treatment as the patient changes in response to therapeutic interventions. There is thus an ongoing interaction between assessment and treatment, with each influencing the other.

The specific psychopathology of bulimia nervosa has been extensively described in the literature (see Fairburn, Cooper and Cooper, 1986). Three major components of the disorder may be identified although these are closely related and mutually interactive. For the purposes of this chapter they will, however, be discussed separately under the headings of disturbed eating habits, extreme methods of weight control, and overvalued ideas concerning shape and weight. According to the DSM-III-R diagnostic criteria (American Psychiatric Association, 1987), disturbances in all three areas are required for a diagnosis of bulimia nervosa to be made.

Assessment of Eating Habits

The eating habits of patients with bulimia nervosa have been described in detail elsewhere (Russell, 1979; Pyle, Mitchell and Eckert, 1981; Herzog, 1982; Fairburn and Cooper, 1984; Mitchell *et al.*, 1985). The pattern of eating is characterized by attempts at stringent dieting punctuated by recurrent episodes of overeating during which large quantities of high-calorie food tend to be consumed. Patients attempt to control their eating in a variety of ways, such as by having strict rules regarding the type of food (usually low in carbohydrates and fat) which may be consumed. Such control may be successfully maintained for varying lengths of time, ranging from a few hours to periods of a week or longer; but inevitably control is eventually lost and overeating occurs. The factors responsible for the loss of control vary and include the breaking of the self-imposed dietary rules as well as dysphoric mood states such as depression, anxiety, loneliness and boredom (Cooper and Bowskill, 1986). The episodes of bulimia are characterized by a loss of self-control and, generally, a powerful urge to eat those foods usually excluded from the diet. In most cases the episodes are followed by feelings of guilt, remorse, shame and self-disgust. The common response is renewed resolve to restrict food intake and further attempts to do so. In addition to the alternating overeating and dieting, some of these patients spit out high-calorie food rather than swallow it and a small number engage in rumination, which involves regurgitating already ingested food, rechewing it and then either swallowing it or spitting it out (Fairburn and Cooper, 1984).

In assessing the eating habits of patients with bulimia nervosa, it is therefore important to obtain an accurate picture of the dietary rules which they obey and to which they aspire, the nature and severity of the bulimic episodes as well as their possible precipitants, and the presence and frequency of other disturbed eating habits such as spitting and rumination. Various techniques may be used to obtain this information, including direct questioning of patients in the context of a clinical interview, examining self-monitoring sheets, and using standardized self-report questionnaires. It has also been suggested that standardized test meals and observation in hospital may provide valuable information.

Interview techniques

The most obvious method for obtaining information about patients' eating habits is to question them directly within the context of a clinical interview. However, since the disorder is characteristically associated with shame, guilt and secrecy, vigilance and sensitivity on the part of the interviewer is required, and the possibility of the denial or minimization of symptoms must be kept in mind. The information elicited during the interview should ideally be both detailed and comprehensive in order to facilitate diagnosis and later clinical management. This may be achieved by the use of one of the two interviews specifically designed for this purpose: the Clinical Eating Disorder Rating Instrument or CEDRI (Palmer *et al.*, 1987) or the Eating Disorder Examination or EDE (Cooper and Fairburn, 1987a). Both are investigator-based, providing a standard set of probe questions concerning the presence of features of anorexia nervosa and bulimia nervosa over the four weeks prior to the interview. Additional subsidiary questions usually need to be asked. On the basis of the patient's responses, ratings are made by the interviewer using a preset scheme. Satisfactory levels of interrater reliability have been obtained with both interviews. No information on the validity of the CEDRI has been published, whereas the EDE has been shown to discriminate well between controls, 'restrained eaters' and patients with anorexia nervosa or bulimia nervosa (Cooper, Cooper and Fairburn, 1989; Wilson and Smith, 1989).

The CEDRI has 35 items. The first 22 items address the specific psychopathology of anorexia nervosa and bulimia nervosa. The remainder of the instrument is concerned with general psychopathology. Fourteen items are concerned with the behavioural components of bulima nervosa. Of these 14, eight items specifically address the eating habits of these patients. The EDE provides a much more detailed assessment of these disorders. The eleventh edition has 60 items all of which are concerned with the specific psychopathology. Twenty-seven of these items address eating habits. Thus, for example, while the CEDRI includes one question assessing dietary restraint, the EDE assesses this feature in more detail, including questions relating specifically to avoidance of eating at all, avoidance of eating particular foods, adherence to self-imposed calorie limits, reactions to dietary rule-breaking, and preoccupation with food and its calorie content. The EDE also includes questions relating to rumination and the effects of mood on eating, neither of

Table 3.1 Social eating (eating concern subscale): example of an EDE item

Over the past four weeks have you been concerned about other people seeing you eat? Have you avoided such occasions? (Rate the degree of concern about eating normal or less than normal amounts of food in front of others, e.g. family, and whether this has led to avoidance. If the possibility of eating with others has not arisen, rate 9. *Do not consider objective bulimic episodes.*)	
0 —	No concern about being seen eating by others and no avoidance of such occasions
1 —	
2 —	Has felt slight concern at being seen eating, but no avoidance
3 —	
4 —	Has felt definite concern, and has avoided some such occasions
5 —	
6 —	Has felt definite concern, and has avoided all such occasions

which are included in the CEDRI. An example of an EDE item together with its probe questions and guidelines for rating is given in Table 3.1.

One of the major difficulties in assessing the eating habits of patients with bulimia nervosa stems from the problem of operationally defining a bulimic episode or 'binge' (Fairburn, 1987). The DSM-III-R diagnostic criteria for bulimia specify that such episodes occur in a discrete period of time and involve the consumption of a 'large amount' of food. However, although most of the episodes of overeating of these patients are of short duration, some patients describe protracted episodes lasting many hours. It is also difficult to specify what constitutes a 'large amount' of food. The number of calories consumed during a bulimic episode is difficult to ascertain under naturalistic conditions and seems to vary widely both between patients and between episodes. For example, based on their observations of hospitalized patients, Mitchell and Laine (1985) reported calorie intake during bulimic episodes varying from 1436 to 25 755. The EDE addresses this difficulty by distinguishing 'objective' from 'subjective' bulimic episodes, where objective episodes involve eating what others would consider a large amount of food and subjective episodes involve eating an amount which others would not consider large. With both types of episode, the subject views the amount eaten as excessive.

Table 3.2 Summary of EDE classificatory scheme

Form of overeating	Loss of control	Consumption of what would generally be regarded as a large amount of food (as judged by the interviewer)
Objective bulimic episodes	+	+
Subjective bulimic episodes	+	–
Objective overeating	–	+
Subjective overeating	–	–

+ Present.
– Absent.

The DSM-III-R criteria also specify that there should be 'a feeling of lack of control over eating behaviour during the eating binges'. Again there are problems of definition since it is not entirely clear what is meant by 'a feeling of lack of control'. These are the guidelines provided in the EDE: 'The interviewer should ascertain whether the subject felt that he or she could have resisted the episodes of eating (i.e. prevented them from occurring) or could have stopped eating once they had started. If the subject reports that this would have been difficult or impossible, even if these episodes had been planned, loss of control should be regarded as having been present.' Episodes of 'excessive' eating (objective or subjective as defined above) are classed as being bulimic episodes or episodes of overeating on the basis of the presence or absence of lack of control (as defined above). Thus the EDE distinguishes four types of overeating. This classificatory scheme is summarized in Table 3.2. Further details are provided in the EDE schedule itself (Cooper and Fairburn, 1987b).

Self-monitoring

Eating diaries in which patients record their daily food and liquid intake have frequently been used to assess the specific psychopathology of bulimia nervosa (Fairburn, 1985; Rosen *et al.*, 1986). Self-monitoring of this type is very useful in assessing the eating habits of individual patients.

Typically, patients are provided with blank monitoring sheets, carefully instructed in their use, and asked to complete them accurately for a period of a week or more. Completed sheets are then discussed in detail at a further assessment session. In order to be maximally effective, monitoring sheets should include information regarding the time and location of eating and drinking and a lay description of the type and amount of food eaten, although details regarding amounts should not include their precise weight or calorie content as this is usually impractical and may encourage undesirable preoccupation with calorie intake. Patients should also indicate on the forms which episodes of eating they consider to be excessive, and which foods were consumed as part of a controlled meal. It is also useful to obtain information regarding the environmental and emotional context in which episodes of overeating occurred since this may help identify possible precipitants of such episodes.

To maximize the accuracy of the recorded information, patients should be asked to record their food intake immediately after eating or if possible in advance. Delay in recording may lead to the inadvertent omission of items, particularly after bulimic episodes, during which awareness of food intake is often impaired and following which associated shame and self-disgust may result in a desire to minimize the amount eaten.

Self-monitoring has certain advantages as an assessment method. Often it reveals aspects of the patient's eating habits which she may inaccurately describe during a clinical interview, or, indeed, of which she may not be aware. The degree of dietary restraint and nature and frequency of bulimic episodes may be elucidated through examination of monitoring sheets, and the precipitants of loss of control may be tentatively identified. Variations in daily eating habits, difficult to elicit and describe within the context of an interview, may also become apparent. Figure 3.1 shows a monitoring sheet which documents the disruption of dietary restraint by two episodes of bulimia.

One major disadvantage of self-monitoring as a method of assessment is the fact that the increased self-awareness induced by monitoring often leads to behaviour change. As a result, self-monitoring is of more value as a means for assessing progress during treatment, and indeed inducing change, than as a method of assessing eating habits in general. Such monitoring also fails to provide precise information regarding nutrient intake, but in practice such detail is rarely required.

In conclusion, self-monitoring is not an adequate substitute for direct questioning during the clinical interview, but as an adjunct to such an interview it may provide valuable information which is otherwise difficult to elicit.

Self-report questionnaires

Largely due to their economy and ease of administration, self-report questionnaires are a popular method for assessing the specific psychopathology of bulimia, nervosa. A number of such questionnaires have been designed which purport to measure the disturbed eating habits of patients with

DATE 7th November DAY Wednesday

TIME	FOOD AND LIQUID CONSUMED	PLACE	B	V/P	CIRCUMSTANCES
7.45	1 apple 1 grapefruit 1 black coffee	Kitchen			Depressed. Feel fat.
3.10	1 egg sandwich	Work	*		Bought more food from canteen. Shouldn't
	1 bread roll	"	*		have eaten the egg
	1 doughnut	"	*		sandwich – too much.
3.45	1 doughnut	"	*		Bound to be a terrible day now.
	1 cup tea	"	*		
	1 danish pastry	"	*		Can't stop eating. Help.
4.00	2 cups of tea	"		V	
					Weighed myself – 9st. 4lbs Cried.
					MUST NOT EAT AGAIN TODAY.
8.20	1 slice of toast	Kitchen	*		
	1 slice of toast	"	*		Lonely, bored I need someone to talk to.
8.35	1 slice of toast	"	*		
	1 Diet Coke	"			
8.40	Whole packet of shortbread biscuits	"	*		Give up. I can't go on like this. Hate
8.52	1 bowl of cereal		*		myself.
	2 glasses of water				Feel completely bloated.
9.05	1 bowl of cereal		*		
				V	
					Weighed 9st 5lb Wish I was dead.
				L	– 16 Nylax

Figure 3.1. A monitoring sheet illustrating the eating habits of a patient with bulimia nervosa. It is typical of a patient in the early stages of treatment (B, bulimic episodes; V/P, vomiting or purgative use; L, laxative use; *episodes of eating viewed by the patient as 'excessive')

bulimia nervosa. These may be broadly categorized into those assessing the presence and severity of bulimic episodes and those focusing on dietary restraint.

Measures of bulimic episodes

The earliest questionnaire of this type was that reported by Hawkins and Clement (1980), who devised a 19-item questionnaire in which nine items constituted a Binge Scale. The scale has adequate internal consistency and test–retest reliability, but when administered to a large sample of university students it defined over two-thirds of the females and half of the males as 'bingers', suggesting that it may be overinclusive. Ortega *et al.* (1987) compared scores on the Binge Scale with objective observer ratings of patients' behaviour based on analysis of their detailed daily eating records and found that improvements in scores on the scale were not reflected in changes in behaviour. It would appear that the scale reflects subjects' perceptions of their episodes of overeating rather than bulimic behaviour *per se*. It is therefore of questionable value as a measure of eating habits.

Gormally *et al.* (1982) subsequently devised a 16-item Binge Eating Scale to assess the severity of bulimic episodes in obese patients. Criterion validity was established by comparison with ratings made during a structured interview and the scale was shown to be internally consistent. Test–retest reliability was not assessed. The scale describes both behavioural features and feelings and cognitions associated with bulimic episodes. These two aspects are combined in a total score. This prevents clear identification of their relative severity.

The Bulimia Test (BULIT) (Smith and Thelen, 1984) is a three-item test designed to assess the symptoms of bulimia nervosa. It has been found to discriminate adequately between groups of patients with bulimia nervosa and normal controls, and validity and test–retest reliability have both been established. In addition to questions assessing eating habits, the test includes questions concerning purging, changes in weight and menstrual function, all of which contribute to a total score, thereby masking the specific contribution of disturbed eating habits.

Recently, Henderson and Freeman (1987) have described the Bulimic Investigatory Test (BITE). This consists of 36 items divided into a 30-item symptom subscale and a six-item severity scale. This test proved to be accurate in distinguishing between patients with bulimia nervosa and normal controls, and internal consistency, validity and test–retest reliability were all satisfactory. Again, however, items included in the test appear to assess a range of heterogeneous features so that a clear picture of eating habits does not emerge.

Measures of dietary restraint

A number of measures have been devised to assess the strength of attempts to diet (so-called 'dietary restraint'). Herman and Polivy (1975) were the first to report such a measure. They noted, on the basis of the face validity of the items, that their scale comprised two factors: 'diet and weight history' and 'concern with dieting'. Factor analysis of the scale conducted by other re-searchers (Blanchard and Frost, 1983; Ruderman, 1983) using normal-weight samples confirmed the presence of these two factors, which Ruderman (1986) termed 'concern with dieting' (CD) and 'weight fluctuation' (WF). However, Drewnowski, Riskey and Desor (1982) point out that in order to be valid, this scale should discriminate clearly between degree of obesity and dietary restraint as a behavioural characteristic. In a study of 150 subjects, half of whom were obese, they confirmed the presence of the two factors of weight history and concern with dieting, but they found that in obese subjects the weight history factor accounted for a much higher proportion of the variance than it did in normal-weight subjects. They concluded that the total score on the restraint scale was influenced by degree of obesity and did not provide a pure measure of dietary restraint. Thus, as Ruderman (1986) points out, the scale is psychometrically valid only for normal-weight subjects and the two factors should be considered separately in measuring restraint, rather than subsumed in a total score. It should also be noted that some items are concerned with the disinhibition of dietary restraint rather than restraint itself and this has introduced a definite element of circularity in much of the work using this measure.

The Three-factor Eating Questionnaire devised by Stunkard and Messick (1985) provides a more satisfactory measure of dietary restraint. This is a 51-item questionnaire which has three subscales derived by factor analysis of the scale as a whole: cognitive restraint, disinhibition of eating, and perceived hunger. Weight change was found to be predicted by the disinhibition of eating subscale but to be unrelated to scores on the cognitive restraint subscale. The measure therefore allows for clearer identification of the separate effects of restraint and weight history, thereby avoiding the pitfalls discussed above. Validity and reliability of this measure have yet to be conclusively established, but Stunkard and Messick (1985) report some preliminary work which has supported the measure's criterion validity and test–retest reliability.

Recently, van Strien *et al.* (1986) devised a similar measure, the Dutch Eating Behaviour Questionnaire (DEBQ). This is a 33-item questionnaire with three subscales: restrained eating, eating in response to emotional stimuli, and 'external' eating (eating in response to environmental food cues). These subscales have been shown to have high internal consistency and factorial validity. In a further validation study (Wardle, 1987), the original factor structure was replicated. In this validation study, the restrained eating subscale was found to discriminate well between normal controls and a mixed group of dieters and patients with bulimia nervosa or anorexia nervosa, but it failed to discriminate between the dieters and patients. Patients with bulimia nervosa scored significantly higher than all other groups on the external eating and emotional eating subscales. Although originally designed for use with obese subjects, this questionnaire therefore shows promise as a measure of dietary restraint as well as certain other aspects of the eating habits of patients with bulimia nervosa.

Conclusions

Self-report questionnaires have general inherent limitations, particularly as regards the assessment of complex psychopathological features. For example, questions relating to the occurrence of 'binges' are of limited value since this term has no generally accepted meaning. At best, these questionnaires give a rough measure of the severity of the symptoms of the disorder. However, since they are easy to administer, they are potentially useful as screening instruments in epidemiological studies and for establishing group effects in, for example, experimental work. They are not well suited to the detailed assessment of eating habits, and they are clearly not capable of providing detailed information of the type which may be derived from a structured clinical interview.

Test meals

Rosen *et al.* (1985) have devised a laboratory procedure for assessing the eating habits of patients with bulimia nervosa. Standard test meals are administered and subsequent vomiting or purging is prevented. They have found that patients with bulimia nervosa show marked dietary restraint in this context, eating significantly less than normal controls. In addition, after eating the test meals, the patients report feelings and thoughts regarding food and eating which are significantly more negative than those expressed by controls.

It is possible that this procedure may provide an objective measure of dietary restraint. The authors claim that eating under these circumstances corresponds with the patients' own report of their food intake, but the artificial nature and perceived demand characteristics of the procedure as well as the problems of constructing meals which are sufficiently representative of patients' usual diet cast doubts on its validity. In addition, the procedure is complex and, if it is true that its findings correspond well with patients' self-report, it is doubtful that it has any advantages over more conventional assessment methods.

Admission and observation

Another means of assessing eating habits is to admit patients to hospital and observe their eating. This involves considerable disruption of the patients' usual routine and is likely to have a significant effect on their behaviour. Its value as a means for assessing patients' usual eating habits is therefore questionable. Nonetheless, Mitchell and Laine (1985) used this method, encouraging patients to maintain their normal behaviour in the context of a period of close observation. Interesting findings emerged, including the fact that over a 24-hour period the patients tended to eat more than they had reported they usually ate. This casts some doubt on the accuracy of self-report procedures as a means for determining the amount eaten. Mitchell and Laine (1985) also obtained interesting information on the types of foods consumed during bulimic episodes and the sequence in which these are eaten, but such detail is probably of limited clinical relevance.

Assessment of Extreme Weight Control Methods

Patients with bulimia nervosa engage in a variety of behaviours designed to control body shape and weight. In addition to the extreme dieting discussed above, these include self-induced vomiting, the misuse of purgatives, diuretics and appetite suppressants, and excessive exercising. Many patients engage in a combination of these behaviours, of which self-induced vomiting and purgative misuse are the most common.

In assessing patients with bulimia nervosa it is important to obtain an accurate description of the ways in which they attempt to control their shape and weight and the circumstances under which these methods are used. The available assessment techniques are the same as those described above.

Interview techniques

Direct questioning about weight control measures is reasonably satisfactory as a means of assessing this aspect of bulimia nervosa. Once again, it is important to remember that patients may feel ashamed and embarrassed about their behaviour and sensitivity is therefore required in the timing and phrasing of questions. It is important to phrase these questions carefully ('This is a question we ask everybody we see here'), perhaps in a manner suggesting that the presence of these symptoms is commonly encountered ('Many people with eating problems tell us that . . . '). The Eating Disorder Examination includes in its standard format questions relating to self-induced vomiting, purgative misuse and exercising. For self-induced vomiting and purgative misuse, separate ratings are made of the total number of episodes and number of days on which these occurred over the preceding four weeks. In the case of purgative misuse, the average number of purgatives taken per occasion is also recorded as well as their type.

Particular caution must be employed when questioning patients about exercising. Exercise for fitness and health is emphasized by contemporary society as being of value and it is therefore important to distinguish between exercising which is normal or healthy and exercising which is symptomatic of an eating disorder. The EDE makes this distinction by only rating exercise that is intended to utilize calories or change shape, weight or body fat composition, although this may not have been the sole reason for exercising.

Self-monitoring

Eating diaries of the type described above may also be used to record behaviour intended to control body weight. It will be apparent from such diaries when and under what circumstances these methods are used; for example whether they are only used after bulimic episodes or whether they also occur after normal meals or on a habitual basis relatively independent of eating.

As with the assessment of eating habits, monitoring sheets have the advantage of being able to reveal aspects of patients' behaviour which are difficult to elicit using an interview or self-report questionnaires, or of which patients may not be aware. Their usefulness is dependent on the honesty of the patient and subject to distortion due to embarrassment and shame. In most cases it is possible to establish a collaborative relationship between the patient and the assessor, particularly if treatment is to be offered, and under these circumstances self-monitoring is likely to provide an accurate and clinically valuable assessment of these behaviours.

Self-report questionnaires

Most of the self-report questionnaires which address the specific psychopathology of eating disorders include questions concerning weight control measures, but responses to these questions are usually subsumed in a total summary score. Few give any indication as to the frequency of this behaviour. They are therefore of little clinical value in this respect.

Test meals

The test meal procedure of Rosen *et al.* (1985) is intended to assess how patients eat when self-induced vomiting is prevented. It may therefore provide an indication of the extent to which self-induced vomiting influences the patients' eating habits. It is not suited to the assessment of the impact on eating of purgative misuse or extreme exercising. The procedure therefore has limited clinical relevance.

Admission and observation

Using this method Mitchell and Laine (1985) were able to assess accurately the timing and frequency of patients' self-induced vomiting over a 24-hour period. As a result interesting information was obtained, but the disadvantages of admission discussed earlier greatly outweigh the value of the accuracy of detail provided.

Assessment of Overvalued Ideas Concerning Shape and Weight

Associated with the behavioural aspects of bulimia nervosa is a characteristic set of extreme concerns about shape and weight. These have been proposed as being of primary importance in the maintenance of the disorder (Fairburn, 1985; Fairburn, Cooper and Cooper, 1986). Patients are preoccupied with their shape and weight and, from their actions, it is clear that one or both is of paramount importance in their life. Unlike patients with anorexia nervosa, a desire to be extremely thin is not frequently described: patients with bulimia nervosa usually give a desired weight which is not significantly different from that of women in the general population (Fairburn and Cooper, 1984). What distinguishes these patients from normal women is their tendency to evaluate their self-worth almost exclusively in terms of shape or weight. Thinness is regarded as desirable, attractive and evidence of self-discipline and personal effectiveness, while fatness is feared and viewed as reprehensible. While similar views are not uncommon in the general population and are to a large extent fostered by current social values, the strength with which these views are held and their personal significance make them dysfunctional.

It is apparent that dietary restriction and other methods of weight control previously described are explicable in terms of these patients' concerns about their shape and weight. Other behaviours are also indicative of the presence of these concerns. Patients may weigh themselves frequently, sometimes several times each day, or, alternatively, they may actively avoid weighing in order to reduce their anxiety about their shape or weight. Avoidance of the sight of their bodies, for example in mirrors or while bathing, is also common, and public exposure in places like communal changing rooms and swimming pools is often experienced as aversive and avoided whenever possible. Bruch (1973) has proposed that patients with eating disorders have a distorted body image and this has been confirmed in bulimia nervosa in several experimental studies which have shown that they tend to overestimate their body size (Cooper *et al.*, 1987).

Interview techniques

By their nature, complex beliefs and values of the type described are difficult to evaluate. Assessment is further complicated by many patients' awareness that their attitudes are somewhat irrational. Thus some are reluctant to acknowledge them if baldly questioned. Obtaining an indication of the presence and extent of these characteristic overvalued ideas concerning shape

Table 3.3 Standardized assessment of the personal importance attached to shape and weight. The 'importance of shape' item from the Eating Disorder Examination (EDE), 11th edition (Cooper and Fairburn, 1987b)

Over the past four weeks has shape been an important issue for you?
Has *your* shape influenced how you think about (judge, feel, evaluate) yourself as a person?
If you imagine the scheme (scale) by which you judge yourself — based on things like . . . (your performance at work, being a parent, your marriage, how you get on with other people) . . . and you put these things in order of importance, where does your shape fit in?

(Rate the degree of importance the subject has placed on body shape and its position in his or her scheme for *self-evaluation*. To make this rating, comparisons need to be made with other aspects of the subject's life which are of importance in his or her scheme for self-evaluation, e.g. quality of relationships, being a parent, performance at work or in leisure activities. Do not prompt with the terms 'some', 'moderate' or 'supreme'. If the subject has regarded both shape and weight as being of equivalent 'supreme' importance, rate 6 on this item and on 'Importance of weight'.)

0 —	No importance
1 —	
2 —	Some importance (definitely an aspect of self-evaluation)
3 —	
4 —	Moderate importance (definitely one of the main aspects of self-evaluation)
5 —	
6 —	Supreme importance (nothing is more important in the subject's scheme for evaluating himself or herself)

and weight may be facilitated by questioning about the behavioural accompaniments of these concerns such as the avoidance of exposure.

One of the major strengths of the Eating Disorder Examination is that it provides detailed information on the attitudinal aspects of the disorder. Indeed, eight items contribute to the 'shape concern' subscale (importance of shape, preoccupation with shape or weight, dissatisfaction with shape, fear of fatness, discomfort seeing body, avoidance of exposure, feelings of fatness, desire for a flat stomach) and five items to the 'weight concern' subscale (importance of weight, reaction to prescribed weighing, preoccupation with shape or weight, dissatisfaction with weight, pursuit of weight loss). One of the key items, 'importance of shape', is shown in Table 3.3. The CEDRI does not address this aspect of the psychopathology of bulimia nervosa in any detail.

Self-monitoring

Eating diaries can include space for patients to record thoughts concerning shape and weight. They should record their thoughts verbatim immediately they occur or as soon as possible thereafter. Beliefs and values concerning shape and weight are rarely directly accessible in this way: instead, they usually have to be inferred from the patient's thoughts and behaviour. The precise nature of underlying beliefs and values may be identified using standard cognitive restructuring procedures (see Fairburn, 1985; Fairburn and Cooper, 1989). Self-monitoring may also assist in identifying the specific situations in which problematic thoughts occur. As such it may be a useful adjunct to the clinical interview. However, it must be noted that this form of self-monitoring is far less straightforward than simply recording behaviour and some patients may experience considerable difficulty in carrying it out. Thoughts about shape and weight are usually 'automatic' and patients require practice identifying them. In addition, because such thoughts are often emotionally charged and directly related to beliefs and values of great personal significance, some patients resist revealing them unless a trusting relationship has been established with the assessor. A minority of patients are unable to identify their thoughts.

Self-monitoring of thoughts and feelings about shape and weight is most effectively used in the ongoing assessment of patients during treatment. It cannot be relied upon as the only source of information about this aspect of the disorder.

Self-report questionnaires

From its title, it would seem reasonable to expect that the Eating Attitudes Test (EAT) (Garner and Garfinkel, 1979; Garner *et al.*, 1982) would provide a specific measure of this aspect of the psychopathology of bulimia nervosa. In fact, the instrument is concerned with the full range of the specific psychopathology of eating disorders and only three of the 40 items directly address concerns about shape and weight. Although several other items assess direct behavioural experiences of these concerns, for example the frequency of weighing, the EAT cannot be regarded as a specific measure of the attitudinal components of bulimia nervosa.

In contrast, the Eating Disorder Inventory (EDI) (Garner, Olmsted and Polivy, 1983) does more directly address these concerns. Four of the seven items of the drive for thinness subscale and all nine of the items of the Body Dissatisfaction Scale are concerned with attitudes to shape and weight. How scores on these individual items and on the two subscales relate to EDE scores has yet to be investigated.

Dissatisfaction with body shape *per se* is most comprehensively assessed by the recently developed self-report Body Shape Questionnaire (BSQ) (Cooper *et al.*, 1987). This is a 34-item measure which focuses exclusively on the phenomenal experience of 'feeling fat'. The questionnaire has been found to discriminate well between patients with bulimia nervosa and samples of normal women and has also been shown to be sensitive to change (Cooper and Steere, 1989).

Objective measures

The Stroop technique

Given the limitations of self-report questionnaires as mean assessing complex constructs and the fact that semistructured interviews require the assessor to make complex clinical judgements, more objective measures are needed. One technique which might provide an objective measure of personal concerns about shape and weight is a variation of the Stroop colour-naming task. In this task subjects are required to name the colour of the ink in which words are written, ignoring the content of the words themselves. The speed of their response is measured. The colour-naming of the words is retarded if attention is paid to the word content. For instance, colour-naming is significantly slowed if the words are the names of colours and there is a clash between the words themselves and the colour of the ink in which they are written, for example, the word 'red' written in blue ink (Jensen and Rohrwer, 1966). In addition, evidence from studies of patients with spider phobias (Watts *et al.*, 1986), patients with generalized anxiety (Mathews and Macleod, 1985), and those who have attempted suicide (Williams and Broadbent, 1986), as well as from studies of normal groups (McKenna, 1986), indicates that words of personal significance to individuals also retard colour-naming. Since clinical experience suggests that patients with bulimia nervosa react strongly to words related to their concerns about eating, shape and weight (for example 'fat'), it would be expected that these patients would be impaired in the colour-naming of such words. The results of a preliminary study suggest that this is indeed the case. Compared with controls matched for age and sex, patients with bulimia nervosa were found to take longer to colour-name words related to their concerns about shape, weight and eating (Fairburn *et al.*, 1989).

Body-size estimation techniques

Disturbances in body image can probably be considered a manifestation of extreme concerns about shape and weight. One aspect of such a disturbance is the dissatisfaction with shape discussed above. A second aspect is more perceptual in nature and involves an inability to assess one's body size accurately such that one sees one's body as larger than it actually is. A related phenomenon is the desire for a body size significantly smaller than one's own. A considerable body of experimental work has been concerned with establish-

Table 3.4 The case-control studies of body-size estimation in bulimia nervosa and bulimia

Authors	Year	Technique[a]	Diagnosis[b]	Patients *N*	Patients *Mean*	Controls *N*	Controls *Mean*	Significance[c]
Norris	1984	MC	B	12	118.5	12	101.5	***
Birtchnell *et al.*	1985	MC	BN	50	123.7	19	117.6	NS
Willmuth *et al.*[d]	1985	MC	BN	20	115.7	20	103.7	**
Whitehouse *et al.*	1986	IM	B	22	110.8	20	102.2	*
		ID	B	22	103.1	20	96.1	**
Freeman *et al.*	1985	ID	BN	47	106.5	33	102.9	*
Garner *et al.*[e]	1985	ID	B	59	107.6	16	95.8	***
Touyz *et al.*[f]	1985	ID	B	19	111.3	15	101.0	*
Collins *et al.*	1987	ID	B	24	110.8	66	98.0	**
Cooper and Taylor	1988	ID	BN	25	118.0	82	105.8	**

[a] MC, movable calliper technique; IM, image-marking technique; ID, image-distortion technique.

For the MC and IM techniques, the data refer to the composite mean scores: that is, the average of the individual body parts assessed.

[b] BN, bulimia nervosa; B, bulimia.

[c] * $p < 0.05$; ** $p < 0.01$; *** $p < 0.001$.

[d] Willmuth *et al.* provide data only on individual body parts. The means in the table are therefore estimates and the significance level an extrapolation from the data they provide.

[e] Control sample derived from Garner *et al.* (1976).

[f] Control sample derived from Touyz *et al.* (1984).

ing whether patients with eating disorders overestimate their body size. Two main methods of assessment have been used: movable calliper techniques and image-distortion methods. The first of these requires patients to adjust the width between two movable markers until the distance between them is judged to correspond to the width of different body regions (e.g. waist, hips, thighs). Image-distortion methods involve projecting an image of the patient's whole body onto a screen and, with the aid of an optical or electrical device, getting the patient to adjust it until it corresponds to her judgement of her actual size. Table 3.4 summarizes the findings from the controlled studies of size estimation in patients with bulimia nervosa.

Although in all but one of the studies patients overestimated their size significantly more than controls, it is apparent that there is considerable variability within both patients and controls. This is less true when a body size dissatisfaction index is generated based on the discrepancy between perceived and desired size, but nevertheless variability remains high (Cooper and Taylor, 1987). At present it must be questioned whether size perception techniques provide any information of value beyond that which can be learned from the simpler measures of shape dissatisfaction discussed earlier.

Conclusion

The clinical assessment of patients with bulimia nervosa must include a comprehensive evaluation of eating habits, weight control methods and concerns about shape and weight. Each of these facets of the specific psychopathology of the disorder is complex and subject to variability both between patients and within the same patient at different times.

The mainstay of assessment is the clinical interview in which patients are directly questioned about relevant aspects of their behaviour, thoughts and attitudes. Recently developed investigator-based interviews, such as the Eating Disorder Examination, represent a significant advance in this respect since they provide a means for thoroughly examining patients' self-reported psychopathology. Their semistructured nature ensures reliability, whilst retaining sufficient flexibility to permit the assessment of complex phenomena. Such measures provide the best means for conducting detailed psychopathological studies and for investigations into the effects of treatment.

References

American Psychiatric Association (1987). *Diagnostic and Statistical Manual of Mental Disorders III-R* (3rd edition revised). American Psychiatric Association, Washington DC.

Blanchard, F. and R. O. Frost (1983). Two factors of restraint: concern for dieting and weight fluctuation. *Behaviour Research and Therapy* **21**, 259–267.

Bruch, H. (1973). *Eating Disorders: Obesity, Anorexia Nervosa and the Person Within.* Basic Books, New York.

Cooper, P. J. and R. Bowskill (1986). Dysphoric mood and overeating. *British Journal of Clinical Psychology* **25**, 155–157.

Cooper, P. J. and J. Steere (1989). Change in body size estimation during treatment for bulimia nervosa, in preparation.

Cooper, P. J. and M. J. Taylor (1989). Body image disturbance in bulimia nervosa. *British Journal of Psychiatry*, in press.

Cooper, P. J., M. J. Taylor, Z. Cooper and C. G. Fairburn (1987). The development and validation of the Body Shape Questionnaire. *International Journal of Eating Disorders* **6**(4), 485–494.

Cooper, Z., P. J. Cooper and C. G. Fairburn (1989). The validity of the Eating Disorder Examination and its subscales. *British Journal of Psychiatry* **154**, 807–812.

Cooper, Z. and C. G. Fairburn (1987a). The Eating Disorder Examination: a semi-structured interview for the assessment of the specific psychopathology of eating disorders. *International Journal of Eating Disorders* **6**, 1–8.

Cooper, Z. and C. G. Fairburn (1987b). Eating Disorder Examination: interview schedule (11th edition). Unpublished manuscript, University of Oxford.

Drewnowski, A., D. Riskey and J. A. Desor (1982). Feeling fat yet unconcerned: self-reported overweight and the restraint scale. *Appetite: Journal for Intake Research* **3**, 273–279.

Fairburn, C. G. (1985). Cognitive-behavioral treatment for bulimia. In *Handbook of*

Psychotherapy for Anorexia Nervosa and Bulimia, ed. by D. M. Garner and P. E. Garfinkel. Guilford Press, New York.

Fairburn, C. G. (1987). The definition of bulimia nervosa: guidelines for clinicians and research workers. *Annals of Behavioural Medicine* **9**, 3–7.

Fairburn, C. G. and P. J. Cooper (1984). The clinical features of bulimia nervosa. *British Journal of Psychiatry* **144**, 238–246.

Fairburn, C. G. and P. J. Cooper (1989). The management of eating disorders. In *Behavioural Approaches to Adult Psychiatric Disorders: A Practical Guide*, ed. by K. Hawton, P. Salkovskis, J. Kirk and D. M. Clark, Oxford University Press, Oxford.

Fairburn, C. G., P. J. Cooper, M. J. Cooper, F. D. McKenna and P. Anastesiades (1989). The use of the Stroop colour-naming task to assess the psychopathology of bulimia nervosa, in preparation.

Fairburn, C. G., Z. Cooper and P. J. Cooper (1986). The clinical features and maintenance of bulimia nervosa. In *Handbook of Eating Disorders*, ed. by K. D. Brownell and J. P. Foreyt. Basic Books, New York.

Garner, D. M. and P. E. Garfinkel (1979). The Eating Attitudes Test: an index of the symptoms of anorexia nervosa. *Psychological Medicine* **11**, 707–711.

Garner, D. M., M. P. Olmsted, Y. Bohr and P. E. Garfinkel (1982). The Eating Attitudes Test: psychometric features and clinical correlates. *Psychological Medicine* **12**, 871–878.

Garner, D. M., M. A. Olmsted and J. Polivy (1983). Development and validation of a multidimensional eating disorder inventory for anorexia nervosa and bulimia nervosa. *International Journal of Eating Disorders* **2**, 15–34.

Gormally, J., S. Black, S. Dastin and D. Rardin (1982). The assessment of binge eating severity among obese persons. *Addictive Behaviors* **7**, 47–55.

Hawkins, R. C. and P. F. Clement (1980). Development and construct validation of a self-report measure of binge eating tendencies. *Addictive Behaviors* **5**, 219–226.

Henderson, M. and C. P. L. Freeman (1987). A self-rating scale for bulimia: the BITE. *British Journal of Psychiatry* **150**, 18–24.

Herman, C. P. and J. Polivy (1975). Anxiety, restraint and eating behavior. *Journal of Abnormal Psychology* **84**, 666–672.

Herzog, D. B. (1982). Bulimia: the secretive syndrome. *Psychosomatics* **23**, 481–484.

Jensen, A. R. and W. D. Rohrwer (1966). The Stroop colour-word test: a review. *Acta Psychologica* **25**, 36–93.

Matthews, A. and C. Macleod (1985). Selective processing of threat cues in anxiety states. *Behaviour Research and Therapy* **23**, 563–569.

McKenna, F. P. (1986). Effects of unattended emotional stimuli on colour-naming performance. *Current Psychological Research Review* **5**, 3–9.

Mitchell, J. E., D. Hatsukami, E. D. Eckert and R. L. Pyle (1985). Characteristics of 275 patients with bulimia nervosa. *American Journal of Psychiatry* **142**, 482–485.

Mitchell, J. E. and D. C. Laine (1985). Monitored binge eating behavior in patients with bulimia nervosa. *International Journal of Eating Disorders* **4**, 177–183.

Ortega, D. F., H. R. Waranch, A. J. Maldonado and F. Hubbard (1987). A comparative analysis of self-report measures of bulimia. *International Journal of Eating Disorders* **6**(2), 301–311.

Palmer, R., M. Christie, C. Cordle, D. Davies and J. Kenrick (1987). The Clinical Eating Disorder Rating Instrument (CEDRI): a preliminary description. *International Journal of Eating Disorders* **6**, 9–16.

Pyle, R. L., J. E. Mitchell and E. D. Eckert (1981). Bulimia: a report of 34 cases. *Journal of Clinical Psychiatry* **42**, 60–64.

Rosen, J. C., H. Leitenberg, C. Fisher and C. Khazam (1986). Binge-eating episodes in bulimia nervosa: the amount and type of food consumed. *International Journal of Eating Disorders* **5**, 255–267.

Rosen, J. C., H. Leitenberg, K. M. Fondacaro, J. Gross and M. Willmuth (1985). Standardized test meals in assessment of eating behavior in bulimia nervosa: consumption of feared foods when vomiting is prevented. *International Journal of Eating Disorders* **4**, 59–70.

Ruderman, A. J. (1983). The restraint scale: a psychometric investigation. *Behaviour Research and Therapy* **21**, 258–283.

Ruderman, A. J. (1986). Dietary restraint: a theoretical and empirical review. *Psychological Bulletin* **99**, 247–262.

Russell, G. (1979). Bulimia nervosa: an ominous variant of anorexia nervosa. *Psychological Medicine* **9**, 429–448.

Smith, M. C. and M. H. Thelen (1984). Development and validation of a test for bulimia nervosa. *Journal of Consulting and Clinical Psychology* **52**, 863–872.

Stunkard, A. J. and S. Messick (1985). The three-factor eating questionnaire to measure dietary restraint, disinhibition and hunger. *Journal of Psychosomatic Research* **29**, 71–83.

van Strien, T., J. E. R. Frijters, G. P. A. Bergers and P. B. Defares (1986). The Dutch Eating Behavior Questionnaire (DEBQ) for assessment of restrained, emotional, and external eating. *International Journal of Eating Disorders* **5**, 295–315.

Wardle, J. (1987). Eating style: a validation of the Dutch Eating Behavior Questionnaire in normal subjects and women with eating disorders. *Journal of Psychosomatic Research* **13**, 161–169.

Watts, F. N., F. P. McKenna, R. Sharrock and L. Trezise (1986). Colour-naming of phobia-related words. *British Journal of Psychology* **77**, 97–108.

Williams, J. M. G. and K. Broadbent (1986). Distraction by emotional stimuli: use of a Stroop task with suicide attempters. *British Journal of Clinical Psychology* **25**, 101–110.

Wilson, G. T. and D. Smith (1989). Assessment of bulimia nervosa: an evaluation of the Eating Disorder Examination. *International Journal of Eating Disorders* **8**, 173–179.

4

The Structured Interview for Anorexia and Bulimia Nervosa (SIAB): development and characteristics of a (semi-) standardized instrument

Manfred M. Fichter
University of Munich
Martin Elton
University of Munich
Klaus Engel
Psychiatric Hospital, Dortmund
Adolf-Ernst Meyer
University Hospital, Hamburg
Fritz Poustka
University of Frankfurt
Hartmut Mall
University of Ulm
and
Sybille von der Heydte
University of Munich

In the past decade significant progress has been made in the methodology of reliable and valid assessment and the diagnostic classification of psychiatric symptoms. Several structured and standardized interviews have been developed in general psychiatry. Examples of interviews of this kind for use by trained professionals are the Present State Examination (PSE) with its CARTEGO computer system for diagnostic classification (Wing, Cooper and Sartorius, 1974a,b) and the Structured Clinical Interview for DSM-III-R Diagnosis (SCID) by Spitzer, Williams and Gibbon (1987). The National Institute of Mental Health Diagnostic Interview Schedule (DIS) (Robins *et al.*, 1981, 1982) has been developed for use by trained lay interviewers. These interviews improve reliability: (1) by using (semi-)standardized probes; (2) by requiring training of the interviewers usually with the use of videotapes; and (3) by supplying a detailed manual with definitions and case examples. This helps to increase the reliability of symptom identification. In addition, diagnostic criteria for psychiatric illnesses have been operationalized and defined more explicitly in the *Diagnostic and Statistical Manual of Mental Disorders* DSM-III-R (American Psychiatric Association, 1987) and the ICD-10 criteria (World Health Organization, 1987) (see Appendix 1). Computer algorithms are used for the present generation of (semi-)standardized interviews in psychiatry to compute diagnoses according to one or more (polydiagnostic) classification systems. The explicitness also increases the reliability of diagnostic classification.

Instruments of various kinds for the assessment of eating disorders have been reviewed by Fairburn, Steere and Cooper (this volume, Chapter 3). Palmer *et al.* (1987) and Cooper, Cooper and Fairburn (1989) recently described the Clinical Eating Disorder Rating Instrument (CEDRI), a 35-item interview; 22 items cover the specific pathology of anorexic and bulimic eating disorders and 13 items cover the more general psychopathology. Cooper and Fairburn (1987) developed the Eating Disorder Examination (EDE), a 60-item interview which covers the specific psychopathology of anorexia and bulimia nervosa in detail but not the general psychopathology. Both instruments showed acceptable interrater reliability. No validity data concerning the CEDRI have been published. The objectives in developing the Structured Interview for Anorexia and Bulimia Nervosa (SIAB) were:

1. to develop a (semi-)standardized interview for the use of trained professionals;
2. to design an interview with standard probes and well-established reliabilities, based on explicit symptom definitions in a detailed manual;
3. to explore the internal structure with the use of factor and cluster analyses;
4. to establish validity by comparison with the results of other expert- and self-rating instruments; and
5. to design an instrument which allows for a direct polydiagnostic classification according to ICD 10 and DSM-III-R.

The sophisticated administration of the interview requires a special training on the basis of the manual and prerated videotapes.

Method of Construction of the SIAB Scale

The first revision of the Structured Interview for Anorexia and Bulimia Nervosa (SIAB) was used in a multicentre study with 346 patients with anorexic and bulimic eating disorders (325 female and 21 male) and 111 female community controls. Interviews were conducted by psychiatrists or psychologists trained in the use of the instrument on the basis of the manual and videotapes. Each item was rated for present status (past two weeks) and for maximum of pathology in the previous years (lifetime). Items were rated on a severity scale from 0 (symptom not present) to 4 (symptom very much/very severely present). Several items covering general psychopathology were derived from the Goldberg Interview (Goldberg *et al.*, 1970) and the Present State Examination (Wing, Cooper and Sartorius, 1974a,b). The second revision of the SIAB is based on analyses of the first revision. It consists of two separately factor-analysed sections: the SIAB-P covers the specific and general psychopathology (62 items; 34 items resulting from factor analyses and 28 items for additional diagnostic classification purposes which will enter factor analyses for the third revision); the SIAB-FAM covers family interactions and family pathology (25 items; 22 items resulting from factor analyses and three additional items).

The sample of 346 anorexic and bulimic patients had an average age of 25.7 ± 7.4 years (healthy controls 20.9 ± 3.2 years), a body weight at the time of assessment of 49.1 ± 10.2 kg (controls 57.2 ± 7.9 kg), and a body-mass index (BMI) of 17.4 ± 3.1 (controls 20.3 ± 2.4). Of 332 anorexic and bulimic patients 34.8 per cent had no binge attacks, 17.1 per cent had binge attacks monthly or weekly, 12.1 per cent had binge attacks twice weekly, and 36.0 per cent had binge attacks daily. Forty-two per cent of all patients showed no vomiting, 12.4 per cent vomited weekly or monthly, 5.4 per cent vomited twice weekly, and 40.2 per cent vomited daily. The control group consisted of a representative community sample of 300 German females aged 15–25 years living in one of the districts of Hamburg (Engel and Höhne, 1989). Onc hundred and eleven females could be contacted and agreed to participate (community controls).

From preliminary cluster analyses the following clusters were derived for the SIAB-P: (1) persistent concern with figure and food (Cronbach's alpha = 0.81; interrater reliability = 0.94); (2) bulimic symptoms (0.74/0.78); (3) sexuality (0.71/0.91); (4) social interactions and isolation (0.94/0.67); (5) demoralization (0.91/0.66). For the SIAB-FAM (family interaction and pathology) the following clusters were derived: (1) relationship with mother (0.91/0.60); (2) relationship with father (0.96/0.91); (3) marital relationship of parents

(0.96/0.83); (4) avoidance of conflicts in the family (0.94/—). Because of methodological limitations of the cluster-analytic approach, the 'classical' methodology of factor analysis was used for exploratory data analysis. Tables 4.1 and 4.2 give a list of the factor-analysed items. They were separately analysed for the SIAB-P (psychopathology) and for the SIAB-FAM (family interaction and family pathology) of the interview for lifetime expression.

Internal consistency of the SIAB components and interrater reliability of the items were established with the interviews. Interrater reliability, as shown by Kendall's coefficient of concordance, was determined for both past and present expression (past — SIAB-P: $W = 0.96$; SIAB-FAM: $W = 0.84$; present — SIAB-P: $W = 0.94$; SIAB-FAM: $W = 0.89$ respectively; all $p < 0.001$).

In the following, two examples of items from the SIAB-P (psychopathology) and one item from the SIAB-FAM (family interaction and pathology) are given:

Disturbances in body image

Probe: How do you judge your figure according to your own standards — too fat, too thin or just right?

Additional probes: Do you see yourself as thicker than other people do (e.g. physicians, therapist)? Are there certain parts of your body which you experience as particularly fat?

	Presently	Maximum of pathology (lifetime)
0 = No body-image disturbances		
1 = Slight body-image disturbances		
2 = Marked body-image disturbances		
3 = Severe body-image disturbances		
4 = Very severe body image disturbances	☐	☐

Depressive thoughts and dysfunctional cognitive schemata

Probe: Do you brood or ruminate about whether you have done something wrong? Do you primarily see negative traits and attributes in yourself when something goes wrong? Do you worry about the future?

Additional probes: Do you often think in an 'all-or-nothing' fashion ('If I don't get a good grade in a certain exam I am a total failure')? Do your negative thoughts tend to generalize to other areas? Do you have difficulties in accepting criticism?

	Presently	Maximum of pathology (lifetime)
0 = No		
1 = Slightly		
2 = Markedly		
3 = Severely		
4 = Very severely	☐	☐

Dominance among parents

Probe: Who of your parents really makes the decisions in the family?

Additional probes: Who of your parents initiates activities within the family such as planning weekends, excursions, vacation, buying furniture for the house, etc.? (Also count more subtle forms of dominance)

0 = Father very dominant, makes all decisions, mother has little say in the family or is frequently absent
1 = Father slightly dominant
2 = Both parents dominant to the same degree

3 = Mother slightly dominant
4 = Mother strongly dominant, makes all important decisions, father has little to say and has a less important role in the family (e.g. frequently absent)

	Presently	Highest score (0–4) (lifetime)
	□	□

The distribution of scores for each individual item was scrutinized and those which demonstrated a gross departure from normality were excluded from further analyses. The method of analysis was performed for item expressions in the past (lifetime) which per definition had the same or higher scores than ratings for the present status. Exploratory principal component analysis (PCA) with varimax rotation was conducted on the combined SIAB-P (psychopathology) and SIAB-FAM (family interaction) interview as well as for parts A and B separately. Attention was initially focused on obtaining a parsimonious number of components which could be used for the application of a meaningful descriptive label to those items for the interview directed to the past (lifetime). The final selection of items, identified in the analysis of lifetime item expressions as contributing to the principal component solution, were adopted for the analysis of the expression of items in the present. Factor scores on the components were determined for both sections of the SIAB.

SIAB (Specific Eating Disorder and General Psychopathology)

Results of factor analyses

A combined analysis of items from the SIAB-P (psychopathology) and the SIAB-FAM (family interaction) did not produce clear component solutions. Therefore, the following principal component analyses focused on the two interview parts separately. Seven items from the psychopathology section and six items from the family interaction and pathology section were excluded *a priori* from the analysis as they did not apply equally to all respondents or demonstrated unacceptable distributions. Thirty-six items from the psychopathology section were entered into the initial principal component analysis with varimax rotation and the number of components to be rotated varied, taking account of the Guttman criterion, so as to obtain the most interpretable component solution. A criterion of 0.40 was adopted as the cutoff for item loadings on the components. As a result of this criterion two items (lack of concentration, hypochondria) were excluded. In the final principal component analysis of 34 items, 10 met the Guttman criterion and accounted for 6.3 per cent of total variance. The rotation of six of these accounted for 53.2 per cent of variance and produced the most meaningful pattern of item allocation to components (Table 4.1). Only two items loaded on more than one component. The components were termed 'body image and slimness ideal', 'social integration and sexuality', 'depression', 'compulsion and anxiety', 'bulimic behaviour' and 'laxative abuse' to reflect the predominant pattern of item loading on any one component. The first three components were the most robust and contributed 35.4 per cent to the proportion of total variance explained in comparison to 17.8 per cent from the last three components.

The items generally demonstrated good components specificity; this is further reflected in the high loadings, whose square may be interpreted as the proportion of item variance accounted for by that component on one component and markedly lower or negligible on the other components. This may best be seen by comparing the squared factor loading with the communality to arrive at the amount of variance accounted for by the rest of the components.

External validity

The factor scores of the components obtained for the past (lifetime and present) were entered into a correlational analysis for subsamples of patients with subscales of the Anorexia Nervosa Inventory for Self-Rating (ANIS; $N = 120$) by Fichter and Keeser (1980) and Fichter *et al.* (1988) and with another interview, the Eating Disorder Examination (EDE; $N = 50$), developed by Cooper and Fairburn (1987) and Cooper, Cooper and Fairburn (1989).

As shown in Table 4.3, correlation coefficients were calculated with the subscales and grand mean of the Anorexia Nervosa Inventory for Self-Rating (ANIS). Since the ANIS ratings refer to the present status, the SIAB ratings for the present and not the lifetime ratings were analysed. Consistent and quite strong correlations were observed between the factor scores for the components 'slimness and body ideal', 'social integration and sexuality' and 'depression' and the ANIS subscales and the ANIS grand mean. These results, shown in detail in Table 4.3, suggest interdependence between these SIAB components and ANIS subscales. The SIAB component 'bulimic behaviour' showed significant but weak correlations with the ANIS subscale 'bulimic symptoms' ($r = 0.26, p < 0.001$). Correlation analyses of the SIAB factor scores with the ANIS subscales and the EDE grand mean produced higher coefficients for the present as compared to the past (lifetime) expression of symptoms. High correlations were observed between the EDE grand mean and the SIAB components 'slimness and body image' ($r = 0.46; p < 0.001$), 'bulimia' ($r = 0.43; p < 0.001$), 'laxative abuse' ($r = 0.31; p < 0.01$) and 'depression' $r = 0.30$/NS) for the present symptom expression.

Table 4.1 SIAB–P psychopathology interview: mean scores for patients and healthy controls and principal component loadings of lifetime item ratings. Loadings are presented without the decimal point

Item	Body image	Social integration	Depression	Anxiety/ compulsion	Bulimic behaviour	Laxative abuse	Communality	Mean scores (0–4) Patients' lifetime	Patients' present	Controls present
I. Body image and slimness ideal										
29. Persistent overconcern with food and eating	79	08	03	18	–01	15	0.69	2.6	1.7	0.5
30. Ideal of slimness	84	04	13	08	09	14	0.76	2.7	1.7	0.7
10. Fasting	82	07	11	–02	–05	14	0.71	2.7	1.5	0.5
15. Body-image disturbances	82	14	17	–04	03	14	0.74	2.6	1.7	0.7
32. Perception of proprio- and interoceptive signals	43	09	10	29	07	–04	0.29	1.9	1.3	0.2
53. Global rating of eating disorder	55	16	21	12	06	02	0.39	3.3	2.1	0.3
II. Social integration and sexuality										
44. Loss of libido	20	60	01	13	–10	28	0.51	2.7	1.6	0.3
45. Sexual anxieties	10	53	05	15	–12	27	0.40	2.6	1.7	0.4
47. Sexual behaviour	15	47	–20	–07	–38	–13	0.45	2.0	1.6	0.4
50. Peer integration	–03	80	27	03	–11	–14	0.75	2.3	1.5	0.3
49. Extent of social contacts	–01	85	20	02	00	–11	0.78	2.3	1.4	0.2
51. Social withdrawal	11	82	17	–01	09	–02	0.72	2.4	1.4	0.4
48. Leisure activities	11	73	21	12	25	10	0.68	2.3	1.4	0.2
III. Depression										
38. Suicide attempts	14	12	60	20	13	05	0.45	1.6	0.7	0.5
36. Self-esteem	20	23	70	07	08	16	0.62	2.2	1.6	0.4
35. Confidence in performance	06	33	62	09	01	19	0.54	2.2	1.6	0.7
31. Feelings of insufficiency	34	11	63	03	20	03	0.57	2.4	1.7	0.5
4. Achievement orientation	05	–02	44	–02	–46	19	0.44	2.4	2.1	0.7
33. Depressed mood	10	12	73	13	03	04	0.58	2.4	1.8	0.8
34. Depressive thoughts	10	03	76	19	–03	10	0.64	2.3	1.8	0.7

(continued)

Table 4.1 (*continued*)

Item	Body image	Social integration	Depression	Anxiety/ compulsion	Bulimic behaviour	Laxative abuse	Communality	Mean scores (0–4) Patients' lifetime	Patients' present	Controls present
IV. Compulsion and anxiety										
6. Anxiety	18	10	38	45	24	–18	0.48	2.1	1.7	0.6
7. Phobia	–06	09	14	58	–05	–02	0.37	1.0	0.9	0.5
25. Compulsive checking	06	00	06	66	02	14	0.46	0.8	0.7	0.3
26. Cleanliness obsessions	–01	04	12	45	–27	28	0.37	0.5	0.4	0.3
27. Obsessive ruminations	14	–08	18	63	11	–05	0.47	1.5	1.4	0.5
28. Compulsive thoughts and behaviours about eating	28	25	–04	53	01	07	0.43	1.4	1.1	0.2
V. Bulimic behaviour										
16. Bingeing	47	–20	28	–04	49	–02	0.58	2.0	1.4	0.7
19. Induced vomiting	29	–14	26	–06	57	03	0.50	1.9	1.3	0.1
24. Motor hyperactivity	27	05	25	10	–49	–02	0.39	2.3	1.7	0.9
52. Denial of illness	32	31	17	–06	–43	–20	0.46	2.0	0.9	—
8. Sleep disturbance	10	08	25	08	40	20	0.29	1.7	1.2	0.3
40. Alcohol abuse	13	11	15	05	52	05	0.33	0.6	0.2	0.2
VI. Laxative abuse										
20. Obstipation	19	08	17	11	09	74	0.64	2.0	1.1	0.2
21. Laxative abuse	20	–02	20	00	14	72	0.62	1.9	0.7	0.2
Total variance explained	4.18	3.97	3.88	2.20	2.14	1.69				
Proportion explained	12.3	11.7	11.4	6.5	6.3	5.0				

Table 4.2 SIAB–FAM family interaction and pathology interview: mean scores for patients and healthy controls and principal component loadings of lifetime ratings. Loadings are presented without the decimal point

Item	Marital satisfaction	Achievement orientation	Rigidity	Family closeness	Communality	Mean scores (0–4) Patients' lifetime	Patients' present	Controls present
I. Marital dissatisfaction (parents)								
65. Perceived rejection by father	59	19	04	00	39	1.3	1.0	0.7
63a. Presence/absence of father in family	55	20	02	−03	34	1.6	1.4	1.2
59. Absence of joint family activities	54	29	−02	08	38	2.1	2.0	1.2
61a. Marital dissatisfaction of mother	80	−19	24	03	73	1.8	1.5	1.3
61b. Marital dissatisfaction of father	73	−27	19	02	64	1.5	1.2	0.9
62. Lack of family conflict resolution	47	22	45	29	56	2.3	1.9	1.0
II. Achievement orientation and performance expectancy								
70b. Performance expectancy of mother	−03	67	44	01	64	1.8	1.6	0.9
69a. Achievement orientation of father	14	71	−13	14	56	2.1	2.1	1.0
69b. Achievement orientation of mother	−16	62	37	00	55	1.8	1.7	0.8
70a. Performance expectancy of father	30	78	−11	02	71	1.9	1.6	1.0
III. Rigidity and family interaction								
58. Family overconcern with food and eating	15	09	49	09	28	1.7	1.6	0.3
66. Perceived rejection by mother	39	19	50	−03	44	1.3	1.0	0.4
68. Dominance by mother	−17	−19	59	−01	41	2.0	2.1	1.9
71. Interactional rigidity	37	06	67	20	63	2.0	1.8	1.2
IV. Family closeness and enmeshment								
72. Enmeshment	13	12	25	52	36	1.8	1.4	0.5
60. Family isolation	18	−07	26	46	32	1.6	1.5	0.7
73a. Restrictive reaction to disorder by mother	16	31	33	49	47	2.2	1.8	—
73b. Restrictive reaction to disorder by father	25	36	−05	40	35	1.6	1.3	—
67a. Distance from mother	−04	−07	−09	74	56	1.7	1.2	0.4
67b. Distance from father	−09	14	−17	66	49	1.2	0.9	0.3
63b. Presence/absence of mother in family	−20	−04	19	40	24	2.3	2.2	1.4
Total variance explained	3.00	2.62	2.26	2.19				
Proportion explained	14.3	12.5	10.8	10.4				

SIAB-FAM (Family Interaction and Family Pathology)

Results of factor analyses

Twenty-one items relating to family life in the past and present were similarly entered into separate principal component analyses with varimax rotation. Six components of the family interview part, accounting for 59.5 per cent of the variance, had an eigenvalue of at least 1.0 per cent in the analyses of the past expression. The rotation of four of these, accounting for 48 per cent of variance, produced the most interpretable results (cf. Table 4.2). These were labelled 'marital satisfaction and disintegration', 'achievement orientation and performance expectancy', 'rigidity and family interaction', and 'family closeness and enmeshment'. Two items loaded on more than one component ('lack of family conflict resolution', and 'performance expectancy of the mother' — cf. Table 4.2). With these exceptions, items generally demonstrated clear loadings on one component, with all other loadings being much lower or negligible. No marked difference in the proportion of variance explained was observed between the four components. The analyses of items concerning family interactions for the present produced seven items, accounting for 64.5 per cent of total variance, which passed the Guttman criterion. The loadings on the components, produced by rotation of four, accounted for 48.3 per cent of the variance. Since the items loaded similarly on the components to the results obtained in the analyses of the past, the same labels were ascribed.

External validity

The component 'marital dissatisfaction' showed high and significant correlations with the Anorexia Nervosa Inventory for Self-rating (ANIS) subscales 'figure consciousness' ($r = 0.26$; $p < 0.01$), 'feelings of insufficiency' ($r = 0.43$; $p < 0.001$), 'sexual anxieties' ($r = 0.24$; $p < 0.01$), 'bulimic symptoms' ($r = 0.33$; $p < 0.001$) and the ANIS grand mean ($r = 0.34$; $p < 0.001$). The SIAB-FAM component 'achievement orientation and performance expectancy' showed significant correlations with the ANIS subscale 'insufficiency' ($r = 0.25$; $p < 0.01$) and with the EDE grand mean ($r = 0.42$; $p < 0.001$). The SIAB-FAM component 'rigidity and family interaction' showed no significant correlations with the ANIS self-rating scale and the EDE interview. The SIAB-FAM component 'family closeness and enmeshment' showed significant correlations with the ANIS subscales 'insufficiency' ($r = 0.26$; $p < 0.01$), 'sexual anxieties' ($r = 0.23$; $p < 0.01$) and with the ANIS grand mean. Thus, of the SIAB-FAM components only 'achievement orientation and performance expectancy' showed a high and significant correlation with specific eating disorder psychopathology as assessed in the Eating Disorder Examination (EDE).

Table 4.3 Correlations between factor scores obtained from principal component analysis of SIAB, Anorexia Nervosa Inventory for Self-rating (ANIS) subscores (N = 120) and Eating Disorder Examination (EDE) (N = 50) based on symptoms expression at the time of assessment (present)

Structured Interview for Anorexia and Bulimia Nervosa	Anorexia Nervosa Inventory for Self-rating							Eating Disorder Examination
	FIG	INS	OBS	NEM	SEX	BUL	Grand mean	EDE
SIAB–P (psychopathology)								
Body image and slimness ideal	0.55**	0.19*	0.36**	0.42**	0.20*	0.31**	0.47**	0.46**
Social integration and sexuality	0.30**	0.32**	0.21*	0.27**	0.41**	0.27**	0.37**	0.13
Depression	0.21*	0.44**	0.24*	0.17	0.19	0.22*	0.32**	0.30
Compulsion and anxiety	–0.03	0.18	0.16	0.06	0.19	–0.08	0.09	–0.03
Bulimic behaviour	–0.09	0.15	–0.11	0.13	0.13	0.26**	0.06	0.43**
Laxative abuse	0.16	0.17	0.19*	0.29**	0.15	0.23*	0.24*	0.31*
SIAB–FAM (family interaction and pathology)								
Marital dissatisfaction	0.26*	0.43**	0.15	0.18	0.24*	0.33**	0.34**	0.06
Achievement orientation and performance expectancy	0.15	0.25*	0.15	0.12	0.17	0.10	0.20	0.42**
Rigidity and family interaction	0.15	0.21	0.21	0.10	0.14	0.11	0.20	–0.10
Family closeness and enmeshment	0.14	0.26*	0.19	0.17	0.23*	0.20	0.24*	–0.06

FIG, figure consciousness; INS, feelings of insufficiency; OBS, obsessionality and ananchasm; NEM, negative effect of meals; SEX, sexual anxieties; BUL, bulimic symptoms.

*$p < 0.01$.

**$p < 0.001$.

Conclusions

Principal component analyses were conducted separately for the SIAB-P (specific eating disorder and general psychopathology) and the SIAB-FAM (family interaction and family pathology) for both their past and present expression. Varimax rotation of six components for the past expression of the SIAB-P (psychopathology) produced the most interpretable solution in terms of ascribing a meaningful label to the components. The first three components ('body image and slimness ideal', 'social integration and sexuality' and 'depression') of the six identified components accounted for the main part of the variance explained by the solution, i.e. potentially better describe the eating disorders during an acute phase in the past. The component 'social integration and sexuality' was the most stable in the comparison of the past and present solutions of the psychopathology part of the interview, while the component 'laxative abuse' was least stable. This suggests that anorexic and bulimic eating disorders may manifest differently over time and particularly when situational aspects are taken into consideration. The components derived from analyses can serve as heuristic devices in describing anorexic and bulimic eating disorders.

The analyses and rotation of the SIAB-FAM (family interaction and family pathology) produced four components, which were labelled 'marital satisfaction and disintegration', 'achievement orientation and performance expectancy', 'rigidity and family interaction', and 'family closeness and enmeshment'. These components demonstrated some changes in the allocation of items to components between analyses of past and present expression.

Correlational analyses for establishing external validity showed low correlations with the Eating Disorder Examination for some SIAB components and significant correlations with others. The Eating Disorder Examination correlated significantly with the SIAB-FAM components 'body image and ideal of slimness', 'bulimic symptoms' and 'laxative abuse', and with the SIAB-FAM component 'achievement orientation and performance expectancy' in the family. As would be expected, high correlations were observed between the SIAB-P component 'body image and ideal of slimness' and the Anorexia Nervosa Inventory for Self-rating (ANIS) subscale 'figure consciousness' (r = 0.55) as well as the ANIS subscale 'negative effect of meals' (r = 0.42). Also, the 'depression' component of the SIAB-P showed a higher correlation with the ANIS depression subscale ('feelings of insufficiency'; r = 0.44). Except for the SIAB-FAM component 'marital dissatisfaction', the components of the SIAB-FAM (family interaction and family pathology) appear to measure different dimensions than those covered by scales on specific eating pathology as measured by the Eating Disorder Examination and the Anorexia Nervosa Inventory for Self-Rating.

We have presented data concerning standard values for single items of the

SIAB-P and SIAB-FAM for eating-disordered patients and healthy controls. Secondly, different components have been established for the SIAB-p (psychopathology) and the SIAB-FAM (family interaction and pathology) using principal component analyses and varimax rotation. The meaning of these components has been further elaborated by the use of correlational analyses with the Eating Disorder Examination and the Anorexia Nervosa Inventory for Self-Rating and its subscales. The SIAB-P and SIAB-FAM can be used in clinical practice and research for the diagnosis of anorexic and bulimic eating disorders, for their detailed specification and the formation of subgroups and can also be useful for therapy evaluation and the assessment of the course of illness. For the SIAB-P (psychopathology) in its second revision a computer algorithm exists for automated diagnoses of eating disorders according to the DSM-III-R criteria and the ICD-10 criteria.

Acknowledgements

We thank Dr Martina Hentze, Delia Höhne and Dr Maren Wittern for assessing the control group.

References

American Psychiatric Association (1987). *Diagnostic and Statistical Manual of Mental Disorders — Revision (DSM-III-R).* American Psychiatric Association, Washington DC.

Cooper, Z. and C. G. Fairburn (1987). The Eating Disorder Examination: a semi-structured interview for assessment of specific psychopathology of eating disorders. *International Journal of Eating Disorders* **6**, 1–7.

Cooper, Z., P. J. Cooper and C. G. Fairburn (1989). The validity of the Eating Disorder Examination and its subscales. *British Journal of Psychiatry* **154**, 807–812.

Engel, K. and D. Höhne (1989). An interaction model of anorexia nervosa. *Psychotherapy and Psychosomatics*, in press.

Fichter, M. M. and W. Keeser (1980). Das Anorexia Nervosa Inventar zur Selbstbeurteilung (ANIS). *Archiv für Psychiatrie und Nervenkrankheiten* **228**, 67–89.

Fichter, M. M., M. Elton, L. Sourdi, S. Weyerer and G. Koptagel-Ilal (1988). Anorexia nervosa in Greek and Turkish adolescents. *European Archives of Psychiatry and Neurological Science* **237**, 200–208.

Goldberg, D. P., P. Cooper, R. R. Eastwood, M. B. Kedward and M. Shepherd (1970). A standardized psychiatric interview for use in community survey. *British Journal of Preventive and Social Medicine* **24**, 18–23.

Palmer, R. L., M. Christie, C. Cordle, D. Davis and J. Kenrick (1987). The Clinical Eating Disorder Rating Instrument (CEDRI): a preliminary description. *International Journal of Eating Disorders* **6**, 9–14.

Robins, L. N., J. E. Helzer, J. Croughan and K. S. Ratcliff (1981). National Institute of Mental Health Diagnostic Interview Schedule. Its history, characteristics and validity. *Archives of General Psychiatry* **38**, 381–389.

Robins, L. N., J. E. Helzer, K. S. Ratcliff and W. Seyfried (1982). Validity of the Diagnostic Interview Schedule, Version II: DSM-III diagnoses. *Psychological Medicine* **12**, 855–870.

Spitzer, R. L., J. B. W. Williams and M. Gibbon (1987). *The Structured Clinical Interview for DSM-III-R (SCID),* German translation by H. U. Wittchen, M. Zaudig, E. Schramm, P. Sprenger, W. Mombour, J. Klug and R. Horn (1987). *Strukturiertes klinisches Interview für DSM-III-R.* Beltz-Verlag, Weinheim.

Wing, J. K., J. E. Cooper and N. Sartorius (1974a). *The Description and Classification of Psychiatric Symptoms: An Instruction Manual for the PSE and CATEGO System.* University Press, London.

Wing, J. K., J. E. Cooper and N. Sartorius (1974b). *Measurement and Classification of Psychiatric Symptoms. An Instruction Manual for the PSE and CATEGO Program.* Cambridge University Press, London, New York.

World Health Organization (1987). *International Classification of Diseases — tenth revision*, chapter V. Mental, behavioral and developmental disorders. (1986) Draft for Field Trials. World Health Organization, Geneva.

5

Medical complications in bulimia nervosa

James E. Mitchell
Claire Pomeroy
and
Eduardo Colon
University of Minnesota, Minneapolis

The disordered eating behavior practiced by individuals with bulimia nervosa often results in physiological disturbances which affect several organ systems. Fortunately, most of these disturbances are not severe, and most resolve quickly if the disorder is effectively treated or abates spontaneously. However, certain physiological changes can cause significant morbidity and at times have resulted in death. For this reason, all patients with bulimia nervosa need to be carefully screened medically and to have certain laboratory parameters assessed. Many patients with this disorder will also require periodic monitoring of vital signs and certain laboratory tests during treatment. In this chapter, we will review the available literature on these disturbances. The chapter encompasses three areas: (1) the behaviors associated with bulimia nervosa which result in physiological disturbances; (2) physical findings which can be useful diagnostically; and (3) specific medical complications by organ system. Certain areas of dysfunction, such as prolonged gastric emptying, will not be described in detail since they are covered elsewhere in this volume.

Table 5.1 Prevalence of disturbed eating behavior reported by women with bulimia nervosa

'Bingeing'	100%
Fasting	92%
Physical abuse for weight control	91%
Self-induced vomiting	88%
Chewing and spitting out of food	65%
Laxatives and dietary aids	61%
Appetite suppressants	50%
Diuretics as weight controls	33%

Behaviors Associated with Bulimia Nervosa

Bulimia nervosa is frequently thought of as a disorder of binge-eating which occurs in individuals who have a marked preoccupation with weight. However, individuals with this disorder commonly engage in several problem behaviors other than binge-eating and, for the most part, it is these associated behaviors that have adverse medical consequences (Table 5.1).

The signs, symptoms and physiological disturbances that are encountered in individuals with bulimia nervosa are explainable and understandable in the context of these behaviors, as will be illustrated further in the text. As an introduction we will offer two examples. Frequent self-induced vomiting causes a loss of hydrogen ion and fluid in the vomitus, engendering a metabolic alkalosis. The enamel erosion caused by exposure of the dental surfaces to the highly acid gastric contents also results from vomiting. Therefore, during the assessment of patients with bulimia nervosa, careful questioning needs to focus on the presence or absence of these behaviors. Appropriate laboratory tests and other diagnostic procedures based on this history should be used to screen for possible complications. For example, serum electrolyte determinations are quite important in a patient who reports self-induced vomiting, and dental consultation is also desirable for these patients.

Symptoms

Patients presenting for treatment with bulimia nervosa frequently report concerns about their physical health, and it is common for these patients to acknowledge that they have previously sought medical evaluation but did not tell the evaluating physician that they had an eating disorder. For example, a young woman might present to a physician with complaints of lethargy, weakness, and dizziness yet fail to report a pattern of self-induced vomiting and laxative abuse. Therefore, physicians must have a high index suspicion concerning the possibility of bulimic behaviors in women in the age group primarily at risk.

Two studies have systematically examined the physical symptoms endorsed by patients with bulimia nervosa presenting for treatment for their eating disorder. Abraham and Beumont (1982) reported that among 32 bulimic patients, the most commonly mentioned physical symptoms were swelling of hands and feet (69 per cent), abdominal fullness (66 per cent), fatigue (47 per cent), headache (38 per cent), and nausea (34 per cent). In a series of 275 women with bulimia, our group found the most common physical complaints to be weakness (84 per cent), feeling 'bloated' (75 per cent), 'puffy cheeks' (50 per cent), presumably related to salivary gland swelling, dental problems (37 per cent), and finger calluses (27 per cent), which will be discussed below (Mitchell *et al.*, 1985).

Signs

There are three signs observable on examination which should alert the clinician to the possible diagnosis of bulimia nervosa. The first is lesions on the skin over the dorsum of the hand. Originally described by Russell in 1979, such lesions result from the use of the hand to stimulate the gag reflex. The lesions vary from calluses to scars to superficial ulceration (Joseph and Herr, 1985; Schiff *et al.*, 1986; Wynn and Martin, 1984).

A second sign of diagnostic utility is hypertrophy of the salivary glands, particularly the parotid glands, a finding also encountered in patients with anorexia nervosa. The swelling is usually bilateral and painless and is often subtle, but in rare cases very obvious and disturbing to patients for cosmetic reasons (Anders *et al.*, 1975; Levin *et al.*, 1980; Simon *et al.*, 1979; Walsh, Croft and Katz, 1984). The exact prevalence of this finding in individuals with bulimia nervosa is unknown, but this complication is probably present in a minority of patients (Jacobs and Schneider, 1985).

The third sign, and the one that is probably most useful diagnostically since it is demonstrable in the highest number of patients, is the presence of dental enamel erosion (Clark, 1985; Hellstrom, 1977; House, Bliziotes and Licht, 1981; Hurst, Lacey and Crisp, 1977; Kerr, 1980; King and Plack, 1983; Simmons, Grayden and Mitchell, 1986; Wolcott, Yager and Gordon, 1984). The highly acid gastric contents erode the surface enamel, resulting in decalcification. In one recent study, the majority of patients who had been self-inducing vomiting at least three times a week for four years demonstrated this finding on examination (Simmons, Grayden and Mitchell, 1986).

Organ System Dysfunction

Fluid and electrolyte abnormalities

Electrolyte abnormalities are common in patients with bulimia nervosa and in related eating disorders. In one series of 168 patients with such disorders, 49 per cent had an electrolyte or acid–base abnormality, most commonly elevated serum bicarbonate suggesting metabolic alkalosis (27 per cent), hypochloremia (24 per cent), hypokalemia (14 per cent), and/or hyponatremia (5 per cent) (Mitchell *et al.*, 1984). These abnormalities result from the bulimia-associated behaviors, most commonly self-induced vomiting which causes loss of fluids, hydrogen ion, and chloride. Laxative abuse and diuretic abuse may also contribute to the volume depletion, and all of these behaviors result in hyperaldosteronism, which facilitates potassium wasting by the kidneys. Although alkalosis is the usual acid–base disturbance, metabolic acidosis can be associated with laxative-induced diarrhea (Mitchell and Boutacoff, 1986; Mitchell *et al.*, 1983).

Gastrointestinal

As mentioned previously, salivary gland hypertrophy has been described in patients with bulimia nervosa; however, the mechanism of hypertrophy is unclear. Various metabolic abnormalities such as alkalosis, malnutrition and high carbohydrate intake associated with binge-eating have been implicated by some authors (Anders *et al.*, 1975; Bennett *et al.*, 1982; Simon *et al.*, 1979). A related abnormality is that of hyperamylasemia (Gwirtsman *et al.*, 1986). In a series of 108 bulimic patients, our group found that 30 (27.8 per cent) had an elevated serum amylase level (Mitchell *et al.*, 1983). However, the elevations were usually modest, at maximum twice normal levels. Subsequently, Jacobs and Schneider (1985) reported that 15 of 24 patients in a series of bulimic patients had elevated serum amylase levels. The amylase elevations usually have been assumed to be salivary in origin, and Humphries *et al.* (1987) and Kaplan (1987) recently documented that most bulimic patients with elevated serum amylase levels have isolated increases in salivary isoamylase activity. However, Gavish *et al.* (1987) recently reported a subgroup of five patients with bulimia in a series of 21 patients with hyperlipidemic pancreatitis. The patients with bulimia were unusual in that they were difficult to manage medically, and their recurrent episodes of pancreatitis were associated with the discrete binge-eating episodes. Elevated pancreatic function has been reported by others as well (Gwirstman *et al.*, 1986). Therefore, an elevated serum amylase may be associated with pancreatic dysfunction in these patients and should be evaluated critically in each patient.

Two rare but very serious GI complications of bulimia nervosa are esophageal perforation and gastric perforation (James, 1984; Kerr, 1980; Larsen, Jensen and Axelsen, 1983; Michel, 1982; Phillips and Cunningham, 1984; Silber, 1978). The first well-documented case of esophageal perforation was published in 1724, when Boerhaave described the demise of Baron John Van Wassener, a Dutch admiral who ruptured his esophagus while self-inducing emesis (Silber, 1978). Other specific cases of esophageal rupture attributed to bulimia nervosa, have not, to our knowledge, been published. However, we have seen one such case in our clinic and it is likely that some of the other case reports of esophageal rupture reported in the literature may have involved bulimic individuals but that the diagnosis was not considered.

The available literature also suggests that gastric rupture can be associated with bulimia nervosa, but the exact incidence is unknown. Saul *et al.* (1981) reviewed the literature on spontaneous rupture of the stomach and noted that in 11 of the cases there was a diagnosis of anorexia nervosa and in 10 additional cases a history of recent weight loss. These authors added the case report of a 22-year-old female described as well nourished who developed gastric infarction and perforation after overeating. Several other cases of gastric dilatation or ischemic bowel changes associated with bulimic behavior have appeared (Breslow, Yates and Shisslak, 1986; Edwards, 1985; Mitchell, Pyle and Miner, 1982). Hiatal hernia has also been attributed to bulimia, but this has not been systematically investigated (Gross, 1983).

Laxative abuse is a common complicating behavior in bulimia nervosa patients (Mitchell and Boutacoff, 1986; Mitchell *et al.*, 1985). Medical complications associated with laxative abuse include laxative dependency, with profound constipation on laxative withdrawal, and, rarely, the development of permanent impairment of colonic function. Other laxative abuse complications which have been described in the literature include gastrointestinal bleeding, steatorrhea, and protein-losing gastroenteropathy (Mitchell and Boutacoff, 1986).

Mediastinum

Several published cases have suggested an association between the development of pneumomediastinum and vomiting behavior. Donley and Kemple (1978) reported the case of a 17-year-old female who developed mediastinal emphysema and the authors speculated that vomiting was a possible etiological factor. Chatfield, Bowditch and Forrest (1979) reported an episode of pneumomediastinum which occurred in a female with hyperemesis gravidarum. Brooks and Martyn (1979) reported the case of a 16-year-old female with anorexia nervosa in which an acute vomiting episode was linked to the development of pneumomediastinum, and Bullimore and Cooke (1982) reported an 18-year-old male with recurrent vomiting who developed subcutaneous emphysema. These reports suggest that vomiting behavior can result in pneumomediastinum or subcutaneous emphysema, but that these complications are most common in patients who are concomitantly emaciated, such as those with anorexia nervosa.

Cardiovascular

Probably the most common hemodynamic change which results from bulimic behaviors is dehydration. This can result in symptomatic hypotension and also contributes to the electrolyte abnormalities which develop in this condition.

Recently there also has been growing concern about the misuse of ipecac by patients with eating disorders and the possibility of myocardial toxicity developing in these patients (Adler *et al.*, 1980; Bennett *et al.*, 1982; Brotman *et al.*, 1981; Dawson and Yager, 1986; Ferguson, 1985; Isner, 1986; Manno and Manno, 1977; Norris, O'Malley and Palmer, 1985; Pope *et al.*, 1986; Schwartz and Clendenning, 1985). The alkaloid emetine contained in ipecac and which has been shown to accumulate in muscle with repeated usage is known to be associated with the development of myopathies, although a causal relationship between emetine use and fatal cardiomyopathy remains a matter of debate (Isner, 1986). Experimentation with this drug appears to be widespread in patients with eating disorders. Pope *et al.* (1986) reported that 28 of a series of 100 patients with bulimia indicated they had used ipecac to induce vomiting and that four of those indicated having used the drug on more than 100 occasions. Therefore, the possibility of a myopathy and, of particular concern, a cardiomyopathy, should be considered in these patients.

Johnson *et al.* (1986) recently reported an apparent excess of mitral valve prolapse in women with bulimia compared to age-matched controls. The significance of this finding is unclear.

Endocrine system

Although several investigators have begun to study neuroendocrine parameters in patients with bulimia nervosa, these data are still limited and preliminary. The results so far, however, are of interest. Most reports have concerned the dexamethasone suppression test (DST). Much of the original interest concerning the DST in bulimia nervosa resulted from the finding of a high rate of non-suppression on the DST in patients with certain types of depression and the observation of a high prevalence of affective disorders in women with bulimia nervosa. These two findings led to the use of the DST as a tool to investigate the relationship between bulimia nervosa and affective disorders. The DST studies in bulimia nervosa have varied as to methodology, but generally the results indicate high rates of non-suppression, with from 20 to 67 per cent of the patients tested failing to suppress (Gwirtsman *et al.*, 1983; Hudson, Pope and Jonas, 1983; Hudson and Hudson, 1984; Hughes, Wells and Cunningham, 1986; Krieg, Backmund and Pirke, 1987; Lindy *et al.*, 1985; Mitchell *et al.*, 1984; Musisi and Garfinkel, 1985). However, the presence or absence of an affective disorder in an individual patient with bulimia nervosa does not appear to be a good predictor of suppression, and the significance of the high rate of non-suppression is unclear.

Three studies have examined thyrotropin-releasing hormone (TRH) effects on thyroid-stimulating hormone (TSH) release, and the findings to date are conflicting. Gwirtsman *et al.* (1983) reported that eight of 10 patients demonstrated blunting. However, Mitchell and Bantle (1983) and Norris, O'Malley and Palmer (1985) found evidence of significant blunting in only a few patients. Also in the Norris *et al.* study, no significant group differences were found between bulimic and control subjects.

Mira and associates reported that many patients with bulimia nervosa had oligomenorrhea or amenorrhea, and that these menstrual changes were associated with low basal luteinizing hormone (LH) and estradiol levels, and with low weight (Mira, Stewart and Abraham, 1985; Mira *et al.*, 1987).

Three studies have systematically examined glucose tolerance in patients with bulimia nervosa. Two found no abormalities in serum glucose levels (Hohlstein *et al.*, 1986; Mitchell and Laine, 1985). However, Schweiger *et al.* (1987) recently demonstrated that bulimic patients had elevated insulin secretion and glucose levels after a test meal compared to age-matched controls. Ferguson (1985) has reported the case of a patient who died with 'acute hypoglycemia', and our group has studied one patient who developed documented symptomatic hypoglycemia after vomiting on several occasions.

There also appears to be an interesting association between diabetes mellitus and both anorexia nervosa and bulimia nervosa (Pirke, Pahl and Schweiger, 1985; Pope *et al.*, 1986). Several authors have reported cases or series of patients who had both an eating disorder and diabetes mellitus, and several of these reports indicated that patients withheld their own insulin as a way to induce glycosuria and cause weight loss. Hudson *et al.* (1985) reported that 35 per cent of the patients who responded to a questionnaire survey administered to patients being seen for diabetes mellitus indicated symptoms suggestive of bulimia. Taken together, these reports suggest that there is an association between diabetes mellitus and eating disorders, which is perhaps not surprising when one considers the amount of emphasis placed on food intake and weight in this population.

Metabolic

In contrast to anorexia nervosa, few metabolic studies have been reported in patients with bulimia nervosa. However, Pirke, Pahl and Schweiger (1985) have reported that patients with bulimia nervosa develop metabolic abnormalities suggestive of starvation, including reduced serum glucose levels, reduced T3 levels, reduced plasma norepinephrine, and elevated levels of free fatty acid and beta hydroxybutyric acid. These findings suggest that despite a normal body weight their metabolic functioning indicates inadequate intake.

Neurological

Interest in the neurological functioning of patients with bulimia nervosa has resulted from both a logical curiosity about the functioning of central neural mechanisms subserving food intake and appetite and from observations that specific CNS lesions can result in abnormal eating behaviors, at times resembling bulimia. The latter include hypothalamic tumors, Huntington's chorea, and certain postictal phenomena (Lewin, Mattingly and Millis, 1972; Remick, Jones and Campos, 1980; Wegner and Struve, 1977; Weller and Weller, 1982).

Much of the work done examining neurological mechanisms in bulimic patients has been reported by Rau, Green and their colleagues. In a series of articles, they reported that 64 per cent of a series of 59 patients with a compulsive eating disorder (a diagnostic grouping with some overlap with bulimia nervosa) demonstrated electroencephalographic (EEG) abnormalities which the authors thought to be of clinical importance (Green and Rau, 1974; Rau and Green, 1975, 1978; Rau, Struve and Green, 1979). However, the significance of the described EEG abnormalities is a matter of debate (Lombrose, Schwartz and Clark, 1966; Long and Johnson, 1968; Maulsby, 1979; Wegner and Struve, 1977), and a subsequent EEG study involving readings of tracings by electroencephalographers blind to patient status found that only four of 25 EEGs were clearly abnormal (Mitchell, Hosfield and Pyle, 1983). More work needs to be done before any firm conclusions can be drawn regarding neurophysiological dysfunction, at least of a type detectable by EEG, and the abnormal eating behaviors of patients with bulimia nervosa.

Lankenau *et al.* (1985) compared the CT scan results of five bulimic patients to those of 14 controls and found no differences, in contrast to the ventricular enlargement demonstrated in patients with anorexia nervosa, a finding also reported by other researchers (Sein, Searson and Nicol, 1981). However, Krieg, Backmund and Pirke (1987) found evidence of CT changes in a larger series of patients with bulimia. The significance of these changes has yet to be determined.

Other complications

Other medical complications not previously discussed include the development of a peripheral myopathy secondary to the use of ipecac or to hypokalemia, and the possible development of hypokalemic neuropathy in patients who have protracted dehydration and hypokalemia. There has also been a case report of a patient who met criteria for bulimia who was binge-eating and self-inducing vomiting and presented with the vitamin K dependent coagulation factor deficiency and evidence of hemorrhagic tendencies on physical examination (Niiya *et al.*, 1983), and a patient with bulimia who developed a folate deficiency (Eedy, Curran and Andrews, 1986).

Discussion

Although the medical complications which occur in individuals with bulimia nervosa can be quite serious, all of the available evidence suggests that the morbidity and mortality is far less than that seen in patients with anorexia nervosa where emaciation is also present. Starvation carries with it a marked risk for numerous other complications in addition to those already described, including osteoporosis, liver function abnormalities, leukopenia, thrombocytopenia, and impaired cardiac functioning. Clinical evidence suggests quite clearly that bulimia nervosa is a more benign condition.

The abnormalities which have been demonstrated in bulimia nervosa are not just of interest because of our concern about the physical status of these patients; some are also of interest as possible clues to the pathophysiology of the disorder. It seems reasonable to speculate that the cycle of binge-eating and starving and the protracted fasting which characterize the eating of patients with bulimia nervosa may engender secondary physiological disturbances which tend to perpetuate or exacerbate the behavior. Therefore, further research which attempts not just to document the prevalence of such abnormalities but also to relate them to the ongoing pattern of eating behavior may prove useful in helping us understand the pathogenesis of this condition.

References

Abraham, S. F. and P. V. Beumont (1982). How patients describe bulimia or binge eating. *Psychological Medicine* **12**, 625–635.

Adler, A. O., P. Walinsky, R. A. Krall and L. Chosy (1980). Death resulting from ipecac syrup poisoning. *Journal of the American Medical Association* **243**, 1927–1928.

Al-Mufty, N. S. and D. H. Bevan (1977). A case of subcutaneous emphysema, pneumomediastinum and pneumoretroperitoneum associated with functional anorexia. *Journal of Clinical Practice* **31**, 160–161.

Anders, D., D. Harms, O. Kriens and H. Schmidt (1975). Zur Frage der Sialadenose als sekundarer Organmanifestation der Anorexia nervosa — Beobachtungen an einem 13 jahrigen Knaben. *Klinische Paediatrie* **187**, 156–162.

Bennett, H. S., A. J. Spiro, M. A. Pollack and P. Zucker (1982). Ipecac-induced myopathy simulating dermatomyositis. *Neurology* **32**, 91–94.

Berke, G. S. and T. C. Calcaterra (1985). Parotid hypertrophy with bulimia: A report of surgical management. *Laryngoscope* **95**, 597–598.

Breslow, M., A. Yates and C. Shisslak (1986). Spontaneous rupture of the stomach: a complication of bulimia. *International Journal of Eating Disorders* **5**, 137–142.

Brooks, A. P. and C. Martyn (1979). Pneumomediastinum in anorexia nervosa. *British Medical Journal* **1**, 124.

Brotman, M. C., N. Forbath, P. E. Garfinkel and J. G. Humphrey (1981). Myopathy due to ipecac syrup poisoning in a patient with anorexia nervosa. *Canadian Medical Association Journal* **125**, 453–454.

Bullimore, D. W. and D. Cooke (1982). Cyclical vomiting with pneumomediastinum. *Acta Paediatrica Scandinavica* **71**, 675–676.

Burke, R. C. (1986). Bulimia and parotid enlargement — case report and treatment. *Journal of Otolaryngology* **15**, 49–50.

Chatfield, W. R., J. D. P. Bowditch and C. A. Forrest (1979). Spontaneous pneumomediastinum complicating anorexia nervosa. *British Medical Journal* **1**, 200–201.

Clark, D. C. (1985). Oral complications of anorexia nervosa and/or bulimia: with a review of the literature. *Journal of Oral Medicine* **40**, 134–138.

Dawson, J. A. and J. Yager (1986). A case of abuse of syrup of ipecac resulting in death. *Journal of the American College of Health* **34**, 280–282.

Donley, A. J. and T. J. Kemple (1978). Spontaneous pneumomediastinum complicating anorexia nervosa. *British Medical Journal* **11**, 1604–1605.

Edwards, G. M. (1985). Case of bulimia nervosa presenting with acute, fatal abdominal distension. *Lancet* **1**, 822–823.

Eedy, D. J., J. G. Curran and W. J. Andrews (1986). A patient with bulimia nervosa and profound folate deficiency. *Postgraduate Medical Journal* **62**, 853–854.

Ferguson, J. M. (1985). Bulimia: a potentially fatal syndrome. *Psychosomatics* **26**, 252–253.

Friedman, E. J. (1984). Death from ipecac intoxication in a patient with anorexia nervosa. *American Journal of Psychiatry* **141**, 702–703.

Gavish, D., S. Eisenberg, E. M. Berry, Y. Kleinman, E. Witztum, J. Norman and E. Leitersdorf (1987). An underlying behavioral disorder in hyperlipidemic pancreatitis: a prospective multidisciplinary approach. *Archives of Internal Medicine* **147**, 705–708.

Green, R. S. and J. H. Rau (1974). Treatment of compulsive eating disturbances with anticonvulsant medication. *American Journal of Psychiatry* **131**, 428–432.

Gross, M. (1983). Aspects of bulimia. *Cleveland Clinical Quarterly* **50**, 19–25.

Gwirtsman, H. E., P. Roy-Byrne, J. Yager and R. H. Gerner (1983). Neuroendocrine abnormalities in bulimia. *American Journal of Psychiatry* **140**, 559–563.

Gwirtsman, H. E., J. Yager, B. K. Gillard and L. Lerner (1986). Serum amylase and its isoenzymes in normal weight bulimia. *International Journal of Eating Disorders* **5**, 355–361.

Hellstrom, I. (1977). Oral complications in anorexia nervosa. *Scandinavian Journal of Dentistry* **85**, 71–86.

Hillard, J. R., M. C. Lobo and R. P. Keeling (1983). Bulimia and diabetes: a potentially life-threatening combination. *Psychosomatics* **24**, 292–295.

Hohlstein, L. A., H. E. Gwirtsman, F. Whalen and M. P. Enns (1986). Oral glucose tolerance in bulimia. *International Journal of Eating Disorders* **5**, 157–160.

House, R. D., M. M. Bliziotes and J. H. Licht (1981). Perimolysis. Unveiling the surreptitious vomiter. *Oral Surgery* **51**, 152–155.

Hudson, J. I. and M. S. Hudson (1984). Endocrine dysfunction in anorexia nervosa and bulimia: comparison with abnormalities in other psychiatric disorders and disturbances due to metabolic factors. *Psychiatric Developments* **4**, 237–272.

Hudson, J. I., M. S. Hudson and S. M. Wentworth (1983). Self-induced glycosuria. A novel method of purging in bulimia. *Journal of the American Medical Association* **249**, 2501.

Hudson, J. I., H. G. Pope, Jr and J. M. Jonas (1983). Hypothalamic–pituitary–adrenal axis hyperactivity in bulimia. *Psychiatry Research* **8**, 111–117.

Hudson, J. I., S. M. Wentworth, M. S. Hudson and H. G. Pope (1985). Prevalence of anorexia nervosa and bulimia among young diabetic women. *Journal of Clinical Psychiatry* **46**, 88–89.

Hudson, M. S. and S. M. Wentworth (1983). Bulimia and diabetes. *New England Journal of Medicine* **309**, 431–432.

Hughes, P. L., L. A. Wells and C. J. Cunningham (1986). The dexamethasone suppression test in bulimia before and after successful treatment with desipramine. *Journal of Clinical Psychiatry* **47**, 515–517.

Humphries, L. L., L. J. Adams, J. H. Eckfeldt, M. D. Levitt and C. J. McClain (1987).

Hyperamylasemia in patients with eating disorders. *Annals of Internal Medicine* **106**, 50–52.
Hurst, P. S., J. H. Lacey and A. H. Crisp (1977). Teeth, vomiting and diet: a study of the dental characteristics of seventeen anorexia nervosa patients. *Postgraduate Medicine* **53**, 298–305.
Isner, J. M. (1986). Effects of ipecac on the heart (Letter). *New England Journal of Medicine* 1253.
Jacobs, M. B. and J. A. Schneider (1985). Medical complications of bulimia: a prospective evaluation. *Quarterly Journal of Medicine* **54**, 177–182.
James, E. C. (1984). Postemetic rupture of herniated cardia of the stomach (Letter). *Journal of the American Medical Association* **251**, 471.
Johnson, D. L. and V. M. Rue (1985). The bulimic dental patient. Recognition and recommendations. *Dental Hygiene* **59**, 372–377.
Johnson, G. L., L. L. Humphries, P. B. Shirley, A. Mazzoleni and J. A. Noonan (1986). Mitral valve prolapse in patients with anorexia nervosa and bulimia. *Archives of Internal Medicine* **146**, 1525–1529.
Joseph, A. B. and B. Herr (1985). Finger calluses in bulimia (Letter). *American Journal of Psychiatry* **142**, 655.
Kaplan, A. S. (1987). Hyperamylasemia and bulimia: a clinical review. *International Journal of Eating Disorders* **6**, 537–543.
Kerr, W. F. (1980). Spontaneous intramural rupture and intramural haematoma of the esophagus. *Thorax* **35**, 890–897.
King, T. M. and W. F. Plack (1983). Perimolysis in a patient diagnosed with anorexia nervosa: case report. *Military Medicine* **148**, 676–677.
Kiriike, N., S. Nishiwaki, Y. Izumiya and Y. Kawakita (1986). Dexamethasone suppression test in bulimia. *Biological Psychiatry* **21**, 325–328.
Krieg, J. C., H. Backmund and K. M. Pirke (1987). Cranial computed tomography findings in bulimia. *Acta Psychiatrica Scandinavica* **75**, 144–149.
Lankenau, H., M. E. Swigar, S. Bhimani, D. Luchins and M. Quinlan (1985). Cranial CT scans in eating disorder patients and controls. *Comprehensive Psychiatry* **26**, 136–147.
Larsen, K., B. S. Jensen and F. Axelsen (1983). Perforation and rupture of the esophagus. *Scandinavian Journal of Thoracic and Cardiovascular Surgery* **17**, 311–316.
Levin, P. A., J. M. Falko, K. Dixon, E. M. Gallup and W. Saunders (1980). Benign parotid enlargement in bulimia. *Annals of Internal Medicine* **93**, 827–829.
Lewin, K., D. Mattingly and R. R. Millis (1972). Anorexia nervosa associated with hypothalamic tumour. *British Medical Journal* **2**, 629–630.
Lindy, D. C., B. T. Walsh, S. P. Roose, M. Gladis and A. H. Glassman (1985). The dexamethasone suppression test in bulimia. *American Journal of Psychiatry* **142**, 1375–1376.
Lombrose, C. T., I. H. Schwartz and D. M. Clark (1966). Ctenoids in healthy youths. *Neurology (Minneapolis)* **16**, 1152–1158.
Long, M. T. and L. C. Johnson (1968). Fourteen- and six-per-second positive spikes in a nonclinical male population. *Neurology* **18**, 714–716.
Manno, B. R. and J. E. Manno (1977). Toxicology of ipecac. A review. *Clinical Toxicology* **10**, 221–242.
Maulsby, R. L. (1979). EEG patterns of uncertain diagnostic significance. In *Current Practice of Clinical Electroencephalography*, ed. by D. W. Klass and D. D. Daly. Raven Press, New York. pp. 411–419.
Michel, L. (1982). Post-emetic laceration and rupture of the gastroesophageal junction.

Acta Chirurgica Belgica **1**, 13–24.
Mira, M., P. M. Stewart and S. Abraham (1985). Hormonal and biochemical abnormalities in women suffering from eating disorders. *Pediatrician* **12**, 148–156.
Mira, M., P. M. Stewart, J. Vizzard and S. Abraham (1987). Biochemical abnormalities in anorexia nervosa and bulimia. *Annals of Clinical Biochemistry* **24**, 29–35.
Mitchell, J. E. and J. P. Bantle (1983). Metabolic and endocrine investigations in women of normal weight with the bulimia syndrome. *Biological Psychiatry* **18**, 355–365.
Mitchell, J. E. and L. I. Boutacoff (1986). Laxative abuse complicating bulimia: medical and treatment implications. *International Journal of Eating Disorders* **5**, 325–334.
Mitchell, J. E. and D. C. Laine (1985). Monitored binge-eating behavior in patients with bulimia. *International Journal of Eating Disorders* **4**, 177–183.
Mitchell, J. E., D. Hatsukami, E. D. Eckert and R. L. Pyle (1985). Characteristics of 275 patients with bulimia. *American Journal of Psychiatry* **142**, 482–485.
Mitchell, J. E., W. Hosfield and R. L. Pyle (1983). EEG findings in patients with the bulimia syndrome. *International Journal of Eating Disorders* **2**, 17–23.
Mitchell, J. E., R. L. Pyle, E. D. Eckert, D. Hatsukami and R. Lentz (1983). Electrolyte and other physiological abnormalities in patients with bulimia. *Psychological Medicine* **13**, 273–278.
Mitchell, J. E., R. L. Pyle, D. Hatsukami and L. I. Boutacoff (1984). The dexamethasone suppression test in patients with bulimia. *Journal of Clinical Psychiatry* **45**, 508–511.
Mitchell, J. E., R. L. Pyle and R. A. Miner (1987). Gastric dilatation as a complication of bulimia. *Psychosomatics* **23**, 96–97.
Musisi, S. and P. Garfinkel (1985). Comparative dexamethasone suppression test measurements in bulimia, depression and normal controls. *Canadian Psychiatric Association Journal* **30**, 190–194.
Niiya, K., T. Kitagawa, M. Fujishita, S. Yoshimoto, M. Kobayashi, I. Kubonishi, H. Taguchi and I. Miyoshi (1983). Bulimia nervosa complicated by deficiency of vitamin K-dependent coagulation factors. *Journal of the American Medical Association* **250**, 792–793.
Norris, P. D., B. P. O'Malley and R. L. Palmer (1985). The TRH test in bulimia and anorexia nervosa: a controlled study. *Journal of Psychiatric Research* **19**, 215–219.
Palmer, E. P. and A. T. Guay (1986). Reversible myopathy secondary to abuse of ipecac in patients with major eating disorders. *New England Journal of Medicine* **313**, 1457–1459.
Phillips, L. G. and J. Cunningham (1984). Esophageal perforation. *Radiologic Clinics of North America* **22**, 607–613.
Pirke, K. M., J. Pahl and U. Schweiger (1985). Metabolic and endocrine indices of starvation in bulimia: a comparision with anorexia nervosa. *Psychiatry Research* **14**, 33–39.
Pope, H. G. Jr, J. I. Hudson, R. A. Nixon and P. L. Herridge (1986). The epidemiology of ipecac abuse. *New England Journal of Medicine* **314**, 245–246.
Rau, J. H. and R. S. Green (1975). Compulsive eating: a neuropsychological approach to certain eating disorders. *Comprehensive Psychiatry* **16**, 223–231.
Rau, J. H. and R. S. Green (1978). Soft neurological correlates of compulsive eaters. *Journal of Nervous and Mental Disease* **166**, 435–437.
Rau, J. H., F. A. Struve and R. S. Green (1979). Electroencephalographic correlates of compulsive eating. *Clinical Electroencephalography* **10**, 180–189.
Remick, R. A., M. W. Jones and P. E. Campos (1980). Postictal bulimia (Letter). *Journal of Clinical Psychiatry* **41**, 256.

Russell, G. (1979). Bulimia nervosa: an ominous variant of anorexia nervosa. *Psychological Medicine* **9**, 429–488.
Saul, S. H., A. Dekker and C. G. Watson (1981). Acute gastric dilatation with infarction and perforation. *Gut* **22**, 978–983.
Schiff, R. J., C. L. Wurzel, S. C. Brunson, I. Kasloff, M. P. Nussbaum and S. D. Frank (1986). Death due to chronic syrup of ipecac use in a patient with bulimia. *Pediatrics* **78**, 412–416.
Schwartz, B. K. and W. E. Clendenning (1985). A cutaneous sign of bulimia. *Journal of the American Academy of Dermatology* **12**, 725–726.
Schweiger, U., J. Poellinger, R. Laessle, G. Wolfram, M. M. Fichter and K.-M. Pirke (1987). Altered insulin response to a balanced test meal in bulimic patients. *International Journal of Eating Disorders* **6**, 551–556.
Sein, P., S. Searson and A. R. Nicol (1981). Anorexia nervosa and pseudo-atrophy of the brain. *British Journal of Psychiatry* **139**, 257–258.
Silber, W. (1978). The spectrum of emetogenic injury to the esophagus. *South African Journal of Surgery* **16**, 111–119.
Simmons, M. S., S. K. Grayden and J. E. Mitchell (1986). Bulimia: the need for psychiatric–dental liaison. *American Journal of Psychiatry* **143**, 783–784.
Simon, D., P. Laudenbach, M. Lebovici and P. Mauvais-Jarvis (1979). Parotidomegalie au cours des dysorexies metales. *Nouvelle Presse Medicale* **8**, 2399–2402.
Szmukler, G. I. (1984). Anorexia nervosa and bulimia in diabetics. *Journal of Psychosomatic Research* **28**, 365–369.
Walsh, B. T., C. B. Croft and J. L. Katz (1981). Anorexia nervosa and salivary gland enlargement. *International Journal of Psychiatry in Medicine* **11**, 255–261.
Wegner, J. T. and F. A. Struve (1977). Incidence of the 14 and 6 per second position spike pattern in an adult clinical population: an empirical note. *Journal of Nervous and Mental Disease* **164**, 340–345.
Weller, R. A. and E. B. Weller (1982). Anorexia nervosa in a patient with an infiltrating tumor of the hypothalamus. *American Journal of Psychiatry* **139**, 824–825.
Whittier, J. R. (1976). Asphyxiation, bulimia, and insulin levels in Huntington's disease (chorea). *Journal of the American Medical Association* **235**, 1423–1424.
Wolcott, R. B., J. Yager and G. Gordon (1984). Dental sequelae to the binge–purge syndrome (bulimia): report of cases. *Journal of the American Dental Association* **109**, 723–725.
Wynn, D. R. and W. J. Martin (1984). A physical sign of bulimia (Letter). *Mayo Clinic Proceedings* **59**, 722.

6

Bulimia in children and adolescents

Helmut Remschmidt
and
Beate Herpertz-Dahlmann
Phillipps-Universität Marburg

Although hyperphagic disorders similar to bulimia have been recognized since ancient times (Ziolko, 1985), bulimia as a specific disorder has only been defined during the past decade. This development is reflected in the fact that bulimia is not listed in the ninth edition of ICD or in the multiaxial classification scheme for psychiatric diseases in children and adolescents by Rutter, Shaffer and Sturge (Remschmidt and Schmidt, 1977). A definition of bulimia together with diagnostic criteria can, however, be found in DSM-III (American Psychiatric Association, 1980) and DSM-III-R. The DSM-III criteria still have shortcomings in that they include neither extreme fears of fatness in female patients and the compulsive desire to control their body weight nor the connection with anorexia nervosa which features in the case history of many bulimic patients.

These problems are not satisfactorily resolved in the revision of the DSM-III criteria (DSM-III-R), although the connection between bulimia and anorexia is more clearly formulated. A differentiation is made between two types of anorexic patients (Halmi, 1985), type 1: patients who manifest reduced food intake without attacks of insatiable hunger (bulimia) or vomiting, abuse of laxatives or diuretics; type 2: patients who manifest reduced food intake together with induced vomiting and abuse of laxatives and diuretics but who do not experience attacks of insatiable hunger (bulimia).

Type 1 and type 2 are patients *without* bulimia. In a third group of patients anorexia *with* bulimia is present; in this group considerable loss of body weight is necessary. Finally, *pure* bulimia is defined by the presence of typical bulimic symptoms; however, body weight remains within the normal range (despite certain fluctuations).

Although DSM-III-R criteria represent a definite advance when compared with the original DSM-III criteria, some issues remain unresolved. Amongst these, the connection with anorexia nervosa remains unclear. In DSM-III-R this connection is mentioned only in the criteria for the diagnosis of anorexia nervosa. In any case, it can be assumed that about 50 per cent of female patients with anorexia nervosa will, at a later stage, manifest bulimic symptoms (Garfinkel, Moldofsky and Garner, 1980; Fairburn and Garner, 1986).

Following a critical discussion of various aspects of the classification of anorexia nervosa and bulimia, Fairburn and Garner (1986) propose the future use of Russell's term 'bulimia nervosa' rather than 'bulimia' for those patients who display the full syndrome. Furthermore, they stress the necessity of including the characteristic concerns with body shape and weight and the desire to control body weight as essential diagnostic criteria. They also argue that those female patients who show the essential symptoms of bulimia nervosa (attacks of insatiable hunger, intense desire to control body weight and characteristic fears concerning body shape and weight) should be diagnosed as having 'bulimia nervosa', independent of their actual body weight. By contrast, the diagnosis 'anorexia nervosa' should be reserved for those patients who do not display bulimic episodes. Thus, these authors express the opinion that the term 'anorexia nervosa' should only be used for those patients whose diagnosis would previously have been 'restrictive anorexia nervosa'.

These issues have been discussed in some detail here since the onset of the disorder can be closely studied and its symptomatology precisely described in young patients. However, this is only possible if the variations in symptomatology are taken into account during the investigations. As this has not previously been done, retrospective evaluations are problematic.

Ziolko (1985) differentiates between three groups of patients with regard to body weight and course of the disorder: (1) patients with bulimia and a body weight within the normal range; (2) patients with bulimia and reduced body weight, with a negative attitude towards a normal body weight and a persistent fear of fatness (in agreement with the original definition of 'bulimia nervosa' by Russell, 1979); (3) patients in whom the illness takes a more phasic (bipolar) course — bulimic eating behaviour and, possibly, weight gain alternate with anorexic eating behaviour and weight loss. Finally, it is possible to establish a connection with 'depressive' symptomatology, which is also included in DSM-III criteria. The positive effect of treatment with antidepressants could be partly explained by the fact that DSM-III criteria were used in a number of studies of eating disorders.

Epidemiology

It appears that in the developed countries of the western world anorexic and bulimic behaviours are increasing. This can be deduced from studies on hospitalized patients and from case history data. Whereas the number of cases registered per year in the fifties and sixties was only 0.45 per 100 000 of the population (Theander, 1970), today it lies between 1.12 (Willi and Grossmann, 1983) and 4.06 (for the period 1978–1982) (Szmukler, 1985). The interpretation of these observations has not been uncontroversial. Thus, Williams and King (1987) ascribed the increasing number of female patients and the increased diagnosis of anorexia solely to the increase in the number of young women in the population and not to an increase in morbidity risk.

It is more difficult to obtain objective information on the frequency of bulimia than on that of anorexia. This is not only due to the problems involved in the definition and demarcation of bulimia; bulimic patients conceal their symptoms to a great extent, which makes it extremely difficult to get an objective estimate of the number of hidden cases. A further problem derives from the fact that patients with bulimic symptomatology may delay seeking treatment much longer than do patients with anorexia nervosa. In a number of epidemiological investigations questionnaires have been used, in the hope that by keeping the responses anonymous the answers will be more honest. Cooper and Fairburn (1983), in a questionnaire investigation of 369 attenders at a family planning clinic, identified bulimia in 2 per cent of the sample. In a population of college students, Schwartz, Thompson and Johnson (1982) found 10 per cent with bulimic symptomatology. Paul, Brand-Jacobi and Pudel (1984) sent questionnaires to more than 600 readers of a women's magazine who had volunteered to assist with research into bulimia; they received 484 answers from persons who could be classified as cases of bulimia nervosa. This investigation demonstrated that the majority of the bulimia cases were in the age group between 20 and 30; only 16 per cent were younger and 22 per cent older than this. The mean duration of the illness was seven years; in most of the cases it began between 14 and 20, most frequently at the age of 18. About 10 per cent became ill between 14 and 16 and less than 20 per cent between 16 and 18. This chapter is concerned largely with the 16–18-year-old patients.

Table 6.1 Number of treatments after hospitalization of female and male patients with anorexia nervosa (Feighner's criteria) and bulimia (according to DSM-III) during the years 1983–1986

	1983	1984	1985	1986
Pure restrictive anorexia nervosa	15	21	30	24
Anorexia nervosa with bulimic episodes (bulimarexia)	3	8	1	2
Bulimia	1	2	1	7
Total	19	31	32	33

Results of Investigations

Anorexia nervosa and bulimia in patients hospitalized in a psychiatric clinic for children and adolescents

The increase in the number of patients with anorexia nervosa and bulimia which has been observed in all western countries is also reflected in the client population of our clinic. Whereas during the period 1952–1980 an average of 2–4 patients per year were treated for this type of disorder, this figure increased in 1981 to 14, in 1982 to 15, in 1983 to 19, in 1984 to 31 and in 1986 to 33 patients.

In addition, during the period between 1983 and 1986 we frequently identified anorexic patients with bulimic episodes and those with pure bulimia (Table 6.1). This may be due to the fact that more care was taken over the differentiation between these illnesses. It may, however, also reflect a real increase in the frequency of bulimic disorders as compared with pure restrictive anorexic disorders.

During the period between 1.7.85 and 15.8.87 we observed a total of 55 girls and boys with anorexia nervosa, bulimia or bulimarexia. Among these were 11 cases (20 per cent) who suffered from a bulimic disorder (six with bulimia nervosa, five with bulimarexia). The most significant data about these 11 cases are provided in Table 6.2.

Table 6.2 shows that at the time of hospitalization the patients were between 13 and 17 years old. In some cases, the onset of the disorder was certainly earlier. Thus, in the first girl (patient No. 1), the bulimic eating behaviour had already started at the age of 13 and did not change during the following three years. By contrast, in patient No. 6, the reason for the first hospitalization was anorexia nervosa without bulimia, but by the time the second hospitalization became necessary bulimia and alcohol abuse had developed. At the time of the

Table 6.2 Data on 11 cases with a bulimic disorder studied between 1.7.85 and 15.8.87

Patient No.	Sex	Age (yr)	Diagnosis	Onset of disorder and preceding periods of hospitalization	Symptoms	Family situation	Menstrual cycle	Ideal body weight (kg)	Actual body weight (kg)	DST
1	f	16	B	Primary bulimic behaviour for 3 years	Binge attacks several times daily 60 DM daily for food; truancy	Parents divorced, lives with mother	Regular	49	44.5	Non-suppressor
2	f	16	BA	Primary bulimic behaviour for 2 years	Originally about 3 times weekly, eventually several times daily	Parents divorced, lives with father	Secondary amenorrhoea	52	40.5	Non-suppressor
3	f	16	B	1. Primary bulimic behaviour for 1 year 2. Anorexic only (no bingeing) attempt at suicide	Laxative abuse, binge attacks and vomiting several times a week No bingeing	Parents divorced, lives with mother	Secondary Amenorrhoea	46	44.8	Non-suppressor
4	f	17	B	Bulimic behaviour for 3/4 years	Vomiting up to 20 times daily, rare attacks of insatiable hunger	Lives with natural parents	Secondary amenorrhoea	46	45.8	Suppressor
5	f	15	BA	'Restrictive' for 1/2 years, bulimic for 3 weeks	Nocturnal (only carbo-hydrate)	Lives with natural parents	Secondary amenorrhoea	49	44.2	Non-suppressor
6	f	17	B	1. Anorexia nervosa without bulimia 2. Bulimia and alcohol abuse 3. Bulimia and suicide attempt	Bingeing on carbohydrate rich foods (butter with sugar), vomiting several times daily	Parents divorced, lives with grand-parents who are separated	Secondary amenorrhoea	48	55.5	Suppressor

7	f	15	B	Primary bulimia for 1/4 years	3 times daily vomiting, isolated binge attacks	Lives with natural parents	Regular	48	45.8	Non-suppressor
8	m	13	BA	Primary 'restrictive', subsequent (two occasions) bingeing and vomiting	1–2 × weekly binge attacks and vomiting, otherwise fasting	Lives with natural parents	—	39	29.2	Non-suppressor
9	f	15	B	'Restrictive' for 4 years (1st hospitalization 3 years ago) bulimic symptoms for 2 years	Oscillates between fasting, bingeing and vomiting (*c*.1–3 × daily), carbohydrates	Lives with natural parents	Primary amenorrhoea	52	46.9	Non-suppressor
10	f	16	BA	1/2 year bingeing hunger stimulated by television, followed by vomiting	Vomiting *c*.1 × daily. Binge attacks several times weekly	Lives with natural parents	Secondary amenorrhoea	50	42.3	Non-suppressor
11	f	17	BA	Anorexic for about 1 year, ½ year binge attacks and vomiting (stimulated by periodicals)	Binge attacks every 2 days and (vomiting induced by salt solution), suicide attempt	Death of natural father 6 years previously. other remarried 4 years previously	Secondary amenorrhoea	47	42.1	Suppressor

Abbreviations: A, anorexia nervosa; B, bulimia; BA, bulimanorexia; DST, dexamethasone suppression test.

third hospitalization the bulimic symptoms had persisted but the reason for hospitalization was a suicide attempt.

A detailed analysis of the onset of the disorder showed that, of the 11 patients, only six exhibited bulimic symptomatology from the start (patients Nos. 1, 2, 3, 4, 7 and 10). In the remaining five patients bulimic symptomatology developed in the context of previously established anorexia. This sequence may also be reversed. For example, one girl (patient No. 3) was first hospitalized because of bulimic eating behaviour which had already been manifested over one year. At the second hospitalization she had no attacks of insatiable hunger but had attempted suicide. With the exception of two girls who were cases of primary bulimia (Nos. 1 and 7), all other girls had primary or secondary amenorrhoea. Five girls came from broken homes (the parents were separated) and three had attempted suicide. In the dexamethasone suppression test eight patients were non-suppressors.

In the course of a longitudinal study (begun in 1985) we paid special attention to the connection between the dexamethasone suppression test and depression during the clinical treatment of patients with anorexia nervosa and bulimia nervosa or bulimarexia (Herpertz-Dahlmann and Remschmidt, 1987a,b).

For the classification of the anorexic patients (group A) Feighner's diagnostic criteria (Feighner *et al.*, 1972) were used. The bulimic patients (group B) were classified according to DSM-III. Individual ideal body weight was calculated according to the relative BROCA formula (for female patients between 14 and 20 years: cm above 1 m body height in kg minus 20 per cent; for male patients between 14 and 20: minus 15 per cent). For girls and boys under 14 we followed Kunze's (1977) tables.

To date, the dexamethasone suppression test (DST) has been conducted once in 30 patients from group A and 11 patients from group B, twice in 26 patients from group A and six patients from group B, and three times in 12 patients from group A and four patients from group B. In accordance with the standardization of the DST by Carroll *et al.* (1981), patients were given 1 mg dexamethasone orally at 23.00 h on the evening before the test day. Blood samples were taken on the following day at 08.00, 16.00 and 23.00 h. None of the patients received any medication before the first investigation. Some of the patients had been treated with tricyclic antidepressants. If medication had already started, it was continued during the second and third test since withdrawal of treatment might have affected the results of the DST (Dilsaver and Greden, 1984). Plasma cortisol concentrations were estimated by radio-immunoassay. The 'mood states' of the patients were assessed at the day of the test by means of the Hamilton Depression Scale (HAMD) (Hamilton, 1960) conducted by the responsible therapist. In parallel, self-report information was obtained from the patient by means of a questionnaire derived from Zung's Self-Rating Depression Scale (SDS) (Zung, 1972). Due to severe weight loss, nourishment by nasogastric tube and confinement to bed was necessary for a number of patients. In these cases, items 7, 12 and 16 of the HAMD could not be considered, since they directly or indirectly assess weight loss, food intake and physical activity. The statistical comparison of the two groups was conducted using the Mann–Whitney–Wilcoxon U-test. In addition, the presence of affective disorders in the families of both groups of patients was compared. The severity of individual family afflictions was scored in 'point values'. Thus, a patient with an afflicted close relative (father, mother or sibling) scored three points, for more distant relatives (grandparent, aunt, uncle) the score was two points, and for even more distant relatives (great-grandparent, cousin) one point. The number of points in the anorexic group and in the control group were compared in the following risk areas: (1) family afflictions of psychiatric disorders in general, (2) family afflictions of affective disorders, (3) family afflictions of eating disorders (anorexia nervosa or bulimia) and (4) family afflictions of alcohol abuse.

Comparison of the two groups did not reveal significant differences with regard to any of these four types of variables. There were, however, statistically significant differences between group A and group B with regard to test weight (actual body weight at the time of the test) expressed as a percentage of 'ideal' body weight and also with regard to the DST. These comparisons are shown in Table 6.3.

Table 6.3 demonstrates that there was a highly significant difference between group A and B with regard to test weight as expressed as a percentage of 'ideal' body weight. As would be expected, patients with bulimia nervosa and bulimarexia showed less weight loss than 'restrictive anorexics'. This difference holds, however, only for the time of the admission to the clinic (T1). At the time of the DST (T2) 8–12 weeks after hospital treatment, the difference had disappeared due to the anorexic patients' increase in weight. This was also the case at the time of discharge from the clinic (T3).

In the DST, blood cortisol concentrations (mean of three estimations) were somewhat higher at the time of admission (T1) in patients from group A compared with those from group B (maximal as well as mean values). This difference was reversed at T2. At T1 and T2 the differences between group A and group B were statistically significant. This was no longer the case at T3.

The results of the DST (maximum values) at T1 indicated 'non-suppression' for both groups (more pronounced in patients in group A than in group B). This finding is illustrated in Figure 6.1. Figure 6.1 shows that between T1 and T2 a significant decrease in cortisol values (for DST maxima as well as for the DST mean values) occurred in anorexic girls (group A). There was no significant difference between these values at T2 and T3. For patients in the bulimic group (B), cortisol values remained about equal at all three test times (T1, T2 and T3).

Table 6.3 Comparison of data from anorexia nervosa patients (group A) and bulimia patients (group B) at admission (T1), after 8–12 weeks' stabilizing treatment (T2) and at discharge (T3)

	t_1		Significant difference		t_2		Significant difference		t_3		Significant difference	
	Group A (N = 30)	Group B (N = 11)	u	p	Group A (N = 26)	Group B (N = 6)	u	p	Group A (N = 12)	Group B (N = 4)	u	p
Test weight (kg)	40.9 ± 7.8	43.7 ± 6.3	NS		49.1 ± 8.6	45.8 ± 4.9	NS		53.6 ± 8.9	44.7 ± 5.6	NS	
Test weight as % of ideal weight	77.3 ± 8.8	92.1 ± 11.7	48	$p \leqslant 0.0006$	94.8 ± 4.9	96.5 ± 4.9	NS		98.5 ± 2.18	96.6 ± 3.5	NS	
DST (Maximum)	14.6 ± 10.5	7.4 ± 5.9	96	$p \leqslant 0.004$	2.6 ± 3.2	7.2 ± 6.7	40	$p \leqslant 0.06$	4.1 ± 4.6	6.1 ± 5.3	NS	
DST (Average)	9.6 ± 6.7	4.7 ± 3.8	74.5	$p \leqslant 0.021$	1.7 ± 2.4	4.3 ± 3.5	35	$p \leqslant 0.03$	2.4 ± 2.3	3.5 ± 3.2	NS	
HAMD (score)	11.7 ± 6.9	10.0 ± 4.5	NS		6.7 ± 4.7	4.8 ± 3.9	NS		6.1 ± 2.5	5.7 ± 4.7	NS	
SDS (score)	42.2 ± 10.9	44.4 ± 9.2	NS		35.4 ± 7.7	36.4 ± 11.9	NS		32.3 ± 6.6	41.3 ± 11.4	NS	

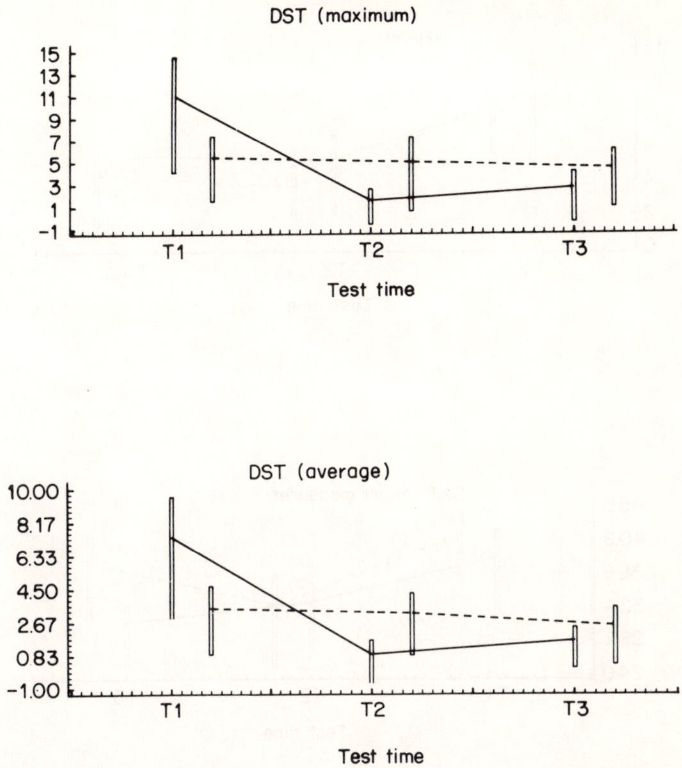

Figure 6.1. Comparison of patients with anorexia nervosa (——) with patients with bulimia (- - -) at time of hospitalization (T1), after 8–12 weeks (T2) and at time of discharge from clinic (T3): DST

In summary, it can be said that, between T1 and T2, patients with anorexia show considerable changes which are obviously connected with weight gain. This is not, however, the case for patients in the bulimia group.

Analysis of the results obtained from the assessment of depressive mood changes (HAMD) revealed no significant differences between the two groups at any of the test times. There were, however, significant changes when each group was regarded on its own. This is shown in Figure 6.2.

The upper part of Figure 6.2 shows the assessment of the patients by the therapist using the Hamilton scale. It is evident that, according to the therapist, patients with anorexia nervosa as well as those with bulimia or bulimarexia showed a definite fall in depressive tendencies between T1 and T2. Between T2 and T3 these stabilized around a mean value. The results obtained *via* the self-

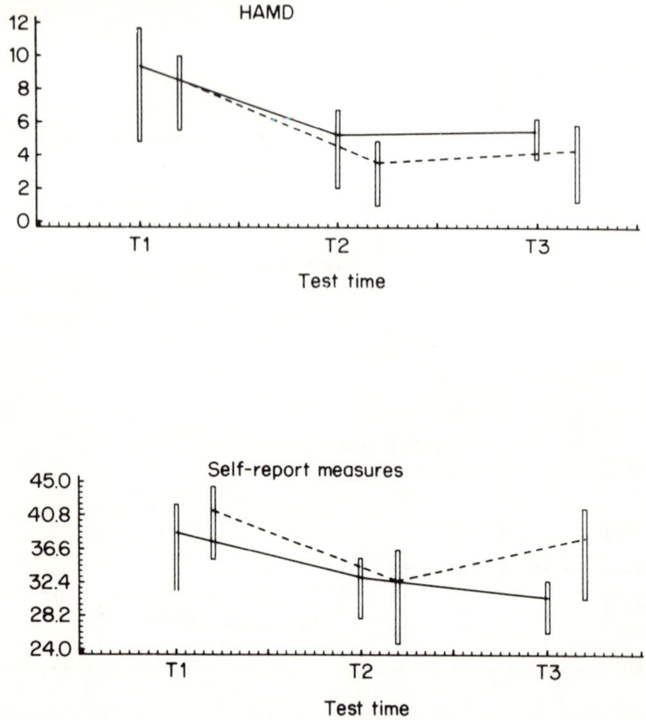

Figure 6.2. Comparison of patients with anorexia nervosa (——) with patients with bulimia (- - -) at time of hospitalization (T1), after 8–12 weeks (T2) and at time of discharge from clinic (T3): HAMD and self-report measures

report measures (lower part of Figure 6.2) are, however, somewhat different; whereas the patients from group A showed a more or less continuous improvement in their mood state, this was not the case for group B. In group B the values at the beginning and end were almost identical. The mean value at T2 was the lowest. These results pose the question as to whether there is a connection between anorexia nervosa and depression or between bulimia/bulimanorexia and depression. Whereas the existence of depressive mood changes in girls with anorexia nervosa and bulimia is well known, the question of an aetiological connection between depression and anorexia nervosa or bulimia still remains open (see Laessle in this volume, Chapter 8). The following observations argue in favour of such a connection (Herzog, 1984): (1) the existence of previous and existing depressive mood changes in patients with anorexia and bulimia; (2) a higher incidence of affective disorders in the family; (3) neuroendocrine abnormalities; and (4) beneficial effect of treatment with antidepressant drugs.

In contrast, those holding the opposite viewpoint (see Strober and Katz, 1987) point out that the occurrence of depressive symptoms in these eating disorders is not necessarily proof of an aetiological connection. There are also counterarguments with respect to symptomatology and family background.

Symptomatology

Many patients with anorexia nervosa show symptoms which are in sharp contrast to depressive symptoms, for example, pronounced hyperactivity, self-assertiveness, sthenic or forceful behaviour and strong achievement drive, which makes them work until exhaustion. These characteristics are in no way typical of depression. Comparative investigations between female patients with anorexia nervosa and patients with pronounced depression (major depression) revealed clear-cut differences between these two groups (Piran *et al.*, 1985). Similar observations were made by Cooper and Fairburn (1986) in a comparison of female patients with bulimia and patients with unipolar endogenous depression. In the female bulimics, depressive mood changes were of shorter duration and their manifestation coincided with episodes of insatiable hunger and vomiting.

Family studies

Depressive disorders are frequently observed in the families of cases of eating disorders such as anorexia nervosa and bulimia nervosa. In contrast, in families with cases of depressive illnesses the incidence of eating disorders is not elevated. The percentage of eating disorders among the relatives of depressive, manic or schizophrenic patients is very low (0.6–1.3 per cent) and not different from the expected value in a normal population (Strober *et al.*, 1987).

These observations emphasize the fact that the connection between depression and eating disorders is highly complex and not yet clarified. Our results agree with those of Herzog (1984), who found a higher percentage of depressive mood changes in anorexic as compared with bulimic patients. In this regard it must be remembered that the values on the Hamilton scale lie only in the middle range and, especially, that in our study three questions on the Hamilton scale could not be used (see above). With regard to the DST, our results do not agree with those of Hudson *et al.* (1987), who found suppression of cortisol secretion in adult patients with bulimia.

Bulimia in a larger follow-up sample

During recent years we have conducted a larger follow-up investigation which included all inpatients of our clinic treated for anorexia between 1952

Table 6.4 Symptomatology at time of hospitalization ($N = 104$)

Amenorrhoea	N=98	94.2%
Constipation	N=72	69.2%
Hyperactivity	N=61	58.7%
Hypothermia	N=52	50.0%
Laxative abuse	N=39	37.5%
Bradycardia	N=37	35.6%
Self-induced vomiting	N=37	35.6%
Lanugo hair	N=28	26.9%
Bulimic episodes	N=28	26.9%

and 1982. The total number of patients analysed was 104, 100 females and four males. Mean age at onset of the disorder was 13 years (9–19 years) and age at first admission to the clinic was (on average) 14.6 years. Mean duration of treatment was 4.7 months, timespan of the catamnesis was 11.6 years and mean age of patients at the time the catamnesis was compiled was 26.6 years.

Reliable information could be obtained on about 85 patients (81.7 per cent). Information on 12 patients (11.5 per cent) was incomplete and no information could be obtained from seven (7.7 per cent) patients. Of these, five refused to collaborate and two could not be traced.

The investigation consisted of a detailed interview about the 'long-term course' of the anorexia nervosa, the Anorexia Nervosa Inventory for Self-Assessment (ANIS; Fichter and Keeser, 1980) and a psychological test investigation. In the following, only those aspects concerning bulimia will be discussed.

Symptomatology at the time of hospitalization of all 104 patients is presented in Table 6.4. It can be seen that 39 female patients (37.5 per cent) reported laxative abuse, 37 reported self-induced vomiting and 28 manifested bulimic episodes.

At the time of the follow-up investigation data were obtained from 96 patients which enabled a diagnosis to be made according to the multiaxial classification scheme (Remschmidt and Schmidt, 1977). Of these 96 patients, 23 (23.9 per cent) still displayed symptoms typical of anorexia nervosa or bulimia. Fifteen patients were still 'restrictive anorexic' (15.6 per cent) and eight (8.2 per cent) suffered from DSM-III 'bulimia'.

It is notable that in this 'long-term course' study 28 patients manifested bulimic episodes, at least at the time of admission to the clinic. Since most of the patients had been treated before 1980, the specific diagnosis 'bulimia' had not been recorded in the case histories, as the required definition was not yet in use. The phenomenon as such was, however, recognized.

References

American Psychiatric Association (1980). *Diagnostic and Statistical Manual of Mental Disorders*, 3rd edn. American Psychiatric Association, Washington DC.

Carroll, B. J., M. Feinberg, J. F. Greden *et al.* (1981). A specific laboratory test for the diagnosis of melancholia. *Archives of General Psychiatry* **38**, 15–22.

Cooper, P. J. and C. G. Fairburn (1983). Binge-eating and self-induced vomiting in the community: a preliminary study. *British Journal of Psychiatry* **142**, 139–144.

Cooper, P. J. and C. G. Fairburn (1986). The depressive symptoms of bulimia nervosa. *British Journal of Psychiatry* **148**, 268.

Dilsaver, S. C. and J. F. Greden (1984). Effects of antidepressant withdrawal on the dexamethasone suppression test. *Psychiatry Research* **14**, 111–122.

Fairburn, C. G. (1981). A cognitive behavioral approach to the management of bulimia. *Psychological Medicine* **11**, 707–711.

Fairburn, C. G. (1984). Bulimia. Its epidemiology and management. In *Eating and its Disorders*, ed. by A. J. Stunkard and E. Sellers. Raven Press, New York.

Fairburn, C. G. (1985a). Cognitive-behavioral treatment for bulimia. In *A Handbook for the Treatment of Anorexia Nervosa and Bulimia*, ed. by D. M. Garner and P. E. Garfinkel. Guilford Press, New York.

Fairburn, C. G. (1985b). Review: The management of bulimia nervosa. *Journal of Psychiatric Research* **19**, 465–472.

Fairburn, C. G. and D. M. Garner (1986). The diagnosis of bulimia nervosa. *International Journal of Eating Disorders* **5**, 403–419.

Feighner, J. P., E. Robins, S. B. Guze *et al.* (1972). Diagnostic criteria for use in psychiatric research. *Archives of General Psychiatry* **26**, 57–63.

Fichter, M. M. (1985). *Magersucht und Bulimia*. Springer, Berlin, Heidelberg, New York.

Fichter, M. M. and W. Keeser (1980). Das Anorexia-nervosa-Inventar zur Selbstbeurteilung (ANIS). *Archiv für Psychiatrie und Nervenkrankheiten* **228**, 67–89.

Garfinkel, B. E., H. Moldofsky and D. M. Garner (1980). The heterogeneity of anorexia nervosa. Bulimia as a distinct subgroup. *Archives of General Psychiatry* **37**, 1036–1040.

Gerlinghoff, M. and G. D. Ploog (1987). Anorexia nervosa und Bulimie — eine mehrdimensionale stationäre Psychotherapie. *Zeitschrift für Psychotherapie und Medizinische Psychologie* **37**, 312–316.

Griffiths, S. A., S. W. Touyz, P. B. Mitchell and W. Bacon (1987). The treatment of bulimia nervosa. *Australian and New Zealand Journal of Psychiatry* **21**, 5–15.

Halmi, K. A. (1985). A review: classification of the eating disorders. *Journal of Psychiatric Research* **19**, 113–120.

Hamilton, M. (1960). A rating scale of depression. *Journal of Neurology, Neurosurgery and Psychiatry* **23**, 56–62.

Herpertz-Dahlmann, B. and H. Remschmidt (1987a). Depressive Symptomatik und Dexamethason-Suppressions-Test im stationären Behandlungsverlauf der Anorexia nervosa. *Nervenarzt* **58**, 610–616.

Herpertz-Dahlmann, B. and H. Remschmidt (1987b). Der Aussgewert des Dexamethason-Suppressions-Tests bei Anorexia nervosa. *Monatsschrift für Kinderheilkunde* **135**, in press.

Herzog, D. B. (1984). Are anorexic and bulimic patients depressed? *American Journal of Psychiatry* **141**, 1594–1597.

Hudson, J. I., D. L. Katz, H. G. Pope, M. S. Hudson, G. T. Griffing and J. C. Melby (1987). Urinary free cortisole and response to the dexamethasone suppression test in

bulimia: a pilot study. *International Journal of Eating Disorders* **6**, 191–198.
Jonas, J. M. and M. S. Gold (1986/7). Treatment of antidepressant-resistant bulimia with naltrexone. *International Journal of Psychiatry in Medicine* **16**, 305–309.
Kunze, D. (1977). Alters-/Grössen- und Grössen-/Gewichtsbeziehung, dargestellt als neue Perzeptilenkurve. *Kinderarzt* **8**, 979.
Lacey, J. H. (1984). Management of bulimia. In *Handbook of Psychotherapy for Anorexia Nervosa and Bulimia*, edited by D. M. Garner and P. E. Garfinkel. Guilford Press, New York.
Lee, N. F. and A. J. Rush (1986). Cognitive behavior group therapy for bulimia. *International Journal of Eating Disorders* **5**, 599–615.
Paul, T., J. Brand-Jacobi and V. Pudel (1984). Bulimia nervosa. Ergebnisse einer Untersuchung an 500 Patientinnen. *Münchner Medizinische Wochenschrift* **126**, 614–618.
Piran, N., S. Kennedy, P. E. Garfinkel and M. Owens (1985). Affective disturbance in eating disorders. *Journal of Nervous and Mental Disease* **173**, 395–400.
Remschmidt, H. and M. H. Schmidt (1977). *Multiaxiales Klassifikatiosschema für Psychiatrische Erkrankungen im Kindes- und Jugendalter*. Huber, Berne, Stuttgart, Vienna.
Russell, G. F. M. (1979). Bulimia nervosa: an ominous variant of anorexia nervosa. *Psychological Medicine* **9**, 429–448.
Schwartz, D. M., M. G. Thompson and C. L. Johnson (1982). Anorexia nervosa and bulimia: the sociocultural context. *International Journal of Eating Disorders* **1**, 20–36.
Strober, M. and J. L. Katz (1987). Do eating disorders and affective disorders share a common etiology? A dissenting opinion. *International Journal of Eating Disorders* **6**, 171–180.
Strober, M., W. Morrell, J. Sadjak and B. Salkin (1987). Are anorexia nervosa and affective disorders related? A blind family interview study. Cited in Strober and Katz (1987).
Szmukler, G. I. (1985). The epidemiology of anorexia nervosa and bulimia. *Journal of Psychiatric Research* **19**, 143–153.
Theander, J. (1970). Anorexia nervosa. *Acta Psychiatrica Scandinavica*. Suppl. 214.
Willi, J. and S. Grossmann (1983). Epidemiology of anorexia nervosa in a defined region of Switzerland. *American Journal of Psychiatry* **140**, 564–567.
Williams, P. and M. King (1987). Die 'epidemische' Anorexia nervosa: ein neuer Mythos? *Lancet* (German edition) **1/4**, 328–331.
Ziolko, H. U. (1985). Bulimie. *Fortschritte der Neurologie und Psychiatrie* **53**, 231–258.
Zung, W. W. K. (1972). The depression status inventory: an adjunct to the self-rating depression scale. *Journal of Clinical Psychology* **28**, 539–543.

7

Bulimia (nervosa) in the male

Manfred M. Fichter
and
Romana Hoffmann
University of Munich

Bulimia in the male is less common than in females. In Russell's (1979) publication on bulimia the proportion of male patients was 6.2 per cent (N = 32). Herzog (1982) found a proportion of 3 per cent (N = 33), Mitchell and Goff (1984) 3.8 per cent (N = 312), Pope, Hudson and Jonas (1986) 12.8 per cent (N = 117) and Robinson and Holden (1986) 4 per cent (N = 223). Thus, the male to female ratio in bulimia is somewhat lower than in anorexia nervosa (8 per cent, see Fichter, 1985). Series of five or more male anorexic patients were described in the seventies and eighties by Andersen and Mickalide (1985), Beumont, Beardwood and Russell (1972), Bruch (1973), Burzig (1981), Crisp, Burns and Bhat (1986), Dally, Gomez and Isaacs (1979), Fichter and Daser (1987), Hall, Delahunt and Ellis (1985), Hasan and Tibbetts (1977), Hay and Leonard (1979), Herzog *et al.* (1984), Hogan, Herta and Lucas (1974), Martin and Dauner (1978), Mester (1981), Sheppard, Jackson and Malone (1984), Taipale, Larkio Miettinen and Valanne (1972) and by Vandereycken and Van den Broucke (1984). The subject of anorexia nervosa in the male has been reviewed by Sterling and Segal (1985) and by Scott (1986). These investigations also include anorexic patients with bulimia.

The present review is chiefly concerned with the bulimic syndrome in boys and men, mainly of normal body weight (bulimia or bulimia nervosa). The few papers dealing with this subject have been published only very recently. Their central findings will be discussed here in conjunction with our own study of 17 patients with bulimia, diagnosed according to DSM-III criteria, a control group of 17 homosexual men and a further control group of 18 heterosexual men. Eight of our 17 bulimic patients were acute cases at the time of the study; the remaining nine had a previous history of the bulimic syndrome. At onset of the eating disorder, our male bulimics were on average 18.0 ± 1.5 (SD) years old (range 7–33) and the mean duration of the disease was 7.7 ± 2.1 years. The figures shown after the mean values are always the standard deviation (or the range).

The age at onset of the eating disorder in the bulimic men in Herzog *et al.*'s (1984) study was 20.7 (in women 17.7) years, in that of Robinson and Holden (1986) 19 years, Schneider and Agras (1987) 19.8 (8–40) years, Turnbull, Freemand and Annadale (1987) 22.4 (19–24) years, and Pope, Hudson and Jonas (1986) 25.8 (women 20.2) years. Thus, age at onset seems to be somewhat higher in men than in women.

The duration of the disorder in bulimic men at the time of the investigation was reported by Herzog *et al.* (1984) as 7.4 (in women 4.2) years, by Schneider and Agras (1987) as 6.9 years (about the same as in women) and by Turnbull, Freeman and Annadale (1987) as 2.2 years. In our study it was 7.75 ± 2.2 years. On average, the duration of the disorder up to the point of assessment was equal or somewhat longer in male bulimic patients than in females. Male bulimics appear to be not only fewer in number but also to have a 'higher threshold' for seeking medical or psychological advice.

As intended, in our investigation all three groups were of the same average age at the time of the investigation (bulimics 28.3 ± 9.1 years, homosexuals 28.9 ± 8.9 years and heterosexual controls 28.6 ± 3.4 years). It was found that the bulimic men commonly lived with their parents (41.2 per cent) or alone (35.3 per cent) and only a small proportion lived together with a partner (17.6 per cent) or in a 'commune'. Of the bulimic men, 29.4 per cent had lower and 5.9 per cent higher secondary education and 17.7 per cent had degrees from a higher technical college or a university. Thus, compared with the population norm (but not in comparison to the control groups), the educational standard of our bulimic men was relatively high. There was no difference between our three groups with regard to social class (chi square = 7.7; df = 4; NS). Furthermore, it should be emphasized that the following disorders were relatively frequent among the immediate relatives of our group of male bulimics: obesity (35.3 per cent), depression including cyclothymia (35.3 per cent), and stomach and intestinal ulcers (29.4 per cent). It is interesting to note that obesity (31.6 per cent) and affective disorders (31.6 per cent) also occurred relatively frequently in the families of the homosexual controls, but not in those of the heterosexual controls. In the literature on bulimics, alcohol misuse and dependency in male patients and/or their relations have frequently been reported (Mitchell and Goff, 1984; Pope, Hudson and Jonas, 1986; Schneider and Agras, 1987). In our investigation no statistically significant differences between the samples were found in this respect.

With regard to eating behaviour there were, on the whole, few differences between male and female bulimics. In our sample of bulimic men the total amount of food consumed during an episode of 'binge-eating' consisted of, on average, 4247 ± 744 kcal (1000–10 000). The duration of self-induced vomiting was 3.7 ± 1.0 (0.5–10) years, i.e. a shorter duration than the eating disorder. In the course of their bulimia, our patients ate large quantities of food during an episode of 'binge-eating'; 82.3 per cent did so very rapidly, 52.9 per cent often or always experienced loss of control at these times and 89.2 per cent felt guilty and angry after an attack; 70.6 per cent experienced an uncontrollable urge to eat until they felt physically unwell; 53 per cent stated with certainty that the eating attacks occurred only when they were alone. On the whole, fewer male than female bulimic patients appeared to succumb to pressure to eat only very small quantities in public, while manifesting a disciplined and restricted eating behaviour in company.

With regard to weight-control or weight-reduction strategies, only a few differences, which did not reach statistical significance, were found between male and female bulimic patients. Taking laxatives appears to occur less frequently in males than in females according to our own findings and those of Mitchell and Goff (1984) and Schneider and Agras (1987). The same trends were found with regard to diuretics and appetite-suppressant drugs in the above studies (i.e. rarer in bulimic men). In our sample, 12 out of 17 male bulimics induced vomiting, nine of them daily or several times per day. Laxatives were taken daily or several times per day by only three patients (17.6 per cent), two took appetite-suppressant drugs (11.8 per cent) and none took diuretics. Seven (41.2 per cent) used frequent fasting as a means of controlling their body weight. It was also remarkable that chewing and spitting out of food was reported by two bulimic men (11.8 per cent) as occasional and by another two (11.8 per cent) as frequent (daily or several times per day). Four male bulimics were ruminants; they regurgitated ingested food, chewed it and swallowed it again; this occurred daily or several times per day. Spitting and rumination have also been observed in female bulimics, but less frequently. It is not clear whether male, as compared with female, bulimics are more active with regard to gymnastic exercises, jogging or other athletic pursuits. In male anorexic patients such activities are very common (Burns and Crisp, 1985; Fichter and Daser, 1987). It appears, however, that this symptom does not occur as frequently in male bulimics as it does in male anorexics. Nevertheless, our clinical observations of male bulimics revealed several extreme cases of compulsive athletic activity despite severe consequent orthopaedic damage.

By definition, our male bulimics were of normal weight (102.4 ± 13.4 per cent of the ideal weight (Broca Index)); the same was true of the heterosexual male control group (101.1 ± 10.7 per cent). The homosexual men were on average somewhat lighter (94.5 ± 6.6 per cent). The height of the homosexual group was 175 cm; they were thus slightly shorter than the bulimics and the heterosexual male controls (both 178 cm). The values given in the literature for weight and height of bulimic males in comparison with healthy men or bulimic females vary. In terms of percentage of ideal weight, the values for male bulimics were lower than those for female bulimics. Pope, Hudson and Jonas (1986) and Turnbull, Freeman and Annadale (1987) found bulimic men to be taller than male controls, an observation which was not confirmed in our investigation. In our study the mean desired body weight of male bulimics was on average 5.8 ± 7 kg lower than the ideal body weight (homosexuals 1.0 ± 4.3 kg; heterosexual controls 4.1 ± 5.7 kg). Since the homosexual group had a lower body weight (in percentage terms), the 'desired' weight of all groups was fairly similar (although there was a slight tendency for a lower 'desired' weight in bulimic males). In our study, compared with the homosexual and heterosexual controls, significantly more of the bulimic men reported having been overweight between the age of six and 12 years (chi square = 9.3; df = 4; $p < 0.05$). Male bulimics also showed greater changes in body weight as compared with the two control groups (chi square = 22.2; df = 6; $p < 0.001$).

In comparison to homosexual and heterosexual controls, the bulimic men were more likely to be dieting (chi square = 11.6; df = 2; $p < 0.003$) and weighed themselves more frequently (chi square = 8.3; df = 2; $p < 0.009$). Their thoughts were significantly more concerned with eating, nutrition and body weight (chi square = 33.4; df = 8; $p < 0.001$), they showed a highly developed thinness ideal (chi square = 17.8; df = 8; $p = 0.02$) and manifested, in general, more serious misperceptions of their body image than did the controls. In men with anorexia nervosa we previously found a somewhat less developed 'thinness ideal' and less severe disturbance of body image than in female anorexic patients (Fichter and Daser, 1987). The same seems to hold for male bulimics. Schneider and Agras (1987) found that according to the Eating Attitudes Test (EAT, Garner and Garfinkel, 1979), male bulimics were less concerned with nutrition and weight than female bulimics; and, according to the Eating Disorder Inventory (EDI, Garner *et al.*, 1983), bulimic men had a less developed drive for thinness and less body dissatisfaction.

The findings of Turnbull, Freeman and Annadale (1987) show the same trends: two out of their five cases had no pathological fear of fatness and scores on the EAT and EDI were so low that the authors concluded that the identification of male cases of bulimia nervosa by this type of self-report scale was problematic.

The fear of fatness (which is apparently not present in all male bulimics), phobias concerning body weight and body-image disturbance all appear to be significant in establishing diagnostic criteria. With regard to eating disorders, these criteria must, however, not apply exclusively to the female sex. Diagnostic criteria which are solely directed towards females will result in an underidentification of bulimic syndromes in males (see Mitchell and Goff,

1984). In the revised edition of the American Psychiatric Association's criteria set out in DSM-III-R (American Psychiatric Association, 1987), the criterion 'persistent overconcern with body shape and weight' has now been added. Observations of male bulimics suggest, however, that this allows a more homogeneous group of bulimic women to be distinguished. This might lead to the exclusion of atypical female cases and may also impair the recognition of bulimia in males.

Psychometric comparisons of female and male anorexic patients did not show significant differences, with the exception of physical hyperactivity and, in our opinion, disturbance of body image (Fichter and Daser, 1987). With respect to psychometrically recognizable personality characteristics, Schneider and Agras (1987) did not find any important differences between the sexes.

Psychosexual Development and Sex-Role Identification

In male patients with anorexia nervosa, disturbances in psychosexual development and sex-role identification have been reported (Fichter and Daser, 1987). An increased prevalence of homosexuality in a mixed group of bulimic and anorexic men has also been found (Herzog *et al.*, 1984). An analysis of male bulimic patients with regard to these factors is especially interesting, since it has implications regarding the aetiology of this disorder, which occurs frequently in young women but is rare in young men.

Reaction to partners

The percentage of married bulimic men is remarkably low, even when age is taken into account. Andersen and Mickalide (1985) found that only four out of 24 (16.7 per cent) male patients with a bulimic syndrome had been married, Mitchell and Goff (1984) found the proportion to be one out of 12 (8.3 per cent) and Schneider and Agras (1987) found one out of 15 (6.7 per cent), a proportion significantly lower than in a control group of female bulimics. In our investigation, because one of the control groups consisted of homosexual subjects, marital status was less relevant than the existence of a stable relationship with a partner. Only four of the 17 bulimics (23.5 per cent), as compared with 10 of the 19 homosexual subjects (52.6 per cent) and 14 of the 18 heterosexual subjects (77.8 per cent), had a permanent partner at the time of the study (chi square = 10.3; df = 2; $p = 0.006$). One item of the Structured Interview for Anorexia and Bulimia Nervosa (SIAB) (Fichter, 1985) is concerned with the dimension of stability and intimacy (*vs* instability and distance) in the relationship with a partner. Of the bulimic group, only five out of 17 (29.4 per cent) had at any time previously, and only four out of 17 (32.5 per cent) at the time of the study, a stable, intimate relationship with a partner. In contrast, in the heterosexual control group, 13 out of 18 cases (72.2 per cent) had a stable relationship with a partner previously or at the time of the study. In the homosexual control group, six (31.5 per cent) had in the preceding years and nine (47.4 per cent) at the time of the study a stable and intimate relationship with a partner. The difference between the three groups was statistically significant at the follow-up assessment (chi square = 16.2; df = 8; p = 0.04). In a further item of the SIAB the nature of the relationship is assessed. According to this item, at the time of the study 68.8 per cent of the male bulimics, 42.1 per cent of the homosexuals and only 29.4 per cent of the heterosexual controls had no partner relationship at all, or had a relationship with infrequent contact and without cohabitation (chi square = 23.1; df = 8; p = 0.003).

Sexuality

According to the few available studies, there are clear indications that homosexual tendencies occur more frequently in bulimic men than in the normal male population. In a combined group of 27 anorexic and bulimic men, Herzog *et al.* (1984) reported homosexuality (which was not closely defined) in 25.9 per cent. By comparison, in a female control group with eating disturbances, only 4 per cent ($p < 0.01$) were homosexual. Pope, Hudson and Jonas (1986) based their investigation on narrow criteria for homosexuality (concrete homosexual experiences including orgasms in a homosexual relationship during the preceding five years). According to this definition, they found that homosexuality was not significantly more frequently manifested in bulimic men (7.1 per cent) than in male students (5.8 per cent). In contrast, Robinson and Holden (1986) reported homosexuality in three out of nine bulimic men (33.3 per cent), and Schneider and Agras (1987) found homosexuality in four out of 15 (26.7 per cent) cases and clearly established bisexuality in a further 26.7 per cent.

In our study, various aspects of homosexuality (behaviour, tendencies, opinions, self-evaluation with regard to homosexuality and masculinity, etc.) were assessed. Homosexual contacts were denied by 11 bulimic men (64.7 per cent); three (17.6 per cent) had such contacts 'rarely' to 'somewhat often' (control group of heterosexual men 5/18 = 27.8 per cent); a further three bulimics (17.7 per cent) had 'rather frequent' to 'very frequent' homosexual contacts (men of the heterosexual control group 0 per cent) (chi square = 3.54; df = 2; p = 0.17 (NS)). Fourteen (82.4 per cent) considered themselves to be 'somewhat' to 'very homosexual' (control group 12.5 per cent) (chi square = 1.1; df = 3; NS). This self-report information may, however, be considerably influenced by anxieties, desires and social norms. Other questions were more explicitly directed towards homosexual tendencies. The following items were included: (1) 'I experience tenderness as more pleasant from other men than from women'; (2) 'During self-satisfaction (masturbation) I imagine the body of another man'; (3) 'I can develop a much closer relationship with men than with women'; (4) 'If I have sexual dreams I dream about men'; (5) 'I am sexually more stimulated by men than by women'; (6) 'Occasionally I fall head over heels in love with a man'. On a scale of 0–4 for each question bulimic men scored a mean of 9.5 ± 13.0 points; the corresponding values for homosexual men were 44.9 ± 3.6 and for heterosexual men 6.8 ± 5.7 points. Thus, in these very explicitly worded items, a slight tendency towards homosexuality was apparent in bulimic men as compared to the heterosexual control group.

In another group of questions all subjects evaluated themselves according to the following categories: (1) explicitly heterosexual (bulimics 70.8 per cent, homosexuals 0 per cent, control group 83.3 per cent); (2) heterosexual with homosexual experiences (bulimics 17.6 per cent, homosexuals 0 per cent, control group 16.7 per cent); (3) bisexual (bulimics 0 per cent, homosexuals 5.3 per cent, control group 0 per cent); (4) homosexual with heterosexual experiences or explicitly homosexual (bulimics 11.8 per cent, homosexuals 94.7 per cent, control group 0 per cent). If categories (1) and (2) or (3) and (4) are combined, there were no significant differences between bulimic men and the heterosexual control group (chi square = 2.2; df = 1; $p = 0.13$ (NS)).

With regard to the self-report of their masculinity, there was no statistically significant difference between the three groups of men (chi square = 5.0; df = 6; NS). Bulimic men showed a tendency to feel uncomfortable in the company of homosexuals; 23.5 per cent were relatively, 5.9 per cent very and 11.8 per cent intolerably uncomfortable in the presence of a homosexual man (chi square = 33.9, df = 12; $p < 0.001$). Both bulimic and homosexual men frequently reported 'disgust and discomfort at the thought of "sleeping with a woman" ' as well as 'fears of having to touch a woman or being touched by a woman'. They also reported marked inhibition during sexual contacts with women, avoided women and kept out of their way (especially bulimic men), and regarded themselves as shy and anxious about heterosexual intercourse. With regard to bisexual behaviour, there were no statistically significant differences between the three groups of men. There was a non-significant trend for bulimic men to report a lack of libido (chi square = 16.6; df = 10; $p = 0.08$).

The results regarding the heterosexual behaviour of bulimic men (see Table 7.1) were very remarkable. At the time of the investigation, all subjects in the male control group, but only 28.6 per cent of the bulimics, had sexual relationships including sexual intercourse (SI). Of the bulimics, 21.4 per cent engaged only in 'petting' without SI, 7.1 per cent had a relationship with a partner without physical contact, and 42.9 per cent avoided any close relationship with a partner. The men of the heterosexual control group more frequently had a sexual relationship including sexual intercourse both at the time of the study and during the preceding years. While 94.4 per cent of the heterosexual control group had mature heterosexual contacts either previously or at the time of the study, this was true of only 56.3 per cent of the bulimics at any time. In 31.2 per cent of the latter group, the most intimate relationship

Table 7.1 Heterosexual behaviour in men

	Present A Bulimics (N = 14) N(%)	Present B Homosexuals (N = 16) N(%)	Present C Controls (N = 18) N(%)	In previous years A Bulimics (N = 16) N(%)	In previous years B Homosexuals (N = 16) N(%)	In previous years C Controls (N = 18) N(%)
I. Sexual relationship including sexual intercourse (SI).	4 (28.6)	4 (25.0)	17 (94.4)	9 (56.3)	6 (37.5)	17 (94.4)
Petting without SI	3 (21.4)	1 (6.3)	0 (0)	5 (31.2)	4 (25.0)	0 (0)
II. Partner relationship without physical contact	1 (7.1)	4 (25.0)	0 (0)	0 (0)	4 (25.0)	0 (0)
III. Avoidance of any closer partner relationship	6 (42.9)	7 (43.8)	0 (0)	2 (12.5)	2 (12.5)	0 (0)
Statistics	A *vs* B *vs* C: chi square = 23.4; df = 2; $p < 0.001$			A *vs* B vs C: chi square = 15.1; df = 2; $p < 0.01$		
	(I/C: $z = 2.65$; $p < 0.01$; II/B: $z = 1.65$; $p < 0.05$; II/C: $z = 2.82$; $p < 0.01$) A *vs* C: chi square = 17.9; df = 1; $p < 0.001$ (I/A: $z = -1.78$; $p < 0.04$; II/A: $z = 2.58$); $p < 0.001$			(I/C: $z = 1.77$; $p < 0.05$; II/B: $z = 1.98$; $p < 0.05$; II/C: $z = -2.43$; $p < 0.01$) A *vs* C: chi square = 9.4; df = 1; $p < 0.05$ (II/A: $z = 1.96$; $p < 0.05$; II/C: $z = 1.9$; $p < 0.05$)		

with women was 'petting' and 12.5 per cent avoided any contact with partners (compare Table 7.1).

There was also a significant difference between experimental groups (chi square = 25.8; df = 6; $p < 0.001$) in the frequency of sexual intercourse (SI) independent of the sex of the partner during the previous six months. Whereas 12 bulimics (70.6 per cent) had no sexual contacts with either men or women (comparative value for the control group 5.6 per cent), one bulimic patient (5.9 per cent) had such contact one to three times per month and only four bulimic patients (23.5 per cent) had sexual contacts more than once a week.

Behaviour during childhood, although distorted by memory, may provide additional information about psychological development and sex-role identification. Whilst none of the heterosexual men admitted to preferring to play with dolls as a child, this was the case in 23 per cent of the bulimic men (chi square = 4.8; df = 1; $p < 0.05$). In a comparison of all three male groups, this question was answered in the affirmative by significantly fewer heterosexual men ($z = -2.1$) and significantly more homosexual men ($z = 2.1$) than by bulimic men ($z = -0.05$) (chi square = 11.4; df = 2; $p < 0.01$). In 47.4 per cent of the homosexual men the answer to this question was 'yes'. A childhood wish to be a girl was somewhat more frequent in homosexuals (10.5 per cent) and in male bulimics (5.9 per cent) than in the heterosexual controls (0 per cent). Bulimic patients reported more frequently than the heterosexual controls that they were *not* 'go-getters' as children (homosexuals 57.9 per cent, bulimics 29.4 per cent, control group 22.2 per cent). This difference was, however, not statistically significant (chi square = 5.7; df = 2; $p = 0.59$).

It is noteworthy that one man in the homosexual control group showed a fully developed bulimic eating disorder according to DSM-III criteria; another four (22.2 per cent) had previously, or at the time of the study, experienced attacks of insatiable hunger without any other bulimic symptoms (control group 11.2 per cent). This finding suggests that homosexual men are at a relatively higher risk for developing an anorexic or bulimic eating disorder. A larger number of homosexual than heterosexual men may be exposed to the social pressure to remain slim. Younger heterosexual men are more influenced by the prevailing 'fitness ideal' than by the 'thinness ideal'; they try to shape their body less by means of reduced food intake (as seems to be the case in women, but also in bulimic men and in homosexuals) than by athletic activities.

A semantic differential for the evaluation of personality characteristics of themselves, their mother and their father produced the following finding: bulimic men saw themselves as being similar to their mothers in terms of being 'soft', 'insecure' and 'weak', and they described their mothers as 'over-concerned', 'warm', 'tense' and 'inhibited'. Fathers were seen as rather 'sure of themselves', 'strong', 'hard', 'distant' and 'withdrawn'. The evaluations of both parents were similar in terms of the following characteristics: 'mean', 'active', 'stiff', 'innocent', 'sick' and 'nagging'. The homosexual and bulimic groups both described their mothers as more active than their fathers. Both groups also regarded their fathers as rather 'distant' and 'withdrawn', while this was not the case in the heterosexual control group.

Indications of increased homosexuality also emerge from other literature on bulimic men as, even more importantly, do inhibitions and insecurity in sexual behaviour. In the series reported by Pope, Hudson and Jonas (1986), three out of 14 (21.4 per cent; mean age of the total group 29.9 years) had no heterosexual experiences and a further four subjects (28.6 per cent) were heterosexually inactive while they were bulimic. One of the nine cases described by Robinson and Holden (1986) had been operated upon for pseudogynecomasty.

In the seminal paper by Russell (1979), two male bulimic patients were described and it was noted that they had extremely little sexual experience as compared with the 38 female bulimic patients. In our study of 29 male patients with primary anorexia nervosa and seven male patients with atypical anorexia nervosa (more than half of these 36 patients showed bulimic symptoms) we found, as an indication of disturbed psychosexual development and sex-role identification, typically 'female' values on the MF scale of the Freiburg Personality Inventory (Fahrenberg, Selg and Hampel, 1973). On the semantic differential there were large similarities with the 'personality profile' of the mother, which may be regarded as a sign of inadequate identification with the father. One-third of these 36 male patients with primary or atypical anorexia nervosa had lost their fathers during their childhood or youth through separation or death (significantly more frequently than female anorexic patients and male controls). A close relationship with the mother, together with physical absence or emotional distance of the father, has often been observed in bulimic or (restricting) anorexic patients; they show strongly developed anxieties about both heterosexual and homosexual contacts (Fichter and Daser, 1987).

According to the results available at present, homosexual behaviour seems to be somewhat more frequent in bulimic than in healthy men. It would, however, be incorrect to assume that all bulimic men are basically homosexual. Disturbed psychosexual development and sex-role identification may be one of several factors which actually lead to the development of bulimia in the few men who show the symptoms of this disorder. Due to strongly developed anxieties about sexuality, heterosexual (and possibly also homosexual) behaviour is inhibited. This sexual inhibition is the most significant finding. In addition, there appears to be disturbed sex-role identification which does not necessarily lead to homosexual behaviour.

A plausible hypothesis is that those men who are at a higher risk of developing this (basically female) disorder are: (1) in general more vulnerable to psychological disorders, and (2) more liable to succumb to the social pressure regarding shape, slimness and physical appearance to which girls and younger women in western industrial nations are nowadays exposed. This applies particularly to those boys and men who are insecure and have problematic psychosexual development and identity. Anderson and Mickalide (1985) assumed a linear relation between the advertising of slimness and dieting on the one hand and the development of bulimic and anorexic eating disorders on the other. Slimness ideals and ideas are, in our present society, directed more frequently at women rather than men. Even if only a minority of bulimic men are homosexual, it remains important for therapy to help patients with possible problems in their psychosexual development and identification to lose overdeveloped sexual inhibitions and achieve mature sexuality.

Further Findings

Very little is known about the *course* of bulimia in men. As noted, it is plausible that bulimic men have disturbed psychosexual development as well as an abnormally high susceptibility to psychological disorders. However, this hypothesis requires further testing. It suggests that in men the course of the bulimic disorder may be worse than in women. Our findings regarding the accumulation of psychological and psychosomatic disorders in the immediate families of male bulimics support this assumption (a comparison with bulimic women is still lacking), Anderson (1985) found a higher rate of obsessive personalities and suspected a higher percentage of affective disorders in the families of bulimic men. Clinically, we observed particularly marked cases of tooth decay in bulimic men; this observation and its cause will have to be reinvestigated in a larger sample.

Recently, King and Mezey (1987) have drawn attention to the unusual eating behaviour of jockeys, who reduce their food intake with the yearly cycles of racing seasons. During these seasons they not infrequently take laxatives, diuretics and appetite-suppressant drugs and often experience attacks of insatiable hunger. Boxers, who are subdivided into weight classes, also adopt unusual eating behaviours for professional reasons and are, thus, at a higher risk of developing eating disorders (Halmi, 1987, personal communication).

References

American Psychiatric Association (1987). *Diagnostic and Statistical Manual of Mental Disorders - Revision (DSM-III-R).* APA, Washington DC.

Anderson, A. E. (1985). *Practical Comprehensive Treatment of Anorexia Nervosa and Bulimia.* The Johns Hopkins University Press, Baltimore.

Anderson, A. E. and A. D. Mickalide (1985). Anorexia nervosa and bulimia. Their differential diagnoses in 24 males referred to an eating and weight disorders clinic. *Bulletin of the Menninger Clinic* **49**, 227–235.

Beumont, P. J. V., C. J. Beardwood and G. F. M. Russell (1972). The occurrence of the syndrome of anorexia nervosa in male subjects. *Psychological Medicine* **2**, 216–231.

Bruch, H. (1973). *Eating Disorders: Obesity, Anorexia Nervosa and the Person Within.* Routledge & Kegan Paul, London.

Burns, T. and A. H. Crisp (1984). Anorexia nervosa in the male. Paper presented at the International Conference on Anorexia Nervosa and Related Disorders, Swansea.

Burns, T. and A. H. Crisp (1985). Factors affecting prognosis in male anorexics. *Journal of Psychiatric Research* **19**, 323–328.

Burzig, G. (1981). Anorexia Nervosa beim Mann. Diagnostische Überlegungen anhand von 20 Fällen. *Therapiewoche* **31**, 971–978.

Crisp, A. H., T. Burns and A. V. Bhat (1986). Primary anorexia nervosa in the male and female: a comparison of clinical features and prognosis. *British Journal of Medical Psychology* **59**, 123–132.

Dally, P., J. Gomez and A. J. Isaacs (1979). *Anorexia Nervosa.* Heinemann Medical, London.

Fahrenberg, J., H. Selg and R. Hampel (1973). *Das Freiburger Persönlickeitsinventar (FDI).* Hogrefe, Göttingen.

Feighner, J. P., E. Robins, S. B. Guze, R. A. Woodruff, G. Winokur and R. Munoz

(1972). Diagnostic criteria for use in psychiatric research. *Archives of General Psychiatry* **26**, 57–63.

Fichter, M. M. (1985). *Magersucht und Bulimia.* Springer Verlag, Heidelberg and New York.

Fichter, M. M. and C. Daser (1987). Symptomatology, psychosexual development and gender identity in 42 anorexic males. *Psychological Medicine* **17**, 409–418.

Fichter, M. M. and W. Keeser (1980). Das Anorexia Nervosa Inventar zur Selbstbeurteilung (ANIS-32). *Archiv für Psychiatrie und Nervenkrankheiten* **228**, 67–80.

Garner, D. M. and P. E. Garfinkel (1979). The Eating Attitudes Test: an index of the symptoms of anorexia nervosa. *Psychological Medicine* **9**, 273–279.

Garner, D. and P. E. Garfinkel (Eds) (1985). *Handbook of Psychotherapy for Anorexia Nervosa and Bulimia.* Guildford Press, New York.

Garner, D. M., M. A. Olmsted and J. Polivy (1983). Development and validation of a multidimensional eating disorder inventory for anorexia nervosa and bulimia nervosa. *International Journal of Eating Disorders* **2**, 15–34.

Hall, A., J. W. Delahunt and P. Ellis (1985). Anorexia nervosa in the male. *Journal of Psychiatric Research* **19**, 315–321.

Halmi, K. (1987). Personal communication.

Harry, J. (1982). *Gay Children Grown up: Gender, Culture and Gender Deviance.* Praeger, New York.

Hasan, M. K. and R. W. Tibbetts (1977). Primary anorexia nervosa (weight phobia) in males. *Postgraduate Medical Journal* **53**, 146–151.

Hay, G. G. and J. Leonard (1979). Anorexia nervosa in the male. *The Lancet* **ii**, 574–576.

Herzog, D. B. (1982). Bulimia: the secretive syndrome. *Psychosomatics* **23**, 481–487.

Herzog, D. B., D. D. Norman, C. Gordon and M. Pepose (1984). Sexual conflict and eating disorders in 27 males. *American Journal of Psychiatry* **141**, 989–990.

Hogan, W. M., E. Herta and A. R. Lucas (1974). Diagnosing anorexia nervosa in males. *Psychosomatics* **15**, 122–126.

King, M. B. and G. Mezey (1987). Eating behaviour of male racing jockeys. *Psychological Medicine* **17**, 249–253.

Martin, M. and I. Dauner (1978). Anorexia bei Knaben- zu ihrer Differentialdiagnose. *Zeitschrift für Kinder- und Jugendpsychiatrie* **6**, 117–130.

Mester, H. (1981). *Anorexia Nervosa.* Springer Verlag, Berlin.

Meyer, J. K. (1985). Ego-dystonic homosexuality. In *Comprehensive Textbook of Psychiatry. IV.* Vol. I, edited by H. I. Kaplan and B. J. Sadock. Williams & Wilkins, Baltimore, pp. 1056–1065.

Mitchell, J. E. and G. Goff (1984). Bulimia in the male patient. *Psychosomatics* **25**, 909–913.

Olmstead, M. P. and J. Polivy (1983). Development and validation of a multidimensional eating disorder inventory for anorexia nervosa and bulimia. *International Journal of Eating Disorders* **2**, 15–34.

Pope, H. G., J. I. Hudson and J. M. Jonas (1986). Bulimia in men. A series of fifteen cases. *Journal of Nervous and Mental Diseases* **174**, 117–119.

Robinson, P. H. and N. L. Holden (1986). Bulimia nervosa in the male: a report of nine cases. *Psychological Medicine* **16**, 795–803.

Russell, G. (1979). Bulimia nervosa: an ominous variant of anorexia nervosa. *Psychological Medicine* **9**, 429–448.

Schneider, J. A. and W. S. Agras (1987). Bulimia in males: a matched comparison with females. *International Journal of Eating Disorders* **2**, 235–242.

Scott, D. W. (1986). Anorexia nervosa in the male: a review of clinical, epidemiological and biological findings. International Journal of Eating Disorders **5**, 799–819.

Sheppard, N. P., A. Jackson and J. P. Malone (1984). Male anorexia nervosa: a review of nine patients. *Irish Medical Journal (Dublin)* **77**, 4–8.

Sterling, J. W. and J. D. Segal (1985). Anorexia nervosa in the male: a critical review. International Journal of Eating Disorders **4**, 559–572.

Taipale, V., K. Larkio Miettinen and E. H. Valanne (1972). Anorexia nervosa in boys. *Psychosomatics* **13**, 236–240.

Turnbull, J. D., C. P. L. Freeman and K. Annadale (1987). Physical and psychological characteristics of five male bulimics. *British Journal of Psychiatry* **150**, 25–29.

Vandereycken, W. and S. Van den Broucke (1984). Anorexia nervosa in males. A comparative study of 107 cases reported in the literature (1970 to 1980). *Acta Psychiatrica Scandinavica* **70**, 447–454.

8

Affective disorders and bulimic syndromes

R. G. Laessle
Max-Planck Institute for Psychiatry, Munich

A close nosological relationship between eating disorders and affective disorders has been a subject for discussion for some time (Wulff, 1932; Zutt, 1948). The possibility of such a relationship in regard to bulimia has recently been reconsidered by American authors (Hudson and Pope, 1987). At the same time, the beneficial effects of antidepressant drugs in bulimic patients have been interpreted as an indication of a common biological basis (diathesis) for bulimia and depression. However, a thorough evaluation of this hypothesis requires the consideration of data from other areas of nosological research in psychiatry. These include studies of the phenomenology, of the course and outcome of the disorder, of family history and of biological changes.

In this contribution empirical observations are presented which may provide a better understanding of the significance of various factors in the co-occurrence of affective disorders and bulimia.

Phenomenology of Depression in Bulimic Syndromes

In 1979 Russell had already described clear symptoms of depression in 87 per cent of his patients with 'bulimia nervosa'. In further studies, using standardized self- and 'third-person' valuation scales for the diagnosis of depression, it was found that depression scores were usually significantly

Table 8.1 Depression scores for bulimic patients and controls (von Zerssen, 1976)

	Mean	SD	Percentage of normal sample
Bulimia (DSM-III) ($N = 32$)	19.1	8.0	98
Major depression (DSM-III) ($N = 38$)	22.3	8.4	99
Normal female controls ($N = 211$)	6.7	5.0	69

higher for bulimic patients than for normal control subjects (Strober and Katz, 1986).

The results of our own study of 32 patients with bulimia are shown in Table 8.1. At the time of hospitalization, patients with an eating disorder had significantly higher scores on the depression scale (von Zerssen, 1976) than normal women and their mean score was the same as that of a group of patients with major depression (DSM-III).

Further information relevant to depressive disorders in patients with bulimia is given in studies on the cross-sectional and lifetime prevalence of operationally defined affective syndromes. The results of investigations in which standardized diagnostic interviews were used are summarized in Table 8.2. The reported cross-sectional prevalence for a 'major affective disorder' lies between 21 and 45 per cent (average 37 per cent) and the lifetime prevalence between 36 and 92 per cent (average 61 per cent). The affective disorders were largely of the depressive type. Bipolar disorders were only seen in the samples of Hudson *et al.* (1983a) and Laessle *et al.* (1987), who found a lifetime prevalence of about 15 per cent.

Thus, more than half of the bulimic patients experienced a phase of a clinically significant affective disorder during the course of their life. Depression occurred most commonly in patients whose eating disorder started as anorexia nervosa and developed into (normal-weight) bulimia (Laessle *et al.*, 1987). In comparison, the prevalence rates for a 'major depression' (DSM-III) in the normal population are as follows: cross-sectional prevalence for women in the USA approximately 3–4 per cent (Robins *et al.*, 1984), in West Germany approximately 3 per cent (Wittchen and von Zerssen, 1987). The lifetime prevalence in the USA is approximately 9 per cent (Robins *et al.*, 1984) and in West Germany approximately 8 per cent (Wittchen and von Zerssen, 1987).

Table 8.2 Prevalence of major depression in bulimia

Authors	Diagnosis of eating disorder*	No. of cases	Proportion of patients with MAD† (%)	Diagnosed duration‡
Hudson *et al.* (1983a)	B	49	73	L
	B-AN	25	92	L
Herzog (1984)	B	55	24	C
Piran *et al.* (1985)	AN-B	33	36	L
Walsh *et al.* (1985)	B	34	71	L
			21	C
	B-AN	7	86	L
			71	C
	AN-B	9	56	L
			33	C
Laessle *et al.* (1987)	B	26	39	L
			27	C
	B-AN	22	50	L
			42	C
	AN-B	18	50	L
			45	C

*At time of interview, B, bulimia (DSM-III) without a history of anorexia nervosa; B-AN, bulimia (DSM-III) with a history of anorexia nervosa; AN-B, anorexia nervosa (DSM-III) with bulimic symptoms.
†Major affective disorder according to DSM-III or RDC.
‡L, lifetime prevalence; C, cross-sectional prevalence.

The data regarding the temporal relationship of the depression and of the eating disorder do not provide a consistent picture. Whereas in Hudson *et al.*'s (1983a) study depression manifested itself in 49 per cent of the cases at least one year before the eating disorder, Walsh *et al.* (1985) observed this in 26 per cent and Laessle *et al.* (1987) in only 9.4 per cent of cases.

Symptom pattern of depression in bulimia and major depression

Since the diagnosis of 'major depression' can be based on different symptom clusters, the question arises of whether the pattern of affective symptoms is the same in bulimic patients as in primary depressive patients. So far, there are hardly any data available on this issue. It appears, however, that important differences exist in the symptom profile. In the study by Walsh *et al.* (1985), and in our own investigations (Laessle *et al.*, 1987), less than 20 per cent of bulimic patients with a 'major depression' fulfilled the criteria for the subgroup 'melancholia'. In a discriminant function analysis of the symptom profiles of 66 bulimic patients and 47 patients with primary depression without a lifetime diagnosis of an eating disorder, a significant difference between the two groups was obtained (Laessle *et al.*, 1988). Patients suffering from primary depression could be clearly separated from bulimics by the more frequent manifestation of symptoms such as loss of energy, suicide attempts, loss of appetite, loss of libido and general retardation. Similar differences had been found earlier by Cooper and Fairburn (1986). These authors further questioned the diagnostic value of single, specific symptoms as indicators of depression in bulimic patients, since symptoms such as dysphoria, pathological guilt and loss of self-esteem can fluctuate greatly with time and are closely related to changes in eating behaviour and cognitive characteristics.

Course and outcome in bulimia and affective disorders

The assumption that bulimic syndromes are a variant of depressive disorders implies a congruent course for both disorders. According to data from a prospective study of the course of unipolar depression (Keller, 1985), the cumulative probability of a complete remission of the depressive phase three months after start of treatment is 42 per cent. After six months it is 64 per cent, after one year 74 per cent and after two years 79 per cent. Thus, 20 per cent of depressive patients show a somewhat chronic course of the disorder. In a methodologically comparable study on the course of bulimia, Keller *et al.* (1986) found that six months after the start of treatment only 35 per cent of the patients fulfilled the criteria for complete remission. Thus, the remission rate in bulimia was only half of that in unipolar depression. At the time of inclusion in this study, 60 per cent of the bulimic patients fulfilled RDC criteria for a 'major' or 'minor affective disorder'. A remission of the affective disorder after six months occurred in 25 per cent of the patients, but simultaneous remission of both syndromes occurred in only one patient. Thus, an improvement of the affective disorder was not necessarily associated with a reduction in bulimic symptomatology. The results of a 2–5 year follow-up of bulimic patients can be similarly interpreted (Swift *et al.*, 1985). On average, the patients showed very low depression scores, although 26 out of 30 fulfilled DSM-III criteria for bulimia even at follow-up examination. In their three-year follow-up, Norman and Herzog (1986) also found on average a significant decrease in depressive symptoms. However, the eating disorder persisted in nearly 50 per cent of the cases.

In summary, it can be concluded that clinically significant depressive disorders occur far more frequently in bulimic patients than in persons without any psychological disorders. This is, however, not only the case for bulimia but also for other psychiatric and psychosomatic illnesses. For example, in 40–60 per cent of patients with schizophrenia (Guze *et al.*, 1985), anxiety disorders (Breier, Charney and Heminter, 1984), alcohol abuse (Cadoret, Troughton and Widmer, 1984) and irritable colon (Young *et al.*, 1976) high lifetime rates for an affective disorder were found. Thus, depressive syndromes are not specific to bulimia. Furthermore, analysis of the symptom patterns indicates substantial differences between bulimic and primary depressive patients. The discontinuity of the remission patterns of both syndromes tends to argue against a common aetiological process for the affective and the bulimic disorder, in spite of the phenomenological similarities which undoubtedly exist at certain times. This interpretation is further supported by the results of studies of the prevalence of eating disorders in young people admitted for treatment of their depression. If a common aetiology is assumed, the probability of developing an eating disorder, especially bulimia, should be high in this group. However, in several follow-up studies Strober and Katz (1987) found no indication of an increased incidence of bulimia up to four years later.

Affective disorders in the families of bulimic patients

Several studies described a high prevalence of affective disorders in the families of bulimic patients (for review see Strober and Katz, 1986). In four studies operational criteria were used for the diagnosis of affective disorders in members of the family. Hudson *et al.* (1983b) found a morbidity risk for a major affective disorder (DSM-III) of 26 per cent amongst first-degree relatives. In a second investigation, the same authors (Hudson *et al.*, 1988) found a morbidity risk of 32 per cent, which was comparable to that of relatives of patients with a major depression. Of the bulimic patients, 49 per cent had at least one close relative with an affective disorder. In both investigations the morbidity risk in a 'non-psychiatric' control group was significantly lower.

Similar morbidity rates have been found by Stern *et al.* (1984) and Blouin *et al.* (1986). However, in these two investigations the difference between the eating-disorder group and the 'non-psychiatric' control group was not significant. It is, however, doubtful whether the control groups were, in fact, representative because the lifetime prevalence for major depression among the relatives of the controls was more than 30 per cent, and thus higher than would be expected for the general population (Robins *et al.*, 1984). At first glance, the consistently reported concentration of affective disorders in the families of bulimic patients suggests a common genetic component for both disorders. Other data, however, make this hypothesis less plausible. A detailed analysis of the results of Hudson *et al.* (1988) shows that the accumulation of affective disorders occurs largely in the families of bulimic patients who were diagnosed as suffering from a major affective disorder in addition to the eating disorder. Similar results have also been reported by Gershon *et al.* (1984) and Strober and Katz (1986). Furthermore, Strober and Katz (1986) did not find a high prevalence of eating disorders in families of patients with an affective disorder. In contrast, eating disorders occurred at an increased rate in the families of patients with eating disorders, and affective disorders in relatives of patients with an affective disorder.

These results indicate that genetic transmission within a family of affective disorders and of eating disorders, such as anorexia nervosa or bulimia, occurs independently. It is possible that affective disorders in family members create specific intrafamilial environmental and psychological conditions which increase the probability of the development of an eating disorder in another 'vulnerable' family member.

Biological Changes and Depressive Symptoms

Disturbances in neuroendocrine functions (e.g. increased plasma cortisol concentrations with abnormal results for the dexamethasone test, decreased secretion of TSH after stimulation with TRH, decreased secretion of growth hormone after stimulation with clonidine) have been observed in numerous studies of depressive patients (for review see Hudson and Hudson, 1984). Many authors have regarded these disturbances as biological markers for endogenous depression. Pathological results in the dexamethasone suppression test and the TRH test have also been observed in patients with bulimia and this has been interpreted as evidence for a close nosological relationship between bulimia and affective disorders (for review see Hudson and Pope, 1987).

Recently, however, data have become available on the effect of weight loss, nutrition and stress on neuroendocrine functions which clearly argue against the specificity of these observations for certain forms of depression (Berger *et al.*, 1983; Fichter and Pirke, 1986). It has also been shown that in normal-weight bulimic patients (Fichter and Pirke, this volume, Chapter 16) there is a significant correlation between disturbances in neuroendocrine functions and qualitative and quantitative aspects of the eating behaviour of these patients.

A further means of comparing affective disorders and bulimia on a biological basis is studies of sleep EEG. The sleep EEG of depressed patients consistently shows characteristic deviations from the norm (e.g. disturbances of sleep duration, sleep structure and disturbances of REM sleep; for review see Kupfer, 1986). For bulimia, polysomnographic data from four studies are available (for review see Lauer *et al.*, 1988). None of these studies showed significant differences between bulimic patients and age-matched control subjects. The EEG results of bulimic patients with the additional diagnosis 'major affective disorder' were also normal. In summary, neither neuroendocrine results nor EEG results support the assumption that an affective disorder forms the basis for bulimia.

Depression and adaptation to starvation

Keys *et al.* (1950) were the first to demonstrate that starvation could result in severe changes in affective state. These include, for example, lack of energy, disturbed sleep, dysphoria, difficulty in concentrating, social withdrawal, loss of libido and loss of interest in general. Fichter (1985) also reported elevated depression scores in young women after two weeks of fasting. Thus, some of the affective symptoms in patients with eating disorders may be closely connected with their nutritional state.

Pirke *et al.* (1985) showed metabolic and endocrine adaptation to starvation not only in seriously underweight patients with anorexia nervosa but also in normal-weight patients with bulimia. In bulimic patients these changes are obviously due to intermittent fasting.

In one of our investigations we have analysed the relationship between malnutrition and depressive symptomatology. Data on depression (DS, von Zerssen, 1976; BDI, Beck and Beck, 1972), on the psychopathology of the eating disorder (EDI, Garner, Olmsted and Polivy, 1983), on body weight and also on indicators of starvation which are relatively independent from body weight (T3, betahydroxybutyric acid (BHBA), cortisol) were collected from 64 patients who fulfilled DSM-III criteria for anorexia or bulimia, controlling for the specific psychopathology of the eating disorder and the diagnostic subgroups (anorexia, bulimia), a multiple regression analysis revealed that 12 per cent of the variance in the DS score could be explained by the indicators or starvation. Significant partial correlations were found for body weight and for BHBA: the lower the body weight, the higher the depression score (independent of other variables measured). In addition, the depression score for patients with pathologically increased BHBA values was significantly higher than for patients with BHBA values in the normal range (also taking into account all other measured variables). If the BDI score was used as a criterion in the regression analysis, no significant effects were observed for the biological indicators of starvation. The BDI is more a measure of cognitive-motivational aspects of the depression, the DS of mood and psychovegetative symptoms. Therefore, our data support the conclusion that specific depressive symptoms in anorexia and bulimia — rather than a global depressive syndrome — might be related not only to severe weight loss, but also the metabolic and endocrine adaptation to starvation, which can be found in normal-weight patients with bulimia.

Depression and alterations in neurotransmitter systems

Changes in eating behaviour influence the function of noradrenergic (Schweiger, Warnhoff and Pirke, 1985) and of serotoninergic neurotransmitter systems (Wurtman, 1983). Many clinical studies indicate changes in peripheral and central neurotransmitter functions in patients with anorexia nervosa and bulimia (see Pirke, this volume, Chapter 15). Neurotransmitters such as norepinephrine and serotonin are involved in the regulation of a number of psychological, and especially of affective functions. It has, therefore, been assumed that depressive disorders are related to neurotransmitter disturbances (Von Praag, 1986). However, Von Praag (1986) concluded from the available data that alterations in these neurotransmitter systems are not so much linked with a general depressive syndrome as with particular components of the syndrome (e.g. mood regulation, vegetative complaints, psychomotoric symptoms).

In two of our studies the relevance of neurotransmitter changes to the depressive symptoms of patients with eating disorders was analysed. The first investigation was designed to examine the relationship between 'depressive mood' (as a specific symptom of depression) and decreased noradrenergic activity. The increase in plasma noradrenaline concentrations (delta-NA) during orthostatic challenge has been used as an indicator for transmitter changes. In 24 inpatients with anorexia nervosa (DSM-III) biological and psychopathological data were collected during the second, fifth, eighth, eleventh and fourteenth week of treatment. Depressive mood was measured three times a week by a standardized self-rating scale (von Zerssen, 1976). An average mood score per week was calculated and correlated with the 'delta-NA' values observed in the same week.

At four out of five measurement points significant correlations between mood and 'delta-NA' were found (second week: $r = -0.40$; eighth week: $r = 0.35$; eleventh week: $r = -0.49$; fourteenth week: $r = -0.42$). The lower the 'delta-NA' values, the worse the mood of the patients was. The severity of the specific psychopathology of the eating disorder (measured by ANIS: Fichter and Keeser, 1980) correlated significantly with mood but not with the 'delta-NA' values.

Taken together, these results indicate that depressive symptoms are associated with changes in the activity of central and peripheral noradrenergic systems which have been induced by starvation. Since such changes occur not only in severely underweight anorexic patients but also in normal-weight bulimics (Pirke *et al.*, 1985), this relationship may also hold for patients in the latter group.

Composition of the diet influences serotonergic activity (Wurtman, 1983). Malnutrition which is characterized by a deficit in carbohydrates can lead to a decreased influx of tryptophan into the brain and thus to decreased central serotonin synthesis.

The influence of such changes on mood has been investigated under conditions of food restriction in 18 healthy young women (aged between 18 and 30 years). During a diet phase of six weeks the subjects ate approximately 1000 kcal per day and lost about 1 kg weight per week. The mean loss in body weight for all participants was 6.1 kg. Food intake was recorded in a diary and mood was rated daily on visual analogue scales. In the fifth week of the diet phase blood samples were taken every hour over a period of 24 hours in order to analyse the large neutral amino acids (LNAA) and tryptophan.

During the last three weeks of the diet phase there was a significant correlation between mean mood score and the proportion of carbohydrates in the diet ($r = -0.74$; $p < 0.01$). The smaller the proportion of carbohydrates, the worse the mood. A close relationship between this observation and changes in serotonin synthesis is also shown by the significant correlation between the quotient tryptophan/LNAA (which is regarded as the best indicator for tryptophan influx into the brain) and mood ($r = -0.52$; $p < 0.05$). Other variables (e.g. stress, feeling of hunger) were not significantly correlated with mood. Similar observations have been reported by Spring (1986) and DeCastro (1987). Thus, a weight-reducing diet with a low proportion of carbohydrates can contribute to depressive mood, as serotonin synthesis in the brain is impaired by decreased availability of its precursor, tryptophan.

More recent results regarding the eating behaviour of bulimic patients show frequent variations in the composition of their food (Schweiger *et al.*, 1988; Woell *et al.*, 1989). As a result of the attempt to eat as little 'fattening' food as possible between bulimic episodes, the diet of many patients is relatively poor in carbohydrates. This can make an essential contribution to the intermittent occurrence of depressive mood changes *via* the mechanism described above.

Depressive Symptoms and Specific Psychological Characteristics of Bulimia

So far, psychological theories regarding the aetiology and maintenance of depressive disorders in patients with bulimia have been hardly even considered. As a heuristic conceptual framework, the cognitive approach of Beck (1976) appears to be especially useful. According to Beck, depressive episodes are partly the consequence of an altered cognitive structure, which is characterized by the person's negative perception of himself, the environment and the future (so-called 'cognitive triad'). Beck assumes that the cognitive triad develops and is maintained on the basis of irrational assumptions (e.g. 'I must not make any mistakes', 'I must be liked by everybody') and cognitive distortions (e.g. dichotomous thinking, overgeneralization, etc.). Many bulimic patients show such dysfunctional cognitions (Phelan, 1987; Ruderman, 1986), particularly with regard to shape and weight. The self-concept of patients is almost exclusively defined by these physical attributes (Striegel-Moore, Silberstein and Rodin, 1986). On the basis of Beck's assumptions, we have investigated the question of the extent to which dysfunctional cognitions (especially regarding one's own body) are related to depressive symptoms in patients with bulimia.

Forty-nine patients with bulimia (DSM-III) have been studied either at the

Table 8.3 Relationship between depression and cognitive characteristics of the eating disorder in 49 patients with bulimia

Variable	Standard regression coefficient	Partial correlation
Negative body attitudes	0.53	0.51***
Body dissatisfaction	0.08	0.08
Drive for thinness	0.19	0.26*
Perfectionism	0.31	0.41***
Body weight	– 0.29	– 0.35**
Time of assessment	– 0.11	– 0.15
Regression equation Multiple $R^2 = 0.58$	$F = 9.7$, df = 6/42, $p < 0.001$)	

*$p < 0.10$; **$p < 0.05$; *** $p < 0.001$

time of hospitalization ($N = 31$) or one year after discharge from the clinic of the Max-Planck Institute for Psychiatry (N = 18). Specific cognitive characteristics were assessed by three subscales of the Eating Disorder Inventory (EDI, Garner, Olmsted and Polivy, 1983): EDI 1, drive for thinness; EDI 3, body dissatisfaction; EDI 5, perfectionism. In addition, a semantic differential (Steinhausen, 1985) was used to measure negative body attitudes. The severity of the depression was assessed by means of a standardized depression scale (DS: von Zerssen, 1976). The scores obtained from all scales for assessing cognitive schemata were significantly correlated with severity of depression (negative body attitudes: $r = -0.59, p < 0.001$; body dissatisfaction: $r = -0.46, p < 0.001$; perfectionism: $r = -0.33, p < 0.05$). Because the independent variables were also interconnected, partial correlations were estimated by regression analysis. Body weight and time of data collection (dichotomized: 0, hospitalization; 1, follow-up examination) were included in the regression equation to control for their possible effects on depression. The results are shown in Table 8.3. Taken together, the four scales measuring cognitive distortion account for 45 per cent of the variance in the depression scores. The highest partial correlations were obtained for the scales negative body attitudes and perfectionism, respectively. This means that the more negatively the body was evaluated and the stronger the desire for perfectionism, the more depressed were the patients (independent of the effects of the other variables in the regression equation).

Similar correlations were found in a study by Swift *et al.* (1985). These results emphasize the possible relevance of psychological factors to the development and maintenance of depression in bulimic patients. Further evidence has been provided by the clinical observations of Fairburn *et al.* (1985), which showed that, in most cases, changes in cognitions regarding body weight and shape are accompanied by an improvement in depressive symptomatology during cognitive-behavioural treatment of bulimia.

Conclusions

The results of phenomenological studies show that clinically significant depression frequently occurs in patients with a bulimic syndrome. A possible explanation for the manifestation of depressive symptoms in eating disorders is the assumption of a common biological–genetic basis for both disorders. Since antidepressant medication has a beneficial effect in some bulimic patients (see Hudson and Pope, this volume, Chapter 22), it is possible that in some cases a severe affective disorder is manifested in the form of a bulimic disorder. However, empirical evidence suggests that there are perceptible boundaries between the two conditions in terms of symptom phenomenology and course over time. Moreover, depression has been shown to be a common concomitant disturbance in a variety of severe psychiatric conditions and detailed analysis of the available studies regarding the occurrence of affective disorders in members of the patient's family also argues against a specific aetiological connection between depression and bulimia.

To date, few studies have investigated the extent to which specific biological and psychological consequences of the eating disturbance are implicated in the development and maintenance of depressive symptoms. The pathological eating behaviour of bulimic patients leads to many biological changes (e.g. metabolic adaptation to malnutrition, neurotransmitter disturbances). As shown in the empirical studies described above, these secondary biological consequences can be closely associated with specific symptoms of depression (e.g. deterioration of mood). For a psychologically oriented explanation of affective disorders in bulimia, specific psychopathological characteristics of the eating disorder must be taken into account. Above all, dysfunctional cognitions regarding the evaluation of shape and weight seem to be closely associated with depression in bulimic patients.

References

Beck, A. T. (1976). *Cognitive Therapy and the Emotional Disorders.* International University Press, New York.

Beck, A. T. and R. W. Beck (1972). Screening depressed patients in family practice: a rapid technique. *Postgraduate Medicine* **52**(6), 81.

Berger, M., K. M. Pirke, P. Doerr, J. C. Krieg and D. v. Zerssen (1983). Influence of weight loss on the dexamethasone suppression test. *Archives of General Psychiatry* **40**, 585.

Blouin, P., V. McAffer, J. Blouin and E. Perez (1986). The incidence of depression in bulimia. Paper presented at the International Conference on Eating Disorders, New York City, April 1986.

Breier, A., D. S. Charney and G. R. Heminter (1984). Major depression in patients with agoraphobia and panic disorder. *Archives of General Psychiatry* **41**, 1129.

Cadoret, R., E. Troughton and R. Widmer (1984). Clinical differences between antisocial and primary alcoholics. *Comprehensive Psychiatry* **25**, 1.

Cooper, P. J. and C. G. Fairburn (1986). The depressive symptoms of bulimia nervosa. *British Journal of Psychiatry* **148**, 268.

DeCastro, J. M. (1987). Macronutrient relationships with meal patterns and mood in spontaneous human feeding behavior. *Physiology and Behavior* **39**, 561.

Fairburn, C. G., P. J. Cooper, J. Kirk and M. O'Connor (1985). The significance of the neurotic symptoms of bulimia nervosa. *Journal of Psychiatric Research* **19**, 135.

Fichter, M. M. (1985). *Magersucht und Bulimia.* Springer, Heidelberg.

Fichter, M. M. and W. Keeser (1980). Das Anorexia-nervosa-Inventar zur Selbstbeurteilung (ANIS). *Archiv. für Psychiatrie und Nervenkrankheiten* **228**, 67.

Fichter, M. M. and K. M. Pirke (1986). Effect of experimental and pathological weight loss upon the hypothalamic–pituitary–adrenal axis. *Psychoneuroendocrinology* **11**, 11.

Garner, D. M., M. P. Olmsted and J. Polivy (1983). The development and validation of a multidimensional eating disorder inventory for anorexia nervosa and bulimia. *International Journal of Eating Disorders* **2**, 15.

Gershon, E. S., J. L. Schreiber, J. R. Hamovit, E. D. Dibble, W. H. Kaye, J. I. Nurnberger, A. Andersen and M. H. Ebert (1984). Clinical findings in patients with anorexia nervosa and affective illness in their relatives. *American Journal of Psychiatry* **141**, 1419.

Guze, S. B., C. R. Cloninger, R. L. Martin and P. J. Clayton (1985). A follow-up and family study of schizophrenia. *Archives of General Psychiatry* **140**, 1273.

Herzog, D. B. (1984). Are anorectic and bulimic patients depressed? *American Journal of Psychiatry* **141**, 1594.

Hudson, J. I. and M. S. Hudson (1984). Endocrine dysfunction in anorexia nervosa and bulimia: comparison with abnormalities in other psychiatric disorders and disturbances due to metabolic factors. *Psychiatric Developments* **4**, 237.

Hudson, J. I. and H. G. Pope (1987). Depression and eating disorders. *Presentations of Depression*, ed. by O. G. Cameron. Wiley, New York, p. 33.

Hudson, J. I., H. G. Pope, J. M. Jonas and D. Yurgelun-Todd (1983a). Phenomenologic relationship of eating disorders to major affective disorder. *Psychiatry Research* **9**, 345.

Hudson, J. I., H. G. Pope, J. M. Jonas and D. Yurgelun-Todd (1983b). Family history study of anorexia nervosa and bulimia. *British Journal of Psychiatry* **142**, 133.

Hudson, J. I., H. G. Pope, J. M. Jonas, D. Yurgelun-Todd and F. R. Frankenburg (1988). A controlled family history study of bulimia. *Psychological Medicine*, in press.

Keller, M. B. (1985). Chronic and recurrent affective disorders: incidence, course, and influencing factors. In *Chronic Treatments in Neuropsychiatry*, ed. by D. Kemali and G. Racagni. Raven Press, New York, p. 111.

Keller, M. B., D. B. Hertzog, P. W. Lavori, A. Bridges, I. Ott and G. L. Klerman (1986). One-year course of bulimia and affective disorder. Paper presented at the annual meeting of the American Psychiatric Association, Washington DC.

Keys, A., J. Brozek, A. Itenschel, O. Mickelson and H. L. Taylor (1950). *The Biology of Human Starvation.* University of Minnesota Press, Minneapolis.

Kupfer, D. J. (1986). The sleep EEG in diagnosis and treatment of depression. In *Depression. Basic Mechanism, Diagnosis, and Treatment*, ed. by A. J. Rush and K. Z. Altshuler. Guilford Press, New York, p. 102.

Laessle, R. G., S. Kittl, M. Fichter, H. U. Wittchen and K. M. Pirke (1987). Major affective disorder in anorexia nervosa and bulimia. A descriptive diagnostic study. *British Journal of Psychiatry* **151**, 785.

Laessle, R. G., U. Schweiger, M. M. Fichter and K. M. Pirke (1988). Eating disorders and depression: psychobiological findings in bulimia and anorexia nervosa. In *The Psychobiology of Bulimia Nervosa*, ed. by K. M. Pirke, W. Vandereycken and D. Ploog. Springer, Berlin, p. 90.

Laessle, R. G., U. Schweiger and K. M. Pirke (1988a). Depression as a correlate of starvation in patients with eating disorders? *Biolology and Psychiatry* **23**, 719.

Laessle, R. G., U. Schweiger and K. M. Pirke (1988b). Mood and orthostatic norepinephrine response in anorexia nervosa. *Psychiatry Research* **24**, 87.

Laessle, R. G., S. Kittl, M. M. Fichter and K. M. Pirke (1988c). Cognitive correlates of depression in patients with eating disorders. *International Journal of Eating Disorders* **7**, 863.

Lauer, C., J. Zulley, J.-C. Krieg and M. Berger (1988). EEC sleep and the cholinergic REM-Induction Test in anorexic and bulimic patients. *Psychiatry Research* **26**, 171.

Norman, D. K. and D. B. Herzog (1986). A 3-year outcome study of normal-weight bulimia: assessment of psychosocial functioning and eating attitudes. *Psychiatry Research* **19**, 199.

Phelan, P. W. (1987). Cognitive correlates of bulimia: the bulimic thoughts questionnaire. *International Journal of Eating Disorders* **6**, 593.

Piran, N., S. Kennedy, P. E. Garfinkel and M. Owens (1985). Affective disturbance in eating disorders. *Journal of Nervous and Mental Disease* **173**, 395.

Pirke, K. M., R. Laessle and U. Schweiger (1988). Psychosomatische Interaktionen bei Anorexia und Bulimia Nervosa. In *Gestörtes Eßverhalten*, ed. by V. Pudel, T. Paul and C. Jacobi. Springer, Heidelberg.

Pirke, K. M., J. Pahl, U. Schweiger and M. Warnhoff (1985). Metabolic and endocrine indices of starvation in bulimia: A comparison with anorexia nervosa. *Psychiatry Research* **15**, 33.

Robins, L. N., J. E. Helzer, M. M. Weissman, H. Orvaschel, E. Gruenberg, J. D. Burke and D. A. Regier (1984). Lifetime prevalence of specific psychiatric disorders in three sites. *Archives of General Psychiatry* **41**, 949.

Ruderman, A. J. (1986). Bulimia and irrational beliefs. *Behaviour Research and Therapy* **24**, 193.

Russell, G. F. M. (1979). Bulimia nervosa: an ominous variant of anorexia nervosa. *Psychological Medicine* **9**, 429.

Schweiger, U., R. G. Laessle, M. M. Fichter and K. M. Pirke (1989). Consequences of dieting at normal weight. In *The Psychobiology of Bulimia Nervosa*, ed. by K. M. Pirke, W. Vandereycken and P. Ploog. Springer, Berlin, p. 74.

Schweiger, U., M. Warnhoff and K. M. Pirke (1985). Norepinephrine turnover in the hypathalamus of adult male rats. *Journal of Neurochemistry* **45**, 706.

Spring, B. (1986). Effects of food and nutrients on the behavior of normal individuals. In *Nutrition and the Brain*, ed. by R. J. Wurtman and J. J. Wurtman. Raven Press, New York, p. 1.

Steinhausen, H.-C. (1985). Das Körperbild bei jungen Mädchen und Frauen im Vergleich zu anorektischen Patientinnen: Prüfung eines Messinstruments. *Nervenarzt* **56**, 1.
Stern, S. L., K. N. Dixon, E. Nemzer, M. D. Lake, R. A. Sansone, D. J. Smeltzer, S. Lantz and S. S. Schrier (1984). Affective disorder in the families of women with normal weight bulimia. *American Journal of Psychiatry* **141**, 1224.
Striegel-Moore, R. H., L. R. Silberstein and J. Rodin (1986). Towards an understanding of risk factors for bulimia. *American Psychology* **41**, 246.
Strober, M. and J. Katz (1986). Depression in the eating disorders: a review and analysis of descriptive, family and biological findings. In *Diagnostic Issues in Anorexia Nervosa and Bulimia*, ed. by D. M. Garner and P. Garfinkel. Bruner and Mazel, New York, p. 101.
Strober, M. and J. Katz (1987). Do eating disorders and affective disorders share a common etiology? A dissenting opinion. *International Journal of Eating Disorders* **6**, 171.
Strober, M., B. Salin, J. Burroughs, W. Morrell and J. Sadjak (1986). A family study of anorexia nervosa and depression. Paper presented at the annual meeting of the American Psychiatric Association, Washington DC, May 1986.
Swift, W. J., N. H. Kalin, F. S. Wambolt, N. Kaslow and M. Rithoz (1985). Depression in bulimia at 2 to 5-year follow-up. *Psychiatry Research* **16**, 111.
Van Praag, H. M. (1986). Monoamines and depression: the present state of the art. In *Emotion, Theory, Research, and Experience*, ed. by R. X. Plunchik and H. Kellerman. Academic Press, Orlando, p. 335.
Walsh, B. T., S. P. Roose, A. H. Glasmann, M. Gladis and C. Sadik (1985). Bulimia and depression. *Psychosomatic Medicine* **47**, 123.
Wittchen, H. U. and D. von Zerssen (1987). *Verläufe behandelter und unbehandelter Depressionen und Angststörungen*. Springer, Berlin, Heidelberg, New York.
Woell, C., M. M. Fichter, K. M. Pirke and G. Wolfram (1989). Eating behaviour of patients with bulimia nervosa. *International Journal of Eating Disorders* **8**, 557–568.
Wulff, M. (1932). Über einen interessanten oralen Symptomenkomplex und seine Beziehung zur Sucht. *Internationales Zeitschrift für Psychoanalytische* **18**, 281.
Wurtman, R. J. (1983). Behavioral effects of nutrients. *Lancet* **1**, 1145.
Young, S. J., D. H. Alpers, C. C. Norland and R. W. Woodruff (1976). Psychiatric illness and irritable bowel syndrome. *Gastroenterology* **70**, 162.
Zerssen, D. von (1976). *Klinische Selbstbeurteilungsskalen aus dem Münchener Psychiatrischen Informationssystem*. Beltz, Weinheim.
Zis, A. P. and F. S. Goodwin (1982). The amine hypothesis. In *Handbook of Affective Disorders*, ed. by E. S. Payke. Livingstone, Edinburgh, London, New York, p. 175.
Zutt, J. (1948). Das psychiatrische Krankheitsbild der Pubertätsmagersucht. *Archiv für Psychiatrie Nervenkrankheiten* **180**, 776.

9

Course and outcome of bulimia nervosa

David B. Herzog, Martin B. Keller
and
Philip W. Lavori
Massachusetts General Hospital and Harvard Medical School, Boston
Isabel S. Bradburn
University of California — Berkeley
and
Ingrid L. Ott
Harvard Medical School, Boston

Bulimia nervosa has only recently been classified as a distinct psychiatric disorder (American Psychiatric Association, 1980) and consequently not much is known about its long-term course. Few studies have reported outcome of more than one-year duration and the reports have described a wide array of outcomes. Furthermore, comparison between these studies is hampered by methodological considerations. In this chapter we will review the long-term outcome studies and present data from our longitudinal study on the course of bulimia nervosa. We conclude with an overview of our current five-year prospective study.

Ten studies on bulimia nervosa reporting outcome data of at least one-year duration have been published since 1980 (Abraham, Mira and Llewellyn-Jones, 1983; Brotman, Herzog and Hamburg, 1988; Fairburn et al., 1986; Hsu and Holder, 1986; Lacey, 1983; Mitchell *et al.*, 1986; Norman and Herzog, 1986; Pope *et al.*, 1985; Swift *et al.*, 1987; Yager, Landsverk and Edelstein,

1987, see Table 9.1). Some of these studies have been reviewed previously (Herzog, Keller and Lavori, 1988). Various methodological issues make comparison between them difficult. First of all, researchers have used differing admission criteria for entry into their studies. Most have used the criteria set forth in the *Diagnostic and Statistical Manual of Mental Disorders*, third edition (DSM-III) (American Psychiatric Association, 1980) to define the subject group, although two studies (Fairburn *et al.*, 1986; Hsu and Holder, 1986) relied on Russell's criteria (Russell, 1979). In order to better define their clinical populations, some investigators imposed minimum frequencies of bulimic episodes, but such frequencies vary across studies.

A second problem with the current studies is the lack of data on the course of the disorder between entry into the study and follow-up. Most of the outcome studies collected cross-sectional data, often with long intervals between follow-up contacts. Since some studies suggest bulimia nervosa is a chronic disorder, with marked fluctuations of symptomatology, cross-sectional data may not accurately reflect the course of the disorder. Several of the studies addressed this issue by maintaining short-term intervals (3–4 months) between follow-up contacts (Fairburn *et al.*, 1986; Lacey, 1983) or by assessing outcome based on behavior averaged across a substantial period of time (Brotman, Herzog and Hamburg, 1988; Swift *et al.*, 1987).

Additional problems include the frequent use of a retrospective design, the differing length of time that patients are followed and the wide variety of measures used to assess outcome. Many of the studies base outcome assessment on instruments with limited or no tested reliability and validity. In addition, some follow-up interviews are administered in person whereas others are given over the telephone.

Another difficulty in comparing the results of the studies is that outcome criteria differ. Only one study reported bulimia syndrome diagnoses at follow-up (Swift *et al.*, 1987). Most investigators have concentrated on eating behavior, reporting frequencies of bulimic symptoms at follow-up. Within this domain, researchers have used different standards of what constitutes good outcome. With respect to binge-eating, some investigators consider a frequency of less than once a month (Swift *et al.*, 1987; Abraham, Mira and Llewellyn-Jones, 1983) or less than once a week (Hsu and Holder, 1986) acceptable for good outcome. Others have focused on complete remission or a high percentage reduction of bulimic symptoms for a specified period of time (Brotman, Herzog and Hamburg, 1988).

In addition to eating behavior, most studies have reported on the incidence of depressive symptomatology at follow-up and many include data on psychosocial functioning. Information regarding study methodology and outcome of eating behavior, psychological symptoms and psychosocial functioning is presented in Table 9.1. Findings from the outcome studies will be discussed by outcome variable.

Table 9.1 Studies of bulimia nervosa

Study	Study design Duration of follow-up prospective/retrospective	Outcome at follow-up Eating behavior symptoms	Psychological symptoms	Psychosocial functioning
Abraham, Mira and Llewellyn-Jones (1983) *N* = 43	14–72 mo retrospective	29–42% 'cured' 17–49% 'improved'	Not reported	Not reported
Brotman, Herzog and Hamburg (1988) *N* = 14	12–60 mo retrospective	57% remission 29% marked improvement	Two 'clinically depressed'	36% at least moderately impaired
Fairburn *et al.* (1986) *N* = 24	12 mo prospective	Median 0 binges/mo; marked improvement in purging	Reduced psychopathology, depressive symptoms	Improved social adjustment
Hsu and Holder (1986) *N* = 56	12–35 mo retrospective	46% binged < 1 ×/wk 18% binged 1–2 ×/wk 21% binged > 2 ×/wk	64% dysphoric 20% dysphoric + > 3 depressive symptoms	36% good 30% intermediate 20% poor
Lacey (1983) *N* = 28	'Up to two years' prospective	71% not bingeing/purging 29% reduced binge episodes to 3 ×/yr	Not reported	Not reported

Michell *et al.* (1986) *N* = 75	12–15 mo retrospective	33% abstinent 13% much improved 17% improved 21% minimally improved 11% unchanged	Not reported	Not reported
Norman and Herzog (1986) *N* = 18	34–36 mo retrospective	56% normal eating attitudes at 3 yr	All psychological symptoms improved at 3 yr; depressive symptoms improved at 1 yr	Improved work functioning at 3 yr; no other improvements in role functioning
Pope *et al.* (1985) *N* = 20	2–28 mo retrospective	50% remitted bulimia 95% improved at least partially	82% of 11 subjects followed 2 yr had marked improvement in depressive symptoms	Not reported
Swift *et al.* (1987) *N* = 30	25–50 mo retrospective	13% did not meet DSM-III 50% did not meet DSM-III-R	One subject probable major depressive episode; 90% scored in normal range on depression measures	Normal social functioning
Yager, Landsverk and Edelstein (1987) *N* = 628	20 mo prospective	2% bulimic anorexia 48% normal-weight bulimic 50% subdiagnostic eating disorder	Not reported	Not reported

Eating Behavior

Several treatment studies have reported favorable outcome in eating behaviors. Fairburn *et al.* (1986) compared individual cognitive-behavioral treatment and insight-oriented short-term focal psychotherapy with 24 female bulimics. They randomly assigned subjects to one of the therapies for 18 weeks, after which the patients received no treatment. Subjects were interviewed at termination of therapy and four, eight and 12 months later. Although subjects in the cognitive-behavioral group improved significantly more than the other subjects, both groups reported substantial improvement at 12 months. The median frequency of bingeing decreased from 20 or more episodes per month to 0 for both groups. The groups also exhibited marked reductions in vomiting. The most dramatic gains followed completion of the treatment course.

A prospective follow-up of a controlled eclectic treatment study also reported positive outcome. Every three months for 'up to two years' Lacey (1983) followed up 28 of 30 bulimic women who participated in a 10-week treatment program. Half of the probands operated initially as a control group. At the end of the 10 weeks, the treated group reported substantial improvement while the control group had not altered their bulimic behavior. The control group then participated in the treatment program. After completion of treatment, 24 patients (80 per cent) had stopped binge-eating and vomiting, with a gradual decline in symptomatology exhibited by all patients during the course of the 10 weeks. During the two-year follow-up 20 patients had no bulimic episodes, while eight experienced an average of three episodes a year.

Pope *et al.* (1985) conducted a follow-up of their six-week, double-blind, placebo-controlled study on imipramine. Up to 28 months after the medication trial period, 17 of 20 subjects had maintained or increased improvement on their initial positive response to imipramine or another antidepressant. Of the 11 followed for more than two years, eight remitted bulimic symptoms entirely while only one made no improvement. Three of those eight were no longer on medication at follow-up. It is noteworthy, however, that during the follow-up period nine patients required trials of more than one antidepressant.

A fourth treatment study reported more mixed results than the previous studies. In an uncontrolled retrospective study, Hsu and Holder (1986) investigated the 12–35-month outcome of 48 female bulimics treated for 2–4 months with a behavioral approach. Eight of those followed up did not complete the treatment program. Outcome was based on the frequency of weekly binge-eating episodes. One year after treatment, 46 per cent had a good outcome, 18 per cent had an intermediate outcome and 21 per cent had a poor outcome; good outcome represented the subject binge-eating less than once a week over the previous three weeks. Those who dropped out of the treatment program were evenly distributed among outcome groups at follow-up.

Other retrospective studies on clinical samples that received a variety of treatments report a range of outcome. In the Eating Disorders Unit (EDU) at Massachusetts General Hospital in Boston, Brotman, Herzog and Hamburg (1988) reported substantial improvement in eating behavior, but only after long, intensive therapy. Fourteen female bulimics were treated for a mean duration of 23 months in a psychodynamic psychotherapy group. Some patients received adjunctive antidepressant medication and most were in individual therapy as well. This group manifested significant impairment as judged by a global rating scale, with 10 subjects diagnosed with a personality disorder and eight with concurrent affective disorder. At follow-up (12–60 months, mean 42 months), eight subjects had sustained remission from bulimia nervosa for at least six months and another four sustained at least a 75 per cent reduction in bulimic behavior. Subjects required an average of 21 months of intensive treatment before entering a period of sustained improvement. The authors noted that prior to the stable abstinence period most subjects experienced short-term remissions followed by relapses.

An Australian study reported 'cure' rates after an unspecified length of multimodal treatment that ranged from 29 to 42 per cent, depending on whether assessment was made by self-rating, interview or questionnaire (Abraham, Mira and Llewellyn-Jones, 1983). Patients were considered cured if they binged less than once a month, used no weight control measures and had a stable body weight.

Mitchell *et al.* (1986) studied 75 patients 12–15 months after presentation for evaluation at a university clinic. At follow-up they found approximately one-third of their sample had become abstinent, one-third improved and one-third had minimal or no reductions in bulimic symptoms. Patients participated in a variety of treatment during the follow-up period, including weekly group or individual therapy (53 per cent), an intensive structured program for bulimics (53 per cent) and self-help groups (57 per cent). Four per cent of the patients had been hospitalized for bulimia nervosa while another 7 per cent had been hospitalized for psychiatric reasons other than the eating disorder. Thirteen per cent received no treatment. During follow-up most patients improved but nearly 60 per cent were still binge-eating and 44 per cent still self-induced vomiting. During the month prior to follow-up one-third of the subjects were free of binge-eating, vomiting or laxative abuse, while 13 per cent had substantially reduced frequencies of all three behaviors. Seventeen per cent had lower frequencies of at least two of the behaviors, 21 per cent had reduced frequency of one bulimic behavior and 11 per cent were unchanged. The investigators also identified a group that relapsed (Mitchell, Davis and Goff, 1985). They noted that 30 patients (40 per cent) who had been free of bulimic behavior for at least two months had relapsed into a regular pattern of bulimic behaviors for two months.

In another naturalistic retrospective study, Norman and Herzog (1986) compared outcome one and three years after presentation to the EDU. Patients exhibited the greatest improvement in eating attitudes/behavior one year after presentation, with no significant change taking place between years 1 and 3. By the third year, 56 per cent of the subjects scored in the normal range in eating attitudes.

In the only long-term study involving a sample of former inpatient bulimic subjects, Swift *et al.* (1987) found that 2–5 years after their discharge from the hospital 26 of 30 subjects (87 per cent) met DSM-III criteria for bulimic syndrome and 50 per cent met DSM-III-R criteria. Although the majority still regularly practiced bulimic behavior, the mean frequency of bulimic episodes per month decreased substantially: bingeing gradually declined by 84 per cent and vomiting by 76 per cent. Swift *et al.* identified three outcome groups based on behavior averaged across the previous six months. Twenty-seven per cent were considered to have 'good' outcome (bingeing and vomiting less than monthly and no laxative–diuretic abuse), 40 per cent had an 'intermediate' outcome (bingeing and/or vomiting more than once a month but less than daily and no laxative–diuretic abuse at follow-up) and 33 per cent had a 'poor' outcome (bingeing/vomiting daily or ongoing laxative–diuretic abuse).

Yager, Landsverk and Edelstein (1987) also report improved though persistent eating-disordered behavior at follow-up in a nationwide survey study. Subjects answered an advertisement in *Glamour* magazine to participate in research on bulimic disorder. Through returned mail questionnaires, the researchers made simulated diagnoses according to DSM-III criteria. They identified three groups of women with bulimic symptoms: 34 anorexic bulimics, 392 normal-weight bulimics and 202 who had a subdiagnostic eating disorder. Twenty months after completing initial questionnaires, 29 per cent of the anorexic bulimics and 43 per cent of the normal-weight bulimics were rediagnosed as having a subdiagnostic eating disorder, 42 per cent of the bulimic anorexics moved into the bulimic category and 33 per cent of those initially diagnosed with a subdiagnostic disorder were reclassified as bulimic. Significant reduction in binge-eating, vomiting and laxative abuse was reported by all groups, ranging from 13 to 25 per cent for the anorexics and 24 to 42 per cent for the others.

These follow-up studies show that most bulimic patients demonstrated intermediate-term improvement in their eating behavior. Some treatments produced a dramatic short-term response that was sustained 1–2 years after initial treatment (Fairburn *et al.*, 1986; Lacey, 1983; Pope *et al.*, 1985). Intensive psychodynamic group treatment in conjunction with other therapies proved effective with one group, but only after nearly two years of treatment (Brotman, Herzog and Hamburg, 1988). Inpatient treatment was associated with reductions in bulimic and comorbid pathology in a group that was the most symptomatic initially (Swift *et al.*, 1987).

Although their eating behaviors improved, the majority of these bulimic patients did not fully recover from bulimia nervosa. In the nine studies that report such data, between 29 and 87 per cent of subjects continued to binge-eat at least occasionally at follow-up.

Psychological Symptoms

Most of the outcome studies provide data on psychological symptoms. Six studies (Norman and Herzog, 1986; Fairburn *et al.*, 1986; Pope *et al.*, 1985; Brotman, Herzog and Hamburg, 1988; Hsu and Holder, 1986; Swift *et al.*, 1987) report on depression at follow-up and most show a decline in depressive symptomatology. At the EDU Norman and Herzog found that all psychological subscales (somatization, obsessive–compulsive, interpersonal sensitivity, depression and anxiety) measured by the Hopkins Symptom Checklist (HSCL) (Derogatis *et al.*, 1974) improved significantly by three years, but that only depressive symptoms improved by one year. Patients whose eating attitudes normalized from initial presentation to year 3 scored significantly lower at year 3 on all but the anxiety HSCL subscales than those patients with disturbed eating attitudes. Fairburn *et al.* (1986) found that the cognitive-behavioral treatment group showed a continuous decrease in general psychopathology and in depressive symptoms during follow-up; the short-term focal treatment group showed more variable improvement. Pope *et al.* (1985) found that improvement in bulimic symptoms inversely paralleled a decrease in depression. Of the 11 patients followed for more than two years, only two showed no clear improvement in depressive scores; one of these discontinued medication and experienced a relapse of bulimic symptoms. In the study by Brotman, Herzog and Hamburg (1988), two of the eight subjects diagnosed at intake with affective disorder remained clinically depressed at follow-up.

Depressive symptoms were common at follow-up in Hsu and Holder's (1986) study, as 64 per cent of their sample reported persistent dysphoria and 20 per cent manifested dysphoria in addition to at least four other depressive symptoms. Swift *et al.* (1987) noted that while none of their sample met research diagnostic criteria (RDC) (Spitzer, Endicott and Robins, 1978) for a major depression at follow-up, one patient had a probable major depressive disorder and two who had serious impairment in psychosocial functioning had elevated depression scores. Although 90 per cent of their sample scored within the normal range on the two depression scales at follow-up, 13 per cent had made a suicide attempt and 10 per cent had intentionally injured themselves since initial discharge from the hospital. Other patterns of psychiatric disturbance present before hospitalization continued after discharge, but with less severity. One-third continued to report stealing food or clothing and some subjects continued to abuse alcohol. In general, Swift *et al.* found that their bulimic subjects reported more psychological distress at follow-up than a normal group but less than psychiatric outpatients.

Overall, the studies show a reduction in depressive symptoms at follow-up, corresponding in most cases to improvement in eating behavior.

Psychosocial Functioning

Several studies report data on psychosocial functioning at the time of follow-up. Norman and Herzog (1986) found that, although their sample had improved overall in their eating attitudes at year 3, mean social adjustment improved only in the work domain, as measured by the work scale of the Social Adjustment Scale (SAS) (Weissman and Rothwell, 1976).

Swift *et al.* (1987) compared their sample to that of Norman and Herzog and at follow-up found their sample showed healthier levels of social adjustment. Swift *et al.*'s sample was comparable to a normal group and considerably less impaired than a group of depressed women. Using a British modification of the SAS (Cooper *et al.*, 1968), Fairburn *et al.* (1986) report significant improvements made in social adjustment by both treatment groups which were maintained during the follow-up period. Hsu and Holder (1986) used a global judgement scale for social outcome and found that 36 per cent of their sample had good outcome (satisfactory in three areas, including work, family and peer relationships), 30 per cent had an intermediate outcome (satisfactory in two of the above three areas) and 20 per cent had a poor outcome (unsatisfactory in two or all of the above three areas). Thus in all but one study better social adjustment approximated improvement in eating behavior.

These studies show that over time bulimic patients tend to decrease their eating-disordered behavior and depressive symptoms while improving their psychosocial functioning. However, data on the natural course of bulimia nervosa are only just beginning to appear. At the EDU we are in the process of completing a 30-month pilot study on the course and outcome of bulimia nervosa. We present six-month data from the study.

Massachusetts General Hospital Prospective Follow-up Study

In order to chart the natural course of bulimia nervosa, we piloted a prospective follow-up study of 30 bulimic outpatients. We assessed the course of bulimia nervosa at frequent intervals and followed the course of affective disorders diagnosed at intake or which developed during follow-up. The study differs from those reviewed above in that we followed the course of both bulimia nervosa and depressive disorders on a weekly basis for the entire 26-week follow-up period. Design features included the use of DSM-III criteria for diagnosing bulimia nervosa and the use of RDC for all other disorders;

structured clinical inverviews with demonstrated reliability and validity to make intake and outcome diagnoses; assessment of recovery and relapse according to specific diagnostic criteria operationally linked to DSM-III or RDC; and detailed recording of all psychotropic medication and psychosocial treatment. This study was designed to pilot the feasibility of these methods and to provide preliminary data to guide the aims and design of a long-term, large-sample prospective study.

Our pilot sample, drawn from consecutive presentations to our Eating Disorders Unit at the Massachusetts General Hospital, is representative of bulimic patients we see, and their group characteristics approximate other patient populations reported in the literature (Mitchell *et al.*, 1985; Hsu and Holder, 1986). Most patients were single, white women who were either college students or working. Subjects were mostly in their late teens or twenties and, on average, had been bingeing and purging for five years. All were between 90 and 120 per cent of ideal body weight for their height and build (Society of Actuaries and Association of Life Insurance Medical Directors of America, 1979). Three of the patients had a history of anorexia nervosa but none met DSM-III criteria for that disorder at intake.

Consistent with the high rate of affective disorder in other bulimic studies (Hatsukami *et al.*, 1984; Walsh *et al.*, 1985), 25 of the subjects (83 per cent) had a lifetime history of affective illness and 17 (57 per cent) met RDC for an affective disorder at intake. Of these 17, five (29 per cent) met a diagnosis for major depression, three (18 per cent) for dysthymia and another five for minor depression. The other four subjects met criteria for major depression comorbid with another affective illness.

Subjects were administered two psychometric measures at intake: the Eating Disorders Inventory (Garner, Olmsted and Polivy, 1983) and the Beck Depression Inventory (Beck *et al.*, 1961). Diagnoses were made by clinical interviewers using the Schedule for Affective Disorders and Schizophrenia — Lifetime version (SADS-L) (Spitzer and Endicott, 1979) and structured questions from the Diagnostic Interview Schedule (DIS) (Robins *et al.*, 1981) for diagnoses of bulimia nervosa. Interviewers also administered the Longitudinal Interval Follow-up Evaluation — Baseline version (LIFE Base) (Keller *et al.*, 1981), which demonstrated high reliability in a five-center study (Keller *et al.*, 1987). Three and six months after entry into the study an interviewer contacted each patient by telephone for an interview. Interviewers collected follow-up data with the follow-up version of the LIFE Base (LIFE II) (Keller, Shapiro and Wolfe, 1982), which records information on medication and non-somatic treatment, psychosocial functioning and severity of the bulimic and affective disorders. We measured psychosocial functioning with the Global Assessment Scale (GAS), which assesses the subjects' worst level of functioning maintained for at least a week during each month. Psychiatric severity was rated according to a scale operationalized to DSM-III that linked

Table 9.2 Psychiatric status rating scale for bulimia nervosa

Code	Term	Definition
6	Definite criteria severe	Meets definite DSM-III criteria for bulimia nervosa and binges and purges at least twice a week. This eating behavior results in major disruption in functioning (e.g. stays home from work to binge, medical problems develop due to bingeing and purging)
5	Definite criteria	Meets definite DSM-III criteria for bulimia nervosa and binges and purges at least twice a week but has no extreme impairment in functioning (e.g. is able to meet responsibilities because arranges binges around work/school or household responsibilities)
4	Marked	Does not meet definite criteria for DSM-III bulimia nervosa but still has obvious symptoms of this disorder
3	Partial remission	Considerably less psychopathology than full DSM-III criteria for bulimia nervosa
2*	Residual	Although the patient no longer meets DSM-III criteria for bulimia nervosa and no longer binges she still feels she has to fight the impulse to binge
1*	Usual self	There is no evidence of bulimia nervosa, and patient does not fight the urge to binge and purge. However, significant symptomatology from an underlying condition/disorder may continue (e.g. rater believes the patient has returned to her 'usual self', which is characterized by a minor depression or dysthymia)

*If patient stays below this level for at least eight consecutive weeks, episode is considered over.

the frequency of symptomatic behavior to the subject's level of impairment. The scale is presented in Table 9.2. Recovery from bulimia nervosa was defined as a rating of 1 or 2, with the subject exhibiting no bingeing or purging for a minimum of eight consecutive weeks. Relapse was defined as meeting full DSM-III criteria for at least two weeks. Further details of the data collection procedure are available elsewhere (Herzog *et al.*, 1988).

The study design was naturalistic: no controls were placed on the type or amount of treatment subjects received. The patients were given recommendations for specific treatment modalities as is the usual procedure at the EDU. Treatment that patients received included individual psychodynamic or behavioral therapy, group therapy, family therapy, pharmacotherapy or a combination of any of the above. Some patients also participated in local self-help groups, such as Overeaters Anonymous. The type and amount of treatment, including medication dosages, were recorded on a weekly basis.

The results of the study indicate that in the short term, patients with bulimia nervosa have a low recovery rate. At the conclusion of the six-month follow-up period, 10 (33 per cent) of the subjects had met criteria for recovery. Recovery times ranged from one to 16 weeks with a median of seven weeks. One subject relapsed into a second bulimic episode at 23 weeks after 11 weeks of sustained recovery. Six of those who recovered from bulimia nervosa had concomitant affective disorder.

Recovery rates from index episodes of affective disorder were also low, with four of 17 subjects (24 per cent) recovering at some point during the follow-up. Mean time to recovery was seven weeks and all four subjects had recovered by week 10. During the follow-up two additional subjects developed short-lived episodes of minor depression from which they recovered.

Since most studies report improvement rates rather than rates of recovery, we examined our data to determine whether the 20 subjects who did not recover from bulimia nervosa had rated lower on the bulimic psychiatric status scales during any point in the follow-up; lower scores would indicate improvement. Five patients showed short-term symptom remissions, ranging from two to seven weeks. Another nine experienced periods of partial remission (a rating of 3) averaging 10 weeks and ranging from one to 21 weeks. Thus, although these nine subjects did not remit symptoms entirely, they did sustain improvement during the follow-up interval.

The presence of concomitant affective disorder did not significantly affect recovery from bulimia nervosa in the short term. Slightly more subjects (35 per cent) with affective disorder recovered from bulimia nervosa than did subjects without comorbid affective disorder (31 per cent). Only one subject recovered from both bulimia nervosa and affective disorder. This patient relapsed into second episodes of both disorders, but the onset and offset of recovery and relapse from the two disorders did not coincide. These preliminary results suggest that the course of the disorders is different.

Twenty-six of the 30 subjects (87 per cent) pursued some type of treatment during the six months of follow-up. Six (23 per cent) subsequently left treatment, leaving 20 (67 per cent) of the original sample in treatment at the 26-week follow-up contact. All those who received treatment had individual therapy and 13 also had somatotherapy. Four subjects participated in group treatment and three had at least one session of family therapy. Eight of the 17 patients who had an intake diagnosis of affective disorder received somatotherapy.

Two of the four subjects who did not have treatment recovered from bulimia nervosa. Of the other eight subjects who recovered from bulimia nervosa, two had somatotherapy prior to recovery in addition to individual treatment while five had individual treatment alone. One subject had individual treatment before recovery from bulimia nervosa and somatotherapy after recovery. Of the six who recovered from affective disorder, three received both individual therapy and somatotherapy, two had individual treatment only and one did not receive any treatment.

To determine whether an association existed between recovery and improved psychosocial functioning, we compared mean GAS scores for those who had recovered from bulimia nervosa and those who did not for the sixth month of follow-up. Six months after entry into the study, the GAS scores of the recovered bulimics averaged 10 points higher (70.5) than the group that remained in the index bulimic episode (60.9); this difference was highly significant ($p < 0.004$, unpaired *t*-test). Although the difference between the groups on intake GAS scores was not significant, at entry the group that later recovered tended to function slightly better than the non-recovered group.

In order to better assess the severity of the recovery rates of affective disorder in our depressed bulimic subjects, we compared these subjects to others who had an affective disorder but no bulimia nervosa. One hundred and one patients with affective disorder were followed in a naturalistic study for a similar length of time using the same follow-up instrument that we used in the bulimic study (Keller, Shapiro and Wolfe, 1982). Seventy-five per cent of the subjects were inpatients and none were diagnosed as having an eating disorder. By 26 weeks, 62 per cent of the depressed subjects had recovered from their affective disorder, compared to 24 per cent of our subjects. Although there are limitations to external comparisons, the finding that in the short term our subjects recovered at half the rate of a sample of depressed inpatients highlights the severity of disturbance in these bulimic subjects with affective disorder.

Directions for Future Research

Our pilot follow-up study confirmed the viability of our longitudinal method for tracking the course and treatment of bulimia nervosa and affective disorders. We are now in the process of entering 225 subjects into a five-year prospective, naturalistic study supported by a grant from the National Institute of Mental Health. Subjects include not only bulimics but also anorexics and patients diagnosed as having both anorexia nervosa and bulimia nervosa. Based on our experience with the pilot study, we have implemented several improvements in design to strengthen the validity of our results.

We have adjusted our entry criteria to meet DSM-III-R (American Psychiatric Association, 1987) specifications. Furthermore, we are now tracking the course of individual symptoms in addition to the course of syndromes to provide a more complete picture of the relationship between symptom constellations within and between the eating disorders.

Another improvement on our pilot study involves gathering treatment data not only through patient self-report but also through interviews with treating clinicians. We are collecting information on the specific type of psychotherapy patients receive as well as ascertaining the rationale behind treatment decisions.

We have added several other standardized measures to our intake battery to assess potential predictor variables such as personality disorders and subjects' attitudes towards their families. To diagnose Axis II disorders, we are administering the Structured Interview for DSM-III Personality Disorders, second edition (SIDP) (Pfohl, Stangl and Zimmerman, 1982). We also assess personality disorders with the psychometric test the Millon Clinical Multiaxial Inventory (Millon, 1983). Family data are collected through the Family Environment Scale (FES) (Moos and Moos, 1981) and the Perceived Family Interaction Scale (Yager, 1987).

This study expands on the existing base of research on the phenomenology of eating disorders. Our long-term prospective study following a large sample of anorexic and bulimic patients could have widespread implications for future research. Documenting the degree of symptom overlap and crossover between anorexia nervosa and bulimia nervosa will help us understand the relationship between the two disorders and validate or refine their nosological classification. These data in turn can provide the foundation for other biological and family-genetic studies to further validate diagnostic distinctions. The stratification of outcome groups can help assess the heterogeneity of the disorders and identify clinical subgroups. Knowledge of these subgroups will help future treatment studies select their probands and determine an adequate duration of follow-up.

From a public health perspective, information on the longitudinal course of eating disorders can be used to develop educational programs that will be of particular importance to those at high risk for an eating disorder. These data can also provide a basis for planning adequate short-term and long-term treatment programs and facilities, such as residential centers, day hospitals and halfway houses.

References

Abraham, S. F., M. Mira and D. Llewellyn-Jones (1983). Bulimia: a study of outcome. *International Journal of Eating Disorders* **2**, 175.

American Psychiatric Association (1980). *Diagnostic and Statistical Manual for Mental Disorders* (3rd edition). American Psychiatric Association, Washington DC.

American Psychiatric Association (1987). *Diagnostic and Statistical Manual for Mental Disorders* (3rd edition — revised). American Psychiatric Association, Washington DC.

Beck, A. T., C. H. Ward, M. Mendelson, J. Mock and J. Erbaugh (1961). An inventory for measuring depression. *Archives of General Psychiatry* **4**, 561.

Brotman, A. W., D. B. Herzog and P. Hamburg (1988). Longterm course of bulimic patients treated with psychotherapy. *Journal of Clinical Psychiatry* **49**, 157.

Cooper, P. J., M. Osborn, D. Gath and G. Feggetter (1968). Evaluation of a modified self-report measure of social adjustment. *British Journal of Psychiatry* **141**, 68.

Derogatis, L. R., K. Rickels, E. H. Uhlenhuth and L. Covi (1974). The Hopkins Symptom Checklist (HCSL): a self-report symptom inventory. *Behavioral Science* **191**, 1.

Fairburn, C. G., P. J. Cooper, J. Kirk and M. O'Conner (1985). The significance of the neurotic symptoms of bulimia nervosa. *Journal of Psychiatric Research* **19**, 135.

Fairburn, C. G., J. Kirk, M. O'Conner and P. J. Cooper (1986). A comparison of two psychological treatments for bulimia nervosa. *Behaviour Research and Therapy* **24**, 629.

Garner, D. M., M. P. Olmsted and J. Polivy (1983). Development and validation of a multidimensional eating disorder inventory for anorexia nervosa and bulimia. *International Journal of Eating Disorders* **2**, 15.

Hatsukami, D. K., E. Eckert, J. E. Mitchell and R. Pyle (1984). Affective disorder and substance abuse in women with bulimia. *Psychological Medicine* **14**, 701.

Herzog, D. B., M. B. Keller and P. W. Lavori (1988). Outcome in anorexia nervosa and bulimia nervosa: a review of the literature. *Journal of Nervous and Mental Disease* **176**, 131.

Herzog, D. B., M. B. Keller, P. W. Lavori and I. L. Ott (1988). Short-term prospective study of recovery in bulimia nervosa. *Psychiatric Research* **23**, 45.

Hsu, L. K. G. and D. Holder (1986). Bulimia nervosa: treatment and short-term outcome. *Psychological Medicine* **16**, 65.

Hudson, J. I., H. G. Pope, J. M. Jonas and D. Yurgelun-Todd (1984). Phenomenologic relationship of eating disorders to major affective disorder. *Psychiatric Research* **9**, 345.

Keller, M. B., P. W. Lavori, B. Friedman, E. Nielsen, J. Endicott, P. McDonald Scott and N. C. Andreason (1987). The LIFE: a comprehensive method for assessing outcome in prospective longitudinal studies. *Archives of General Psychiatry* **44**, 540.

Keller, M. B., P. W. Lavori, P. McDonald-Scott, W. A. Scheftner, N. C. Andreasen, R. W. Shapiro and J. Croughan (1981). Reliability of life-time diagnosis and symptoms in patients with a current psychiatric disorder. *Journal of Psychiatric Research* **16**, 229.

Keller, M. B., R. W. Shapiro and N. Wolfe (1982). Recovery in RDC major depressive disorder: analysis with the LIFE table and regression models. *Archives of General Psychiatry* **39**, 905.

Lacey, H. (1983). Bulimia nervosa, binge eating, and psychogenic vomiting: a controlled treatment study and long term outcome. *British Medical Journal* **286**, 1609.

Millon, T. (1983). *The Millon Clinical Multiaxial Inventory — Third Edition*. Interpretive Scoring Systems, Minneapolis.

Mitchell, J. E., L. Davis, and G. Goff (1985). The process of relapse in patients with bulimia. *International Journal of Eating Disorders* **4**, 457.

Mitchell, J. E., L. Davis, G. Goff and R. Pyle (1986). A follow-up study of patients with bulimia. *International Journal of Eating Disorders* **5**, 441.

Moos, R. and B. Moos (1981). *Family Environment Scale Manual*. Consulting Psychologists Press, Palo Alto, CA.

Norman, D. K. and D. B. Herzog (1986). A three year outcome study in normal-weight bulimia: assessment of psychosocial functioning and eating attitudes. *Psychiatric Research* **19**, 199.

Pfohl, B., D. Stangl. and M. Zimmerman (1982). *The Structured Interview for DSM-III Personality Disorders (SIDP)*. Department of Psychiatry, University of Iowa, Iowa City.

Pope, H. G., J. I. Hudson, J. M. Jonas and D. Yurgelun-Todd (1985). Antidepressant treatment of bulimia: a two-year follow-up study. *Journal of Clinical Psychopharmacology* **5**, 320.

Robins, L. N., J. E. Helzer, J. Croughan *et al.* (1981). National Institute of Mental Health Diagnostic Interview Schedule: its history, characteristics and validity. *Archives of General Psychiatry* **38**, 381.

Russell, G. F. M. (1979). Bulimia nervosa: an ominous variant of anorexia nervosa. *Psychological Medicine* **9**, 429.

Society of Actuaries and Association of Life Insurance Medical Directors of America (1979). Build Study, Chicago.

Spitzer, R. L. and J. Endicott (1979). *Schedule for Affective Disorders and Schizophenia — Lifetime version* (SADS-L), ed. 3. New York State Psychiatric Institute, New York.

Spitzer, R. L., J. Endicott and E. Robins (1978). Research Diagnostic Criteria: rationale and reliability. *Archives of General Psychiatry* **35**, 773.

Swift, W. J., N. H. Kalin, F. S. Wamboldt, N. Kaslow and M. Ritholz (1985). Depression in bulimia at 2 to 5 year follow-up. *Psychiatric Research* **16**, 111.

Swift, W. J., M. Ritholz, N. H. Kalin and N. Kaslow (1987). A follow-up study of thirty hospitalized bulimics. *Psychosomatic Medicine* **49**, 45.

Walsh, B. T., S. P. Roose, A. H. Glassman, M. Gladis and C. Sadik (1985). Bulimia and depression. *Psychosomatic Medicine* **47**, 123.

Weissman, M. and S. Rothwell (1976). Assessment of social adjustment by self-report. *Archives of General Psychiatry* **33**, 1111.

Yager, J. (1987). *Perceived Family Interaction Scale.* University of California — Los Angeles, Neuropsychiatric Institute.

Yager, J., J. Landsverk and C. K. Edelstein (1987). A 20-month follow-up study of 628 women with eating disorders, I: Course and severity. *American Journal of Psychiatry* **144**(9), 1172.

Part III

Biological Basis

10

Brain mechanisms concerned with food intake and body-weight regulation

Sebastian P. Grossman
The University of Chicago, Chicago

Traditionally, the regulation of food intake and body weight has been viewed exclusively in terms of energy expenditure, resupply and storage. Although individual cases of extreme obesity or voluntary starvation have been discussed in the context of neural and/or psychiatric disorders for more than a century, systematic clinical investigation of eating disorders is only of recent origin. The experimental literature lags even farther behind, although it is becoming increasingly clear that the results of many experimental procedures may be subject to far more complex interpretations than a simple energy expenditure and resupply model would suggest.

In the following discussion, only a few seminal papers and reviews are cited; detailed bibliographies and more extensive discussions of specific issues can be found in earlier reviews (Grossman, 1975, 1978, 1979, 1983, 1986).

The Hypothalamocentric Theory

Many different regions of the brain have been implicated in the regulation of food intake and body weight. However, components of the hypothalamus appear to play a unique role in the neural circuits which integrate and process neural and hormonal signals that influence hunger and satiety as well as neural and hormonal mechanisms responsible for the deposition and utilization of fat stores.

The 'hypothalamocentric' theory was first stated explicitly by Eliot Stellar (1954), on the basis of this own research and work conducted earlier in the laboratory of John Brobeck (Brobeck, 1946; Anand and Brobek, 1950) at the University of Pennsylvania. This seminal work demonstrated that bilateral destruction (electrolytic lesions) of the ventromedial hypothalamus (VMH) produced overeating (hyperphagia) and, in time, obesity, whereas lesions lateral to the VMH, in the dorsolateral hypothalamus (DLH), abolished voluntary food intake (aphagia) and eventually resulted in death unless the animal was fed by intragastric intubation.

Stellar and his associates replicated these important findings in detail and demonstrated that partial recovery from the effects of the lesions occurred (Stellar, 1954; Teitelbaum and Epstein, 1962).

Rats with VMH damage overeat most dramatically during the first few days after surgery (Brobeck had termed this the 'dynamic' phase of the syndrome). After they gain a significant amount of fat, often doubling their initial body weight, food intake decreases to the point where it is just sufficient to maintain the newly acquired body mass. When animals in this 'static' phase of obesity are fasted until they reached preoperative weights, they again overeat dramatically. Conversely, when they are induced to overeat and gain additional weight as a result of insulin treatments or electrical stimulation of DLH, they fast voluntarily until returning to their static phase baseline. This has suggested to some investigators that the lesion may have reset something like a 'ponderostat' or setpoint for body weight. (Recent investigations have shown that rats with VMH lesions which have *ad libitum* access to food eventually break through the self-imposed restrictions, enter a new dynamic phase and return to maintenance feeding only after reaching a still higher level of body weight.)

Rats with DLH lesions lose significant amounts of body weight even when food is administered by intragastric intubation. After a few days or weeks, they accept highly palatable, moist food and eventually eat enough laboratory food to maintain their new, significantly lower body weight. However, unlike neurologically intact animals, the 'recovered' rat with DLH lesions does not increase its food intake in response to experimental treatments which reduce blood glucose levels and/or cellular glucose utilization. Its food intake also remains highly sensitive to the palatability of the diet and it has been suggested that it may eat mainly for hedonic reasons, i.e. to appease the appetite induced by the presence of palatable food.

Keesey *et al.* (1976) have pointed out that the 'recovered' DLH rat does appear to defend its significantly lowered body weight in response to starvation, dietary dilution, etc. (as long as the palatability of the diet is high) and may thus be responsive to metabolic signals from the body's fat stores. This hypothesis of a lesion-related lowering of body fat setpoint receives support from investigations which have shown that preoperative starvation can reduce or abolish the acute effects of DLH lesions on food intake.

The hypothalamocentric theory is supported by data from other experimental paradigms:

1. Electrical stimulation of the DLH elicits feeding in sated rats and results in obesity when repeated on a daily basis. Stimulation of the VMH inhibits ingestive behavior in food-deprived animals, although opposite, facilitatory effects have also been reported.
2. Microinjections of norepinephrine or gamma-amino-butyric acid (GABA) into the medial hypothalamus elicit feeding in sated rats. Chemical compounds known to specifically block the action of these inhibitory neurotransmitters reduce food intake. Microinjections of beta-adrenergic or dopaminergic agonists and antagonists into more lateral hypothalamic sites produce opposite effects on food intake, suggesting important catecholaminergic inputs to DLH as well as VMH systems. Food deprivation and refeeding after a fast modify the metabolism of these transmitters in the hypothalamus (Grossman, 1967; Leibowitz, 1980).
3. Single neurons in the medial hypothalamus decrease their activity during fasting and increase it during and shortly after a subsequent meal. Cells in the lateral hypothalamus display opposite reactions to fasting and refeeding (Oomura, 1973, 1976).

The activity of about 30 per cent of single nerve cells in the hypothalamus is also predictably affected by local or systemic injections of glucose and/or insulin (Oomura, 1976). In direct support of Jean Mayer's (1955) glucostatic theory of hunger, cells in the ventromedial hypothalamus have been shown to increase their firing rate when glucose is applied locally. These cells respond more vigorously when both glucose and insulin are administered, suggesting that these neurons, unlike the rest of the brain, may require insulin for the utilization of glucose. An increase in their activity thus would be appropriate to the state of satiety when both plasma glucose and insulin are high.

Cells in the DLH, in contrast, have been shown to *decrease* their firing rate in response to local increases in glucose alone. These neurons increase their activity in response to insulin alone (a response which might account for the increased hunger and food intake seen after systemic injections of insulin). This response pattern suggests that these nerve cells act as insulin-independent glucoreceptors which are, however, subject to a direct *neuromodulary* influence of insulin.

These are but the highlights of a large and generally consistent literature which supports the hypothalamocentric theory of food intake and body-weight regulation. Few attempts to relate brain structure and function can boast a more solid base. It is none the less true that significant questions have been raised in recent years which have led some investigators to the conclusion that the notion of hypothalamic regulation should be abandoned.

I do not share this pessimistic view, not only because there is, in my opinion, no viable alternative, but also because I believe that many of the issues which seem to argue against hypothalamic regulation do not, in fact, invalidate the concept but instead invite a broader and intuitively more acceptable interpretation of what is being regulated. I will try to briefly present a summary of the problems and the resulting modifications in our conceptualization of the determinants of 'hunger' and 'satiety'.

The Role of the Hypothalamus in Satiety

Anatomical considerations

I should begin by slaying a dragon that has haunted the field for many years. Mainly for the sake of semantic convenience, some early investigators used the phrase ventromedial 'satiety center'. Unfortunately, this has fostered the tacit assumption that the ventromedial *nucleus* autonomously controls this complex function. Nothing could be further from the truth. The early papers in the field were, in fact, quite specific in pointing out that effective lesions were ventral and lateral to the nucleus itself. Subsequent research has shown that (1) lesions confined to the nucleus do not produce hyperphagia (although they may elevate insulin secretion and thus promote obesity); (2) lesions confined to the periventricular nucleus, just rostral and dorsal to the VMN, do produce hyperphagia and obesity; (c) surgical knife cuts anterior and posterior to the ventromedial hypothalamus (which sever noradrenergic projections to the PVN, albeit not selectively) result in hyperphagia and obesity. The latter effects appear to be additive to those of VMH lesions, suggesting that the PVN influence may be an independent one.

In addition, it is quite clear that the region must have extensive connections with other, satiety-related regions of the brain (such as the frontal cortex and amygdala) as well as both sympathetic and parasympathetic branches of the autonomic nervous system which execute many satiety-related hormonal and metabolic commands of hypothalamic origin (Bray, Inoue and Nishizawa, 1981).

Hedonic factors

It has been known for more than 40 years that lesions in the ventromedial hypothalamus induce a behavioral syndrome which, unfortunately, was labeled 'hypothalamic rage' by early investigators. Subsequent study of the phenomenon has indicated that such lesions induce a general state of hyperreactivity to sensory inputs of all modalities (including tactile stimulation incident to restraint and normal handling). Strictly speaking, this is not an effect on sensory processing *per se* (the absolute and differential thresholds appear to be normal) but a disinhibitory effect on affective reactions to the hedonic properties of stimuli.

This raises the intriguing possibility that animals with VMH lesions may overeat, at least in part, because they cannot resist the lure of *haute cuisine* rather than because of an inability to meter the metabolic consequences of the nutrients ingested.

This 'hedonic disinhibition hypothesis' (Grossman, 1966) is supported by a substantial body of experimental evidence, including the following:

(a) Rats with VMH lesions overeat and become obese only when a palatable diet is available. When fed a less preferred powdered diet there is typically no sign of hyperphagia. The animals will indeed starve rather than accept roughage or quinine-adulterated diets that are readily tolerated by neurologically intact rats.
(b) This 'finickiness' can also be demonstrated to be a factor in water intake. Normal tap water appears to be hedonically neutral and most investigators report only feeding-related changes in water intake after VMH lesions. However, when the hedonic valence of water is altered by non-nutritive sweeteners, quinine, etc., the rat with VMH lesions overreacts much as it does to palatable or unpalatable foods.
(c) Although rats with VMH lesions overeat a palatable diet, they refuse to work for it when their efforts are only infrequently rewarded (e.g. on a high fixed or variable interval schedule of reinforcement). It would appear that in this case the negative influence of frequent frustrative non-reward cancels the occasional gratification of appetite.
(d) Prelesion experience with intermittent reward or unpalatable diets attenuates their postoperative inhibitory effect on food-rewarded operant as well as ingestive behavior.

These observations indicate a far more complex role for the ventromedial hypothalamus than the traditional view suggests but do not, in my opinion, invalidate the notion that it is the source of signals which lead to the termination of ingestive behavior. It is, indeed, intuitively obvious that satiety is a relative rather than absolute phenomenon which is strongly influenced by hedonic factors that may well, at least in the short term, exert more powerful effects on food intake than nutritional considerations themselves. Most of us eat far more than metabolic needs dictate when served a meal consisting of many varied courses, and find still more room when our host surprises us with a tempting dessert. On the other hand, we find it relatively easy to adhere to a stringent reducing diet when offered the same tasteless dish day after day.

Endocrine and metabolic effects

Lesions in the VMH increase plasma insulin levels and greatly exaggerate the preabsorptive release of insulin which occurs during the first minutes of a meal. The secretion of growth hormone, which normally modulates the effects of insulin, is inhibited. The hyperinsulinemia is associated with (and undoubtedly at least in part responsible for) increased lipogenesis and fat deposition.

This constellation of endocrine and metabolic disturbances, which results in the rapid removal of nutrients from the circulation, is accompanied by reduced lipolysis that reduces access to the increased fat deposits. It has been argued that the animal with VMH lesions may not 'gain weight because it overeats but overeats because it is gaining weight' (Friedman and Stricker, 1976). This perspective leads to the position (LeMagnen, 1985) that the ventromedial hypothalamus is not concerned with satiety at all but acts as a 'lipo-regulatory' mechanism which controls the body's fat mass.

Before we take a closer look at some of the experimental data which have led to these conclusions, I would like to offer an alternative interpretation.

It is generally agreed that the regulation of food intake and body weight has a short-term component which controls meal size and intermeal interval as well as a long-term component which corrects the errors made by the short-term controller due to variations in the nature or availability of the diet. The proposed 'lipo-regulatory' function of the VMH, far from negating its role in satiety, offers a perfect model of the long-term controller which modulates food intake on the basis of information from the body's energy reserves. As we shall see shortly, there is also evidence for an additional role in short-term satiety which affects meal size (most investigators report an increase in meal size as well as more frequent daytime meals after VMH lesions).

In considering the experimental literature in this area, one must distinguish between hyperphagia and obesity, since metabolic disturbances disrupt the normally close correlation between the two.

One of the earliest clues to the importance of metabolic factors in hypothalamic obesity was the demonstration that animals with VMH lesions gain weight faster than pair-fed controls. The effect is not as large as that seen in animals allowed *ad libitum* access to food but clearly demonstrates the metabolic effects of the lesion.

That insulin is essential for the development of the VMH syndrome has been demonstrated in studies of experimentally diabetic animals who have undergone surgical or pharmacological destruction of the insulin-secreting pancreatic beta cells. Such animals do not overeat or become obese after VMH lesions unless exogenous insulin is administered chronically. It is, however, interesting to note that the quantity of insulin required for the expression of hypothalamic hyperphagia and obesity produces only low levels of plasma insulin which do not result in overeating or obesity in neurologically intact animals. It would appear that an excess of insulin is not essential.

This point is reinforced when one considers the effects of vagotomy. Transection of this major parasympathetic nerve abolishes hypothalamic control over pancreatic insulin secretion. Early studies indicated that vagotomy reversed the hyperphagia and obesity normally seen after VMH lesions. However, significant increases in food intake and body weight have been seen in more recent experiments when the order of experimental treatments was reversed so that the animals could recover from the acute affects of vagotomy (which include mechanical difficulties in swallowing and gastric emptying) before the VMH lesion was made.

These results indicate that hyperinsulinemia, while normally a contributing factor, may not be essential for the expression of hypothalamic hyperphagia and obesity.

This conclusion receives support from reports of overeating and obesity after surgical knife cuts lateral to the VMH which did not affect basal insulin levels. Conversely, it has been reported that only lesions *within* the ventromedial nucleus consistently produce hyperinsulinemia, whereas hyperphagia appears to be the product of damage ventral and lateral to it. It would appear likely that the typically quite extensive lesions used to produce hypothalamic hyperphagia and obesity may affect several distinct though probably interacting neural mechanisms which modulate sensory, endocrine and metabolic reactions in concert with food intake and body weight.

In closing, I should point out that a purely metabolic explanation of VMH functions is unlikely in view of the acute effects of stimulation or inhibition of VMH neural activity in conscious animals. Thus, local infusions of the local anesthetic procaine or the inhibitory neurotransmitter norepinephrine elicit feeding almost instantaneously, certainly long before significant metabolic changes could have occurred. Electrical stimulation of the region has been reported to stop feeding in deprived animals within seconds of its onset.

The Role of the Hypothalamus in Hunger

Anatomical considerations

Lesions in the dorsolateral hypothalamus produce transient aphagia (as well as adipsia). Given extensive postoperative care, including intragastric intubation of food and water, a gradual process of recovery occurs which culminates in the reappearance of voluntary ingestive behavior adequate to maintain life unaided. The acute effects of DLH lesions are dramatic and often persist for weeks or even months. It is therefore surprising that attempts to specify the exact location of effective lesions have not produced a coherent picture.

To be optimally effective, lesions have to be quite large and extend into the far lateral corner of the hypothalamus which is immediately adjacent to major fiber tracts, including the internal capsule and lateral lemniscus. Moreover, the critical area is, itself, rather thinly populated by nerve cell bodies but contains not only the pallido-fugal fiber system but also a significant proportion of the fibers of the medial forebrain bundle (MFB), which constitutes one of the principal connections between the brainstem and forebrain. Electrolytic or surgical lesions in the dorsolateral hypothalamus cannot avoid extensive damage to these fibers of passage and this has been the focus of much controversy and debate.

The problem is vastly complicated by the fact that DLH lesions not only inhibit ingestive behavior but also result in a pattern of sensory motor and arousal deficits (below) which may well be due to an interference with one or more of these fiber systems. Whether these 'non-specific' effects of DLH lesions are responsible, fully or in part, for their devastating influence on ingestive behavior has been the subject of much debate.

Morgane (1961) demonstrated more than 25 years ago that lesions in the globus pallidus produced effects on food and water intake that appeared similar to, though possibly even more severe than, those seen after DLH lesions. He proposed that the effects of the latter might be due to an interruption of the pallido-fugal fiber system, which is a major branch of the extrapyramidal motor system. Subsequent investigations demonstrated that the effects of a unilateral lesion in the DLH (which has only minor effects on food intake and body weight) produced the complete syndrome of hypothalamic aphagia and adipsia when added to a contralateral lesion in the globus pallidus or in portions of the lower brainstem (e.g. the red nucleus) that are targets for pallido-fugal efferents.

Interest in the role of sensory-motor pathways intensified when Ungerstedt (1971) reported that neurotoxin-induced lesions in the substantia nigra, just behind the lateral hypothalamus, also produced aphagia and adipsia. The neurotoxin used in these studies, 6-hydroxy-dopamine (6-OHDA), does not affect fibers of passage and selectively destroys nerve cells which rely on the catecholaminergic neurotransmitters dopamine, epinephrine or norepinephrine. Subsequent experiments, using intracerebroventricular injections of 6-OHDA in conjunction with compounds that protect epinephrine- as well as norepinephrine-producing nerve cells, have shown that the effects of 6-OHDA injections into the substantia nigra are due to the destruction of dopaminergic cells. These neurons give rise to the nigro-striatal pathway, a major bridge which interconnects cerebellar and lower brainstem components of the extrapyramidal motor system with the striatum.

Sensory-motor and arousal dysfunctions

Microinjections of the neurotoxin 6-OHDA into the substantia nigra, dorsolateral hypothalamus or the ventricular system of the brain produce severe sensory-motor and arousal deficits (Ungerstedt, 1971). For days and sometimes weeks, the animal remains rigidly motionless, even catatonic when placed in unnatural positions, but actively resists attempts to displace it. There is no overt response to stimuli of all sensory modalities unless they are extremely intense, in which case the animal briefly becomes activated from coma. That there is no ingestive behavior during this acute response to the neurotoxin may have no significance in the context of the general debilitation.

Gradually, the animal's level of general arousal and activity as well as its responsiveness to external stimuli increases and voluntary food and water intake reappear. However, regulatory deficits, typical of those seen in rats with DLH electrolytic lesions (e.g. unresponsiveness to experimental treatments that elicit feeding or drinking in neurologically intact animals), remain indefinitely. It is not clear, at this point, whether 'subclinical' deficits in arousal and/or sensory-motor functions are responsible for these apparently specific impairments in ingestive behavior.

Electrolytic lesions in the DLH produce a similar though typically less severe syndrome of general apathy, decreased responsiveness to sensory input and motor dysfunctions similar to those seen in catatonia (Levitt and Teitelbaum, 1975). Although apparently overlooked for several decades by the early investigators of the lateral hypothalamic lesion syndrome, it now appears quite likely that these sensory-motor and/or arousal deficits may well play a significant, if as yet poorly understood role in the acute effects of DLH lesions on ingestive behavior.

It has, in fact, been suggested that even the apparently permanent deficits in responding to such experimental treatments which reduce the availability and/or utilization of glucose and elicit feeding in neurologically intact rats may be due to persisting 'subclinical' deficits in arousal or reactivity to internal stimuli. Such an interpretation is difficult to disprove at the present time, but I would like to summarize briefly some experimental observations which lead me to believe that specific effects on food intake and body-weight regulation may well be present after DLH lesions.

Before I present some of the evidence for this conclusion, I should point out yet another potential complication. As indicated above, DLH lesions which affect food intake and body-weight regulation involve an area that is immediately adjacent to the medial lemniscus. It has been shown that damage to his important fiber system impairs sensory feedback from the mouth and interferes wih coordinated motor acts such as biting, licking and chewing that are essential for successful ingestive behavior (Zeigler, 1983). In some instances, these complications are readily apparent in rats with DLH lesions which 'shred' an enormous amount of food while ingesting only little. In other animals, such overt difficulties are not in evidence but covert impairments of sensory feedback from the mouth may be difficult to detect.

The Case for Specific Hypothalamic Mechanism

To return to the principal issue whether an interruption of the dopaminergic nigro-striatal fiber system is responsible for the effects of DLH lesions on food intake and body-weight regulation, the following experimental observations should be considered:

(a) DLH lesions which produce persisting disturbances in food intake and body-weight regulation typically reduce striatal dopamine by only 40—60 per cent, indicating that approximately half of the nigro-striatal fibers are intact and functional. Indeed, we have observed major effects on food intake in animals which sustained striatal dopamine depletions as low as 25 per cent. Yet, when the neurotoxin 6-OHDA is injected intraventricularly, little or no change in food intake or body weight is seen unless striatal dopamine is depleted by 95 per cent or more.

(b) When one transects the lateral, rostral, or caudal connections of the hypothalamus by means of surgical knife cuts which inflict little damage to nerve cell bodies in the region, a broad spectrum of behavioral and neurochemical effects can be observed which range from the severe sensory-motor and arousal deficits seen after electrolytic or neurotoxin lesions that result in a near-complete depletion of striatal dopamine to a syndrome of persisting deficits in food-intake regulation in animals that have no detectable overt sensory-motor dysfunctions. Detailed statistical analysis of the biochemical, sensory-motor and food-intake related effects of these cuts has not indicated close associations except when one considers only the acute postoperative phase of complete aphagia and adipsia (Grossman, 1978).

(c) While voluntary ingestive behavior tends to reappear in parallel with other behaviors and sensory reactivity in general, several investigators have reported that the recovery of voluntary food intake can be dissociated from the general return of motoric functions.

(d) We, as well as others, have shown that microinjections of the neurotoxin kainic acid (KA) into the DLH of rats produced transient aphagia and adipsia as well as the persisting regulatory deficits typical of animals with electrolytic lesions in the area, including unresponsiveness to experimentally induced cellular glucopenia or dehydration. The neurotoxin did not destroy all cells in the DLH and produced effects on food and water intake that were less severe than those seen after electrolytic lesions. The results are none the less important because kainic acid does not affect fibers of passage while destroying nerve cell bodies which have an affinity for the compound, possibly because they are equipped with glutamate receptors. Because of these properties, KA injections into the DLH did not deplete striatal dopamine and failed to reproduce the sensory-motor and arousal dysfunctions which complicate the interpretation of the effects of electrolytic lesions in the area.

The effects of intrahypothalamic KA injections suggest that nerve cell bodies indigenous to the region do, in fact, exert important influences on food and water intake. This conclusion is further strengthened by subsequent experiments aimed at avoiding some complications which might have affected the results of the initial KA studies. (Intrahypothalamic injections of this neurotoxin not only failed to produce the lethargy and somnolence seen after electrolytic lesions but did, in fact, induce apparently random hyperactivity which might have interfered with normal ingestive behavior. Also, the toxin readily spread from the injection site to adjacent regions such as the zona incerta and ventral thalamus, both sites where electrolytic lesions have been shown to affect the regulation of ingestive behavior, although not entirely in the same way as DLH lesions do.)

To circumvent these problems, we ejected KA ions electrophoretically from the tip of a glass micropipette aimed at the DLH. This procedure produced even smaller depletions of neurons in the DLH than previous injections of the toxin but succeeded in producing transient aphagia and adipsia as well as decreased reactivity to glucoprivic challenges without detectable damage to adjacent structures or producing hypo- or hyperactivity or any overt changes in sensory reactivity or spontaneous arousal.

(e) Last, but not least, we need to consider data from experimental paradigms which have sought to stimulate the DLH or attempted to relate its activity to ingestive behavior. As mentioned earlier, electrical stimulation of the lateral hypothalamus has been shown to elicit food intake in sated animals. The effect is typically stimulus-bound (i.e. begins quite promptly after the onset of the stimulation and terminates shortly after it is turned off). At first glance, this would seem to offer strong support for the hypothalamocentric theory of food-intake regulation, but there have been major questions which are in an important sense complementary to the issue of sensory-motor or arousal dysfunctions after DLH lesions.

Once again, the facts are not in doubt. Electrical stimulation of the DLH does elicit feeding and does so quite reliably. However, such stimulation may also elicit other behaviors, including drinking, gnawing on inedible objects, and hoarding (i.e. carrying food rather than eating it). Some investigators have argued that at a particular electrode site, only one of these behaviors is elicited at threshold intensities of stimulation and that others are observed only when the intensity is increased so that a wider population of nerve cells is affected. However, other investigators have reported that stimulation at the same intensity and electrode site can elicit a variety of behaviors, the nature of the specific behavior being determined by environmental factors. Thus, in the presence of food, a rat may feed in response to electrical stimulation and do so reliably. However, when the same stimulation is presented in a situation where food is not available but a drinking spout permits the ingestion of water, the same stimulation may come to elicit drinking. Indeed, when food is subsequently added, the animal may continue to drink in response to the stimulation.

Valenstein (1969) has suggested that the behavioral effects of stimulation of the DLH may not be due to an activation of specific hunger- or thirst-related neural events, but instead reflect activation of the medial forebrain bundle which courses through the area. According to this interpretation, DLH stimulation increases general arousal and alerts the animal to the presence of potential reinforcers in the environment. What emerge are 'prepotent' behaviors which are relevant to the environment. When the environment changes, so does the behavior.

Matters are further complicated by the fact that electrical stimulation which elicits ingestive behavior tends to be 'rewarding' (i.e. the animal will emit an operant such as lever-pressing in order to obtain such stimulation) and the desirability of the reward (i.e. the rate of self-administration) covaries with variables (such as the duration of deprivation, exogenous insulin, intragastric infusions, etc.) which affect food or water intake and, presumably, hunger and thirst itself. It is most curious that an animal should exert effort in order to create a condition in its nervous system which appears to be interpreted as an increase in a basic 'drive' such as hunger or thirst.

The conceptual issues which are raised by this apparent paradox go beyond the context of the present discussion. However, the close association between the rewarding effects of hypothalamic stimulation (rarely found in other brain regions which also sustain brain stimulation self-administration) is a substantial argument for the representation of hunger-related neural mechanisms in the DLH.

Chemical 'brain stimulation' (a term often used uncritically to refer to the administration of chemical compounds to the brain even when they may, in fact, inhibit neural activity) has not so far contributed to our understanding of DLH function, except, perhaps, in a negative fashion.

Microinjections of beta-adrenergic or dopaminergic compounds into the hypothalamus have been shown to exert inhibitory effects on food intake. However, the doses required have generally been high and the effective target sites have been medial to the DLH in the perifornical region. The data support the general conclusion that the hypothalamus contains neurons concerned with the regulation of food intake but tell us little about the specific functions of the DLH.

Microinjections of glucose or glucose analogues such as 2-deoxy-D-glucose (2-DG) into the DLH apparently do not affect food intake even though intracerebroventricular injections of 2-DG are quite effective in eliciting feeding, presumably because they inhibit glucose utilization by a central receptor mechanism which influences food intake in accordance with glucose availability.

Intrahypothalamic infusions of very low doses of insulin have been reported to reduce food intake (or produce a curious pattern of inhibitory effects on night-time feeding, combined with a compensatory increase in daytime intake). Unfortunately, the effects are not large and attempts to localize the responsible site(s) of action within the hypothalamus have not yet been successful. As mentioned earlier, electrophysiological experiments have indicated that insulin may act as a neuromodulator in both medial and lateral hypothalamic portions of the diencephalic feeding system. The recently reported effects of intrahypothalamic injections support such an interpretation but do not, as yet, clearly define the nature of the interaction.

The fact that central infusions of very small doses of insulin tend to reduce food intake has given rise to the hypothesis (Woods and Porte, 1978) that the insulin level of the cerebrospinal fluid (CSF) (which is related to body fat mass) may be a channel of information for hypothalamic mechanisms concerned with food intake. According to this hypothesis, increases in body fat result in a rise in CSF insulin. This is communicated to hypothalamic nerve cells by means of a 'window' in the CSF/brain barrier located in the postero-medial hypothalamus, near the stalk of the pituitary gland.

Conclusions

Twenty-five years ago few individuals would have questioned the conclusion, based on a voluminous and generally consistent literature, that the diencephalon or, more specifically, the ventromedial hypothalamus in cooperation with the dorsolateral region, exerts primary effects on food intake and body weight. Today we are no longer quite as sure, not because the basic experimental findings have come into question but because further study has provided a wealth of additional data which increasingly support alternative interpretations.

There are, indeed, investigators in the field who reject the hypothalamocentric theory of food intake and body-weight regulation on the basis of the data I have summarized above. This is a tempting, 'hard-nosed' position which any scientist eager not to extrapolate too far from his database will consider seriously. I, for one, would do so gladly were it not for the inconvenient fact that the research of the past decades has successfully questioned traditional interpretations without providing more palatable (or, indeed, any) alternatives. Are we to believe that physiological and psychological processes which are as essential for the survival of the individual (and, by implication, the species) as the regulation of food intake and body weight are not subject to control at all? Or that the brain mechanisms responsible for such regulation are so cleverly disguised that nearly a century of active investigation has not even provided a hint of their existence?

I find it more appealing to subscribe to the thesis that the voluminous and varied experimental evidence which point towards hypothalamic regulation does, in fact, direct us to the basic mechanisms we seek to understand. Our investigative tools may well still be sufficiently crude to permit the contamination of our results by inadvertent damage or stimulation of a variety of possibly unrelated neural mechanisms, but I cannot believe that the convergence of findings so characteristic of this particular topic should be accidental.

References

Anand, B. K. and J. R. Brobek (1950). Localization of a feeding center in the hypothalamus of the rat. *Proceedings of the Society for Experimental Biology and Medicine*. **77**, 323–324.

Bray, G. A., S. Inoue and Y. Nishizawa (1981). Hypothalamic obesity: the autonomic hypothesis and the lateral hypothalamus. *Diabetologia* **20**, 366–378.

Brobeck, J. R. (1946). Mechanisms of the development of obesity in animals with hypothalamic lesions. *Physiological Review* **26**, 541–559.

Friedman, M. I. and E. M. Stricker (1976). The physiological psychology of hunger: a physiological perspective. *Psychological Review* **83**, 409–431.

Grossman, S. P. (1966). The VMH: a center for affective reactions, satiety or both? *Physiological Behaviour* **1**, 1–10.

Grossman, S. P. (1967). Neuropharmacology of central mechanisms contributing to control of food and water intake. In *Handbook of Physiology, Section on the Alimentary Canal*, ed. by C. F. Code. Williams and Wilkins, Baltimore, pp. 287–302.

Grossman S. P. (1975). Role of the hypothalamus in the regulation of food and water intake. *Psychological Review* **82**, 200–224.

Grossman, S. P. (1978). Correlative analysis of ingestive behavior and regional amine depletions after surgical transections of neural pathways in the mesencephalon, diencephalon and striatum. In: *Central Mechanisms of Anoretic Drugs*, ed. by S. Garattini and R. Samanin. Raven Press, New York, pp. 1–38.

Grossman, S. P. (1979). The biology of motivation. *Annual Review of Psychology*. **30**, 209–242.

Grossman, S. P. (1983). Contemporary problems concerning our understanding of brain mechanisms that regulate food intake and body weight. In *Psychobiology of Eating and its Disorders*, ed. by A. J. Stunkard and E. Stellar. Raven Press, New York, pp. 5–13.

Grossman, S. P. (1986). The role of glucose, insulin and glucagon in the regulation of food intake and body weight. *Neuroscience and Neurobehavioral Review* **10**, 295–315.

Keesey, R. E., P. C. Boyle, W. Kemnitz and J. S. Mitchel (1976). The role of the lateral hypothalamus in determining the body weight set point. In *Hunger: Basic Mechanisms and Clinical Implications*, ed. by D. Novin, W. Wyrwicka and G. A. Bray. Raven Press, New York, pp. 243–256.

Leibowitz, S. F. (1980). Neurochemical systems of the hypothalamus: control of feeding and drinking behavior and water-electrolyte excretion. In *Handbook of the Hypothalamus*, Vol. 3, ed. by P. J. Morgane and J. Panksepp. Marcel Dekker, New York, pp. 299–437.

LeMagnen, J (1985). *Hunger*. Cambridge University Press, Cambridge.

Levitt, D. R. and P. Teitelbaum (1975). Somnolence, akinesia and sensory activation of motivated behavior in the lateral hypothalamic syndrome. *Proceedings of the National Academy of Sciences of the USA* **72**, 2819–2923.

Mayer, J. (1955). Regulation of the energy intake and the body weight. The glucostatic theory and the lipostatic hypothesis. *Annals of the New York Academy of Sciences* **63**, 15–42.

Morgane, P. J. (1961). Alterations in feeding and drinking behavior of rats with lesions in globi pallidi. *American Journal of Physiology* **201**, 420–428.

Oomura, Y. (1973). Central mechanisms in feeding. In *Advances in Biophysics*, Vol. 5, ed. by M. Kotani. University of Tokyo Press, Tokyo, pp. 65–142.

Oomura, Y. (1976). Significance of glucose, insulin and free fatty acids on the hypothalamic feeding and satiety neurons. In *Hunger: Basic Mechanisms and Clinical Implications*, ed. by D. Novin, W. Wyrwicka and G. A. Bray. Raven Press, New York, pp. 145–157.

Stellar, E. (1954). The physiology of motivation. *Psychological Review* **61**, 5–22.

Teitelbaum, P. and A. N. Epstein (1962). The lateral hypothalamic syndrome: recovery of feeding and drinking after lateral hypothalamic lesions. *Psychological Review* **69**, 74–90.

Ungerstedt, U. (1971). Aphagia and adipsia after 6-hydroxydopamine induced degeneration of the nigro-striatal dopamine system. *Acta Physiologica Scandinavica* (Suppl.) **367**, 97–122.

Valenstein, E. S. (1969). Behavior elicited by hypothalamic stimulation: A prepotency hypothesis. *Brain Behavior and Evolution* **2**, 295–316.

Woods, S. C. and D. Porte, Jr (1978). The central nervous system, pancreatic hormones, feeding and obesity. *Advances in Metabolic Disorders* **9**, 283–312.

Zeigler, H. P. (1983). The trigeminal system and ingestive behavior. In *Handbook of Neurobiology, Vol. 6, Motivation*, ed. by E. Satinoff and P. Teitelbaum. Plenum Press, New York, pp. 265–327.

11

Gastric control of food intake

Paul Robinson
King's College School of Medicine and Dentistry and The Institute of Psychiatry, London

The physiological signals that contribute to the initiation or termination of a bout of eating are likely to include central monoamine levels, secretion of neuropeptides, the concentration of nutrients in the plasma, the activity of hypothalamic neurons and the state of tension in the gastric wall. Information from these and other sources is integrated, at least in man, with cognitive influences and the resulting behavioural response may be the beginning of a meal, its continuance, a change in the type of nutrient selected or the end of the meal. The contribution of gastric distension to this complex process has been investigated by observing the effect on feeding of changes in gastric emptying rate, most commonly delayed gastric emptying. Some of the disturbances of eating behaviour observed in bulimia nervosa and anorexia nervosa may be related to changes in gastric function, particularly slowing of gastric emptying, and an understanding of the mechanisms by which gastric inhibitory agents, administered as drugs and produced in the body, affect feeding can generate hypotheses about the factors leading to over- and undereating in morbid states. In the present discussion we will examine the role of delayed gastric emptying in two models of experimentally induced satiety, that occurring after administration of cholecystokinin, and fenfluramine anorexia, and in abnormal satiety occurring in anorexia and bulimia nervosa.

Cholecystokinin-induced Satiety

Cholecystokinin (CCK) is the name given to a group of peptides sharing a common biologically active octapeptide sequence. It is present in the mammalian nervous system (Vanderhaegen, Signeau and Gepts, 1975) and it inhibits feeding in rats (Gibbs, Young and Smith, 1973a), rhesus monkeys (Gibbs, Falasco and McHugh, 1976; Moran and McHugh, 1982) and in man (Kissileff *et al.*, 1982; Sturdevant and Goetz, 1976). The mechanism of action of CCK satiety has not been fully elucidated, and, because of the relatively high doses required to elicit an effect on feeding, it has not been established that CCK has a physiological role in the control of food intake. The studies designed to investigate these two areas of uncertainty have, however, provided a number of important insights into the control mechanisms of feeding which may have relevance to understanding of disturbances of feeding observed in patients with bulimia nervosa.

Receptors for CCK are found in several body tissues although only the brain (Innis and Snyder, 1980), vagal (Zarbin *et al.*, 1981) and pyloric (Smith *et al.*, 1984) receptors have been suggested as mediating its satiety action. CCK has powerful stimulatory effects on isolated brain slices in tissue baths (Brooks and Kelly, 1985). However, peripherally administered CCK, or CCK secreted from the proximal small intestine, would have limited access to central receptors (Passaro *et al.*, 1982) so a direct central effect of peripheral CCK seems unlikely. Moreover, CCK receptors in the CNS differ from peripheral binding sites, for example in the pylorus. Identification of the receptor type may be performed by determining the relative ability of CCK and closely associated peptides, such as desulphated CCK, which does not have a satiety action, to displace radiolabelled CCK from the binding sites in an autoradiographic study (Moran *et al.*, 1986). It is found that, while sulphated and desulphated CCK are approximately equally potent in displacing radiolabelled CCK from central receptors, pyloric sites demonstrate a much higher relative affinity for sulphated CCK (Moran, Robinson and McHugh, 1985). Thus pyloric receptors show a higher degree of specificity than brain receptors and the two classes of CCK receptor have been labelled type A (for alimentary) and type B (for brain) respectively (Moran *et al.*, 1986). Their relative specificity should be compared with that of the behavioural effect of CCK, the sulphated variety of which is active in reducing food intake but not, under the limited range of circumstances reported, the desulphated form (Gibbs, Young and Smith, 1973b; Robinson, Moran and McHugh, 1988). This evidence points, therefore, to the periphery as the site of the satiety action of CCK. Recently, however, type A CCK receptors have been located in the central nervous system of the rat, specifically in the area postrema, the interpeduncular nuclei and the nucleus tractus solitarius (Moran *et al.*, 1986). The first of these locations is known to have a porous blood–brain barrier (Wislocki and Putnam, 1920), and the area postrema appears to overcome the two objections to a central mediation for CCK satiety — the inaccessibility of CCK to the CNS and the properties of the receptor. Of the peripheral CCK receptor sites, the pylorus and vagus may both be involved in mediating the effect of CCK on food intake. Pyloric receptors are found in the circular muscle of the pyloric sphincter (Smith *et al.*, 1984), and are therefore well placed to influence gastric emptying. The relationship between inhibition of gastric emptying and satiety has been demonstrated in the rhesus monkey, where an intragastric saline load potentiates the effect of intravenous CCK on feeding (Moran and McHugh, 1982). The saline, which is normally rapidly emptied from the stomach and, given alone, has no effect on feeding, appears to be held in the stomach where it can exert a satiety effect. CCK inhibits gastric emptying in man (Shaw *et al.*, 1985) and the effect of the peptide on feeding in man is to shorten a meal but not to decrease the rate of eating (Kissileff *et al.*, 1982). An early end to a meal is just what would be expected of an agent which increased satiety by inhibiting gastric emptying rate. Another possible mode of action of CCK is *via* the abdominal vagus nerve. Attention was drawn to the vagus because of the finding that abdominal vagotomy blocked the inhibitory effects of CCK on feeding (Smith *et al.*, 1981). Further elegant experiments have demonstrated that the essential lesion is of the sensory vagus. Smith, Jerome and Norgren (1985) performed a sensory vagotomy by cutting the dorsal (sensory) root of the one vagus as it enters the brainstem. The other vagus was cut in the abdomen. A unilateral vagotomy does not influence CCK satiety, but when combined with a contralateral sensory vagotomy no effect of CCK on feeding was demonstrable. Moreover, it has been shown that the branch of the vagus required for CCK satiety is that leading to the stomach (Smith *et al.*, 1981). Cutting the hepatic or coeliac branches of the vagus has no effect on CCK satiety.

Inhibition of feeding by CCK is therefore likely to be mediated by the sensory gastric vagus. Two different mechanisms have been postulated for the role of the vagus. First, it has been suggested that when CCK inhibits gastric emptying, food builds up in the stomach during a meal and the result is gastric distension (Moran and McHugh, 1982). The distension signal is transmitted to the brain *via* the sensory vagus and acts as a cue to trigger the end of feeding. It has also been suggested that CCK may act on the terminals of the abdominal vagus itself (Smith and Gibbs, 1985), on CCK receptors that have been described on the vagus which have been observed to flow distally in the nerve (Zarbin *et al.*, 1981).

The proposition that gastric distension, stimulated by CCK-induced inhibition of gastric emptying, is an important mechanism in CCK satiety has been challenged using evidence from sham feeding rats (Gibbs, Young and Smith, 1973b). In these animals, food reaches the stomach but is then diverted through a metal fistula from the stomach through the abdominal skin, thereby preventing the development of gastric distension. CCK inhibits this form of feeding, and, in this situation, CCK is not, of course, acting *via* inhibition of gastric emptying. The only apparent way to reconcile this evidence with that in favour of the gastric inhibition hypothesis is to postulate at least two mechanisms for CCK satiety. Considering the complexity of the CCK receptor systems identified, this would not be unreasonable. Inhibition of sham feeding requires larger doses of CCK than are needed to inhibit feeding in the intact animal (Gibbs, Young and Smith, 1973b) and there is some evidence suggesting that abdominal vagotomy, which blocks CCK satiety in normally feeding animals, does not affect the response of sham feeding rats to CCK (Kraly, 1984). The effect of CCK on sham feeding could, therefore, be mediated *via* the central receptors located in the brainstem, particularly in the area postrema (Moran *et al.*, 1986).

A different line of research has been to adopt a developmental approach and to use the differential ontogeny of CCK systems to dissect out the mediators of its behavioural actions. Suckling is very resistant to inhibitory influences, including CCK (Blass, Beardsley and Hall, 1979), but, using rat pups taking milk independently of the dam from a milk-soaked paper towel, it has been shown that CCK has a powerful inhibitory effect on milk ingestion as early as day 1 (Robinson, Moran and McHugh, 1988) (Figure 11.1). The distribution of CCK receptors in the newborn rat is very different from that in the adult. The brain contains only low levels of CCK binding and autoradiographic studies have shown only a small area in the rhinencephalon bearing CCK receptors at day 1 (Garcha *et al.*, 1987; Hays *et al.*, 1981), in contrast to the adult, which shows widespread binding throughout the forebrain grey matter (Gaudreau *et al.*, 1985). In the stomach, however, extensive CCK binding has been observed at day 1 (Robinson *et al.*, 1987). The adult stomach contains binding sites for CCK confined to the distal part of the circular muscle of the pyloric sphincter. In the neonate, binding is found in the pylorus, the antral circular muscle and the gastric mucosa and this distribution was also noted in the stomach of the foetal rat at day 17 gestation (Figure 11.1). Thus, although CCK receptors are present in the brain to a minor extent at birth, their wide distribution in the stomach points to a gastric mechanism for CCK satiety in the neonate and gastric studies in neonatal rats have demonstrated that, as in adults, CCK significantly reduces the rate of gastric emptying (Robinson, Moran and McHugh, 1988) (Figure 11.1). Receptors in the vagus, another possible site of action of CCK, have not been studied in the neonate.

Studies of the mode of action of CCK have demonstrated the complexity of the mechanisms underlying control of food intake, and may provide a useful model for approaching other candidate satiety peptides. The hormone is secreted in the proximal small intestine (Dockray, 1977), and may act on the nearby pyloric sphincter, on the vagus nerve, or on the alimentary type A receptors in the floor of the fourth ventricle, the area postrema. It may contribute to the physiological control of food intake and gastric function and is worthy of study in eating disorders some of which are characterized by abnormal gastric function, in addition to having a potential role in the treatment of hyperphagic states.

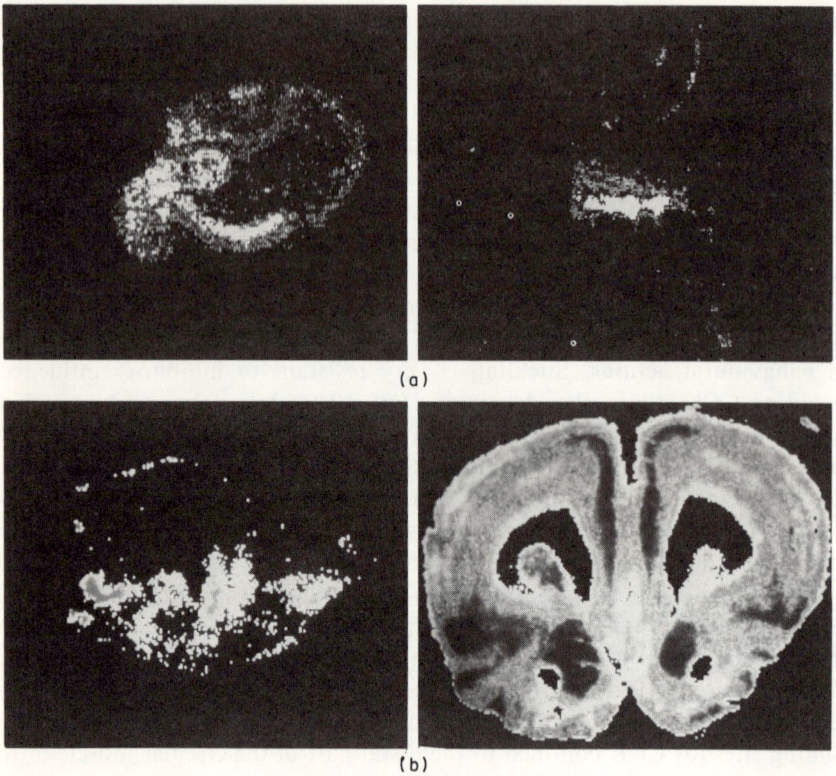

Figure 11.1 (caption opposite)

Fenfluramine Anorexia

The drug *dl*-fenfluramine has long been known to inhibit food intake in several species, including man (Kyriakides and Silverstone, 1979), and consideration of the mode of action of the drug might, as in the case of cholecystokinin, help in the generation of hypotheses about the control of food intake in general. Fenfluramine has also been found to reduce food intake in bulimia nervosa (Robinson, Checkley and Russell, 1985), an eating disorder characterized by episodes of massive overeating (Russell, 1979). These bulimic episodes are generally followed by behaviours aimed at reducing the effects of the ingested food on body weight, most commonly self-induced vomiting, abuse of laxatives and prolonged starvation; the syndrome is also defined by the presence of a morbid fear of weight gain and a desire to reduce weight or keep it at an unrealistically low level. Patients, who are usually young females, may be of any weight, but a distinction is generally made between patients who are severely underweight and may be categorized as having anorexia nervosa complicated by bulimia (Garfinkel, Moldofsky and Garner, 1980) and those

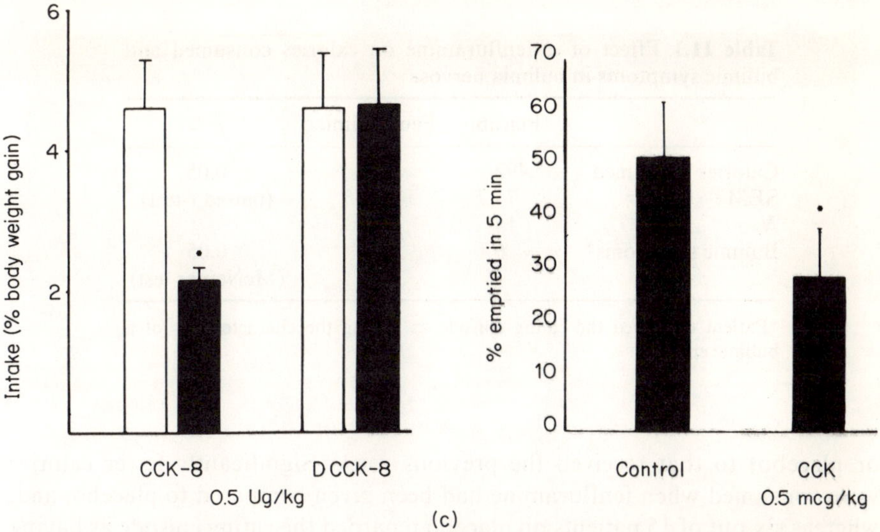

Figure 11.1. (a) Receptors for cholecystokinin, labelled using ^{123}I-CCK-33, in rat stomach. Left: foetal day 17 (duodenum left, oesophagus top left, greater curve on right). Right: adult gastroduodenal junction (gastric antrum at top, duodenum below). Autoradiographs analysed using computerized microdensitometry (Loats Co) showing high densities of receptors in white, lower densities in grey. (b) Brain receptors for CCK, labelled with ^{123}I-CCK-8, in, left, newborn and, right, adult rat. CCK receptors are found at the gastroduodenal junction, gastric mucosa and oesophagus in the foetus, but are confined to the pyloric sphincter in the adult. CCK binding sites in the brain increase from low levels at birth to a wide distribution in the adult grey matter. (c) Left: effect of intraperitoneal sulphated and desulphated CCK-8 on ingestion of warm milk from the floor of an incubator by day 1 rats. Quantity ingested is assessed by per cent weight gain over 30 min. Right: effect of sulphated CCK-8 on gastric emptying of physiological saline, 5 ml/kg, measured by weighing the stomach 5 min after gavage administration of the saline meal. Sulphated CCK inhibits both ingestion and gastric emptying (* $p < 0.05$). Desulphated CCK has no effect on ingestion. (Autoradiographs courtesy of Professor P. McHugh, Dr T. Moran and Dr J. Stephenson (Garcha *et al.*, 1987; Robinson *et al.*, 1987; Robinson, Moran and McHugh, 1988))

who are not underweight. The latter group are the patients referred to here as having bulimia nervosa.

In a study of the action of fenfluramine in bulimia nervosa (Robinson, Checkley and Russell, 1985), 15 patients with bulimia nervosa were given dl-fenfluramine, 60 mg orally, or an inert placebo, under double-blind conditions. Two hours later they were presented with a weighed excess of food, previously selected by them as being the food they were likely to consume during an episode of bulimia. After half an hour, during which time the subjects were left alone, the food was reweighed and the number of calories ingested was calculated. The following week the identical procedure was followed, but the patient was given the alternative preparation (fenfluramine

Table 11.1 Effect of *dl*-fenfluramine on calories consumed and bulimic symptoms in bulimia nervosa

	Placebo	Fenfluramine	$p<$
Calories consumed	492	234	0.05
SEM	74.7	43.5	(paired *t*-test)
N	15	15	
Bulimic symptoms*	6	0	0.05 (McNemar test)

*Patient described the eating episode as having the characteristics of a bulimic episode.

or placebo) to that received the previous week. Significantly fewer calories were consumed when fenfluramine had been given compared to placebo, and, whereas six out of 15 patients on placebo regarded the eating episode as having some characteristics of an 'eating binge', none did after placebo, a significant difference (Table 11.1). During the experiment patients completed visual analogue scale ratings of their feelings of hunger, fullness and urge to eat and other scales. For comparison, 15 normal controls were given a placebo tablet (presented, as to the patients, as a preparation which might or might not affect eating) and were asked to eat the same amount of food as had been consumed by patients under control conditions. Patients with bulimia nervosa showed abnormal responses to eating. Normal controls, after eating, had significant increases in ratings of fullness and decreases in hunger and urge to eat. The patients had normal changes in ratings of fullness, but hunger and urge to eat often did not fall after the food, and sometimes rose substantially. Overall, there was no significant change in rating of hunger attributable to the meal, and a significant increase in urge to eat (Figure 11.2). After fenfluramine, although the amount of food consumed was less than on placebo, hunger ratings and urge to eat tended to fall after eating and the difference between postprandial ratings of urge to eat on fenfluramine and on placebo was significant. Thus, fenfluramine tended to correct the disturbances observed in patients with bulimia nervosa eating a meal in which a large amount of highly calorific food was presented.

Since fenfluramine decreases calories consumed and bulimic symptoms in bulimia nervosa, understanding of the mode of action of the drug might suggest physiological mechanisms that could be disturbed in the disorder. Fenfluramine is thought to act in two main ways: by inhibiting the reuptake in the septal region of the forebrain of serotonin (Duhault *et al.*, 1978) and by inhibition of gastric emptying (Davies *et al.*, 1983; Robinson, Moran and McHugh, 1986; Rowland and Carlton, 1984). In the usual test employed in feeding experiments, measurements of the quantity of food consumed by rats

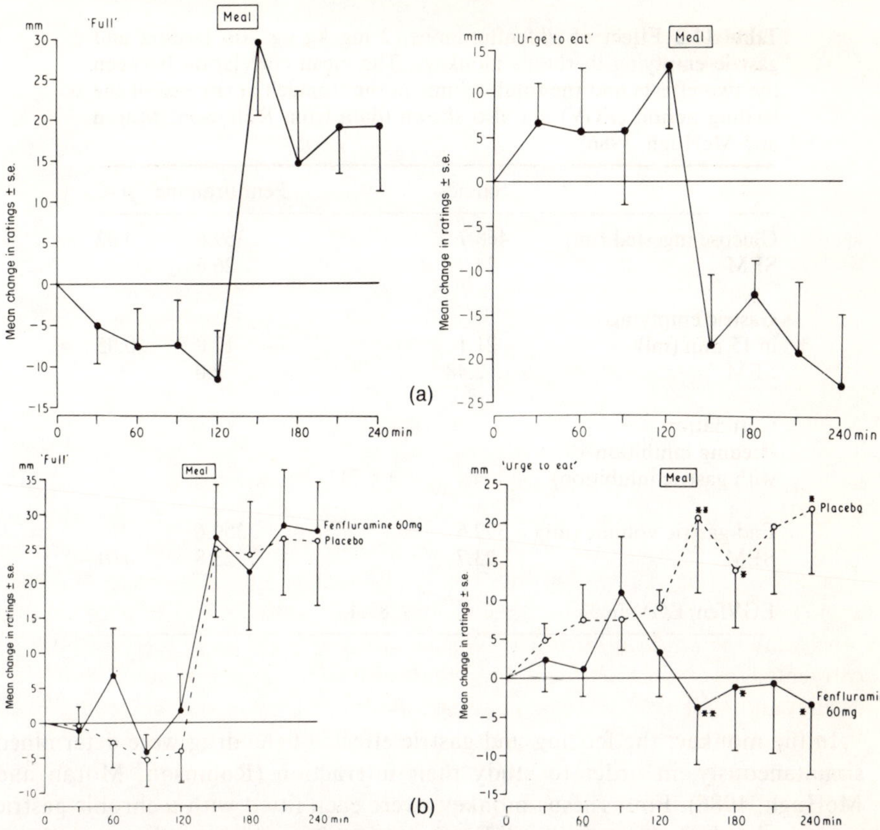

Figure 11.2. (a) In 15 control subjects, having had a placebo at time 0 min, consumption of a meal at 120 min produced a large increase in ratings of fullness and a decrease in urge to eat, measured using 100 mm visual analogue scales. (b) In 15 patients with bulimia nervosa, fullness ratings increased as expected on placebo (broken lines) and after fenfluramine, 60 mg p.o. (solid lines). However, urge to eat tended to *increase* after the meal when placebo had been given. Fenfluramine significantly corrected this response. (* $p < 0.05$, ** $p < 0.01$. Placebo *vs* fenfluramine in patients)

after a fast of 18 hours, fenfluramine shows a marked anoretic effect. If a lesion is made in the serotonergic neurons of the forebrain septum, the effect can no longer be demonstrated. However, if a freely feeding animal with a septal lesion is given fenfluramine, a clear feeding-inhibitory response is observed (Davies *et al.*, 1983). One possible interpretation of this finding is that the drug is enhancing the satiating potency of the food that is in the stomach, perhaps by inhibiting gastric emptying. A gastric inhibitory effect of fenfluramine has been demonstrated in the rat (Rowland and Carlton, 1984), the rhesus monkey (Robinson, Moran and McHugh, 1986) and in man (Horowitz *et al.*, 1985), although the precise mechanism whereby fenfluramine delays gastric emptying is unknown.

Table 11.2 Effect of *dl*-fenfluramine, 2 mg/kg i.g., on feeding and gastric emptying in rhesus monkeys. The mean correlation between the two effects and the total volume in the stomach at the end of the feeding period (EGV) are also shown (data from Robinson, Moran and McHugh, 1986).

	Saline		Fenfluramine	$p <$
Glucose ingested (ml)	468.7		369.6	0.02
SEM	24.9		26.6	
Gastric emptying in 15 min (ml)	21.1		12.8	0.05
SEM	2.48		2.0	
Correlation (feeding inhibition with gastric inhibition)		+ 0.71		
End gastric volume (ml)	399.6		359.6	
SEM	23.7		23.8	0.01
EGVfen/EGVsln %		89.4		

In the monkey, the feeding and gastric effects of the drug were determined simultaneously, in order to study their interaction (Robinson, Moran and McHugh, 1986). Four rhesus monkeys were each fitted with a chronic gastric cannula, implanted surgically. *dl*-Fenfluramine, 2 mg/kg, or saline control was given under blind conditions and gastric emptying of solutions of normal saline or d-glucose was determined using the serial test meal method. A test meal (e.g. 150 ml of saline) was introduced into the stomach *via* the gastric cannula and a variable time later the gastric contents were removed and measured. A correction for secretions was introduced using a dye dilution technique (phenol red in the original solution), the procedure was repeated for different emptying periods and a curve of gastric contents remaining against time was generated. Fenfluramine significantly inhibited gastric emptying of both saline and glucose solutions.

In a second experiment, the results of which are summarized in Table 11.2, the same dose of fenfluramine or saline control was given prior to a meal in which monkeys drank from a bottle of d-glucose, 0.5 kcal/ml. At the end of 15 minutes, the volume consumed was noted and the amount of glucose solution remaining in the stomach measured by means of the gastric cannula. Each of four monkeys was tested 16 times, eight on fenfluramine and eight on saline control. Fenfluramine significantly inhibited both gastric emptying and glucose consumption, as expected. The two effects were correlated in a number of ways, however. The more gastric emptying was inhibited, the more feeding was suppressed, and in one subject in which gastric emptying was not affected by fenfluramine, feeding was also resistant to its effects. In the three remaining animals, the degree of inhibition of glucose intake was significantly correlated with the extent to which gastric emptying was slowed by the drug. In order to estimate the relative contributions of peripheral and central influences to the feeding-inhibitory action of fenfluramine, the total gastric volume at the end of the 15-minute feeding test was measured. It was reasoned that if gastric volume after fenfluramine was the same as after control, the reduced intake could be explained entirely as a consequence of reduced gastric emptying. The results showed a mean gastric volume after fenfluramine that was about 90 per cent of that after control, and that, under the conditions of this experiment, the drug's inhibitory action on feeding could be attributed largely to delayed gastric emptying.

Delayed Gastric Emptying in Anorexia and Bulimia Nervosa

The aforementioned pharmacological studies in animals have shown that delayed gastric emptying is an important mediating influence in drug-induced inhibition of feeding. Anorexia nervosa and bulimia nervosa are conditions in which control of feeding and body weight are profoundly disturbed, and early studies indicated that in anorexia nervosa delayed gastric emptying was a feature of the illness (Dubois *et al.*, 1979; Holt *et al.*, 1981). In these conditions, therefore, gastric stasis may contribute to undereating by enhancing satiety. It may also lead to a rare, but potentially fatal, consequence of rapid refeeding in starvation, acute gastric dilatation (Russell, 1966), in which a severely underweight patient develops a distended, atonic stomach soon after the onset of vigorous refeeding, sometimes progressing to gastric perforation and peritonitis.

The first studies of gastric function in eating disorders left unanswered a number of questions. What are the antecedents of delayed gastric emptying in anorexia nervosa? Is it a primary condition or secondary to the symptoms of the disorder? What are the influences of body weight, diet, bulimia, vomiting and abuse of laxatives? The present studies (Robinson, Clarke and Barrett, 1988) were designed to address these questions.

Gastric emptying rate was measured in 42 subjects. Three different meals were used: a solid mixed meal consisting of radio-labelled poached egg white, bread and butter and orange juice, a caloric liquid meal of 200 ml of a d-glucose solution, 0.5 kcal/ml, and a non-caloric liquid meal of 200 ml physiological saline. Each meal was labelled with 3.7 MBq of technetium 99m-sulphur colloid and gastric scans were acquired using a gamma camera. To compensate for antero-posterior movement of the meal within the stomach,

Table 11.3 Gastric emptying of three radio-labelled meals (a solid, egg-white based meal, 200 ml *d*-glucose solution and 200 ml physiological saline) in controls, patients with bulimia nervosa, patients with anorexia nervosa receiving a refeeding diet at low weight and after weight restoration, and in a group of patients with anorexia nervosa selecting their own diet

Controls		Bulimia Nervosa	Anorexia nervosa		
			Inpatient low wt	Refeeding wt restored	Self-selection diet
Weight (kg)					
	61.67[a]	66.62[a]	40.8[b]	51.60	45.34[b]
SD	7.9	18.21	5.2	7.07	5.95
N	10	10	12	8	10
Solid meal					
% remaining at 100 min					
	21.1[a]	22.59[a]	30.0[a]	28.38	45.84[b]
SD	14.42	14.5	18.1	18.16	20.38
Glucose meal					
% remaining at 30 min					
	73.88[a]	72.86[a]	73.7[a]	77.25	87.20[b]
SD	11.97	13.40	13.6	6.61	9.46
Saline meal					
% remaining at 30 min					
	37.25	39.24	46.6	57.74	48.15
SD	26.16	24.39	19.5	27.06	28.34

Means with different superscripts are significantly different in an ANOVA including: controls, bulimia nervosa, anorexia nervosa, refeeding diet, low weight, and anorexia nervosa, self-selection diet.

both anterior and posterior scans were acquired every few minutes for 120 minutes after the solid meal. For the liquid meals, scanning was continuous using a single anterior detector for 60 minutes.

In order to determine the influence of each of the aforementioned factors on gastric emptying, five conditions were designated in advance. They were: (1) control subjects ($N = 10$); (2) patients with anorexia nervosa at low weight selecting their own diet ($N = 10$). These patients all had very abnormal diets. Some restricted continuously, while others alternated severe restriction with episodes of bulimia and self-induced vomiting; (3) patients with anorexia nervosa at low weight receiving a substantial diet of at least 2500 kcal per day on an inpatient unit for anorexia nervosa ($N = 12$); (4) patients in group (3), having gained weight on the ward, were retested at the higher weight ($N = 8$); (5) patients (none underweight) suffering from bulimia nervosa, with a history of bulimic symptoms occurring at least once during the past week ($N = 10$).

It was confirmed that delayed gastric emptying indeed occurs in patients with anorexia nervosa. However, only patients in group (2), who were selecting their own diet, were found to have significantly delayed emptying (Table 11.3). After two weeks on the ward refeeding diet, gastric emptying was normal. Weight gain did not affect gastric function, and bulimia nervosa patients (group (5)) had normal gastric emptying. It seemed, therefore, that severe self-starvation was necessary for the appearance of delayed gastric emptying. Moreover, starvation could take the form of food restriction or vomiting of gastric contents as long as the quantity of nutrient passing through the pylorus was sufficiently reduced to result in severe weight loss. It should be noted that the patients with bulimia nervosa who were not underweight had normal gastric emptying so that bulimia and vomiting, if not severe enough to cause emaciation, do not result in delayed gastric emptying. Severe starvation appears to be the key determinant, and similar delays in gastric emptying have been noted in human volunteers on semistarvation diets (Keys *et al.*, 1950) and in rats subjected to a restricted diet which caused their weight to fall by about 15 per cent over four months (Robinson, Shim and Stephenson, 1988). Gastric emptying in the starving anorexic patients was sometimes so slow that a meal could be expected to take 24 hours or more to empty from the stomach. It is likely that this physiological change results in enhanced satiety and exacerbates undereating in anorexia nervosa. It does not, however, necessarily protect patients from episodes of massive overeating, as gastric stasis was observed in underweight bulimic patients. In these patients, delayed emptying would increase the time after a bulimic episode that patients could induce vomiting and dispose of the majority of the ingested food. In this way, changes in gastric emptying as starvation becomes more severe could make vomiting a more efficient means of disposing of ingested food and contribute to further weight loss.

The specificity of the effect of diet and weight on gastric emptying was established in a further way. Delayed emptying was only observed after the mixed solid and the glucose meals. Emptying of saline was normal in all groups. The saline meal differed from the others in two respects: it was acaloric and isotonic to plasma. The solid and glucose meals both contained calories and were hypertonic. Duodenal receptors respond to osmotic pressure and caloric content (Hunt, 1956; Hunt and Stubbs, 1975) and delayed gastric emptying could be mediated by hypersensitivity to either stimulus. The gastric studies demonstrated no disturbance in the latency between the end of the meal and the onset of gastric emptying. This 'lag period' was seen for all meals and was longer after the solid meal compared to the liquid meals. At the onset of the lag period, the solid (labelled) part of the meal was seen in the upper part of the gastric fundus, and during the lag phase food was slowly 'fed' towards the antrum. Abnormal gastric emptying was only seen after nutrient had entered the duodenum, suggesting that an alteration in the sensitivity of duodenal receptors underlies the gastric disturbance observed in anorexia nervosa. Cholecystokinin is released from the duodenum by the arrival of nutrients, particularly fat and protein (Liddle *et al.*, 1985) and the gastrointestinal physiology of this peptide, together with its feeding-inhibitory action, makes it a candidate for mediating the disturbance of gastric function observed in anorexia nervosa.

Pharyngeal and Oesophageal Function in Bulimia Nervosa

Regurgitation of gastric contents (rumination) has been described in a proportion of patients with bulimia nervosa (Fairburn and Cooper, 1984) and it has been suggested that an opioid mechanism might underlie this symptom (Blinder, Bain and Simpson, 1986). During measurement of gastric emptying of solid food it is not unusual in a patient with bulimia nervosa to observe gastro-oesophageal reflux of the solid food (Robinson, 1989). This disturbance may reflect incompetence of the lower oesophageal sphincter secondary to prolonged vomiting and could act to make vomiting easier to induce in patients with bulimia nervosa. In this way, a change in gastrointestinal physiology exacerbates and perpetuates the bulimic disorder. The characteristic aversiveness of the act of vomiting is usually lost in bulimia nervosa, perhaps related to a diminution in pharyngeal sensitivity and a loss of the gag reflex (Robinson, 1987), which appears to act as another change in physiology that perpetuates the eating disorder.

Gastric Perceptivity in Anorexia and Bulimia Nervosa

Delayed gastric emptying in anorexia nervosa presumably leads to undereating by causing feelings of prolonged gastric fullness after meals and there is some evidence that this occurs in anorexic patients (Garfinkel, 1974). To examine whether gastric stasis was associated with subjective evidence of prolonged satiety, subjects in the gastric emptying study described above were asked to complete 10 cm visual analogue scale ratings of fullness, hunger and other states during the scans (Robinson, 1989).

Patients with anorexia nervosa rated themselves as significantly fuller than controls, both before the solid mixed meal and during the following two hours. Ratings of hunger were significantly lower than controls. Absolute ratings of hunger and satiety were not significantly different for patients who had delayed gastric emptying compared to those with normal emptying rate; both groups had evidence of prolonged satiety.

In order to assess the degree to which the subjects were able to sense the degree of gastric fullness, hedonic ratings were correlated with the percentage of the meal remaining at the times the ratings were made. Bruch (1962) suggested that patients with anorexia nervosa have disordered perception or interpretation of signals arising in the stomach. There was no significant difference between controls and anorexic patients in mean values of the correlation coefficient (Spearman's rho) between gastric contents and the rating 'full'. However, the patients did have lower correlations for the ratings 'hungry' and 'urge to eat' than controls, suggesting that, while patients were able to perceive the sensation of gastric fullness, they were unable to process or interpret it. Patients with bulimia nervosa who were not underweight had normal correlations between gastric contents and hunger and satiety ratings, while disturbances were observed in underweight bulimic patients, suggesting a greater degree of disruption of normal satiety as weight declines. In control subjects, gastric contents correlated with hunger and fullness ratings at a level of Spearman's rho of about 0.6, and other ratings that were made of mood, feelings of fatness, nausea and urge to be sick did not show a correlation with gastric contents. In anorexic patients, and in patients with bulimia nervosa, however, these ratings frequently did correlate with the amount of food remaining within the stomach. Thus, one bulimic anorexic patient (Figure 11.3) felt no urge to be sick before the meal, and an extreme urge afterwards which declined over the next two hours, giving a correlation coefficient of ± 0.91 between gastric contents and this rating. Overall, both anorexia nervosa and bulimia nervosa patients were significantly more likely to associate ratings of fatness and urge to be sick with gastric contents and patients with bulimia nervosa also had higher correlations for the scale 'nausea'. The patients were apparently using gastric fullness as an indicator of their symptoms, which were triggered by eating and declined with gastric emptying. The abnormal association of gastric contents (or, indeed, of any visceral signal) with a morbid symptom may be termed 'paraceptivity' (distorted perceptivity).

Summary and Conclusions

Modulation of gastric emptying rate is an important factor in the control of food intake. The putative satiety peptide cholecystokinin acts, at least in part, by inhibiting gastric emptying and this action is probably mediated by specific pyloric receptors for CCK. These receptors are present before birth, in contrast to brain CCK receptors, which develop, in the rat, over the first two weeks of life, and the gastric CCK receptors are likely to represent the main site of action for CCK satiety in the neonate. In adults, the gastric inhibitory action of CCK contributes significantly to its satiety effect.

Fenfluramine also exerts part of its feeding inhibitory action by reducing the rate of gastric emptying, although the precise mechanism for this action is uncertain and the demonstration that fenfluramine reduces bulimic symptoms in bulimia nervosa suggests a possible therapeutic approach to the disorder which has been pursued, with equivocal results, in a controlled trial of the *d*-isomer of fenfluramine (Russell *et al.*, 1988).

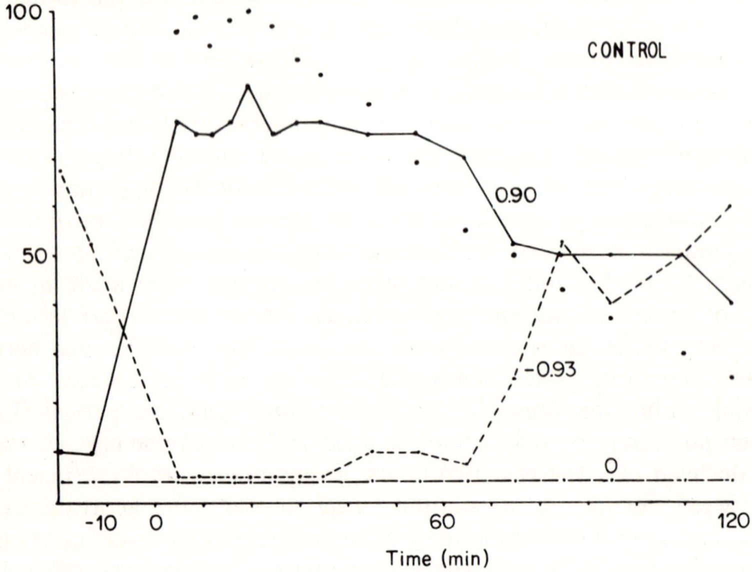

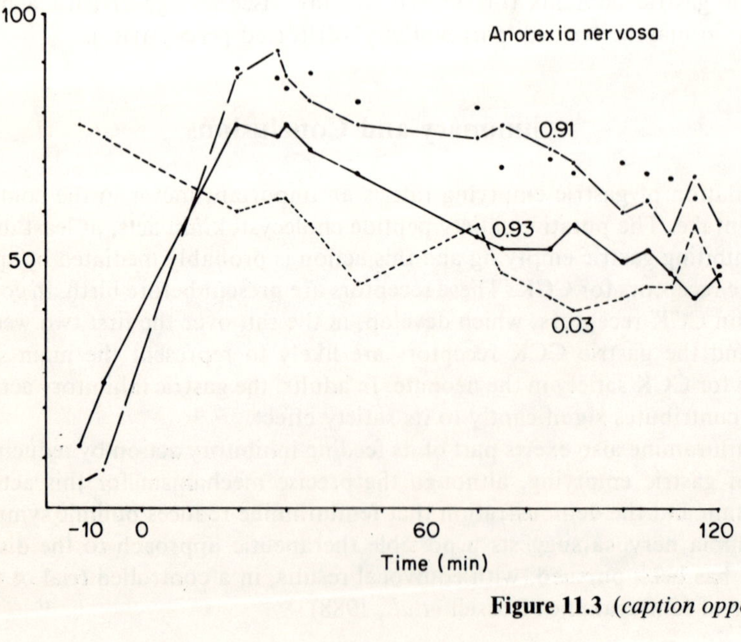

Figure 11.3 (*caption opposite*)

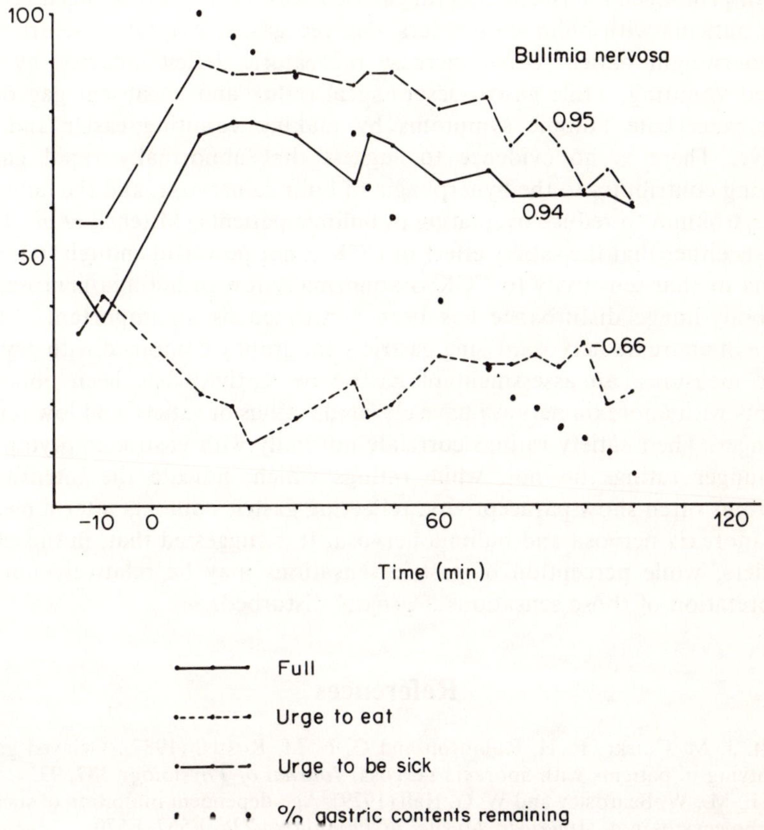

Figure 11.3. Time–activity curves for gastric emptying from three subjects with superimposed VAS scores from the same subjects. Correlation coefficients (Spearman's rho) between gastric counts and VAS are given. Gastric contents are indicated by dots. Fullness is accurately perceived by the three groups. Urge to eat is appropriately rated by controls and patients with bulimia nervosa and urge to be sick is related to gastric contents for both patients but not controls

Delayed gastric emptying has also been demonstrated in patients with anorexia nervosa who were acutely starving, but not those on a refeeding diet, and the replication of this finding in rats given a restricted diet suggests that delayed gastric emptying may be a general characteristic of starvation. This has implications not only for undereating in anorexia nervosa, which may well be exacerbated by delayed gastric emptying, but for the general problem of starvation, which may be complicated by acute gastric dilatation and in which gastric emptying and satiety merit further study. It may be that satiety is modulated, *via* gastric emptying, by the available food supply, so that during times of prolonged intermeal interval gastric stasis results in prolonged satiety.

For patients with bulimic disorders, delayed gastric emptying occurring in an underweight patient could increase the caloric deficit incurred by self-induced vomiting, while gastro-oesophageal reflux and an absent gag reflex might exacerbate bulimic symptoms by making vomiting easier and less aversive. There is no evidence to suggest that abnormally rapid gastric emptying contributes to the hyperphagia of bulimia nervosa, and the failure of cholecystokinin to reduce overeating in bulimic patients (Mitchell *et al.*, 1986) suggests either that the satiety effect of CCK is not powerful enough to inhibit bulimia or that sensitivity to CCK is abnormally low in bulimia nervosa.

A body-image disturbance has been confirmed as an important clinical feature in anorexia nervosa. Using gastric scintigraphy combined with psychometric measures, an assessment of gastric perceptivity has been obtained. Patients with anorexia nervosa have elevated ratings of satiety and low ratings of hunger. Their satiety ratings correlate normally with gastric emptying rate but hunger ratings do not, while ratings which indicate the intensity of symptoms often show paraceptivity, reflecting gastric contents after a meal in both anorexia nervosa and bulimia nervosa. It is suggested that, in the eating disorders, while perception of gastric sensations may be relatively normal, interpretation of those sensations is grossly disturbed.

References

Barrett, J. M. Clarke, P. H. Robinson and G. F. M. Russell (1987). Delayed gastric emptying in patients with anorexia nervosa. *Journal of Physiology* **387**, 92.

Blass, E. M., W. Beardsley and W. G. Hall (1979). Age-dependent inhibition of suckling by cholecystokinin. *American Journal of Physiology* **236**, E567–E570.

Blinder, B. J., N. Bain and R. Simpson (1986). Evidence for an opioid neurotransmission mechanism in adult rumination. *American Journal of Psychiatry* **143**, 225.

Brooks, P. A. and J. S. Kelly (1985). Cholecystokinin as a potent excitant of neurons of the dentate gyrus of rats. *Annals of the New York Academy of Sciences*. **448**, 361–374.

Bruch, H. (1962). Perceptual and conceptual disturbances in anorexia nervosa. *Psychosomatic Medicine* **24**, 187–194.

Davies, R. F., J. Rossi III, J. Panksepp, N. Bean and A. I. Zolovick (1983). Fenfluramine anorexia: a peripheral locus of action. *Physiology and Behavior* **30**, 723–730.

Dockray, G. J. (1977). Immunoreactive component resembling cholecystokinin octapeptide in intestine. *Nature* **270**, 359–361.

Dubois, A., H. A. Gross, M. H. Ebert, and D. O. Castell (1979). Altered gastric emptying and secretion in primary anorexia nervosa. *Gastroenterology* **77**, 319–323.

Duhault, J., L. Beregi, P. Gonnard and M. Boulanger (1978). Brain serotonergic systems and anorectic drugs. In *Central Mechanisms of Anorectic Drugs*, ed. by S. Garattini and R. Samanin. Raven Press, New York, pp. 205–215.

Fairburn, C. G. and S. J. Cooper (1984). Rumination in bulimia nervosa. *British*

Medical Journal **228**, 826–827.
Garcha, G. S., P. R. McHugh, T. H. Moran, P. H. Robinson and J. D. Stephenson (1987). Development of cholecystokinin receptors and suppression of ingestion and gastric emptying in the rat. *Journal of Physiology* **387**, 93.
Garfinkel, P. E. (1974). Perception of hunger and satiety in anorexia nervosa. *Psychological Medicine* **4**, 309–315.
Garfinkel, P. E., H. Moldofsky and D. M. Garner (1980). The heterogeneity of anorexia nervosa: bulimia as a distinct subgroup. *Archives of General Psychiatry* **37**, 1036–1040.
Gaudreau, P., S. St-Pieree, C. B. Pert and R. Quirion (1985). Cholecystokinin receptors in mammalian brain. *Annals of the New York Academy of Sciences* **448**, 198–219.
Gibbs, J., J. D. Falasco and P. R. McHugh (1976). Cholecystokinin-decreased food intake in rhesus monkeys. *American Journal of Physiology* **230**, 15–18.
Gibbs, J., R. C. Young and G. P. Smith (1973a). Cholecystokinin decreases food intake in rats. *Journal of Comparative Physiology and Psychology* **84**, 488–495.
Gibbs, J., R. C. Young and G. P. Smith (1973b). Cholecystokinin elicits satiety in rats with open gastric fistulas. *Nature* **245**, 323–325.
Hays, S. E., S. H. Houston, M. C. Beinfeld and S. M. Paul (1981). Postnatal ontogeny of cholecystokinin receptors in rat brain. *Brain Research* **213**, 237–241.
Holt, S., M. J. Ford, S. Grant and R. C. Heading (1981). Abnormal gastric emptying in primary anorexia nervosa. *British Journal of Psychiatry* **139**, 550–552.
Horowitz, M., P. J. Collins, V. Tuckwell, J. Vernon-Roberts and D. J. C. Shearman (1985). Fenfluramine delays gastric emptying of solid food. *British Journal of Clinical Pharmacology* **19**, 849–851.
Hunt, J. N. (1956). Some properties of an alimentary osmoreceptor mechanism. *Journal of Physiology* **132**, 267–283.
Hunt, J. N. and D. F. Stubbs (1975). The volume and energy content of meals as determinants of gastric emptying. *Journal of Physiology* **245**, 209–225.
Innis, R. B and S. H. Snyder (1980). Distinct cholecystokinin receptors in brain and pancreas. *Proceedings of the National Academy of Sciences USA* **77**, 6917–6921.
Keys, A., J. Brozck, A. Henschel, O. Michelson and H. Taylor (1950). *The Biology of Human Starvation*. University of Minnesota Press, Minneapolis.
Kissileff, H. R., F. X. Pi-Sunyer, J. Thornton and G. P. Smith (1982). C-terminal octapeptide of cholecystokinin decreases food intake in man. *American Journal of Clinical Nutrition* **34**, 154–160.
Kraly, F. S. (1984). Vagotomy does not alter cholecystokinin's inhibition of sham feeding. *American Journal of Physiology* **246**, R829–R831.
Kyriakides, M. and T. Silverstone (1979). A double-blind comparison of fenfluramine and dextroamphetamine on feeding behaviour in man. *Current Medical Research Opinions* **6**, Suppl. 1, 180–187.
Liddle, R. A., I. D. Goldfine, M. S. Rosen, R. A. Taplitz and J. A. Williams (1985). Cholecystokinin bioactivity in human plasma. *Journal of Clinical Investigation.* **75**, 1144–1152.
Mitchell, J. E., D. E. Laine, J. E. Morley and A. S. Levine (1986). Naloxone but not CCK-8 may attenuate binge-eating behavior in patients with the bulimia syndrome. *Biology and Psychiatry* **21**, 1399–1406.
Moran, T. H. and P. R. McHugh (1982). Cholecystokinin suppresses food intake by inhibiting gastric emptying. *American Journal of Physiology* **242**, R491–R497.
Moran T. H., P. H. Robinson and P. R. McHugh (1985). The pyloric cholecystokinin receptors: a site of mediation for satiety? *Annals of the New York Academy of Sciences* **448**, 621–623.
Moran, T. H., P. H. Robinson, M. Goldrich and P. R. McHugh (1986). Two brain

CCK receptors: implications for behavioral actions. *Brain Research* **362**, 175–179.

Passaro, E., H. Debas, W. Oldendorf and T. Yamada (1982). Rapid appearance of intraventricularly administered neuropeptides in the peripheral circulation. *Brain Research* **241**, 335–340.

Robinson, P. H. (1989). Perceptivity and paraceptivity in anorexia and bulimia nervosa. *British Journal of Psychiatry* **154**, 400–405.

Robinson, P. H. (1989). Control of food intake in eating disorders. In *Principles and Practice of Biological Psychiatry*, ed. by T. Dinan. Clinical Neuroscience, London.

Robinson, P. H. and L. Grossi (1987). Gag reflex in bulimia nervosa (Letter). *Lancet* **ii**, 221.

Robinson, P. H., S. A. Checkley and G. F. M. Russell (1985). Suppression of eating by fenfluramine in patients with bulimia nervosa. *British Journal of Psychiatry* **146**, 169–176.

Robinson, P. H., M. Clarke and J. Barrett (1988). Determinants of delayed gastric emptying in anorexia nervosa and bulimia nervosa. *Gut* **29**, 458–464.

Robinson, P. H., T. H. Moran, M. Goldrich and P. R. McHugh (1987). Development of cholecystokinin receptors in rat upper gastro-intestinal tract. *American Journal of Physiology* **252** (*Gastrointestinal and Liver Physiology* 15): G529–G534.

Robinson, P. H., T. H. Moran and P. R. McHugh (1988). Cholecystokinin inhibits independent ingestion in neonatal rats. *American Journal of Physiology* **255** (*Regulatory Integrative Comparative Physiology* 24): R14–R20.

Robinson, P. H., T. H. Moran and P. R. McHugh (1986). Inhibition of gastric emptying and feeding by fenfluramine. *American Journal of Physiology* **250** (*Regulatory Integrative Comparative Physiology* 19): R764–R769.

Robinson, P. H., J. I. Shim and J. S. Stephenson (1988). Delayed gastric emptying in rats caused by dietary restriction. *Journal of Physiology* **398**, 62.

Rowland, N. and J. Carlton (1984). Inhibition of gastric emptying by peripheral and central fenfluramine in rats: correlation with anorexia. *Life Sciences* **34**, 2495–2499.

Russell, G. F. M. (1966). Acute dilatation of the stomach in a patient with anorexia nervosa. *British Journal of Psychiatry* **112**, 203–207.

Russell, G. F. M. (1979). Bulimia nervosa: an ominous variant of anorexia nervosa. *Psychological Medicine* **9**, 429–448.

Russell, G. F. M., S. A. Checkley, J. Feldman and I. Eisler (1988). A controlled trial of d-fenfluramine in bulimia nervosa. *Clinical Neuropharmacology* **11** (Suppl. 1): in press.

Shaw, M. J., J. J. Hughes, J. E. Morley, A. S. Levine, S. E. Silvis and R. B. Shafer (1985). Cholecystokinin octapeptide action on gastric emptying and food intake in normal and vagotomized man. *Annals of the New York Academy of Sciences* **448**, 640–641.

Smith, G. P. and J. Gibbs (1984). The satiety effect of cholecystokinin: recent progress and current problems. *Annals of the New York Academy of Sciences* **448**, 417–423.

Smith, G. P., C. Jerome, B. J. Cushin, R. Eterno and K. J. Simansky (1981). Abdominal vagotomy blocks the satiety effect of cholecystokinin in the rat. *Science* **213**, 1036–1037.

Smith, G. P., C. Jerome and R. Norgren (1985). Afferent axons in abdominal vagus mediate satiety effect of cholecystokinin in rats. *American Journal of Physiology* **249**, R638–R641.

Smith, G. T., T. H. Moran, J. T. Coyle, M. J. Kuhar, T. L. O' Donahue and P. R. McHugh (1984). Anatomic localization of cholecystokinin receptors to the pyloric sphincter. *American Journal of Physiology* **246** (*Regulatory Integrative Comparative Physiology* 15): R127–R130.

Sturdevant, R. and H. Goetz (1976). Cholecystokinin both stimulates and inhibits human food intake. *Nature* **261**, 713–715.

Vanderhaegen, J.-J., J. C. Signeau and W. Gepts (1975). New peptide in the vertebrate CNS reacting with antigastrin antibodies. *Nature* **257**, 604–605.

Wislocki, G. B. and T. J. Putnam (1920). Note on the anatomy of the areae postremae. *Anatomical Record* **19**, 281–287.

Zarbin, M. A., J. K. Wamsley, R. B. Innis and M. J. Kuhar (1981). Cholecystokinin receptors: presence and axonal flow in the rat vagus nerve. *Life Sciences* **29**, 697–705.

12

Perception of satiety in bulimia (nervosa)

Katherine A. Halmi
Cornell University Medical College, New York

The patterns of eating and weight changes in bulimia nervosa patients indicate that an aberration may be present in the perception of satiety in these patients. It is of interest to note that periods of food restriction are the most common precipitant to the development of bulimia (Fairburn and Cooper, 1984). Periods of food restriction or dieting are not uncommon and surveys have shown that almost all women have dieted or are dieting during the primary age of risk for developing an eating disorder (between the ages of 12 and 40) (Nylander, 1971). Of all these women, less than 3 per cent develop the psychiatric diagnosis of bulimia nervosa (Stangler and Printz, 1980). The question is, what is unique about the individual who goes on to develop bulimia nervosa? Slade (1982) has succinctly categorized disturbances such as adolescent conflicts, interpersonal problems, stress and failure experiences, dissatisfaction with life and self, and perfectionistic tendencies as being common premorbid factors in women whose initial dieting develops into bulimia nervosa. Obviously, these premorbid conditions are not unique to bulimia nervosa patients. It is reasonable to hypothesize, therefore, that an impairment in physiological mechanisms that regulate food intake is present in bulimia nervosa.

Bulimia nervosa patients begin eating, lose control, or rather do not experience satiety, and eat anything in the range 2000–10 000 kcal, purge and then starve until the next binge–purge episode. Somehow normal-weight bulimics eat enough between purges or absorb enough during the bingeing episodes to maintain a normal weight. The bingeing behavior or bulimia becomes a well-established chronic eating behavior pattern. It seems reasonable to suspect that the mechanism of satiety which ends a meal is impaired in bulimia nervosa patients.

Based on the observation that animals with satiety center (paraventricular and medial hypothalamic) lesions overeat only when their food is palatable and become anorectic when its taste or other sensory properties is mildly aversive, Grossman (1979) formulated the 'hedonic disinhibition hypothesis'. An impairment to the satiety center is associated with exaggerated affective reactions and exaggerated response to hedonic factors. Satiety is a relative rather than absolute phenomenom which takes hedonic as well as nutritive considerations into account. A more extensive discussion of the physiological and pharmacological aspects of satiety is presented in other chapters of this volume.

Identification of disturbances in these psychological processes of satiety could provide cogent clues for impaired central mechanisms. These clues could be followed up more specifically with pharmacological perturbation tests, which could provide pertinent information needed to develop effective treatment interventions for bulimia nervosa. Differences in the detection of satiety and the effect of pharmacological perturbations on satiety could best be assessed with a test meal paradigm. In this chapter, some careful documentations of satiety perceptions in test meal paradigms in bulimic patients and control subjects will be described.

There is a high association of taste preferences with food intake (Drewnowski, Gruen and Grinker, 1982). Normal-weight bulimics may well have taste preferences that are similar to obese subjects who prefer mixtures with a high percentage of lipids compared with normal-weight adults (Drewnowski and Greenwood, 1983). Impairment of central mechanisms regulating feeding behavior may be reflected in taste preferences. We know from animal studies that some lateral hypothalamic cells alter their rate of firing in response to the taste of a palatable food and fire with a background rate that is correlated with food deprivation (Nishino, 1982). There is a possibility that the foods the patient selects to overeat may represent specific taste preferences which, in turn, could be related to specific satiety impairments. These specific taste preferences may provide a clue to which neurotransmitter system is primarily involved with the bingeing. Because of the relationship of taste preferences to eating, some taste preference studies in bulimics will also be presented in this chapter.

Satiety Studies

In order to study the hypothesis that bulimic patients may have an impairment of the perception of satiety, Owen *et al.* (1985) devised an experiment during which the patients and control subjects marked how hungry they were and how full they were before, during and after a test meal which consisted of a liquid formula. The subjects marked how hungry and full they were on 10 cm scales that were marked 'not at all hungry' at one end and 'extremely hungry' at the other and 'not at all full' at one end and 'extremely full' at the other. They made these ratings every two minutes. Underweight anorectic patients were tested during their first week of admission to a hospital treatment program when they were emaciated. They were tested again after weight restoration and at a time when they were eating normally. Bulimic patients were tested during their first week of admission to the hospital and after treatment when they were eating normally and no longer purging. The liquid formula was in a large glass cylinder which was connected to a tube and a straw for the patients to suck through. They were tested twice on admission and twice after treatment. In the first testing, half of the patients were allowed to watch the liquid formula go down the glass cylinder. The other half of the patients were not able to see the liquid formula in the glass cylinder because it was covered from view. In the second testing, patients who watched the liquid in the cylinder were now unable to watch it because it was hidden from view, and likewise those who had previously been unable to watch the liquid go down the cylinder were now able to do so. The same pair of experiments was conducted on admission and at the time of discharge from the hospital treatment program.

There were both quantitative and qualitative differences in the hunger and satiety responses between the eating disorder patients and the control subjects. These responses were examined in three types of eating disorder patients: anorectic restrictors ($N = 23$), anorectic bulimics ($N = 17$), normal-weight bulimics ($N = 12$), and controls ($N = 16$).

The normal-weight bulimics consumed significantly less than the anorectics and normal controls during the pretreatment testing period. This may be due to the fact that bulimics rarely eat normal meals and alternate between binge episodes and severe food restriction. After treatment, the bulimic patients significantly increased the calorie consumption during this test meal. Perhaps this reflects the beneficial effect of treatment. The bulimic patients at this time were no longer binge-eating and therefore may have felt more comfortable in taking in a larger amount of calories during a scheduled meal.

Palatability was assessed by the patients on 10-cm visual analog scales similar to the scales for hunger and fullness. Palatability ratings did not have a consistent effect on meal consumption. When the patients were ill before treatment, there was no relationship between patients' diagnosis and degree of palatability. After treatment, however, the anorectics had lower palatability rating of the meal compared with the bulimic patients and normal control subjects. Most likely this reflects a general tendency on the part of anorectic patients to be cautious of their caloric intake.

All eating disorder patients scored higher on 'restrained eating' than controls during pretreatment. After treatment, there was no difference in the amount of restrained eating between the patients and control subjects.

The amount of test meal consumed had no relationship to hunger and satiety levels in the pretreatment period. Hunger levels were related to diagnosis only in the pretreatment period. The anorectic restrictors had lower premeal, postmeal and 12-minute postmeal hunger levels compared to the other groups. Whether the food was hidden from view or whether it could be observed had no consistent effect on the patients' and controls' ratings on hunger and fullness.

Satiety levels during pretreatment were related to diagnosis. The anorexia nervosa patients had higher satiety levels compared to the other groups. The anorectic patients began a meal and ended a meal feeling more full than the other groups. This may represent a denial of hunger feelings. There was an exception of five anorectic patients who took in a large amount of calories during the pretreatment test meal. These patients were 'not at all full' at the beginning of the meal, but they did end the meal feeling very full. The five patients who took in the large caloric meal were the most severely emaciated of the anorectic restrictors. It is possible their physiological state overrode their wish to restrict caloric intake and they lost control of their perceptual denial of hunger and fullness.

After treatment, there were no differences in satiety levels among the eating disorder subgroups and control subjects. Satiety levels at this time were related only to the amount consumed. The difference in satiety levels among patient subgroups and controls before treatment may be related to the difference in weight status and/or the 'cognitive set' or degree of denial of hunger and satiety.

The hunger and satiety curves generated from the ratings every two minutes were inversely proportional in normal control subjects (Owen *et al.*, 1985). As the meal progressed, the control subjects' hunger curve dropped so that at the end of the meal they were 'not at all hungry' and stayed this way for 20 minutes. In contrast, their fullness or satiety curves were very low before the meal and increased during the meal so that at the end of the meal they were extremely full and stayed in this condition for 20 minutes. The bulimic patients' curves were disturbed both before and after treatment. In fact, treatment seemed to have little effect on the bulimic patients' curves. Most bulimics had flat curves extending from before, throughout and after the meal. That is, they had very little dip in their hunger curve during the meal and stayed very hungry throughout the meal and after the end of the meal. Likewise, they had very little dip in their satiety curve during the meal and stayed not at all full after the end of the meal. Some of the bulimics who had a little dip in their hunger curve had a rapid hunger rebound near the end of the meal or shortly after the end of the meal. This was particularly true of the anorectic bulimics. It is of interest to note that restoration to a normal weight had no effect on the satiety curves of the anorectic bulimic patients. If the satiety responses in bulimics are stable over a long period of time, even when the bulimics have recovered from their binge-eating behavior, then it is reasonable to assume that the disturbed perception of satiety may be a trait associated with the diagnosis of bulimia nervosa.

In another study of hunger perceptions and satiety responses comparing bulimia nervosa patients with healthy controls, Chiodo and Latimer (1986) had subjects fill out a hunger–satiety questionnaire before and after eating an ice-cream sundae. In this study, the bulimics reported feelings of irritability, nervousness, tenseness and depression which lasted 30 minutes after eating the calorie-dense ice-cream sundae. It is not possible to determine whether these feelings and sensations represented hunger, fullness, or neither. Since bulimics tend to binge on calorie-dense foods, it is likely the one hot fudge ice-cream sundae stimulated their urge to binge.

Kissileff, Walsh and Krall (1987) successfully conducted laboratory studies of eating behavior in eight women with normal-weight bulimia. All patients ate to excess when asked and all vomited following the meal.

Two other studies by Mitchell and Laine (1985) and Kaye, Gwirtsman and George (1989) studied the composition of bulimic binges in laboratory settings. The composition of the binges was surprisingly similar in all three of the above studies and resembled the average American diet (46 per cent carbohydrate, 42 per cent fat, and 12 per cent protein). All of these studies indicated that the bulimics seemed to consume more as they ate rather than less. This suggests that bulimic patients have a disorder of satiety.

Taste Studies

Preference for sweetness and 'fattiness' in eating disorder patients was tested in a taste study by Drewnowski, Halmi and Pierce (1987). The aim of this testing was to track the oral perception of sweetness and fat content using a model system that was both palatable and bore a resemblance to real foods. Taste stimuli included commercially available mixtures of milk with varying degrees of fat content to which were added different amounts of sucrose. Thus, two solutions of skim milk (0.1 per cent fat wt/wt), whole milk (3.5 per cent), half and half (10. 5 per cent), heavy cream (37.6 per cent) and heavy cream blended with a 15 per cent admixture of safflower oil (50 per cent fat wt/wt) were added for sucrose levels. The four sucrose levels were 0 per cent wt/wt, 5 per cent, 10 per cent and 20 per cent. The subjects spat out each solution after tasting it and rinsed their mouth with distilled water before tasting the next solution.

Bulimic, anorectic and normal controls were asked to taste each solution and rate it on the degree of sweetness, degree of fattiness and how much they liked the solution. All these ratings were made on nine-point scales.

There were no significant differences in the perceived sweetness intensity or fat content among the eating disorder patients and normal controls prior to treatment. Treatment had no effect on estimates of sweetness intensity and fat content. Neither did treatment have an effect on hedonic response profiles. Individual preferences for sweetness and fat were not systematically influenced by weight gain to target levels or by the sensation of bingeing and vomiting in the bulimic patients.

Both normal-weight bulimic patients and anorectic patients preferred sweeter stimuli compared with volunteer controls. Underweight anorectic patients preferred stimuli of lower fat content compared with normal controls. There were no differences in the optimal preferred fat preference between normal-weight bulimic patients and controls.

This taste study showed that patients with eating disorders have no deficits in sensory perception of increasing sweetness and fatty stimuli. Underweight anorectic restrictors and anorectic bulimics disliked intense 'fat' taste measured by the magnitude of their preference for high-fat stimuli relative to that of control subjects. Anorectic restrictor and anorectic bulimic patients showed significantly larger sweet/fat ratios than did controls, reflecting elevated preference for sweetness relative to fat stimuli. No significant differences in taste response profiles or hedonic optima were obtained even following an average gain of 10.6 kg, suggesting that taste responsiveness may not be tied directly to acute changes in body weight. Taste profile may be a highly enduring characteristic of individuals with eating disorders. Identification of factors responsible for sensory preferences may have important implications for nutritional intervention strategies in bulimia patients. It may be that the pattern of sensory responsiveness to sweetness and fat during childhood or early adolescence predates changes in body weight and serves as a psychobiological early marker for eating disorders.

Garfinkel, Moldofsky and Garner (1978) showed in an earlier study that anorexia nervosa patients had an absence of satiety aversion to sucrose or 'sweet taste' using the Cabanac testing method. This absence of satiety aversion to sucrose was stable at a one-year follow-up and was not affected by significant weight gain to normal levels.

In summary, all of these studies seem to indicate a disturbance of satiety in bulimic patients. But what is the nature of this disturbance? For example, how much does the 'cognitive set' or attitudes about food influence the actual consumption of foods and perception of satiety? Are specific macronutrients such as carbohydrates or fats or combinations of these especially effective in stimulating binge-eating in bulimics?

Hill, Magson and Blundell (1984) found that the ratings of hunger and desire to eat two hours after consumption of highly preferred food were significantly higher compared to those ratings after eating a less preferred food. All of these healthy subjects tracked hunger and satiety or fullness ratings in curves that were inversely proportional and similar to the ratings by controls in the Owen *et al.* (1985) study. In the Hill, Magson and Blundell study (1984), preferred foods seemed to stimulate hunger. Studies measuring the influence of both 'cognitive set' and macronutrient content of foods on satiety responses in bulimics compared with control subjects should provide useful information for treatment strategies including both nutritional counseling and pharmacological interventions.

References

Chiodo, J. and P. Latimer (1986). Hunger perceptions and satiety responses among normal-weight bulimics and normals to a high calorie, carbohydrate rich food. *Psychological Medicine* **16**, 343–349.

Drewnowski, A. and M. Greenwood (1983). Cream and sugar: human preferences for high fat foods. *Physiology and Behavior* **30**, 629–633.

Drewnowski, A., R. Gruen and J. Grinker (1982). Carbohydrates, sweet taste and obesity: changing consumption patterns and health implication. In *Basic Symposium on Food Carbohydrates*, ed. by D. R. Lineback and G. E. Inglett. AVI Publishing, New York.

Drewnowski, A., K. Halmi, and B. Pierce (1987). Taste and eating disorders. *American Journal of Clinical Nutrition* **46**, 442–450.

Fairburn, C. and E. Cooper (1984). The clinical features of bulimia nervosa. *British Journal of Psychiatry* **144**, 238–246.

Garfinkel, P., H. Moldofsky and D. Garner (1978). Body awareness in anorexia nervosa: disturbances in body image and satiety. *Psychosomatic Medicine* **40**, 487–497.

Grossman, S. (1979). The biology of motivation. *Annual Review of Psychology* **30**, 209–242.

Hill, A., L. Magson and J. Blundell (1984). Hunger and palatability: tracking rating of subjective experience before, during and after the consumption of preferred and less preferred foods. *Appetite* **5**, 361–371.

Kaye, W., H. Gwirtsman and T. George (1989). Relationship of mood alterations to bingeing behavior in bulimia. *British Journal of Psychiatry*, in press.

Kissileff, H., T. Walsh and J. Krall (1987). Laboratory studies of eating behavior of women with bulimia. *Physiology and Behavior* **38**, 563–570.

Mitchell, J. and D. Laine (1985). Monitored binge-eating behavior in patients with bulimia. *International Journal of Eating Disorders* **4**, 177–184.

Nishino, H. (1982). Lateral hypothalamic neuron activity during monkey bar press feeding: modulation by glucose, morphine, and naloxone. In *The Neurobasis of Feeding and Reward*, ed. by B. Hoebel and D. Noven. Hair Institute, Brunswick, Maine, pp. 355–372.

Nylander, I. (1971). The feeling of being fat and dieting in a school population: epidemiological interview investigation. *Acta Psychologica Medica Scandinavica* **3**, 17–26.

Owen, W., K. Halmi, J. Gibbs and G. Smith (1985). Satiety responses in eating disorders. *Journal of Psychiatric Research* **19**, 279–284.

Slade, P. (1982). Towards a functional analysis of anorexia nervosa and bulimia nervosa. *British Journal of Clinical Psychology* **21**, 176–179.

Stangler, R. and A. Printz (1980). DSM-III: psychiatric diagnosis in a university population. *American Journal of Psychiatry* **137**, 937–940.

13

Psychopharmacology of hunger and satiety

John E. Blundell, Clare L. Lawton, Andrew J. Hill
and
Peter J. Rogers
University of Leeds, Leeds

The way in which drugs and other chemical agents affect the expression of hunger and food consumption is becoming increasingly important in these last decades of the twentieth century. An understanding of the psychopharmacology of hunger has theoretical and practical significance. First, drugs may be used as tools to investigate the neurochemical and physiological mechanisms involved in appetite control. One way to conceptualize this is to consider drugs as pharmacological scalpels which may be used to dissect the structure of eating behaviour and conscious experiences. Under appropriate experimental circumstances, drugs can be used with a degree of finesse to disclose salient features of the biopsychological systems underlying the manifestation of appetite (e.g. Blundell, 1980, 1984a). Secondly, drugs may have an important role to play in the treatment of disorders of eating and body weight. Obesity is a major social–medical problem in the affluent economic cultures of Western Europe and North America. There is no safe, certain and reliable treatment for obesity and over the years drugs have been used with about as much success as any other form of therapy (e.g. Scoville, 1975). Certain classes of drugs seem particularly promising (e.g. Nathan and Rolland, 1987), and used selectively and judiciously they could probably be made even more effective by tailoring the drug to the needs of the patient (Blundell, 1976). In addition to disorders of overweight, drugs may make specified contributions to the treatment of underweight (e.g. anorexia nervosa, cancer anorexia) and to disorder of appetite, food preferences and eating (e.g. bulimia, bulimanorexia, bulimia nervosa, dietary chaos).

Thirdly, drug effects on appetite may have a more sinister practical significance. There is evidence that three major classes of psychotropic drugs — antipsychotic agents, tranquillizers and hypnotics, and antidepressants — all cause changes in either hunger, food intake or body weight (see Blundell and Rogers, 1978). In general, the changes induced by these drugs involve an augmentation of appetite and increase in body weight. Consequently, serious consideration should be given to the possibility of a subclass of iatrogenic eating or weight problems. Drugs administered for unrelated psychological (or physiological) conditions may induce undetected adjustments leading to unwanted and apparently inexplicable alterations in appetite and body weight.

Taken together, the above considerations draw attention to the importance of adopting an appropriate methodology for investigating the psychopharmacology of hunger. Implications are apparent for the use of drugs at home, in workplaces and in the clinic. The field embraces the use of socially institutionalized drugs such as nicotine and caffeine — both of which have appreciable effects on appetite — illicit drugs such as marijuana and cocaine, and medically prescribed therapeutic agents. It is worth considering how heavy smoking or an excessive intake of caffeine in tea, coffee or soft drinks (colas, lemonade, etc.) could prompt a loss of control over appetite or hinder the maintenance of appetite control in a vulnerable individual. Only some of these issues can be covered in the present chapter. The objective will be to present a conceptual framework and methodology for the scientific study of the psychopharmacology of appetite.

Hunger, Appetite, Satiation and Satiety — a Conceptualization

The terms hunger, appetite, satiation and satiety are widely used in both the scientific literature and non-technical discourse to refer to states and processes which control and guide food consumption. For a full discussion of these issues see Blundell (1979) and Blundell and Burley (1987). It is useful to clarify the use of these terms. Satiation and satiety can be functionally distinguished. Satiation can be regarded as the process which brings a period of eating to a close, whereas satiety is the state of inhibition over further eating once a period of eating has ended. Satiety therefore has a precise technical definition. Although there are many vicarious reasons why eating could be halted, satiety refers only to the inhibition of eating as a result of prior food ingestion. The terms satiation and satiety distinguished above appear to be identical to the notions of 'intrameal satiety' and 'intermeal satiety' defined by Van Itallie and

Vanderweele (1981). In research on animals the operation of these two processes can be distinguished by effects upon meal size (satiation) and intermeal interval (satiety). This distinction can also be used in the description of human eating patterns if the experimental designs permit the disclosure of these effects (see Hill and Blundell, 1986).

The logical status of the term hunger often causes confusion since it is widely used in more than one sense. Hunger is clearly a word which implies a drive or motivational impetus to eat. On the one hand, hunger is a motivational construct with the logical status of a mediating concept or intervening variable (McQuorquodale and Meelh, 1948; Royce, 1963). That is, the term refers to an explanatory principle which itself cannot be directly measured but which is inferred from other observable and measurable events. For example, hunger can be operationally defined as the number of hours since a person or animal was last fed. The number of hours without food therefore quantifies the intensity of the (hunger) drive without reference to any further or physiological phenomena. On the other hand, hunger may be used to refer to certain conscious sensations or feelings linked to a desire to obtain and eat food. This is the sense in which the layman recognizes the notion of hunger and reflects the way in which the term is used in day-to-day discourse. The term is given understanding through a social consensus: that is, use of the term is generally understood as implying a willingness or desire to eat. It is this articulated hunger which researchers attempt to capture by means of rating scales and other devices.

Hunger the motivational construct and hunger the perceived desire to eat can both be seen to be biologically functional. Hunger is a force which impels organisms to seek food to satisfy nutritional requirements. Consciously perceived hunger is one aspect of this and partly exists as detectable physical sensations provoked by physiological events. This may occur in animals but there is no way of revealing this so objective measures of hunger drive are employed (e.g. measuring the amount of effort expanded to obtain food). With humans we can ask directly about hunger feelings.

Hunger and satiety — a clarification

In much of the literature on the control of eating and body-weight regulation, hunger and satiety are used as if they were polar opposites. For example, the question has been posed whether obese people eat because of excessive hunger or defective satiety (e.g. Blundell, 1977a for discussion). This implies that the reason must be one or the other. However, when hunger is used as a motivational construct it can be seen that hunger and satiety really refer to the same process; hunger is the force impelling eating (arising from lack of food) and satiety is the resistance to eating (arising from having eaten). The strengths of hunger and satiety are therefore reciprocally related.

However, in considering hunger the conscious sensation or articulated desire to eat, it is clear that the perception of this feeling can be assessed before eating, during eating or after eating. Therefore the intensity of perceived hunger can reflect the tendency to start eating (hunger construct), the willingness to stop eating (satiation) and the maintenance of inhibition over further eating (satiety). The measured sensation of hunger therefore becomes one index of the strength of satiety. If hunger sensations are weak or low then satiety will be maintained; the restoration of perceived hunger represents the dissipation or weakening of satiety. This conceptualization reflects the different status of these two terms: hunger a conscious sensation and satiety a state or process. Measuring the hunger feeling can therefore be used to evaluate the development of satiation and the durability of satiety. But of course this assessment will be most powerful when combined with the actual measurement of food consumed.

The satiety cascade

Eating food has the capacity to take away hunger and, after satiation has occurred, further eating is inhibited for a period. What mechanisms are responsible for these processes? It is likely that the mechanisms involved in terminating eating and in maintaining inhibition range from those which occur when food is initially sensed to the effects of metabolites following digestion and absorption. By definition, satiety is not an instantaneous event but occurs over a considerable time period; it is therefore useful to distinguish different phases of satiety which can be associated with different mechanisms. This concept is illustrated in Figure 13.1. Four mediating processes are identified: sensory, cognitive, postingestive and postabsorptive. These maintain inhibition over eating (and hunger) during the early and late phases of satiety. Sensory effects are generated through the smell, taste, temperature and texture of food and it is likely that these factors help to bring eating to a halt and inhibit eating (of foods with similar sensory properties) in the short term. Such a mechanism is embodied in the idea of sensory-specific satiety first disclosed by Le Magnen (1960). Cognitive effects represent the beliefs held about the properties of foods and their presumed effect upon the eater and, under certain experimental conditions, they have been demonstrated to operate (e.g. Wooley, 1972). The category identified here as postingestive processes includes a number of possible actions including gastric distension and rate of gastric emptying, the release of hormones such as cholecystokinin from the duodenum, and the stimulation of physicochemically-specific receptors along the gastrointestinal tract (see Mei, 1985). The postabsorptive phase of satiety includes those mechanisms arising from the action of metabolites after absorption across the intestine and into the blood system. This category embraces the actions of chemicals such as glucose and the amino acids which may act directly upon the

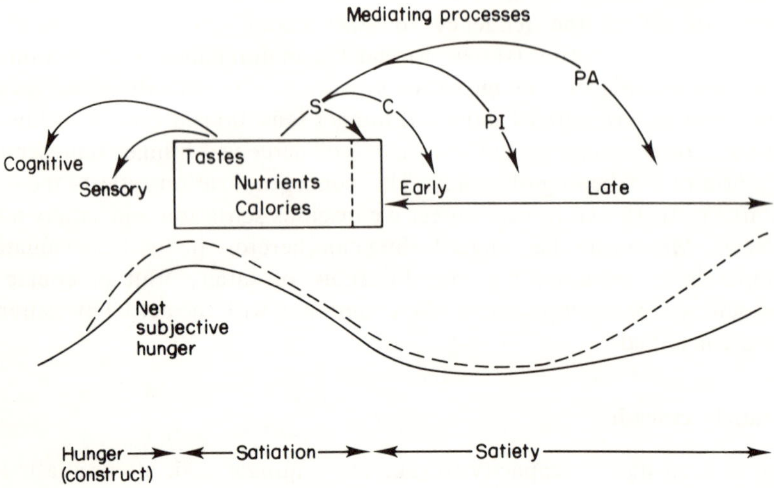

Figure 13.1. Illustration of the major components of the satiety cascade (S, sensory; C, cognitive; PI, postingestive; PA, postabsorptive) and postulated changes in motivation (perceived hunger) accompanying the ingestion of a meal. The diagram also shows the anticipatory effects of food consumption

brain after crossing the blood–brain barrier or which may influence the brain indirectly *via* neural inputs following stimulation of peripheral chemoreceptors.

The approximate anticipated moment of action of these mediating processes is shown in Figure 13.1 but of course the mechanisms will overlap and their effects will be integrated to produce a conjoint effect. It should also be kept in mind that the psychobiological system for appetite control has the capacity to learn, that is, to form associations between the sensory and postabsorptive properties of foods (e.g. Booth, 1977; Le Magnen, 1985). Therefore the sensory aspects of a food may come to predict the absorptive consequences, thereby allowing the sensory-mediating processes to exert an augmented effect.

Role of hunger in food consumption

It is clear that food itself is a potent and natural anorectic substance; eating food takes away our hunger and being deprived of food generally leads to a build-up of hunger (although there are one or two special circumstances where this does not occur). The processes responsible for the inhibition of hunger are shown in Figure 13.1. However, a dilemma arises when foods are produced to deal with a popular demand for low-calorie items in support of an obsession with dieting and slimming. It can be seen from Figure 13.1 that reducing the amount (or nature) of food eaten will weaken those processes (postingestive and postabsorptive) which maintain a low level of hunger and postpone further eating. Changing food composition will alter the capacity of food to influence the satiety cascade. It is well known that casual or planned dieting leads to chronic low levels of hunger and acute intense hunger episodes. This illustrates well the biological function of the hunger sensation, which is to motivate eating. Hunger reminds us that the body requires food. The importance of this is reflected in the nature of hunger; it is a nagging, irritating feeling whose presence constantly serves to stimulate thoughts of food and eating. These attributes of hunger are one reason why casual dieting almost always ends in failure. It appears to be very difficult to cope with unregulated hunger.

Facilitatory and inhibitory effects of foods

The satiety cascade in Figure 13.1 illustrates those processes which mediate the inhibitory effects of food upon further consumption. This diagram also shows that some attributes of food act proactively. These responses are called cephalic phase reflexes and they involve the mouth, stomach, duodenum and lower intestine together with related endocrine glands. In man the sight and smell of food are sufficiently potent to trigger cephalic phase insulin responses (Sjostrom *et al.*, 1980; Simon *et al.*, 1986), and the response in obese subjects is four times that in lean people. The taste of saccharine can provoke a cephalic phase insulin response in rats (Berthoud *et al.*, 1981) and in man (Halter *et al.*, 1975). The stimulus-induced cephalic phase responses are accompanied by an augmentation of the desire to eat. Consequently, one action of salient sensory components of food is to provoke physiological responses which anticipate ingestion and which may facilitate appetite.

Psychopharmacology and the Satiety Cascade

One way to understand the psychopharmacology of hunger is to consider the action of drugs in relation to the satiety cascade. In adjusting hunger or food consumption, drugs act upon mechanisms within the psychobiological system which controls appetite. Food is the natural operator in this system (Blundell, Rogers and Hill, 1987). Consequently, drugs can be conceived as agents which act upon those mechanisms through which food normally expresses its actions. At the physiological or neurochemical level of analysis this means identifying those receptors, pathways, enzymes, hormones, etc., in the periphery of the central nervous system which are modulated by food consumption or a lack of food. At the level of analysis of processes, psychopharmacological agents could modify the sensory, cognitive, postingestive or postabsorptive actions of foods. It is likely that drugs act upon the target organs or receptors through which these processes are mediated. An intensification of the processes of the satiety cascade would lead to a depression of hunger whilst a weakening of the signals or their reception would have the opposite effect — either a maintenance or augmentation of perceived hunger. However, foods also exert facilitatory actions on hunger *via* cephalic phase reflexes. One other way in which drugs could modulate hunger is by amplifying or suppressing the size of these anticipatory cephalic phase responses. In addition, drugs could modify the learned relationships between tastes and metabolic consequences of food.

Accordingly, drawing attention to the processes through which food interacts with the psychobiological appetite systems provides a means of interpreting the action of drugs on hunger.

Which Drugs Alter Appetite?

Laboratory studies have shown that a wide range of chemical agents affect the food consumption of experimental animals (e.g. Blundell, 1987; Blundell and Thurlby, 1987). A suppression of intake is more commonly observed than an elevation. These chemicals include almost all of the common psychotropic drugs which are widely prescribed for various forms of psychopathology. Some drugs have ambivalent effects — increasing or decreasing food intake according to the dose or experimental circumstances. Consequently, drugs are extremely potent agents for altering feeding, and some may produce quite unexpected consequences.

Nicotine

In humans only a limited number of chemicals have received attention but all are of practical or theoretical significance. For example, the compound nicotine has been shown to decrease food intake in experimental animals (Munster and Battig, 1975) and the depressant effect appears to be greater with highly palatable food (Grunberg, Bowen and Morse, 1984). A similar action on sweet-tasting foods occurs in man (Grunberg, 1982). These effects may contribute to the weight-reducing (or weight-maintaining) effects of nicotine and provide a mechanism for the commonly observed increase in appetite and weight gain following the cessation of cigarette smoking.

Classical anorexic drugs

Drugs affecting the biogenic amines probably exert the most dramatic effects on food intake and experimental studies have indicated that there is an interplay between the catecholamines (e.g. Hoebel and Leibowitz, 1981) and serotonin (e.g. Blundell, 1984) within the basal forebrain. Among the drugs which act upon the amine neurotransmitters are the beta-phenylethylamines (see Figure 13.2), which constitute the major class of anorexic agents. The most prominent member of this series is amphetamine but also included are other substituted phenylethylamines such as fenfluramine, which has a contrasting neurochemical profile and pharmacological action (see Silverstone and Kyriakides, 1982 for review). The suppressant effect of amphetamine on subjective hunger using visual analogue rating scales to quantify the strength of hunger generation was formally investigated some 20 years ago (Silverstone and Stunkard, 1968). More recently receptor blocking drugs have been used in conjunction with amphetamine in an attempt to define the specific neurotransmitters involved (Goodall, Trenchard and Silverstone, 1987). Amphetamine will remain a drug of interest until its mode of action is fully understood but its potent effects on other systems militate against its use as a precise tool to investigate the pharmacology of appetite control.

Serotoninergic drugs

Among the anorexic drugs illustrated in Figure 13.2 all but one are believed to exert their effect *via* the catecholaminergic neurotransmitters. The action of fenfluramine is mediated *via* serotonin (e.g. Garattini, 1978). The isolation of the isomers of this drug has produced a compound (*d*-fenfluramine) with greatly enhanced specificity for serotonin neurons (Garattini, Mennini and Samanin, 1987). This agent, together with other drugs acting on serotonin, displays potent anorexic effects. It has been recognized for more than 10 years that the pharmacological activation of serotonin leads to large changes in hunger and food consumption (e.g. Blundell, 1977b; Silverstone and Schuyler, 1975), but the recent disclosure of subtypes of serotonin receptors has stimulated a new era of research on serotonin and feeding. At the present time little is known about the role of the subtypes in the expression of human appetite and eating. Indeed, the 5-HT_{1B} receptor which seems to mediate potent anorexia in animals may not be present in the human brain (Hoyer *et al.*, 1986).

Further interest in serotonin arises from the development of second-generation antidepressant drugs. Classical antidepressant drugs such as amitriptyline have been shown to lead to weight gain with maintenance therapy which subsided when the amitriptyline was stopped (Paykel, Mueller and De la Vergne, 1973). The patients on amitriptyline complained of weight gain and displayed a desire for sweet foods rich in carbohydrate and fat. Similar effects have been described elsewhere (e.g. Harris, Young and Hughes, 1984; Stein, Stein and Linn, 1985). In contrast, more specific uptake blockers (second-generation antidepressants) with a selective action upon serotonin (fluoxetine, fluvoxamine, sertraline, etc.) do not appear to induce weight gain in depressed

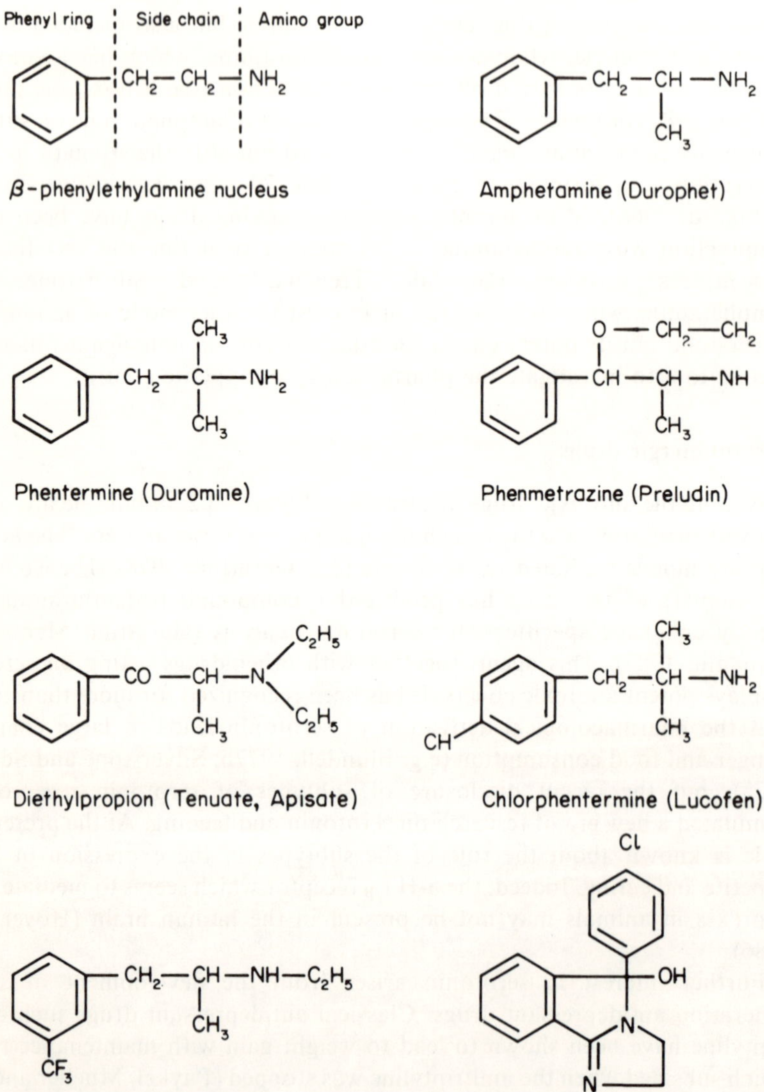

Figure 13.2. Chemical structures and brand names of anorexic drugs

patients and may even promote weight loss. Such an effect would be quite expected from the accepted function of serotonin systems in appetite control. However, in view of the existence of different types of serotonin receptors, it should be kept in mind that drugs stimulating 5-HT_{1A} receptors may well lead to an enhancement of appetite. In animal studies the novel anxiolytic agents gepirone, buspirone and ipsapirone caused an increase in food consumption (Gilbert and Dourish, 1987).

Peptides

In the last decade it has been demonstrated that many peptides present in the central nervous system alter food intake when administered to experimental animals (Morley *et al.*, 1985). These peptides can be divided into those which increase food consumption and those producing inhibition. Of those peptides which enhance intake there is the opioid family and the pancreatic polypeptide group. The latter group includes the very potent agent neuropeptide Y (Clark *et al.*, 1984). Of the inhibitory peptides the most research has been carried out on cholecystokinin. Only a few investigations have been carried out in man.

Considering the opioid group, intravenous injections of the opiate agonist butorphanol tartrate increased food intake but apparently exerted no effect on a crude measure of subjective hunger (Morley, Parker and Levine, 1985). Conversely, it is interesting that naloxone, an opioid receptor antagonist, has been shown to reduce food intake but again caused no significant changes in perceived hunger (Trenchard and Silverstone, 1983). In a 10-week trial of naltrexone (opiate antagonist) in obese subjects, the administration of 100 mg of the compound twice daily did not lead to significantly greater weight loss than placebo (Malcolm *et al.*, 1985). However, it is worth pointing out that in this investigation considerable therapeutic effort was invested in the placebo condition, which included instruction in behaviour modification and nutrition counselling.

The action of opioid agents on food intake but not on subjective hunger is puzzling. However, understanding is advanced by one further study which demonstrated that naltrexone reduced the perceived pleasantness of sucrose (its hedonic value) and diminished the preference for sweet solutions (Fantino, Hosotte and Apfelbaum, 1986). This may indicate that there are two subjective components of the satiety process — a diminution in perceived hunger and a decrease in the perceived pleasantness of food. Elsewhere it has been reported that the serotoninergic drug *d*-fenfluramine reduces hunger but does not influence hedonic value (Blundell and Hill, 1988). Consequently there may be separate opioid and serotoninergic components of the satiety process.

The inhibitory action of gut peptides on eating in humans has been reviewed by Smith and Gibbs (1987). Of the 10 experiments carried out on glucagon, cholecystokinin or bombesin, all but one revealed a reduction in food intake.

The most intensively studied peptide is cholecystokinin. When food intake at a meal is reduced by prior injection of cholecystokinin this does not appear to be followed by later compensatory hunger (Kissileff *et al.*, 1981). The release of cholecystokinin, its action on receptors in the stomach wall and the relay of neural information to the brain *via* the gastric branch of the vagus is one of the likely mechanisms for the mediation of satiety.

Summary

A wide variety of chemicals have been shown to have some effect on food consumption, hunger, food preference or body weight in humans (Table 13.1). Some information has been derived from planned, well-controlled experiments; some has been collected from clinical observation of patients and informal studies. There are three main implications of these data:

1. Drugs can be used as tools to explore the mechanisms underlying the control of food intake, subjective hunger and the processes of satiety.
2. Some drugs have the potential to be used effectively in the treatment of eating disorders
3. The biological system underlying appetite control is vulnerable to the influence of chemicals. It appears that many drugs may produce unexpected and undesirable effects on food intake and the expression of appetite.

Model System for Investigating Drugs and Satiety: A Case Study

It is likely that information about pharmacological effects upon hunger motivation and the satiety process will continue to accumulate through both formal and informal channels. However, knowledge about the role of pharmacological agents in the psychobiological control system underlying appetite will only arise from carefully planned studies with a sound methodology. There is no single unique means of accomplishing this, but we have recently assembled a battery of procedures which provides a way of examining drug-induced changes in subjective motivation, the pattern of eating and nutrient intake over varying time periods. The alterations in these structural parameters reveal modifications taking place in the underlying processes of satiation and satiety.

The first study employing this approach involved the serotoninergic drug *d*-fenfluramine (Isomeride). The plan of the investigation is set out in Figure 13.3. The diagram shows that subjects were given test meals on experimental days 1 and 5 together with visual analogue rating scales, bodily sensations questionnaires, food preferences checklists and forced-choice procedures (see

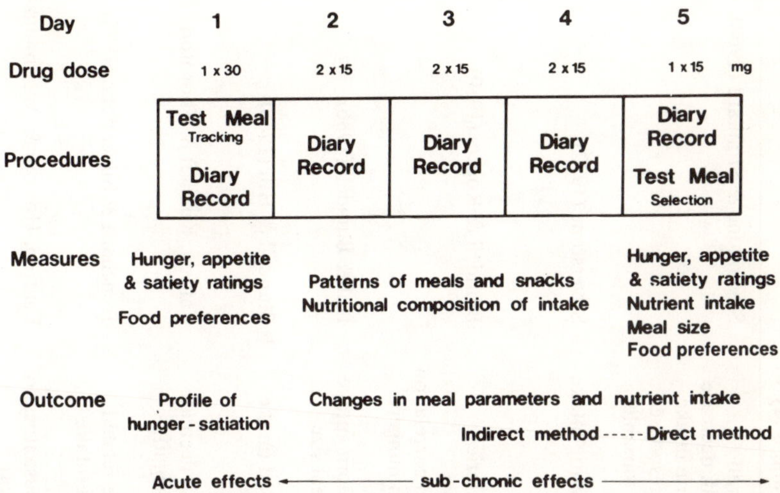

Figure 13.3. Plan of the research model showing the relationship between drug administration, measures of nutrition and behaviour, and the experimental outcome

Blundell and Hill, 1982/3). Subjects were trained to keep accurate diary records of all foods and drinks consumed during the course of the investigation. These records were later analysed to produce profiles of the episodes of eating and patterns of nutrient intakes. The first test meal (day 1) was of fixed size and macronutrient proportions and motivational ratings were carried out before, during and after the meal. This technique is known as temporal tracking (Blundell and Hill, 1985) and provides an indication of the fluctuations in perceived hunger and desire to eat which occur during the act of eating and in the postprandial period (Hill, Magson and Blundell, 1984). The test meal on day 5 was a free-selection meal which contained ample amounts of foods with varying (but precisely known) amounts of carbohydrate, protein and fat. This meal served to indicate the action of the drug on meal and size and selection of macronutrients whilst the first meal revealed the effect of the drug on the profile of hunger during the meal and on the suppression of hunger after eating. The diary records indicated whether the drug produced changes in the number or size of eating episodes and in the consumption of particular nutrients.

The detailed outcome of this investigation has been described elsewhere (Hill and Blundell, 1986; Blundell and Hill, 1987b) but a summary of the major findings is set out in outline form in Figure 13.4. The diagram, derived from

Table 13.1 Effects of some interesting and important chemicals on hunger, food consumption and body weight in man

Chemical	Type of study	Hunger and food preference	Caloric intake and body wt	Authors
Amphetamine 5–20 mg	Lab. expt 16 male subjects	↓ Hunger but great individual variability	Overall signif. decrease calorie intake but responses very variable	Silverstone & Stunkard (1968)
Phentermine 15–30 mg	Lab. expt Six mildly overweight women	Signif. ↓ hunger with 30 mg	↓ Calorie intake	Silverstone (1972)
dl-fenfluramine (Ponderax, Pondermin)	Lab. expt	Signif. ↓ hunger and other sensations (60 mg)	↓ Calorie intake (high correlation with hunger)	Blundell & Rogers (1980)
d-fenfluramine (Isomeride)	Lab. expt Normal wt ss	↓ Hunger (30 mg)	↓ Calorie intake ↓ Meal size	Hill & Blundell (1986)
d-fenfluramine (Isomeride)	Obese ss (BMI > 35)	↓ Hunger (30 mg)	↓ Food intake	Blundell & Hill (1988)
Phenylpropanolamine 37.5 mg	Lab. expt Non-obese women	Small decrease non-signif.	Small decrease non-signif.	Caffrey, Kissileff & Thornton (1987)
Naloxone 0.8 and 1.6 mg i.v.	Lab. expt Normal ss	No effect	Dose-related ↓ food intake	Trenchard & Silverstone (1983)
Naltrexone 120 mg p.o.	Lab. expt Eight healthy adults	Little effect	↓ Pleasantness of sucrose	Fantino, Hosotte & Apfelbaum (1986)
2-deoxy-d-glucose 50 mg/kg	Lab. expt Five males	↑ Hunger ↑ Pleasantness of	Not measured	Thompson & Campbell (1977)

Amitryptiline 100–150 mg	Clinical trial	Little effect on appetite	Marked craving for sweet food correlated with weight gain	Paykel, Mueller & De la Vergne (1973)
Isocarboxazid plus trimipramine	Double-blind clinical trial	↑ Preference for CHO	↑ Body weight gain	Harris, Young & Hughes (1984)
Tricyclic antidepressants	Outpatient treatment, minimum 1 month	38% ↑ appetite 34% ↑ sweet craving	Food pref. related to weight gain	Stein, Stein & Linn (1985)
Chlorpromazine	Exp. study on 32 psychiatric patients	↑ Rating of appetite	Marked gain of body weight	Robinson, McHugh & Folstein (1975)
Cyproheptadine 4 mg t.d.	Lab. study 16 thin ss, four weeks	Signif. ↑ hunger	↑ Food intake, signif. wt gain	Silverstone & Schuyler (1975)
Butorphanol tartrate 1 μg/kg	Lab. expt 10 normal wt ss	No effect	Doubling of food intake in 2 h	Morley *et al.* (1985)
Metergoline 1987	Lab. expt Male subjects	No signif. effect	↑ Intake of sweet food	Goodall & Silverstone (1987)
Tryptophan 0.5, 1.0, 2.0 g	Lab. expt 16 healthy ss	Not reported	↓ Intake (2.0 g)	Silverstone & Goodall (1984)
Tryptophan 1.0 g	Lab. expt	Hunger depends on time	↓ CHO intake after protein meal	Blundell & Hill (1987a)
Phenylalanine up to 10.8 g	Lab. expts	Results variable	Non-signif. ↓ food intake	Fincham, Silverstone & Saha (1977) Silverstone & Goodall (1984) Ryan-Harshman, Leiter & Anderson (1987)

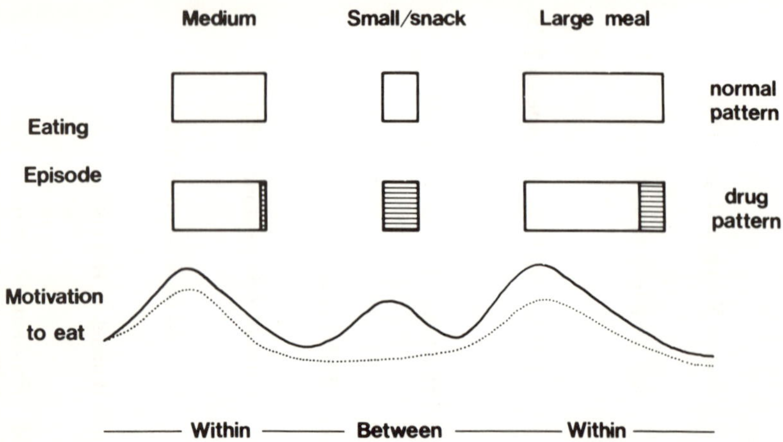

Figure 13.4. Diagrammatic representation of a normal meal pattern of a medium-sized meal, snack and large meal together with the proposed effect of *d*-fenfluramine

measured changes in food intake, eating profiles and hunger motivation, indicates that this drug exerted two major effects on food consumption: first, a reduction in meal size (particularly of large meals) and secondly a decrease in the frequency of small meals and snacks. Accompanying these adjustments in the pattern of eating were fluctuations in the temporal profile of perceived hunger. The drug depressed hunger (and desire to eat) during a meal and maintained this suppression for a considerable period after eating. The postponement of the rehabilitation of hunger after eating coincided with the absence of snacks from the eating repertoire.

This model experimental system has revealed detailed information about the action of this drug (*d*-fenfluramine) on significant parameters reflecting the expression of appetite. The drug exerts an action both during periods of eating (when they occur) and in the periods between eating. Consequently it affects the process of satiation (terminating eating episodes) and intensifies the action of food upon satiety. This intensive mode of investigation provides a way of describing pharmacological action on the short-term control of appetite.

Pharmacology of Appetite: Some Implications for the Eating Disorders

Study of the relationship between drugs and appetite in man is of considerable significance when interpreted with regard to the biopsychological system underlying the expression of eating and its motivation. There are implications for various aspects of the eating disorders and for bulimia in particular.

1. Drugs used as tools (pharmacological scalpels) can help understanding of eating disorders by probing the relationship between subjective motivation (and other conscious states) and the act of eating. For example, the technique of temporal tracking (Blundell and Hill, 1982/3) has been used in patients with eating disorders (Owen *et al.*, 1985). The relationship between drug-induced modulation of hunger profiles (Blundell and Hill, 1987b) and the pathological profiles can further our knowledge of the mechanisms underlying perceived hunger and their role in the expression of eating.

2. Drugs with particular neurochemical actions and behavioural profiles could, if used judiciously, be of help as adjunctive treatments for eating disorders. Already a number of agents have been tried including anticonvulsant drugs for compulsive or binge-eating (Green and Rau, 1974; Wermuth *et al.*, 1977), antidepressant drugs and serotoninergic drugs (Russell, Checkley and Robinson, 1986; Freeman and Hampson, 1987).

3. It is extremely important to investigate possible ways in which various classes of psychotropic drugs may undermine or corrupt the psychobiological control of appetite. Owing to the interaction between the biogenic amines and neuropeptides in the central control of appetite, many drugs which act upon these neurochemicals are likely to influence hunger, eating and body weight. In particular, the benzodiazepines are known to have potent effects (e.g. Blundell, 1977b), and have been referred to as appetite-enhancing compounds (Cooper, 1980). It is therefore possible that the administration of psychotropic drugs could help to induce eating problems (by impeding the regulation of appetite) or exacerbate the course of eating disorders (by making it difficult to regain appetite control).

4. The relationship between drugs and nutrition should be taken seriously. There is some evidence (see Pirke, Chapter 15, and Fichter and Pirke, Chapter 16, this volume) that the consumption of particular nutrients affects brain neurotransmitter function. In turn, this would be expected to modify the action of drugs acting through such neurotransmitters. This would apply to drugs used in treatment or to those drugs for which appetite changes represent an unintended consequence. There is also evidence that dieting or starvation alters transmitter receptor sensitivity (e.g. Goodwin, Fairburn and Cowen, 1987) and this could make certain vulnerable individuals more susceptible to drug actions.

5. Institutionalized drugs such as nicotine and caffeine which are habitually used may exert tonic effects on appetite control which could pass unnoticed. Individuals who smoke heavily and who drink large amounts of tea, coffee or canned beverages may sustain a permanent pharmacological constraint over appetite control. Indeed, it is possible that such domestic pharmacological agents could be deliberately used to aid maintenance to a restrictive eating

regime. The role of such common chemicals in bulimia deserves further investigation.

Taken together a rational approach to the understanding of appetite control — and in particular the satiety cascade — coupled with knowledge of drug action can produce a framework for the psychopharmacological study of appetite. Some of the findings in this field, and their interpretation, are of considerable importance for the study and treatment of bulimia.

Acknowledgements

The authors are grateful to Betty Fowbert for help with the preparation of the text.

References

Berthoud, H. R., D. A. Bereiter, E. R. Trimble, E. G. Siegel and B. Jeanrenaud (1981). Cephalic phase, reflex insulin secretion. *Diabetologia* **20**, 393–401.

Blundell, J. E. (1976). Strategies and tactics in the use of anti-obesity drugs. *Lancet* **1**, 804–805.

Blundell, J. E. (1977a). Hunger and satiety in the control of food intake: implications for the treatment of obesity. *Clinical Dietology*. **23**, 257–272.

Blundell, J. E. (1977b). Is there a role for serotonin (5-hydroxytryptophan) in feeding? *International Journal of Obesity* **1**, 15–42.

Blundell, J. E. (1979a). Hunger, appetite and satiety — psychological constructs in search of identities. In *Nutrition and Lifestyles*, ed. by M. Turner. Applied Science Publications, London, pp. 21–42.

Blundell, J. E. (1980). Pharmacological adjustment of the mechanisms underlying feeding and obesity. In *Obesity*, ed. by A. J. Stunkard. Saunders, Philadelphia, pp. 182–207.

Blundell, J. E (1984a). Serotonin and appetite. *Neuropharmacology* **23**, 1537–1552.

Blundell, J. E. (1984b). Systems and interactions: an approach to the pharmacology of eating and hunger. In *Eating and its Disorders*, ed. by A. J. Stunkard and E. Stellar. Raven Press, New York, pp. 39–65.

Blundell, J. E. (1987). Structure, process and mechanism: case studies in the psychopharmacology of feeding. In *Handbook of Psychopharmacology*, ed. by L. L. Iversen, S. D. Iversen and S. H. Snyder. Plenum, New York, pp. 123–182.

Blundell, J. E. and V. J. Burley (1987). Satiation, satiety and the action of fibre on food intake. *International Journal of Obesity*, Suppl. 1, **11**, 9–25.

Blundell, J. E. and A. J. Hill (1985). Analysis of hunger: interrelationships with palatability, nutrient composition and eating. In *Recent Advances in Obesity Research* IV, ed. by T. D. Van Itallie and J. Hirsch. Libby, London, pp. 118–129.

Blundell, J. E. and A. J. Hill (1987a). Influence of tryptophan on appetite and food selection in man. In *Amino Acids in Health and Disease: New Perspectives*, ed. by S. Kaufman. Alan Liss, New York, pp. 403–419.

Blundell, J. E. and A. J. Hill (1987b). Serotonergic modulation of the pattern of eating and the profile of hunger-satiety in humans. *International Journal of Obesity*, Suppl. 3, **11**, 141–153.

Blundell, J. E. and A. J. Hill (1988). On the mechanisms of action of dexfenfluramine: effect on alliesthesia and appetite motivation in lean and obese subjects. *Clinical Neuropharmacology*, in press.

Blundell, J. E. and P. J. Rogers (1978). Pharmacological approaches to the understanding of obesity. *Psychiatric Clinics of North America* **1**, 629–650.

Blundell, J. E. and P. J. Rogers (1980). Effects of anorexic drugs on food intake, food selection and preferences, hunger motivation and subjective experiences: pharmacological manipulation as a tool to investigate human feeding processes. *Appetite* **1**, 151–165.

Blundell, J. E. and P. L. Thurlby (1987). Experimental manipulations of eating: advances in animal models for studying anorexic agents. *Pharmacology and Therapeutics*. **34**, 349–401.

Blundell, J. E., P. J. Rogers and A. J. Hill (1987). Evaluating the satiating power of foods: implications for acceptance and consumption. In *Chemical Composition and Sensory Properties of Food and their Influence on Nutrition*, ed. by J. Solms. Academic Press, London, pp. 205–219.

Booth, D. A. (1977). Satiety and appetite are conditioned reactions. *Psychosomatic Medicine* **39**, 76–81.

Caffrey, E. W., H. R. Kissileff and J. C. Thornton (1987). Assessment of the effects of phenylpropalolamine on appetite and food intake. *Pharmacology, Biochemistry and Behavior*. **26**, 321–325.

Clarke, J. J., P. S. Kalra, W. R. Crowley and S. P. Kalra (1984). Neuropeptide Y and human pancreatic polypeptide stimulate feeding behaviour in rats. *Endocrinology* **115**, 427–429.

Cooper, S. J. (1980). Benzodiazepines as appetite-enhancing compounds. *Appetite* **1**, 7–19.

Fantino, M., J. Hosotte and M. Apfelbaum (1986). An opioid antagonist, naltrexone reduces preferences for sucrose in humans. *American Journal of Physiology* **251**, R91–R96.

Fincham, J., T. Silverstone and B. Saha (1977). The effect of l-phenylalanine on subjective hunger and satiety in man. Proceedings of 6th ICPFFI, Paris, July 25–28.

Freeman, C.P.L. and M. Hampson (1987). Fluoxetine as a treatment for bulimia nervosa. In *Drugs Regulating Food Intake and Energy Balance*, ed. by G. A. Bray and M. Cairella. Libby, London, pp. 171–178.

Garattini, S. (1978). Importance of serotonin for explaining the action of some anorectic agents. In *Recent Advances in Obesity Research: II*, ed. by G. A. Bray. Newman, London, pp. 433–441.

Garattini, S., T. Mennini and R. Samanin (1987). From fenfluramine racemate to d-fenfluramine: specificity and potency of the effects on the serotoninergic system and food intake. *Annals of the New York Academy of Sciences*, **449**, 156–166.

Gilbert, F. and C. T. Dourish (1987). Effects of the novel anxiolytics gepirone, buspirone and ipsapirone on free-feeding and on feeding induced by 8-OH-DPAT. *Psychopharmacology* **93**, 349–352.

Goodall, E. and T. Silverstone (1987). The effect of the 5-HT releasing drug d-fenfluramine and the 5-HT receptor blocker, metergoline, on food intake in human subjects. In *Human Obesity*, ed. by R. J. Wurtman and J. J. Wurtman *Annals of the New York Academy of Sciences* **449**, 321–323.

Goodall, E., E. Trenchard and T. Silverstone (1987). Receptor blocking agents and amphetamine anorexia in human subjects. *Psychopharmacology* **92**, 484–490.

Goodwin, G. M., C. G. Fairburn and P. J. Cowen (1987). Dieting changes serotonergic function in women, not men, implications for the aetiology of anorexia nervosa? *Psychological Medicine* **17**, 839–842.

Green, R. S. and J. H. Rau (1974). Treatment of compulsive eating disturbances with anticonvulsant medication. *American Journal of Psychiatry* **131**, 428–432.

Grunberg, N. E. (1982). The effects of nicotine and cigarette smoking on food consumption and taste preference. *Addictive Behaviors* **7**, 317–331.

Grunberg, N. E., D. J. Bowen and D. E. Morse (1984). Effects of nicotine on body weight and food consumption in rats. *Psychopharmacology* **83**, 93–98.

Halter, J., P. Kulkosky, S. Woods, W. Makous, M. Chen and D. Porte (1975). Afferent receptors, taste perception endocrine function in man. *Diabetes* **24**, 414.

Harris, B., J. Young and B. Hughes (1984). Changes occurring in appetite and weight during short-term anti-depressant treatment. *British Journal of Psychiatry* **145**, 645–648.

Hill, A. J. and J. E. Blundell (1986). Model system for investigating the actions of anorectic drugs: effect of d-fenfluramine on food intake, nutrient selection, food preferences, meal patterns, hunger and satiety in healthy human subjects. *Advances in the Biosciences*. Pergamon, Oxford, pp. 377–389.

Hill, A. J., L. D. Magson and J. E. Blundell (1984). Hunger and palatability: tracking ratings of subjective experience before, during and after the consumption of preferred and less preferred food. *Appetite* **5**, 361–371.

Hoebel, B. G. and S. F. Leibowitz (1981). Brain monoamines in the modulation of self-stimulation, feeding, and body weight. In *Brain, Behaviour and Bodily Disease*, ed. by H. A. Weiner, M. A. Hofer and A. J. Stunkard. Raven Press, New York, pp. 103–142.

Hoyer, D., A. Pazos and J. M. Palacios (1986). Serotonin receptors in the human brain I. Characterisation and autoradiographic localization of 5-HT_{1A} recognition sites. Apparent absence of 5-HT_{1B} recognition sites. *Brain Research* **376**, 85–96.

Kissileff, H. R., F. X. Pi-Sunyer, J. Thornton and G. P. Smith (1981). C-terminal octapeptide of cholecystokinin decreases food intake in man. *American Journal of Clinical Nutrition* **34**, 154–160.

Le Magnen, J. (1960). Effets d'une pluralite de stimuli alimentaires sur le determinisme quantitif de l'ingestion chez le rat blanc. *Archives des Sciences Physiologiques* **14**, 411–419.

Le Magnen, J. (1985). *Hunger*. Cambridge University Press, Cambridge.

McQuorquodale, K. and P. E. Meehl (1948). On the distinction between hypothetical constructs and intervening variables. *Psychological Review* **55**, 95–109.

Malcolm, R., P. M. O'Neil, J. D. Sexauer, E. Riddle, H. S. Currey and C. Counts (1985). A controlled trial of naltrexone in obese humans. *International Journal of Obesity* **9**, 347–353.

Mei, N. (1985). Intestinal chemosensitivity. *Physiological Review* **65**, 211–237.

Morley, J. E., A. S. Levine B. A. Gosnell and D. D. Krahn (1985). Peptides as central regulators of feeding. *Brain Research Bulletin* **14**, 511–519.

Morley, J. E., S. Parker and A. S. Levine (1985). Effect of butorphanol tartrate on food and water consumption in humans. *American Journal of Clinical Nutrition* **42**, 1175–1178.

Munster, G. and K. Battig (1975). Nicotine-induced hypophagia and hypodipsia in deprived and hypothalamically stimulated rats. *Psychopharmacologia* **41**, 211–217.

Nathan, C. and Y. Rolland (1987). Pharmacological treatments that affect CNS activity: serotonin. *Annals of the New York Academy of Sciences* **499**, 277–296.

Owen, W. P., K. A. Halmi, J. Gibbs and G. P. Smith (1985). *Journal of Psychiatric Research* **19**, 279–284.

Paykel, E. S., P. S. Mueller and P. M. de la Vergne (1973). Amitriptyline, weight gains and carbohydrate craving: a side effect. *British Journal of Psychiatry* **123**, 501–507.

Robinson, R. G., P. R. McHugh and M. F. Folstein (1975). Measurement of appetite disturbances in psychiatric disorder. *Journal of Psychiatric Research* **12**, 59–68.

Royce, J. R. (1963). Factors as theoretical constructs. *American Psychologist* **18**, 522–528.

Russell, G. F. M., S. A. Checkley and P. H. Robinson (1986). The limited role of drugs in the treatment of anorexia and bulimia nervosa. In *Pharmacology of Eating Disorders: Theoretical and Clinical Advances*, ed. by M. O. Carruba and J. E. Blundell. Raven Press, New York, pp. 151–168.

Ryan-Harshman, M., L. A. Leiter and G. H. Anderson (1987). Phenylalanine and aspartate fail to alter feeding behaviour, mood and arousal in men. *Physiology and Behaviour* **39**, 247–253.

Scoville, B. (1975). Review of amphetamine-like drugs by the Food and Drug Administration. In *Obesity in Perspective*, Pt 2, ed. by G. A. Bray. US Government Printing Office, Washington DC, pp. 441–448.

Silverstone, T. (1972). The anorectic effect of a long-acting preparation of phentermine (Duromine). *Psychopharmacologia* **25**, 315–320.

Silverstone, T. and E. Goodall (1984). The clinical pharmacology of appetite suppressant drugs. *International Journal of Obesity* **8**, Suppl. 1, 23–33.

Silverstone, T. and M. Kyriakides (1982). Clinical pharmacology of appetite. In *Drugs and Appetite*, ed. by T. Silverstone. Academic Press, London, pp. 93–123.

Silverstone, T. and D. Schuyler (1975). The effect of cyproheptadine on hunger, calorie intake and body weight in man. *Psychopharmacologia* **40**, 335–340.

Silverstone, J. T. and A. Stunkard (1968). The anorectic effect of dexamphetamine sulphate. *British Journal of Chemotherapy* **33**, 513–522.

Simon, C., J. L. Schlienger, R. Sapin and M. Imler (1986). Cephalic phase insulin secretion in relation to food presentation in normal and overweight subjects. *Physiology and Behaviour* **36**, 465–469.

Sjostrom, L., G. Garellick, M. Krotkiewski and A. Luyckx (1980). Peripheral insulin in response to the sight and smell of food. *Metabolism* **29**, 901–909.

Smith, G. P. and J. Gibbs (1987). The effect of gut peptides on hunger, satiety and food intake in humans. *Annals of the New York Academy of Sciences* **499**, 132–136.

Stein, E. M., S. Stein and M. W. Linn (1985). Geriatric sweet tooth. A problem with tricyclics. *Journal of the American Geriatric Society* **33**, 687–692.

Thompson, D. A. and R. G. Campbell (1977). Hunger in humans induced by 2-deoxy-d-glucose: glucoprivic control of taste preference and food intake. *Science* **198**, 1065–1068.

Trenchard, E. and J. T. Silverstone (1983). Naloxone reduces the food intake of human volunteers. *Appetite: Journal of Intake Research* **4**, 43–50.

Van Itallie, R. B. and D. A. Vanderweele (1981). The phenomenon of satiety. In *Recent Advances in Obesity Research III*, ed. by P. Bjorntorp, M. Cairella and A. N. Howard. Libbey, London, pp. 278–289.

Wermuth, B. M., K. L. Davis, L. E. Hollister and J. L. Stunkard (1977). Phenytoin treatment of the binge-eating syndrome. *American Journal of Psychiatry* **134**, 1249–1253.

Wooley, S. C. (1972). Physiologic versus cognitive factors in short term food regulation in the obese and non-obese. *Psychosomatic Medicine* **34**, 62–68.

14

Stress as a modulator of ingestive behaviors

John E. Morley
St Louis University, St Louis

'A stomach full of food also soothes by drawing the blood away from a disgruntled and maladaptive brain.' Hans Selye (1956)

Stress is defined as the non-specific response of the body to a demand which alters the normal homeostatic state to a new level. It is now well recognized that both physical and psychological stressors can modulate ingestive behaviors. Internal physical stressors such as the response to infection can lead to anorexia, while phaeochromocytomas and hyperthyroidism are associated with hyperphagia, albeit in the face of weight loss. Bereavement commonly is associated with anorexia, while overeating in response to minor psychological stresses or boredom is a commonly observed phenomenon. Physical exercise can be associated with either hyperphagia or anorexia. In laboratory animals, mild tail pinch produces overeating, while restraint stress or exposure to a novel environment produces undereating. Strongman (1965) has provided evidence that the duration of the stressor may play an important role in the response. Brief (3 sec) shocks of 2.6 mA increased food intake of rats during the next hour but longer durations of shock (30 and 300 sec) decreased it. In an attempt to explain the various eating disturbances associated with different stressors, Robbins and Fray (1980) suggested that multiple stressors 'have in common interoceptive stimulus changes which are sufficiently similar to be

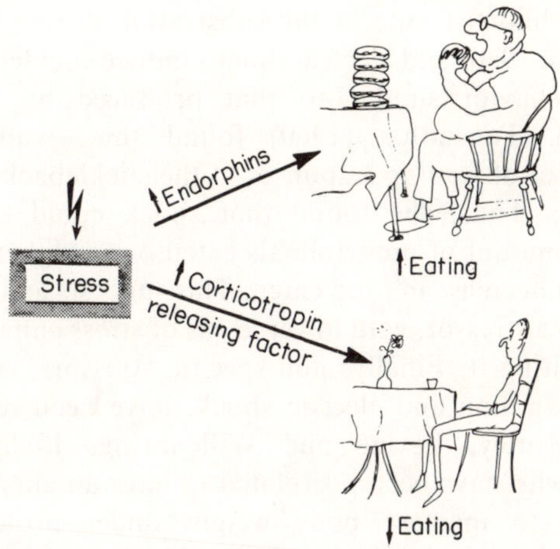

Figure 14.1. Diagrammatic representation of pathways by which stress increases or decreases eating

indiscriminable to the response selection mechanism and which can, therefore, elicit responses apparently irrelevant to the particular motivational state present'.

There is mounting evidence that the common pathway by which different stressors produce their effect is the activation of corticotropin-releasing factor (CRF). Much evidence has been accumulated that CRF is the neurotransmitter responsible for producing anorexia. Similarly, it appears that activation of the endogenous opiods is responsible for stress-induced eating (Figure 14.1). In this chapter we will review the available knowledge of the neurotransmitter substrates which are responsible for the effects of stress on ingestive behaviors.

Stress-induced Eating

Animal studies

The ethology literature is replete with examples of stress-induced eating, which has been considered a displacement phenomenon. During an approach to danger, animals indulge in bouts of grooming or preening before making the decision to 'flee or fight' (Bendra and Spinner, 1958; Manning, 1972). Eating occurs commonly during boundary disputes between birds (Tinbergen, 1937). When Barbary doves were experimentally frustrated in drinking or courtship behavior, they would peck at the ground (McFarland, 1965). This pecking was increased in the presence of grain and by food deprivation. Further, when the doves were trained to retrieve food, this behavior partially replaced pecking. These experiments strongly suggest that stress preferentially activates the feeding system. Cichlid fish bite at the substratum during intervals between fighting (Immelman, 1980) and electric shocks induce sticklebacks to engage in hurried feeding behavior similar to that produced by food deprivation (Immelman, 1980). Tugendhat (1960) found that, while electric shock increased the number of feeding responses of the sticklebacks, it decreased the time spent feeding. Thus, she found that shock could either increase or decrease the total amount of prey animals eaten, with higher shock intensities tending to lead to a decrease in food eaten. This suggests an inverted U-shaped feeding response to a stressor, with lower levels of stress enhancing feeding and higher levels inhibiting it. Finally, non-specific stressors, such as water jets, acoustic stimuli, handling and electric shock, have been reported to induce eating in rats (Morley, Levine and Willenbring, 1986). Spontaneously hypertensive rats, who have been postulated to have an altered opioid system, have been shown to increase body weight under prolonged behavioral stimulation (Niewadomska and Lukazewska, 1986).

In 1963, Sprague *et al.* (1963) demonstrated that mild tail pinch induced biting of a wooden block and swallowing of wet paper or food in cats. Later, Antelman *et al.* (1975; Antelman and Szechtman, 1975) reported that a sustained mild tail pinch in the rat could induce a variety of oral behaviors, including gnawing, eating and licking. Levine and Morley (1982b) demonstrated that mild pinch to other parts of the body would also induce feeding. Tail pinch also induces chewing and eating in mice (Levine *et al.*, 1982b) and reduces the latency to feeding in the mollusk *Apylsia* (Kupferman and Weiss, 1981).

Stress-induced overeating in laboratory animals has also been reported following a cold swim stress (Vaswani, Tejwani and Mousa, 1983), though we found that this model was more likely to result in anorexia (Waggoner *et al.*, 1985). Neck scruff pinch in Siberian hamsters also results in overeating. Teskey, Kavaliers and Hirst (1984) reported that following fighting in mice, the defeated mouse displays stress-induced hyperphagia.

Stress and feeding in humans

St Matthew was the first to correlate the onset of depression and anxiety with the muscles of mastication: '. . . and there shall be a weeping and gnashing of teeth'. In 1955, Stunkard, Grace and Wolff produced the classic article describing the night-eating syndrome in stressed individuals. Subsequently, numerous formal psychological studies have confirmed the presence of stress-induced eating in humans (reviewed in Morley, Levine and Willenbring, 1986).

In our study of the prevalence of stress-induced eating, we found that 44 per cent of subjects increased eating when stressed, 48 per cent decreased eating, and 8 per cent did not change eating when stressed (Willenbring, Levine and Morley, 1986). Boredom was responsible for increased eating in 46 per cent.

Psychodynamic theories of stress eating have suggested that it may develop as a response to conflicting parental signals to 'eat more' but 'stay slim' or because as a child the subject was encouraged to eat to allay generalized anxiety (Nash, 1987). As Hilde Bruch has theorized, stress eating can become a learned response rather than a physiological response to a need state such as hunger (Bruch, 1973). A group which is at particular risk to develop stress-induced eating and obesity is the so-called 'restrained eaters' (Herman and Mack, 1975). This group is obsessed by food and is in a continuous state of dieting and restrained eating to maintain weight loss. In these subjects, cognitive control of eating is easily disrupted and, thus, an emotional upset can cause loss of control and open the floodgates of overeating.

Konner has developed an anthropological theory of the mechanism by which stress-induced eating can lead to obesity (Konner, 1982). His theory is based on the observation that in advanced industrial societies the rich tend to be thin and the poor fat, whereas in poor societies the reverse is the case. In poor societies, rich people become obese because of the uncertainty of how long their ample food supply will last. Besides this stressor, they are also constantly stressed by the general economic instability. In industrialized societies, the poor suffer the constant threat of famine and the condition of subordination, both of which enhance the syndrome of anxiety-induced overeating. Thus, in the absence of better or more specifically predictive explanations, Konner (1982) feels that 'it seems reasonable to postulate the anxiety theory as a provisional model for the obesity of the industrial poor and the agricultural rich'.

Bulimarexia is a syndrome characterized by episodic binge-eating followed by, in most cases, vomiting. The onset of bulimic behavior is often triggered by a traumatic event occurring during a period of voluntary dieting (Pyle, Mitchell and Eckert, 1981). The commonest stressful trigger appears to be the loss of, or separation from, a significant person in one's life.

Does stress induce chewing or true ingestive behavior?

In our studies on stress-eaters, we found that, while unhappy with their weight, they were rarely overweight. They also tended to prefer sweet foods and, most importantly, they showed a preference for high-density foods (Willenbring, Levine and Morley, 1986). These high-density foods represented highly chewable food, suggesting that stress alleviation may be related more to chewing than actual food ingestion.

In children with Lesch-Nyhan syndrome, oral stereotypy (compulsive biting of the fingers, lips and tongue) is markedly increased during periods of emotional upset (Seegmiller, 1980). This has suggested that this condition may represent an amplified version of the far more common compulsive biting of lips and fingernails produced in certain individuals by stressful situations.

Animal studies have strongly supported the concept that it is chewing which produces stress alleviation and that ingestion is merely an epiphenomenon. Mice placed into novel cages have elevated corticosterone levels (Hennessy and Foy, 1987). When the mice were allowed to chew on foil or cardboard, the magnitude of the corticosterone increase was diminished. A highly palatable, soft food (peanut butter chips) produced little chewing and failed to attenuate the cortiscosterone response to novelty.

While tail pinch induced eating occurs at normal rates of feeding (0.2–0.3 g/min), there is evidence against this representing normal eating. Pinched rats will chew sand (Watson *et al.*, 1980) or wood chips (Robbins and Fray, 1980) during the pinch. In naive rats, simple grinding of the food will depress eating, whereas rats will chew at a novel hard food (hard candy) (Levine and Morley, 1982a). When offered a choice of wood chips or ground food during tail pinch, rats prefer the non-edible wood chips (Levine and Morley, 1982a).

Opioid modulation of stress-induced eating

Much evidence supports the concept that opioids are the primary mediators of stress-induced eating. This has been summarized in detail elsewhere (Morley, Levine and Rowland, 1983) and will only be briefly reviewed here:

1. The opiate antagonist naloxone attenuates stress-induced eating in rats (Morley and Levine, 1980a; Lowy, Maickel and Yim, 1980) and mice (Levine *et al.*, 1982b).
2. Dexamethasone, which inhibits ACTH and beta-endorphin release, decreased tail-pinch eating (Lowy and Yim, 1980).
3. The suppressive effect of a number of peptides on tail-pinch eating is partially reversed by a long-acting methionine-enkephaline agent (Morley *et al.*, 1982).
4. Tail pinch will suppress wet-dog shakes in rats in a manner similar to opiates (Ornstein, 1981).
5. Tail pinch produces naloxone-reversible analgesia when writhing is used as a nociceptive stimulus (Levine *et al.*, 1982a).
6. Tail pinch produces catalepsy which is naloxone-reversible (Amir *et al.*, 1981) and can facilitate morphine-induced catalepsy in mice and rats, as well as potentiate morphine-induced caudate spindles in freely moving rats (Ariyanayagum and Handley, 1975; Amir and Ornstein, 1981).
7. Prolonged tail-pinch stimulus applied intermittently over a number of days led to naloxone-precipitable withdrawal symptoms (Morley and Levine, 1980a). It should be noted that this may be a useful model of post-traumatic stress syndrome.
8. Tail pinch alters ir-dynorphin levels in rat cerebral cortex (Morley and

Levine, 1982b). Dynorphin, the endogenous kappa receptor ligand, has been considered to play an integral role in the regulation of ingestive behaviors.

Similar to the situation for tail pinch induced eating, it appears that the stress-induced eating observed after fighting in mice is opioid dependent (Teskey, Kavaliers and Hirst, 1984). The pattern of eating is similar to that seen after morphine administration and the eating is inhibited by naloxone. In humans, naloxone has been demonstrated to decrease 2-deoxyglucose-induced food intake while not altering the perception of hunger (Thompson *et al.*, 1982).

Thus, it seems clear that at least some portions of stress-induced eating are mediated through endogenous opioid activation. In view of the ability of opioids to stimulate dopamine release and turnover (Morley, Levine and Rowland, 1983), this system may well be dopamine independent as well.

Other neurotransmitter systems and tail pinch induced eating

As was mentioned towards the end of the previous section, dopamine may well play a role in tail pinch induced behaviors. Dopamine antagonists inhibit tail pinch induced eating while noradrenergic alpha-blockers have no effect on these behaviors. Similarly, 6-hydroxydopamine injections into the substantia nigra attenuate tail-pinch behaviors (Rowland, Marques and Fisher, 1980). Present formulations suggest that dopaminergic systems may be critical for the chewing behavior, while opioids are more important for the ingestive component of tail-pinch behavior.

A number of agents have been demonstrated to inhibit tail-pinch behavior. These include: cholecystokinin (Nemeroff *et al.*, 1978); calcitonin (Morley, Levine and Prasad, 1981); somatostatin (Levine and Morley, 1981a); substance P (Morley and Levine, 1980b); corticotropin-releasing factor (Levine *et al.*, 1983) prostaglandins (Levine and Morley, 1981b); and serotonergic agonists (Morley, Levine and Rowland, 1983). In all these cases, the predominant effect appears to be on ingestive behavior, with relatively little effect on chewing response as quantitated by measurement of spillage (Morley *et al.*, 1982).

Summary

Careful pharmacological dissection of the tail-pinch model of stress-induced feeding has suggested that mild stressors activate these behaviors through endogenous opioids (primarily responsible for ingestion) and dopaminergic systems (chewing). Animal and human studies have allowed the formulation of a hypothesis that stress alleviation is more closely related to oral behaviors than to actual food ingestion. This suggests that non- (or low)-calorie chewable substances may prove to be extremely useful in the management of stress-induced eating.

Stress-induced Anorexia

Anorexia nervosa represents a dramatic form of stress-induced anorexia. This syndrome occurs primarily in young women but is also seen in middle-aged men in cultures when there is an emphasis on thinness, such as Norway. The syndrome is characterized by self-starvation, laxative abuse and hyperactivity. The starvation and weight loss are also associated with a variety of other pathophysiological changes, such as amenorrhea and lanugo hair. Anorexia and bulimia often occur together, or at different times, in the same individual. The role of secondary malnutrition in producing some of these symptoms and perpetuating the anorexia remains unclear.

Recently, we have observed a number of older subjects who have many characteristics suggestive of anorexia nervosa. They are often in nursing-home situations and have lost their locus of control and appear to be using their refusal to eat as a method by which they can regain control. Interestingly, Jay Weiss' animal model of controllability has shown that weight loss occurs in the yoked animal (Weiss, 1968). These subjects are often males who refuse to eat, chew their food and then spit it out, and fail to perceive their weight loss. Concomitant laxative abuse may be present. The syndrome is often missed, with the subjects eventually dying from infection associated secondarily to malnutrition. Recognition of this syndrome creates a major ethical conundrum, as it needs to be distinguished from the more rational refusal to eat seen in some patients with terminal illness.

Anorexia related to interpersonal loss is well recognized. Bereavement is commonly associated with anorexia and weight loss, particularly in the elderly (Morley, 1986). Food, which may be considered as a symbol of life, can become taboo at the time of bereavement. This symbolic role of food is well recognized in the Jewish 'shivah' and the Irish 'wake', where food is brought into the home of the bereaved. Grief-induced anorexia is not unique to the elderly but has also been observed in infants 8–10 months old in response to loss of parent (Spitz, 1965).

Major depression is associated with anorexia and depression in approximately two-thirds of subjects. Weight loss has been associated with sleep disturbance in depressives, as characterized by early morning awakening (Levine and Morley, 1982a) or mid-night awakening, but not with difficulty in falling asleep. A similar correlation between sleep disturbance and anorexia has been reported in patients with anorexia nervosa (Kalin *et al.*, 1981). In these patients, the sleep disturbance tends to resolve with weight gain. It has been suggested that in depressive patients, decreased appetite, sleep disturbance and decreased sexual drive may not be distinctive for endogenous depression, but rather may represent a non-specific response to stress (Nelson and Charney, 1980). The presence of these vegetative symptoms tends to correlate more strongly with dexamethasone non-suppressibility than do the

Table 14.1 Classification of stress-induced anorexias

Psychological	
(a)	Anorexia nervosa
(b)	Age-related marasmic syndrome (anorexia nervosa variant in the elderly)
(c)	Bereavement-associated anorexia
(d)	Major depression
(e)	Psychosocial dwarfism
Physical	
(a)	Infection
(b)	Cancer
(c)	Exercise-induced (? anorexia nervosa variant)

symptoms associated with lack of interest, anhedonia and lack of reactivity (Miller and Nelson, 1987).

An example of stress-induced anorexia in young children is psychosocial dwarfism. In this condition, physically or psychologically abused children develop malnutrition and associated stunting of growth associated with low somatomedin levels.

Infectious processes represent a physical stressor associated with anorexia. It appears that the release of interleukin-1 is the primary triggering event which leads to the anorexia (McCarthy, Kluger and Vander, 1985). Interleukin-1 also releases cachexin (tumor necrosis factor), which causes both anorexia and weight loss secondary to inhibition of lipogenic enzymes (Beutler and Cerami, 1987).

Cancer is another physical stressor commonly associated with anorexia. In many cases, the mechanism appears to involve interleukin-1 and cachexin release. In addition, some cancer patients produce ectopic hormones, such as bombesin, which are associated with anorexia (Moody *et al.*, 1981).

Excessive physical exercise can be associated with weight loss, relative anorexia and amenorrhea in women. While this is classified under physical stressors, it seems likely that it represents a variant of anorexia nervosa. Table 14.1 summarizes the main forms of stress-induced anorexia.

Does Corticotropin-releasing Factor (CRF) Mediate Stress-induced Anorexias?

CRF is a 41 amino acid peptide which produces many of the effects predicted by Selye in 1936 for a central factor responsible for the coordination of the multiple responses (the general adaptation syndrome) elicited by noxious stimuli (stressors) that threaten to alter homeostasis (Vale *et al.*, 1981). When administered intracerebroventricularly, CRF is a potent anorectic agent in rodents (Britton *et al.*, 1982; Morley and Levine, 1982a). CRF inhibits spontaneous and starvation-induced feeding, as well as feeding induced by a variety of pharmacological agents (Levine *et al.*, 1983; Morley and Levine, 1982a). The CRF decrease in feeding is accompanied by an increase in grooming, suggesting a shift in the normal satiety sequence. The effects of CRF are similar to those reported by Krujt (1964) in defeated jungle fowl. The effect of CRF on feeding is still present in hypophysectomized animals (Morley and Levine, 1982a). The CRF effect is partially, but not completely, dependent on an intact adrenal medulla (Gosnell, Morley and Levine, 1983).

Evidence for a physiological role of CRF in stress-induced anorexia comes from a number of sources. The CRF antagonist alpha-helical CRF [9–41] not only reverses the decrement in feeding induced by CRF but also attenuates the reduction in food intake associated with restraint stress (Krahn *et al.*, 1986; Shibaski *et al.*, 1987). Restraint stress has been demonstrated to be associated with a significant short-term reduction in hypothalamic CRF, suggesting release of CRF during acute stress (Moldow *et al.*, 1987). In these studies, the changes in CRF after use of the protein synthesis inhibitor cycloheximide suggest that prolonged restraint stress is associated with increased CRF synthesis. Kelly and Silverman (1987) have shown alterations in CRF in the paraventricular nucleus associated with their chronic stress paradigm. Weight loss is a prominent feature of their model.

Many of the neurotransmitters involved in the regulation of feeding have been demonstrated to produce their effects within the paraventricular nucleus (PVN). Lesions of the PVN result in hyperphagia (Leibowitz, 1980), suggesting that PVN tonically inhibits feeding. As both CRF cell bodies and receptors are present within the PVN, we studied whether or not the PVN was the site within the central nervous system where CRF exerted its effect. CRF inhibited feeding when injected into the PVN, but not when injected into the ventromedial hypothalamus, striatum, lateral hypothalamus, or globus pallidus (Krahn *et al.*, 1984). Within the PVN, CRF also inhibited norepinephrine-induced feeding. We felt that CRF represented the inhibitory substance produced by the PVN to tonically inhibit feeding.

Within the PVN, norepinephrine acting through alpha-2 receptors enhances feeding (Leibowitz, 1986) and serotonin inhibits feeding (Weiss *et al.*, 1986). The effect of norepinephrine on feeding is inhibited by adrenalectomy, which leads to an increase of CRF within the PVN. Biochemical studies have suggested that norepinephrine inhibits CRF release from the hypothalamus (Rivier and Plotsky, 1986). On the other hand, stressful procedures increase serotonin turnover (Thierry, Fedkete and Glowinski, 1968) and serotonin promotes the release of CRF from the hypothalamus (Buckingham, 1980). It

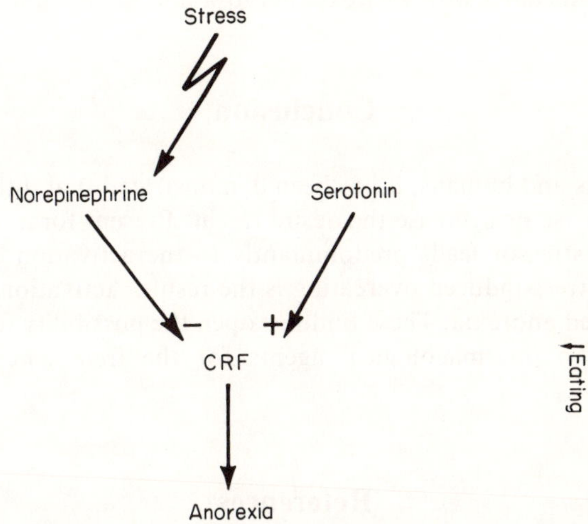

Figure 14.2. Stress-induced anorexia depends on an interplay between norepinephrine and serotonin activating corticotropin-releasing factor (CRF)

seems likely that inhibition of CRF release by norepinephrine is responsible for norepinephrine-induced feeding and CRF release promoted by serotonin is responsible for serotonin inhibition of feeding (Figure 14.2).

CRF has been postulated to play a role in the pathophysiology of anorexia nervosa. Activation of the hypothalamic–pituitary–adrenal axis is a well-recognized concomitant of anorexia nervosa (Beumont, 1983). Elevated cerebrospinal fluid levels of CRF have been demonstrated to be present in patients with anorexia nervosa (Hotta *et al.*, 1986; Kaye *et al.*, 1987). Further, CRF has been shown to inhibit luteinizing hormone levels and the stress-induced inhibition of luteinizing hormone release appears to be secondary to CRF release (Rivier, Rivier and Vale, 1986). Thus, CRF may be partially responsible for the secondary hypogonadism that occurs in patients with anorexia nervosa.

As previously pointed out, anorexia and weight loss occur in many patients with major depression. As in the case of patients with anorexia nervosa, these patients have a hyperactive hypothalamic–pituitary–adrenal axis. Patients with major depressive disorders have been shown to have elevated cerebrospinal fluid CRF levels (Herman and Mack, 1975; Davis, Davis and Mohs, 1984; Roy *et al.*, 1987). CRF may therefore be responsible for the anorexia and weight loss associated with depression. CRF also produces sleep disturbances and decreased sex drive, which are vegetative symptoms included in the DSM-III diagnosis of major depressive disorders.

CRF appears to be a major mediator of stress-induced anorexias. In particular, it appears to play a role in the pathophysiology of the eating disturbances associated with anorexia nervosa and depression.

Conclusion

Both in animals and humans, it has been demonstrated that different stressors can either increase or decrease the desire to eat. Present formulations suggest that when the stressor leads predominantly to the activation of endogenous opioids, then stress-induced overeating is the result. Activation of CRF leads to stress-induced anorexia. These findings open the possibility for the development of specific pharmacological agents for the treatment of the eating disorders.

References

Amir, S. and K. Ornstein (1981). Pinch-induced catalepsy: a natural defensive response involving blockage of central dopamine systems by endogenously-released opioids. *Neuroscience Abstracts* **7**, 49.

Amir, S., S. W. Brown, Z. Amit and K. Ornstein (1981). Body pinch induces long-lasting cataleptic-like immobility in mice: behavioral characterization and the effect of naloxone. *Life Sciences* **28**, 1189–1194.

Antelman, S. M. and H. Szechtman (1975). Tail pinch induces eating in sated rats which appears to depend on nigrostriatal dopamine. *Science* **189**, 731–733.

Antelman, S. M., H. Szechtman, P. Chin and A. E. Fisher (1975). Tail pinch-induced eating, gnawing, and licking behavior in rats: dependence on the nigrostriatal dopamine system. *Brain Research* **99**, 219–237.

Ariyanayagum, A. D. and S. L. Handley (1975). Effect of sensory stimulation on the potency of cataleptogens. *Psychopharmacology* **41**, 165–167.

Beumont, P. J. V. (1983). The endocrinology of anorexia nervosa. *Medical Journal of Australia* **2**, 225–228.

Bendra, D. and N. Spinner (1958). Response to different degrees of novelty: the incidence of various activities. *Journal of Experimental and Analytical Behaviour* **1**, 341–347.

Beutler, B. and A. Cerami (1987). Cachectin: more than a tumor necrosis factor. *New England Journal of Medicine* **316**, 379–384.

Britton, D. R., G. Koob, J. Rivier and W. Vale (1982). Intraventricular corticotropin-releasing factor enhances behavioral effects of novelty. *Life Sciences* **31**, 363–367.

Bruch, G. (1973). *Eating Disorders: Obesity, Anorexia Nervosa, and Person Within.* Basic Books, New York.

Buckingham, J. C. (1980). Corticotropin-releasing factor. *Pharmacological Review* **31**, 253–274.

Davis, K., B. Davis and R. Mohs (1984). CSF corticotropin-releasing factor in neuropsychiatric diseases. *New Research Abstracts, 137th Annual Meeting of American Psychiatric Association.* APA, Washington DC.

Gosnell, B. A., J. E. Morley and A. S. Levine (1983). Adrenal modulation of the inhibitory effect of corticotropin-releasing factor on feeding. *Peptides* **4**, 807–812.

Hennessy, M. B. and T. Foy (1987). Nonedible material elicits chewing and reduces the plasma corticosterone response during novelty exposure in mice. *Behavioral Neuroscience* **101**, 237–245.

Herman, C. and D. Mack (1975). Restrained and unrestrained eating. *Journal of Personality* **43**, 647–660.

Hotta, M., T. Shibaski, A. Masuda, T. Imaki, H. Demura, N. Ling and M. Shizume (1986). The responses of plasma adrenocorticotropin-releasing hormone (CRH) and cerebrospinal fluid immunoreactive CRH in anorexia nervosa patients. *Journal of Clinical Endocrinology and Metabolism* **62**, 319–321.

Immelman, K. (1980). *Introduction to Ethology*. Plenum, New York.

Kalin, N. H., S. C. Risch, D. S. Janowsky and D. L. Murphy (1981). Use of the dexamethasone suppression test in clinical psychiatry. *Journal of Clinical Psychopharmacology* **1**, 64–69.

Kaye, W. H., H. E. Gwirtsman, D. T. George, M. H. Ebert, D. C. Jimesson, T. P. Tomai, G. P. Chrousos and P. W. Gold (1987). Elevated cerebrospinal fluid levels of immunoreactive corticotropin-releasing hormone in anorexia nervosa: relation to state of nutrition, adrenal function and intensity of depression. *Journal of Clinical Endocrinology and Metabolism* **64**, 203–207.

Kelly, D. D. and A.-J. Silverman (1987). Plasticity of hypothalamic peptidergic neurons in response to stress. *Abstracts, Neuronal Control of Bodily Function — Basic and Clinical Aspects: IV. New Frontiers of Stress Research*. Trier, West Germany, p. 11.

Konner, M. (1982). *The Tangled Wing*. Harper and Row, New York.

Krahn, D. D., B. A. Gosnell, M. Grace and A. S. Levine (1986). CRF antagonist partially reverses CRF- and stress-induced effects on feeding. *Brain Research Bulletin* **17**, 285–289.

Krahn, D. D., B. A. Gosnell, A. S. Levine and J. E. Morley (1984). Localization of the effects of corticotropin-releasing factor on feeding. *Proceedings of the Society for Neuroscience Abstracts* **10**, 302.

Kruijt, J. P. (1964). Ontogeny of social behavior in Burmese red jungle fowl (*Gallus gallus spadiceus Bonnateme*). *Behavior*, Suppl. 12, 1–201.

Kupferman, I. and K. R. Weiss (1981). Tail pinch and handling facilitate feeding behavior in apylsia. *Behavior and Neural Biology* **32**, 126–132.

Leibowitz, S. F. (1980). Neurochemical systems of the hypothalamus: control of feeding and drinking behavior and water electrolyte excretion. In *Handbook of the Hypothalamus*, Vol. 3, ed. by P. J. Morgane and J. Panksepp. Raven Press, New York, pp. 299–437.

Leibowitz, S. F. (1986). Brain monoamines and peptides: role in the control of eating behavior. *Federation Proceedings* **45**, 14–21.

Levine, A. S. and J. E. Morley (1981a). Reduction of feeding in rats by calcitonin. *Brain Research* **222**, 187–191.

Levine, A. S. and J. E. Morley (1981b). The effect of prostaglandins (PGE_2 and PGF_2 alpha) on food intake in rats. *Pharmacology, Biochemistry and Behavior* **15**, 735–738.

Levine, A. S. and J. E. Morley (1982a). Gnawing is the preferred consummatory behavior initially induced by tail pinch. *Appetite* **3**, 135–138.

Levine, A. S. and J. E. Morley (1982b). Tail pinch-induced eating: is it the tail or the pinch. *Physiology and Behavior* **28**, 565–567.

Levine, A. S., B. Rogers, J. Kneip, M. Grace and J. E. Morley (1983). Effect of centrally administered corticotropin-releasing factor (CRF) on multiple feeding paradigms.

Neuropharmacology **22**, 337–339.
Levine, A. S., G. L. Wilcox, M. Grace and J. E. Morley (1982a). Tail pinch-induced consummatory behaviors are associated with analgesia. *Physiology and Behavior* **28**, 959–962.
Levine, A. S., J. E. Morley, G. Wilcox, D. M. Brown and B. S. Handwerger (1982b). Tail pinch behavior and analgesia in diabetic mice. *Physiology and Behavior* **28**, 39–43.
Lowy, M. T. and G. K. W. Yim (1980). Selective reduction by dexamethasone of stress-related hyperphagias. *Life Sciences* **27**, 2553–2558.
Lowy, M. T., R. P. Maickel and G. K. W. Yim (1980). Naloxone reduction of stress-related feeding. *Life Sciences* **26**, 2113–2118.
Manning, A. (1972). In *An Introduction to Animal Behavior*. Addison-Wesley, Reading, Mass.
McCarty, D. O., M. J. Kluger and A. J. Vander (1985). Suppression of food intake during infection: is interleukin-1 involved? *American Journal of Clinical Nutrition* **42**, 1179–1182.
McFarland, D. J. (1965). Hunger, thirst and displacement pecking in the Barbary dove. *Animal Behaviour* **13**, 293–300.
Miller, K. B. and J. C. Nelson (1987). Does the dexamethasone suppression test relate to subtypes, factors, symptoms or severity? *Archives of General Psychiatry* **44**, 769–774.
Moldow, R. L., A. J. Kastin, M. Graf and A. J. Fischman (1987). Stress-mediated changes in hypothalamic corticotropin-releasing factor immunoreactivity. *Life Sciences* **40**, 413–418.
Moody, T. W., C. B. Pert, A. F. Gazdor, D. N. Carney and J. D. Minna (1981). High levels of intracellular bombesin characterize human small cell lung carcinoma. *Science* **214**, 1266–1277.
Morley, J. E. (1986). Nutritional status of the elderly. *American Journal of Medicine* **81**, 679–695.
Morley, J. E. and A. S. Levine (1980a). Stress-induced eating is mediated through endogenous opiates. *Science* **209**, 1259–1261.
Morley, J. E. and A. S. Levine (1980b). Substance P suppresses stress-induced eating. *European Journal of Pharmacology* **67**, 309–311.
Morley, J. E. and A. S. Levine (1982a). Corticotropin-releasing factor, grooming, and ingestive behavior. *Life Sciences* **31**, 1459–1464.
Morley, J. E. and A. S. Levine (1982b). Opiates, dopamine, and feeding. In *The Neural Basis of Feeding and Reward*, ed. by B. G. Hoebel and D. Novin. Haer Institute, Brunswick, ME, pp. 449–506.
Morley, J. E., A. S. Levine and C. Prasad (1981). Histidyl-proline diketopiperazine decreases food intake in rats. *Brain Research* **210**, 475–478.
Morley, J. E., A. S. Levine and N. E. Rowland (1983). Stress-induced eating. *Life Sciences* **32**, 2169–2182.
Morley, J. E., A. S. Levine and M. L. Willenbring (1986). Stress-induced feeding disorders. In *Psychopharmacology of Eating Disorders: Theoretical and Clinical Advances*, ed. by J. E. Blundell and M. O. Caruba. Raven Press, New York, pp. 71–99.
Morley, J. E., A. S. Levine, S. S. Murray, J. Kneip and M. Grace (1982). Peptidergic regulation of stress-induced eating. *American Journal of Physiology* **243**, R159–R163.
Nash, J. D. (1987). Eating behavior and body weight: psychosocial influences. *American Journal of Health Promotion* **2**, 5–13.

Nelson, J. C. and D. S. Charney (1980). Primary effective disorder criteria and the endogenous–reactive distinction. *Archives of General Psychiatry* **37**, 287–293.

Nemeroff, C. B., A. J. Osbahr III, G. Bissette, G. Jahnke, M. A. Lipton and A. J. Prange Jr (1978). Cholecystokinin inhibits tail pinch-induced eating in rats. *Science* **200**, 793–794.

Nemeroff, C. B., E. Widerlow and G. Bisette (1984). Elevated concentrations of CSF corticotropin-releasing factor-like immunoreactivity in depressed patients. *Science* **226**, 1342–1343.

Niewiadomska, G. and I. Lukazewska (1986). Increase in body weight of spontaneously hypertensive rats (SHR) under prolonged behavioral stimulation. *Physiology and Behavior* **40**, 681–684.

Ornstein, K. (1981). Suppression of wet-dog shakes by tail and scruff pinch. *Physiology and Behavior* **27**, 13–17.

Pyle, R. L., J. E. Mitchell and E. D. Eckert (1981). Bulimia: a report of 34 cases. *Journal of Clinical Psychiatry* **42**, 60–64.

Rivier, C. L. and P. M. Plotsky (1986). Mediation by corticotropin-releasing factor (CRF) of adenohypophyseal hormone secretion. *Annual Review of Physiology* **48**, 475–494.

Rivier, C., J. Rivier and W. Vale (1986). Stress-induced inhibition of reproductive functions: role of endogenous corticotropin-releasing factor. *Science* **231**, 607–609.

Robbins, T. W. and P. J. Fray (1980). Stress-induced eating: fact, fiction or misunderstanding. *Appetite* **1**, 103–133.

Rowland, N., D. M. Marques and A. E. Fisher (1980). Comparison of the effects of brain dopamine-depleting lesions upon oral behaviors elicited by tail pinch and electrical brain stimulation. *Physiology and Behavior* **24**, 273–281.

Roy, A., D. Pickar, S. Paul, A. Doran, G. P. Chrousos and P. W. Gold (1987). CSF corticotropin-releasing hormone in depressed patients and normal control subjects. *American Journal of Psychiatry* **144**, 641–645.

Seegmiller, J. E. (1980). *Metabolic Control and Disease*. W. B. Saunders, Philadelphia, p. 777.

Shibaski, T., A. Masuda, T. Imaki and N. Yamauchi (1987). CRF and somatostatin in stress-induced suppression of food intake in rats. *Endocrinology* **120**, 85A.

Spitz, R. (1965). *The First Year of Life* International University Press, New York.

Sprague, J. M., M. Levitt, K. Robson, C. N. Lui, E. Stellar and W N. Chambers (1983). A neuroanatomical and behavioral analysis of the syndromes resulting from midbrain lemniscal and reticular lesions in the cat. *Archivio Italiano di Biologia* **101**, 225–295

Strongman, K. T. (1965). The effect of anxiety on food intake in the rat. *Quarterly Journal of Experimental Psychology* **17**, 255–260.

Stunkard, A. J., W. J. Grace and H. G. Wolff (1955). The night eating syndrome. *American Journal of Medicine* **19**, 78–86.

Teskey, G. C., M. Kavaliers and M. Hirst (1984). Social conflict activates opioid analgesic and ingestive behaviors in male mice. *Life Sciences* **35**, 303–315.

Thierry, A. M., M. Fedkete and J. Glowinski (1968). Effects of stress on the metabolism of noradrenaline, dopamine, and serotonin (5-HT) in the central nervous system of the rat. *European Journal of Pharmacology* **4**, 384–389.

Thompson, D. A., S. L. Welle, U. Lilavivat, L. Pinicaud and R. G. Campbell (1982). Opiate receptor blockade in man reduced 2-deoxy-d-glucose induced food intake but not hunger, thirst, and hypothermia. *Life Sciences* **31**, 847–852.

Tinbergen, N. (1937). Uber das Verhalten Kampfender Kohlmeiser (Paries M. major L.). *Ardea* **26**, 222–223.

Tugendhat, B. (1960). The disturbed feeding behavior of the three-spined stickleback. I. Electric shock is administered in the food area. *Behavior* **16**, 159–187.

Vale, W., J. Spiess, C. Rivier and J. Rivier (1981). Characterization of a 41-residue ovine hypothalamic peptide that stimulates secretion of corticotropin and beta-endorphin. *Science* **213**, 1394–1396.

Vaswani, K., G. A. Tejwani and S. Mousa (1983). Stress-induced differential intake of various diets and water by rat: the role of the opiate system. *Life Sciences* **32**, 1983–1996.

Waggoner, D., S. Srdar, A. S. Levine and J. E. Morley (1985). A model of stress-induced anorexia. *Federation Proceedings* **44**, 1281A.

Watson, P. J., M. A. Short, D. H. Munroe and D. R. Warfield (1980). Digging and biting induced by pinch stimuli and lateral hypothalamic electrical stimulation. *Physiology and Behavior* **24**, 267–271.

Weiss, G. F., P. Papadakos, K. Knudson and S. F. Leibowitz (1986). Medial hypothalamic serotonin: effects on deprivation and norepinephrine-induced eating. *Pharmacology, Biochemistry and Behavior* **25**, 1223–1230.

Weiss, J. M. (1968). Effects of coping responses on stress. *Journal of Comparative Physiology and Psychology* **65**, 251–260.

Willenbring, M. L., A. S. Levine and J. E. Morley (1986). Stress-induced eating: a pilot study. *International Journal of Eating Disorders* **5**, 855–864.

15

Central neurotransmitter disturbances in bulimia (nervosa)

K. M. Pirke
Max-Planck Institute for Psychiatry, Munich

Neurotransmitters are chemical substances which are released during the transmission of an electrical signal from one neuron to another or to the target organ. Their action at the innervated tissue is mediated through specific receptors to which the neurotransmitters bind.

Neurotransmitters transmit signals in the peripheral as well as in the central nervous system. Under certain physiological conditions their turnover in different regions of the brain can vary significantly. Changes in peripheral transmitter metabolism may, but do not necessarily, occur in parallel with those in the central transmitter metabolism.

In this chapter, studies of two neurotransmitters, namely noradrenaline and serotonin, will be discussed, since most of the studies published so far have been largely concerned with these two compounds.

Noradrenaline

The central noradrenergic system has numerous functions. Noradrenaline plays a role in the regulation of hunger and satiety (Leibowitz, 1984) as well as in the regulation of many neuroendocrine systems, for example the hypothalamo–hypophyseal–gonadal axis, the hypothalamo–hypophyseal–adrenonocortical axis and the hypothalamo–hypophyseal–thyroid axis.

In patients suffering from bulimia, these neuroendocrine systems are as equally disturbed as the regulation of appetite (see Halmi, Chapter 12 this volume). The noradrenaline system apparently plays an important role in the development of depression (van Praag, 1980; Zis and Goodwin, 1982). Depression occurs frequently in patients with bulimia (Laessle, Chapter 8, this volume). A significant connection between degree of depression and orthostatic increase in the noradrenaline concentrations in peripheral blood plasma has been observed in anorexic patients (Laessle, Chapter 8, this volume). These observations point towards a possible disturbance of the noradrenergic system in bulimia and to a causal link between noradrenaline and some symptoms of bulimia.

MHPG (3-methoxy-4-hydroxy-phenylglycol sulphate) is a metabolite of noradrenaline in the central and in the peripheral nervous systems; it is excreted in the urine. We studied MHPG in the urine (24-hour samples) of 30 female patients with bulimia aged between 20 and 36 years (mean 24.5 years). Twelve young women of similar age served as controls. The diagnosis 'bulimia' was based on DSM-III criteria. The weight of the patients with bulimia was 22.3 ± 0.26 kg/m^2 BMI (body mass index). The BMI of the controls was 21.9 ± 2.4 kg/m^2. Both groups collected urine over periods of 24 hours.

The mean excretion of MHPG sulphate in the patients with bulimia amounted to 0.83 ± 0.27 mg/24 h ($\bar{x}$ – ± SD) and was significantly lower ($p < 0.01$) than the MHPG excretion of the controls (0.98 ± 0.25 mg/24 h).

In a further investigation (Heufelder, Warnhoff and Pirke, 1985) we studied the effect of orthostatic stress on plasma noradrenaline concentrations in patients with bulimia and in controls. Blood was collected from 24 females with bulimia and 20 control females of corresponding age when in the prone position and after standing upright for 10 min. In the prone position noradrenaline levels in the patients with bulimia were low but not significantly depressed. Orthostatic increase in plasma noradrenaline was, however, diminished in bulimia (0.64 ± 0.14 *vs* 1.11 ± 0.12 pmol/ml). In the same study we investigated the α_2-adrenoreceptors of the blood platelets. In patients with bulimia there was a significant increase in the capacity of the receptors (297 ± 37 *vs* 192 ± 8 nmol/mg protein). The α-adrenoreceptors of the blood platelets have two binding sites; one of these has a stimulatory (prostaglandin E_1), and the other an inhibitory (adrenaline, noradrenaline) effect on adenylate cyclase (cAMP). Figure 15.1 shows the stimulatory effect of PGE_1 on cyclic AMP formation by the platelets. Figure 15.2 shows the inhibitory effect of adrenaline on adenylate cyclase. Because of the increased receptor capacity, the ability to stimulate or to inhibit adenylate cyclase is increased in bulimia.

Further information on the function of the noradrenaline system was obtained in a study of 12 controls and 13 patients with bulimia who were first

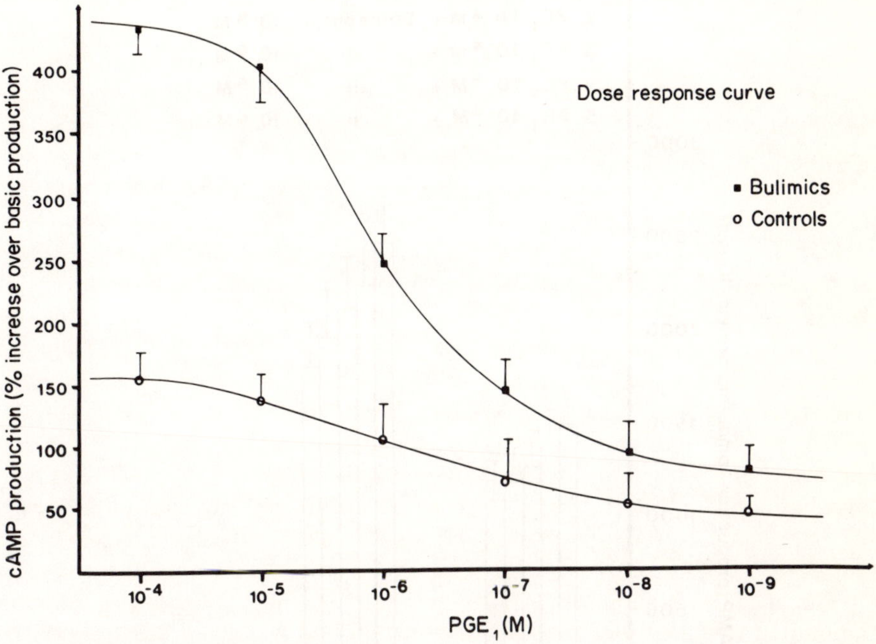

Figure 15.1. Stimulating action of prostaglandin E_1 (PGE_1) on adenylate cyclase (cAMP) production by thrombocytes from female patients with bulimia and from controls (mean values ± SEM)

given a test meal rich in proteins (500 kcal; 82 g protein, 37 g carbohydrates and 1 g fat) and, during a second session, a meal rich in carbohydrates (500 kcal; 124 g carbohydrates) (Pirke *et al.*, 1988).

Figure 15.3 shows the time course of the plasma noradrenaline concentrations before and after the meals. Both groups exhibited a significant increase in noradrenaline after both types of test meals. In the patients with bulimia, the increase (areas below the curves) was significantly smaller.

Physical exertion constitutes a strong stimulus for activation of the noradrenaline system in the periphery and in various regions of the central nervous system (Leifeld, Schweiger and Pirke, 1986). We investigated the effect of a standardized ergometric workload on pulse rate, blood pressure and plasma noradrenaline concentrations in 12 female patients with bulimia (diagnosis according to DSM-III) and 11 healthy controls of similar age (Figure 15.4 a–d). From Figure 15.4a it can be seen that both groups performed the same amount of work. Before the work, pulse rate, systolic blood pressure and noradrenaline were significantly lower in patients with bulimia than in the

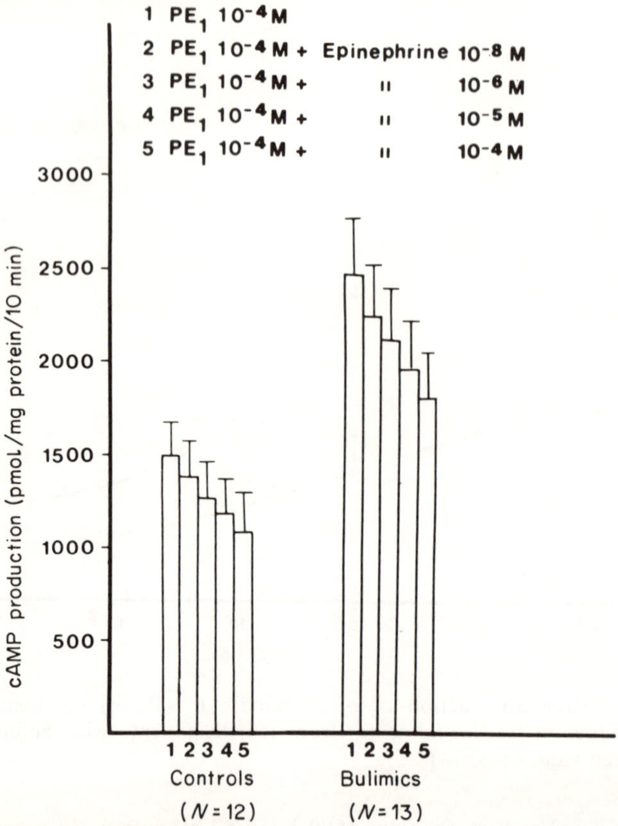

Figure 15.2. Inhibitory effect of adrenaline on adenylate cyclase (cAMP) production by thrombocytes from patients with bulimia and from controls (mean values ± SEM)

control group. During the work there was, however, a normal increase in the parameters measured (Figure 15.4 b–d).

Kaye *et al.* (1989a) found that there were significantly lower noradrenaline concentrations in the plasma of patients with bulimia whether the subjects were lying down or standing up. Noradrenaline concentrations in the cerebrospinal fluid (CSF) were also significantly lower. These results were obtained after the subjects had been in hospital for 30 days and were not observed three days after hospitalization. We obtained similar results from anorexic patients whose noradrenaline values were normal (or even elevated) when they entered hospital; in the course of treatment their noradrenaline concentration fell to subnormal values; with progressive increase in body weight they gradually increased again.

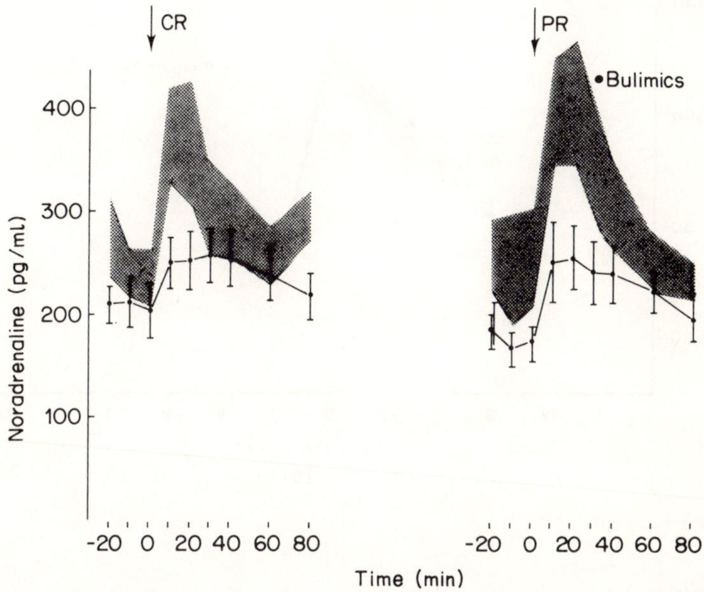

Figure 15.3. The effect of a carbohydrate-rich (CR) and a protein-rich (PR) test meal on plasma noradrenaline concentrations in patients with bulimia (mean values ± SEM) and in controls (stippled area)

In summary, the studies discussed above have led to the following picture:

In bulimia, the activity of the peripheral sympathetic nervous system is slightly, but significantly, decreased. Thus, the capacity of adrenoreceptors is increased, as shown by the example of α_2-adrenoreceptors of the blood platelets and an increase in the ability to stimulate and inhibit the 'second messenger' systems.

Under conditions of general stimulation, the sympathetic nervous system can be easily activated, although the increase in plasma noradrenaline concentration in certain test conditions (orthostasis, test meals) remains subnormal.

The results on the CSF, as well as the neuroendocrine observations (decreased secretion of gonadotrophins; Pirke, Chapter 17, this volume) and the activation of the pituitary–adrenal axis (Fichter, Chapter 18, this volume), point towards a decreased central noradrenaline turnover. All three results are not proof of a diminution in the central noradrenaline turnover, because noradrenaline in the CSF is derived not only from the brain but can also come from the bloodstream. Furthermore, many other neurotransmitter substances

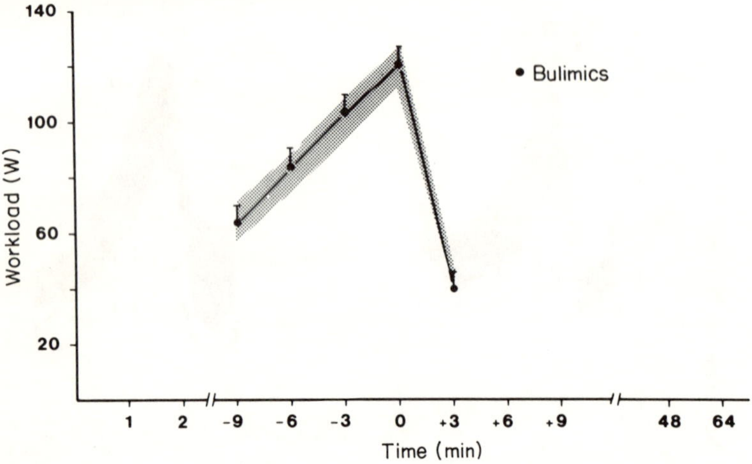
140
100
60
20
Workload (W)
• Bulimics
1
2
-9
-6
-3
0
+3
+6
+9
48
64
Time (min)

(a)

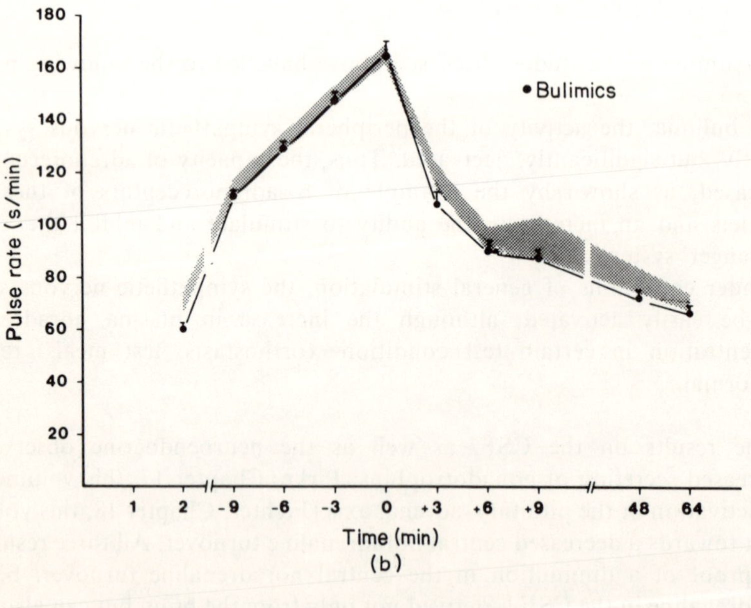
180
160
140
120
100
80
60
40
20
Pulse rate (s/min)
• Bulimics
1
2
-9
-6
-3
0
+3
+6
+9
48
64
Time (min)

(b)

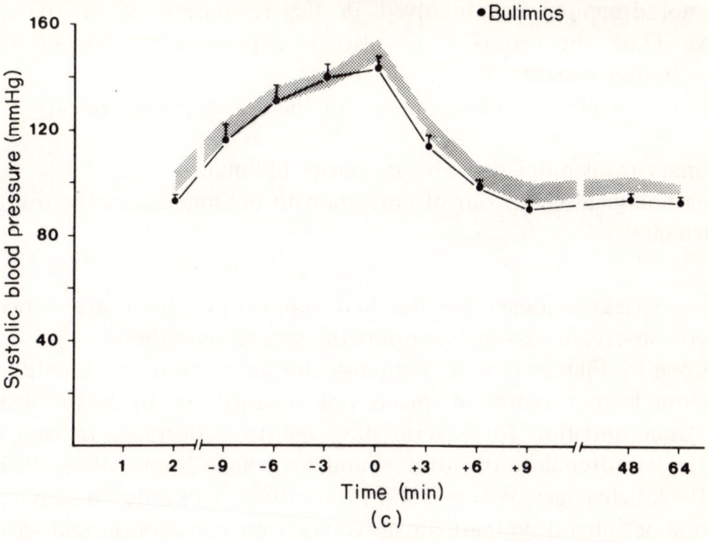

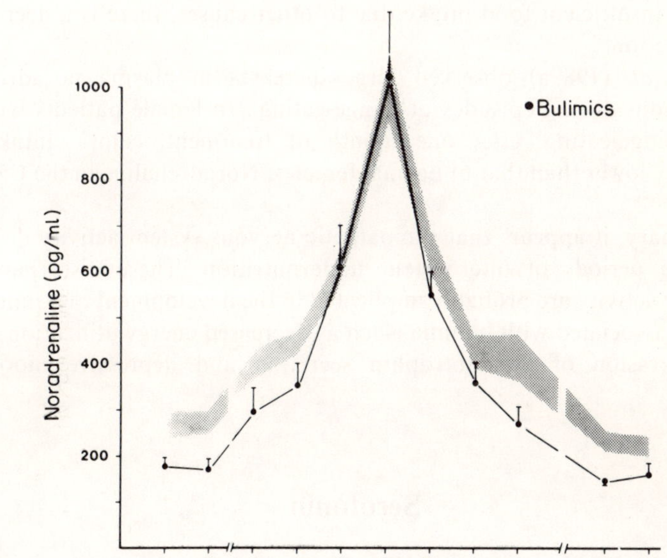

Figure 15.4. Effect of (a) a standardized ergometric workload (watt) in supine position on (b) pulse rate, (c) systolic blood pressure (SBP) and (d) plasma noradrenaline concentrations (NA) in patients with bulimia (mean values + SEM) and in controls (stippled areas)

besides noradrenaline are involved in the regulation of neuroendocrine functions. Thus, the results could also be explained by changes in other neurotransmitter systems.

There are two possible explanations for the noradrenaline results:

1. A primary transmitter disturbance causes bulimia.
2. The pathological behaviour of patients with bulimia causes the transmitter disturbance.

There is no clear evidence for the first supposition; there are, however, a number of observations which support the second hypothesis.

As shown by Fichter *et al.* (Chapter 4, this volume), many female patients with bulimia have intermittent episodes of malnutrition. In the rat, acute and chronic undernutrition for several days led to a decrease in central and peripheral noradrenaline turnover (Landsberg and Young, 1978; Pirke and Spyra, 1982; Schweiger, Warnoff and Pirke, 1985). This reduced activity of the central and peripheral sympathetic nervous system is one of the endocrinological adaptation mechanisms which help the body to adjust to decreased caloric intake and causes a reduction in energy utilization. In the anorexic patient, as in cases of insufficient food intake due to other causes, there is a decrease in sympathetic tone.

Kaye *et al.* (1989a) observed large increases in plasma noradrenaline concentrations during episodes of 'binge-eating'. In female patients who had stopped 'binge-eating' after one month of treatment, calorie intake was significantly lower than that of normal females. Noradrenaline in the CSF was decreased.

In summary, it appears that sympathetic nervous system activity decreases due to the periods of intermittent undernutrition. These disturbances in transmitter activity are probably implicated in the development of a number of symptoms associated with bulimia, such as decreased energy utilization during rest, suppression of gonadotrophin secretion and depressive mood disturbances.

Serotonin

Jimmerson, Brandt and Brewerton (1988) proposed the hypothesis that decreased activity of the central serotonin system may be a predisposing factor for the development of bulimia. This hypothesis is based on animal experiments in which the role of serotonin in the regulation of hunger and satiety has been studied (Blundell, 1984). The administration of serotonin antagonists led to the consumption of larger meals, causing an increase in body weight. In contrast, administration of serotonin agonists led to a decrease in food intake. As a consequence of these observations, serotonin agonists were introduced in the treatment of obesity (Stunkard, Craighead and O'Brien, 1980). Serotonin agonists such as fenfluramine and dexfenfluramine were also tried in the treatment of bulimia. Because of methodological difficulties in these studies, it has not, so far, been possible to reach a clearcut opinion on the therapeutic effects of these drugs (G. Russell, personal communication).

As evidence for the validity of their hypothesis, Jimmerson, Brandt and Brewerton (1988) cite studies in which an increase in prolactin secretion after treatment with m-chlorophenylpiperazine (a serotonin agonist) was observed. In patients with bulimia, the increase in prolactin was significantly less than in normal persons. As prolactin secretion is dependent on oestrogens, and as oestrogen levels are lowered in females with bulimia (see Pirke, Chapter 17, this volume), this interpretation has to be regarded with caution.

Decreased concentration of 5-hydroxyindolylacetic acid (5-HIAA) in the CSF of patients suffering from anorexia nervosa whose body weight was diminished has been reported by Kaye *et al.* (1984). This observation suggests reduced activity of central serotonin systems. In a second investigation (Kaye *et al.*, 1988a), these authors studied anorexic patients with normal body weight. Those female patients who did not experience 'binge-eating' had normal 5-HIAA values in the CSF, but in patients experiencing episodes of 'binge-eating' followed by vomiting the values were not normal. Whether this also occurs in patients with bulimia without a history of anorexia nervosa has not yet been investigated.

In addition to studies of the CSF, there is a second way to obtain information about central serotonin activity. Fernstrom and Wurtman (1971) have observed that the serotonin content of the brain is regulated by the uptake into the brain of the serotonin precursor tryptophan. For the six 'large neutral amino acids' (leucine, isoleucine, phenylalanine, valine, tryptophan and tyrosine) there is a common transport mechanism at the blood–brain barrier. Thus, tryptophan influx into the brain is dictated by the ratio of tryptophan to the other large neutral amino acids (LNAA). After a protein-rich meal only small amounts of tryptophan will enter the brain, as the ratio between tryptophan and its competitors is low (Figure 15.5). The reason for this lies in the fact that animal protein contains little tryptophan but large amounts of its competitors. After a carbohydrate meal there is a release of insulin. Insulin stimulates the influx of both glucose and the LNAA into the peripheral tissues. Tryptophan is an exception. This means that after a carbohydrate meal, the plasma levels of the neutral amino acids are decreased; the tryptophan concentrations, however, remain unaltered. The tryptophan quotient is therefore increased. More tryptophan will be transported into the brain and the serotonin content of the brain increases. If there is a decrease in the effectiveness of insulin, the tryptophan quotient will be reduced. Such a

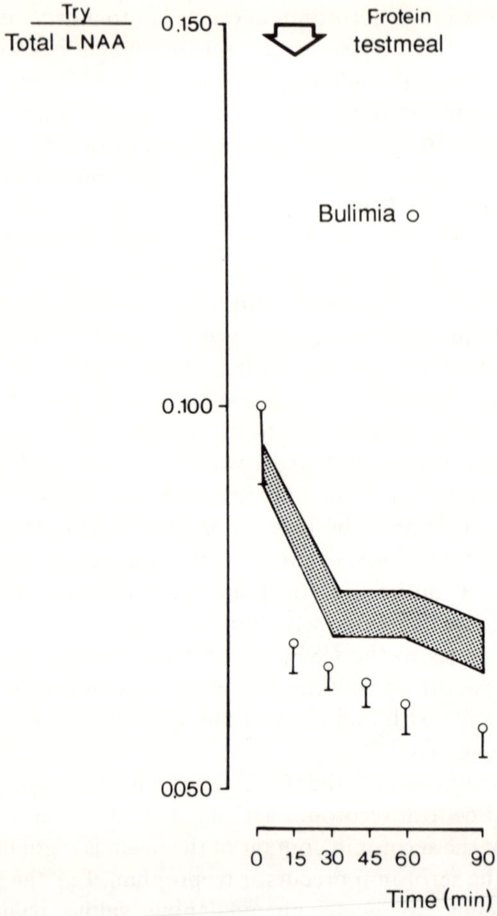

Figure 15.5. The ratio between the plasma concentrations of tryptophan (Try) and the sum of the large neutral amino acids (total LNAA) after a standardized protein test meal in patients with bulimia (mean values ± SEM) and in controls (stippled area)

decreased effectiveness of insulin occurs in anorexia nervosa (Schweiger *et al.*, 1986a) and also in bulimia (Schweiger *et al.*, 1987).

A group of 13 female bulimic patients with normal body weight and 12 normal females of corresponding age were given a protein-rich test meal (for composition see above). Figure 15.5 shows that a decrease in the tryptophan quotient occurred in the blood of both groups. In the bulimic patients, the decrease was significantly larger. This means that less tryptophan entered the brain. In addition to the results of the CSF, this is further (although only indirect) evidence for decreased activity of the serotoninergic neurons in the central nervous system of bulimic patients. Kaye *et al.* (1989b) measured the tryptophan quotient in the blood of bulimic patients during and after episodes of 'binge-eating'. They observed that bulimic episodes ceased when the tryptophan quotient increased. From this finding, the authors concluded that a diminished serotonin activity in the brain could facilitate or even precipitate a bulimia attack. Accordingly, 'binge-eating' would be a form of self-medication in the bulimic patient, used to combat the negative consequences of a diminished serotonin activity in the brain.

The cause of a decreased serotonin activity in the brain of bulimic patients is unknown. The following observations suggest the possibility that the intermittent undernutrition in bulimic patients (Fichter, Chapter 16, this volume) may be the reason for their decreased central serotonin activity: healthy females with normal body weight who go on a weight-reducing diet develop a reduced tryptophan quotient (Schweiger *et al.*, 1986b). A decreased tryptophan quotient together with decreased 5-HIAA concentrations in the CSF also occurs in anorexic patients when they are at low body weight, but not after their weight has normalized (an exception is the bulimic anorexic patient with normal body weight).

References

Blundel, J. E. (1984). Serotonin and apetite. *Neuropharmacology* **23**, 1537.

Fernstrom, J. D. and R. J. Wurtman (1971). Brain serotonin content: increase following ingestion of carbohydrate diet. *Science* **174**, 1023.

Heufelder, A., M. Warnhoff and K. M. Pirke (1985). Platelet $alpha_2$-adrenoceptor and adenylate cyclase in patients with anorexia nervosa and bulimia. *Journal of Clinical Endocrinology and Metabolism* **61**, 1053.

Jimmerson, D. C., H. A. Brandt and T. D. Brewerton (1988). Evidence for altered serotonin function in bulimia and anorexia nervosa: behavioral implications. In *Psychobiology of Bulimia Nervosa*, ed. by K. M. Pirke, W. Vandereycken and D. Ploog. Springer, Berlin, Heidelberg, New York, pp. 83–89.

Kaye, W. H., N. H. Ebert, M. Raleigh and R. Lake (1984). Abnormalities in CNS monoamine metabolism in anorexia nervosa. *Archives of General Psychiatry* **41**, 350.

Kaye, W. H., H. E. Gwirtsman, D. T. George, D. C. Jimmerson, M. H. Ebert and C. R. Lake (1989a). Disturbances in noradrenergic systems in normal-weight bulimia: sympathetic activation with bingeing, reduced noradrenergic activity after a month of abstinence from bingeing. *Archives of General Psychiatry*, in press.

Kaye, W. H., M. H. Ebert, H. E. Gwirtsman and S. R. Weiss (1989b). Brain serotonergic metabolism differentiates between patients with anorexia nervosa that fast or binge. *American Journal of Psychiatry*, in press.

Kaye, W. H., H. E. Gwirtsman, T. D. Brewerton, T. D. George and R. J. Wurtman (1989c). The role of serotonin in producing satiety during bulimic episodes: bingeing and vomiting induced elevations of plasma L-tryptophan associated with self-termination of bulimic episodes. *American Journal of Psychiatry*, in press.

Landsberg, L. and J. B. Young (1978). Fasting, feeding and regulation of the sympathetic nervous system. *New England Journal of Medicine* **298**, 1295.

Leibowitz, S. F. (1984). Noradrenergic function in the medial hypothalamus: potential relation to anorexia nervosa and bulimia. In *The Psychobiology of Anorexia Nervosa*, ed. by K. M. Pirke and D. Ploog. Springer, Berlin, pp. 35–45.

Leifeld, J., U. Schweiger and K. M. Pirke (1986). Exercise-induced increase of hypothalamic norepinephrine turnover in the rat is reduced by semistarvation. *Acta Endocrinologica*, Suppl. 274, 99.

Pirke, K. M. and B. Spyra (1982). Catecholamine turnover in the brain and the regulation of luteinizing hormone and corticosterone in starved male rats. *Acta Endocrinologica* **100**, 168.

Pirke, K. M., W. Riedel, R. J. Tuschl, U. Schweiger, M. Schweiger and B. Spyra (1988). Effect of standardized test meals on plasma norepinephrine in patients with anorexia nervosa and bulimia. *International Journal of Eating Disorders* **7**, 356.

Schweiger, U., J. Poellinger, R. G. Laessle, G. Wolfram, M. M. Fichter and K. M. Pirke (1987). Altered insulin response to a balanced test meal in bulimic patients. *International Journal of Eating Disorders* **6**, 551.

Schweiger, U., M. Warnhoff and K. M. Pirke (1985). Norepinephrine turnover in the hypothalamus of adult male rats: alteration of circadian patterns by semistarvation. *Journal of Neurochemistry* **45**, 706.

Schweiger, U., R. G. Laessle, S. Kittl, B. Dickhaut, M. Schweiger and K. M. Pirke (1986b). Macronutrient intake, plasma large neutral amino acids and mood during weight-reducing diets. *Journal of Neural Transmission* **67**, 77.

Schweiger, U., M. Warnhoff, J. Pahl and K. M. Pirke (1986a). Effects of carbohydrate and protein meals on plasma large neutral amino acids, glucose, and insulin plasma levels of anorectic patients. *Metabolism* **35**, 938.

Stunkard, A. J., L. W. Craighead and R. O'Brien (1980). Controlled trial of behaviour therapy, pharmacotherapy, and their combination in the treatment of obesity. *Lancet* **2**, 1045.

Van Praag, H. M. (1980). Central monoamine metabolism in depressions. II. Catecholamines and related compounds. *Comprehensive Psychiatry* **21**, 144.

Zis, A. P. and F. S. Goodwin (1982). The amine hypothesis. In *Handbook of Affective Disorders*, ed. by E. S. Paykel. Livingstone, Edinburgh, London, New York, S.175.

16

Endocrine dysfunctions in bulimia (nervosa)

M. M. Fichter
University of Munich and Klinik Roseneck, Prien
and
K. M. Pirke
Max-Planck Institute for Psychiatry, Munich

Hypothalamic centres play an important role in the regulation of eating (see Ploog *et al.*, 1981). The functions of the hypothalamus also include the regulation of fluid balance, temperature, physical activity, sexual behaviour, hunger and satiety and hormone secretion. All these functions can be disturbed in the course of anorexic or bulimic eating disorders. To what extent are these functional disturbances primary or secondary in nature? Although Simmonds' (1916) hypothesis that a deficiency of the pituitary gland is the primary cause of anorexia nervosa has been shown to be incorrect, it has for several decades stimulated extensive endocrinological research in this area. In the proposed diagnostic criteria according to the new international diagnostic scheme ICD 10 (WHO, 1987), disturbances in neuroendocrine functions are a necessary criterion for the diagnosis of anorexia nervosa. However, almost all the available neuroendocrine findings in anorexia nervosa indicate that the neuroendocrine changes are not specific to this disorder but are rather the consequence of decreased body weight and insufficient food intake. In Table 16.1 endocrine observations in starvation, anorexia nervosa and bulimia nervosa are listed. Parallels between the findings in anorexia nervosa and those in starvation are impressive. Subsequently, some observations of cases with bulimia nervosa have also become available. Some of these patients show neuroendocrine dysfunctions, but these are not as pronounced as in anorexia nervosa. Two hypotheses have been suggested for the interpretation of these results.

Table 16.1 Endocrine observations in starvation, anorexia nervosa and bulimia nervosa

	Starvation literature		Anorexia nervosa literature		Bulimia literature	
	First author	Own obs.	First author	Own obs.	First author	Own obs.
Thyroid gland						
T4 normal	Palmblad (1977)		Miyai (1975) Moshang (1975)	N.i.	?	N.i.
T3 decreased	Palmblad (1977)	Yes	Miyai (1975) Moshang (1975)	N.i.	?	Yes
Decreased basal metabolism	Brozek (1946)	N.i.	Warren (1973)	N.i.	N.i.	N.i.
TSH normal to slightly decreased	Palmblad (1977)	Yes	Vigersky (1976a)	N.i.		N.i.
TSH response to TRF reduced	N.i.	Yes	Vigersky (1976b)	Yes	N.i.	Yes
Adrenal gland						
Increased plasma cortisol	Alleyne (1967)	Yes	Vigersky (1976a)	Yes	No	No
	Palmblad (1977) Smith (1975)		Walsh (1978) Warren (1973)		Walsh (1987)	
	Alleyne (1967)	Yes	Boyar (1977)	Yes	No	No
Path. 24 h plasma cortisol secretory pattern			Walsh (1978)		Walsh (1987)	
Insufficient suppression of dexamethasone test	Alleyne (1967) Smith (1975)	Yes	Boyar (1977) Walsh (1978)	Yes	Walsh (1987)	Yes
	Alleyne (1967)	Yes	Walsh (1978)	Yes		No
Retarded cortisol catabolism	Smith (1975)	Yes				

Increased cortisol production rate	Smith (1975)	Yes	Boyar (1977) Walsh (1981)	Yes	No Walsh (1987)	No
Growth hormone (HGH)						
Increased	Kling (1978)*	Yes	Virgersky (1976a)	N.i.	N.i.	(Yes)
HGH release after stimulation with clonidine decreased	N.i.	Yes	N.i.	N.i.	N.i.	Yes
Prolactin (PRL)						
Decreased nocturnal PRL secretion	N.i.	Yes	Brown (1979)	N.i.	N.i.	(Yes)
PRL secretion after TRF reduced	N.i.	N.i.	Brambilla (1981) Waldhauser (1984)	N.i.	N.i.	Yes
Gonadotrophins						
Decreased plasma gonadotrophin (LH, FSH)	Pirke (1981)†	Yes	Boyar (1974)	Yes		Yes
Reduced response to LH–RH	Pirke (1981)†	N.i.	Halmi (1975)	N.i.	N.i.	N.i.
Reduced response to clomiphen	N.i.	N.i.	Marshall (1971)	N.i.	N.i.	N.i.
Regression of the 24-h plasma LH secretory pattern	N.i.	Yes	Boyar (1974)	Yes		Yes

* Observations on subjects with increased body weight.
† Animal experiments.
N.i., not investigated; Own obs., own observations in anorexic patients, in fasting test subjects or in bulimia.

1. The affective disorder hypothesis. According to this hypothesis, bulimia is regarded as a nosological subgroup of the typical (major) depression (affective disorder) (Hudson, Laffer and Pope, 1982; Hudson *et al.*, 1983 a, b). Common to both disorders are depressive symptoms in the patient, a family history of depression, beneficial effects of antidepressant medication, and comparable neuroendocrine findings. In the search for so-called 'biological markers' for certain psychiatric diseases, a common denominator for these four disparate findings has been sought.

2. Nutrition hypothesis. This hypothesis is more direct and parsimonious; it accounts for neuroendocrine observations in anorexia nervosa and in bulimia (nervosa) on the basis of a temporarily reduced food intake. According to this hypothesis, depressive mood change in bulimia (nervosa) may be the consequence of a diet which is relatively low in carbohydrates. In this context the theory of Richard Wurtman, which describes the association between carbohydrates and tryptophan intake and serotonin concentrations in the central nervous system, is of special interest. According to this theory, tryptophan, the amino acid precursor of serotonin, competes with the other large neutral amino acids (LNAA) at the blood–brain barrier for transport into the brain (Wurtman and Wurtman, 1984). The tryptophan/LNAA quotient in the blood plasma determines the amount of trypotophan which can pass across the blood–brain barrier and become available in the brain for the synthesis of the neurotransmitter serotonin. Serotonin metabolism and carbohydrate appetite are interlinked in a complicated nutrition–neurotransmitter feedback loop. Carbohydrate intake increases tryptophan content of the brain. On the basis of this by now relatively well-founded theory, one may assume that episodes of excessive hunger and overeating occur in bulimic patients especially in conditions associated with a decreased serotonin content in the central nervous system (CNS). Thus, 'binge-eating' would cause a temporary increase in the serotonin content of the CNS. It is possible to treat central depletion of serotonin temporarily either by supplying the serotonin precursor tryptophan or by eating carbohydrates. The effect of carbohydrates can be explained as follows. Carbohydrates stimulate insulin secretion and insulin increases uptake of LNAA with the exception of tryptophan into the peripheral tissues. Thus the tryptophan/LNAA ratio in the blood plasma increases after carbohydrate ingestion, more tryptophan will enter the brain and more serotonin can be synthesized. Thus, depressive symptoms in bulimia (nervosa) may be explained às a nutritional deficiency, i.e. as a consequence of insufficient carbohydrate intake and ensuing decrease in central serotonin (see Schweiger *et al.*, 1986; Pirke, Chapter 15, this volume).

In bulimic patients with normal body weight, malnutrition is less obvious than in underweight anorexic patients. There are two reasons for assuming that bulimic patients are relatively undernourished:

(a) Bulimic patients typically alternate between periods of fasting and reduced food intake *via* a diet low in carbohydrates and fats, and periods of excessive hunger and 'binge-eating' followed by weight gain. According to the nutrition hypothesis, neuroendocrine dysfunctions should occur during phases of dieting and fasting; they should be absent during phases when body weight remains constant or increases.

(b) Despite an apparently normal or even elevated body weight, a considerable number of patients with bulimia (nervosa) have a suboptimal body weight with respect to their 'individual normal weight'. Following the slimness ideal, they have decreased their 'individual normal weight' by fasting. According to the nutrition theory, the absolute or relative body weight of a bulimic or an anorexic patient is not sufficient to predict the presence of neuroendocrine dysfunctions. In addition, the time dimensions (records of body weight for days, weeks, months or years) are of great importance.

The nutrition hypothesis helps to clarify the connections between the development of neuroendocrine functional disorders in anorexia nervosa and in bulimia (nervosa). Endocrine disturbances in bulimia (nervosa) appear to be largely dependent on actual nutritional state (state-dependency). Since actual food intake has not been taken into account in most of the papers published on the endocrinology of anorexia nervosa or bulimia (nervosa), results are not easy to interpret. In order to be able to manipulate nutritional state experimentally, we studied the effects of fasting ('total food abstinence') on neuroendocrine function in healthy test subjects under controlled conditions.

Experimental Investigations of Healthy Persons Under Conditions of Fasting

Physiology of hunger and fasting

After approximately one day (12–14 hours) of food restriction, glycogen reserves in the body are utilized and glucose and free fatty acids (deriving from liposomes) contribute to the energy supply. Only 10–20 per cent of the energy supply derives from oxidation of amino acids (Owen *et al.*, 1978). After longer periods of fasting (several days), glycogen deposits are exhausted and up to 90 per cent of energy requirements are supplied by free fatty acids and their metabolites (β-hydroxybutyric acid and acetoacetate). The rest of the energy is supplied by amino acids (gluconeogenesis or direct oxidation). After several weeks of fasting, the body adapts itself to reduced food intake by a decrease in the secretion of triiodothyronine (T3) and a reduction in catecholamine synthesis (Young and Landsberg, 1977). This leads (in a cold environment) to decreased body temperature, blood pressure and heart rate. It is well known that blood glucose concentrations are also reduced under conditions of starvation.

Scientific research into the effects of fasting-induced undernutrition in healthy persons began only at the end of the last century with a self-experiment by the physician Tanner (see Keys *et al.*, 1950). At the beginning of this century Benedict *et al.* (1919; Benedict, 1915) conducted the classic 'Carnegie-Nutrition Laboratory fasting experiment' on male test subjects under conditions of semistarvation. After only a few days of fasting, the oxidation of carbohydrates had almost completely ceased. This was confirmed later with newer, more refined analytical techniques. The volunteers studied by Benedict lost about 10 per cent of their original body weight over the course of several months.

To date, the most extensive, and, in terms of design, execution and assessment, most comprehensive experimental study of fasting is the 'Minnesota experiment' by Keys *et al.* (1950). In their extensive monograph *The Biology of Human Starvation*, they reported the physical and psychological effects of a 168-day low-calorie diet in male test subjects. According to the test subjects' self-report, under conditions of semistarvation the following disturbances (in order of frequency of occurrence) were most common; tiredness, loss of appetite, sensitivity to noise, irritability, apathy, hunger, loss of concentration, loss of libido, loss of vigilance, emotional instability, depression and decreased motor activity. Keys *et al.* discussed these results in terms of an 'experimental neurosis', since the symptoms were induced by semistarvation and were reversible by appropriate nutrition. After six months of semistarvation, Keys *et al.* observed an increased variance, compared with the baseline, in the neurosis scales of the Minnesota Multiphasic Personality Interventory (MMPI): hypochondria, depression and hysteria. Individual psychological reactions to the conditions of fasting appeared to vary considerably.

At the time of the Minnesota experiment, detailed neuroendocrine studies had not been possible. During the 1960s experiments on fasting were carried out by Kollar *et al.* (1964) and by Consolazio *et al.* (1967). Palmblad *et al.* (1977) measured the plasma concentrations of a number of hormones such as growth hormone, TSH, cortisol, T3, T4 and rT3 in volunteers during a short period of absolute food deprivation.

In a large number of studies of patients with anorexia nervosa (see Fichter, 1985) many endocrine changes have been observed. It has, however, been clearly demonstrated that disturbances in anorexia nervosa concerning the hypothalamo–hypophyseal–adrenocortical axis (Doerr *et al.*, 1980; Fichter *et al.*, 1982) and –gonadal axis (Pirke *et al.*, 1979) are associated with decreased food intake and loss in body weight. The fact that endocrine dysfunctions in anorexia nervosa are indeed the consequences of reduced food intake was confirmed in follow-up experiments on anorexic patients whose endocrine functions normalized after successful treatment of the weight loss. A further proof was obtained in a fasting investigation on healthy subjects.

The Munich fasting experiment

The aim of this experiment was a detailed analysis of several endocrine systems in healthy female subjects under conditions of complete food deprivation (Fichter, 1985; Fichter, Pirke and Holsboer, 1986; Fichter and Pirke, 1986 a,b). The first fasting experiment in modern psychiatry was conducted at the Department of Psychiatry at the University of Munich in 1981/82 on five healthy young women with a mean age of 23.3 ± 0.98 (SEM) years. These women were paid volunteers. Before the start of the study their suitability for these investigations was very carefully assessed by personal examination, questionnaire and laboratory tests. The experiment was divided into four time phases: (a) baseline I, during which body weight was maintained at baseline; (b) fasting for three weeks (total food abstinence) under stationary conditions with a mean loss in body weight of 8.0 kg; this corresponded to a decrease in body weight from 103 per cent to 88 per cent of ideal weight (Metropolitan Life Insurance Company, 1959); (c) a phase in which body weight was restored to the baseline level; and (d) baseline II, body weight was maintained at the same level as in baseline I.

The following assessments were carried out. During periods of 24 hours (blood samples taken every 30 min) the plasma concentrations of cortisol (Co), luteinizing hormone (LH), follicle-stimulating hormone (FSH), growth hormone (HGH), TSH and prolactin (PRL) were measured. In addition, the following functional tests were conducted: (1) dexamethasone suppression test (DST); (2) TRF test; and (3) clonidine test (see Fichter and Pirke, 1986 a,b). The following observations were recorded.

Hypothalamo-pituitary-adrenocortical axis

The DST assesses the degree to which secretion of cortisol from the adrenal cortex is suppressed by the administration of the synthetic steroid dexamethasone. In healthy people this suppression is pronounced; in some diseases it may be reduced. As can be seen from Figure 16.1, in healthy subjects under conditions of fasting there was a partial reduction in suppression of cortisol secretion. This was more pronounced after three weeks than after two weeks of total food abstinence. Despite the small number of test subjects, this decrease in cortisol suppression under fasting conditions was statistically significant. With regard to the hypothalamo-hypophyseal-adrenocortical axis, considerable changes in cortisol secretion also occurred over 24 hours. Comparing the situation at the start of the experiment with that at the end of the fasting period, a number of changes occurred in the healthy female test subjects. These were: a statistically significant increase in plasma cortisol concentrations over 24 hours, an increase in minimum plasma cortisol

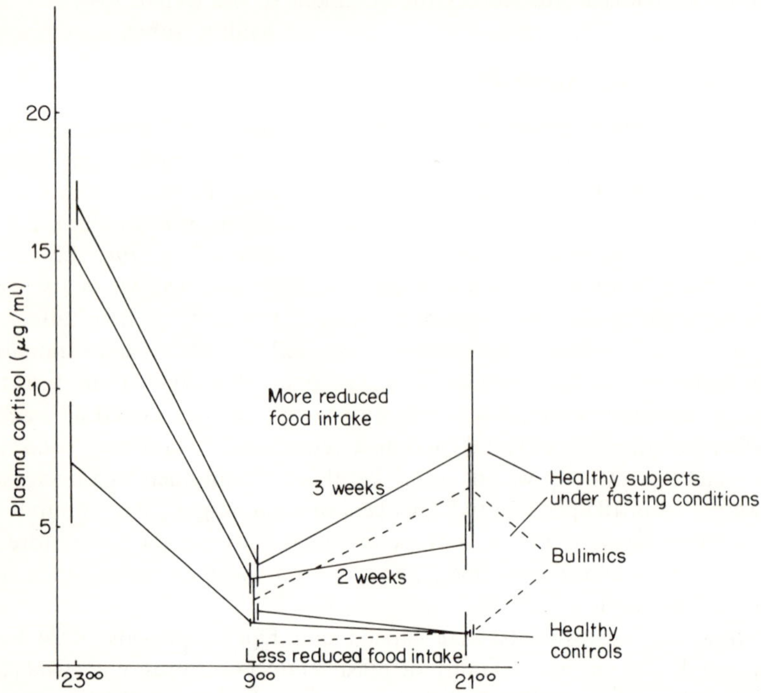

Figure 16.1. Plasma cortisol concentrations in the dexamethasone suppression test (DST) in healthy subjects and in patients with bulimia during normal and reduced food intake (mean ± SEM)

concentrations in 24 hours, an increase in total duration of secretory activity (probably due to a retarded catabolism in the liver), and a prolonged half-life of cortisol in plasma. In addition, the number of episodic cortisol secretions over 24 hours showed a tendency to increase (not statistically significant). Figure 16.2 shows the considerable changes in cortisol secretion occurring in healthy women under conditions of fasting. It is remarkable that all pathological changes in cortisol secretion disappeared completely after restoration of body weight. This is convincing evidence for a connection between reduced food intake and pathological changes in the functioning of the hypthalamo–pituitary–adrenocortical axis. Increased plasma cortisol concentrations and changes in the 24-hour plasma cortisol pattern, prolonged half-life for plasma cortisol (indicating a slower cortisol catabolism) and decrease in the suppression of cortisol secretion by dexamethasone have also been observed in undernourished people in the third world and in patients suffering from malnutrition due to various organic diseases (Cooke *et al.*, 1964; Alleyne and Young, 1967; Smith, Bledsoe and Chetri, 1975).

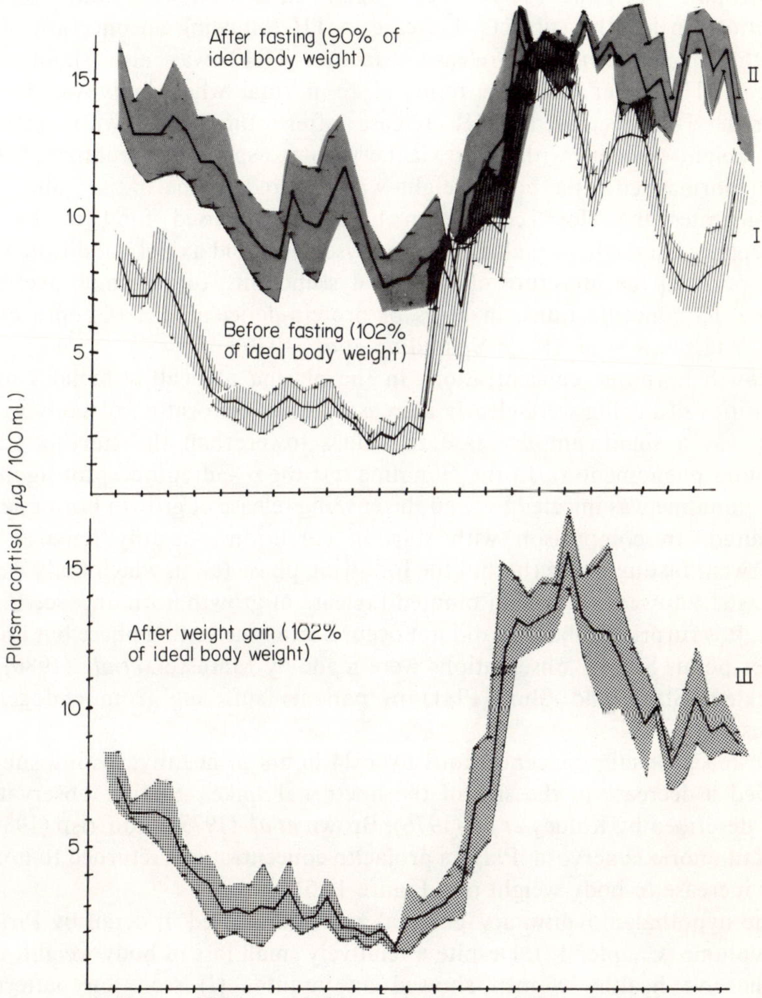

Figure 16.2. Munich fasting experiment. 24-hour plasma cortisol concentrations in five healthy women before and after 21 days of fasting and after final weight gain (mean values ± SEM)

Considerable changes were also found in the *hypothalamo-pituitary-thyroid* axis. The values for plasma T3 and the 'basal metabolism' were decreased under starvation conditions (Alleyne and Young, 1967; Smith, Bledsoe and Chetri, 1975) and the T4 values were usually normal (Palmblad *et al.*, 1977; Brozek and Keys, 1946). As shown in Figure 16.3, basal values for the thyrotrophic hormone (TSH) were significantly decreased under fasting conditions in healthy subjects. Increase in TH following an injection of the hypothalamic thyrotrophin-releasing factor (TRF) was also significantly reduced. The latter response returned to normal when body weight was restored. The decreased TSH release after stimulation with TRF in underweight patients with anorexia nervosa (Casper and Frohman, 1982), which normalized after body weight was restored to the initial value, also demonstrates the close connection between decreased food intake and disturbances in the hypothalamo–hypophyseal–thyroid axis. In addition, there are reports in the literature of thyroid dysfunctions, for example decreased plasma T3 concentrations, in cases of protein-deficient diet (Chopra *et al.*, 1975; Vagenakis *et al.*, 1975; Spaulding *et al.*, 1976).

Growth hormone concentrations in the plasma of healthy females under conditions of fasting were clearly increased. After restoration of body weight there was a significant decrease to values lower than the starting values (rebound phenomenon). In the clonidine test the α_2-adrenoreceptor agonistic drug clonidine was injected i.v. and the ensuing release of growth hormone was measured. In comparison with starting conditions, healthy females who underwent fasting phase (b) and the following phase (c), in which body weight increased, showed a reduced ('blunted') release of growth hormone (see Figure 16.4). It is surprising that this did not occur during the fasting phase but only at a later point. Similar observations were made by Matussek *et al.*, (1980) and Checkley, Slade and Slur (1981) in patients suffering from endogenous depression.

Plasma prolactin concentrations over 24 hours in healthy, fasting subjects showed a decrease in the size of the nocturnal spikes. Similar observations were described by Kalucy *et al.* (1976), Brown *et al.* (1979) and Crisp (1980) in cases of anorexia nervosa. Plasma prolactin concentrations returned to normal after increase in body weight (see Figure 16.5).

The hypothalamo–pituitary–gonadal axis is discussed in detail by Pirke in this volume (Chapter 17). Despite a relatively small loss in body weight, three of the five healthy women showed an infantile (I) secretion pattern of luteinizing hormone (LH).

Further fasting studies

Our results, based on the dexamethasone test under fasting conditions, have been confirmed by von Mullen *et al.* (1987) in an investigation of 14 healthy

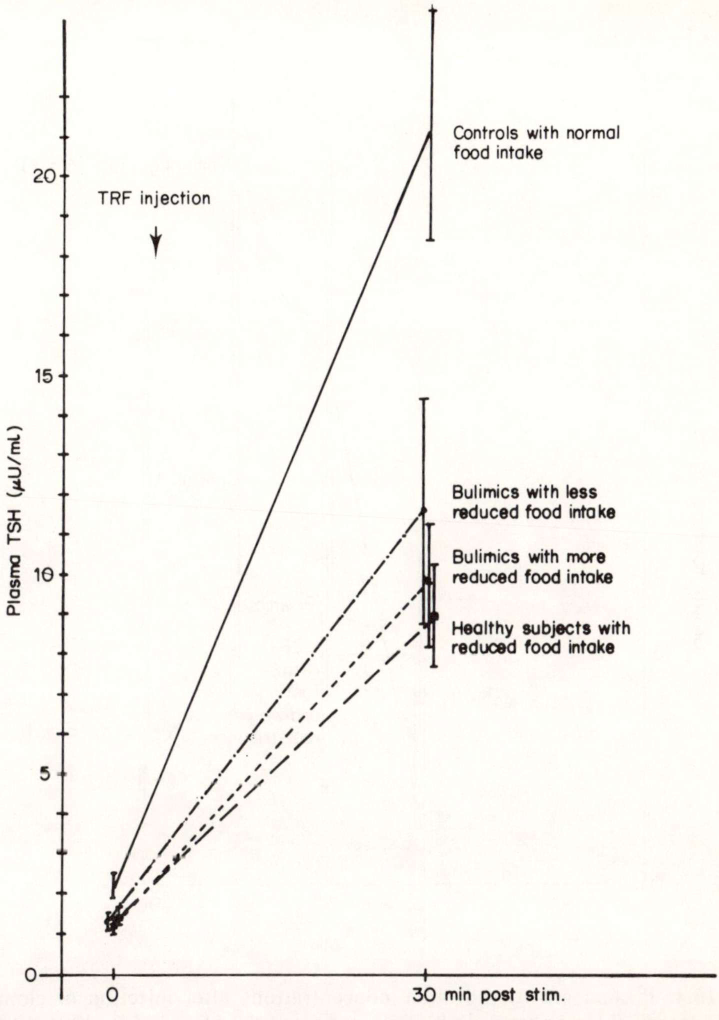

Figure 16.3. Plasma TSH concentrations 0 and 30 min after stimulation with thyrotrophin-releasing factor (TRF) in healthy subjects and in patients with bulimia nervosa during normal and reduced food intake (mean values ± SEM)

female test subjects on a low-calorie diet (1000–1200 kcal/day). In this investigation REM latencies were also shortened in the sleep EEG under conditions of reduced calorie intake. Reduction in REM latencies as well as increased plasma cortisol concentrations and impaired cortisol suppression in the DST have been referred to as 'biological markers' for endogenous (typical) depression in many publications in recent years. However, these results depend to a large extent on nutritional conditions.

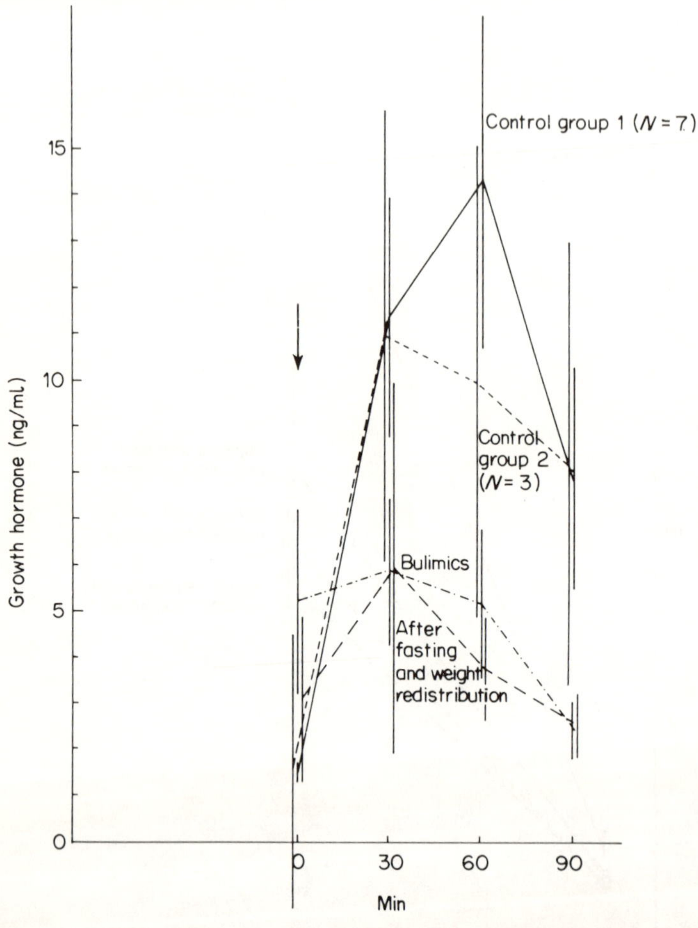

Figure 16.4. Plasma growth hormone concentrations after injection of clonidine in healthy controls (luteal phase), in bulimia patients ($N = 5$) and in healthy test subjects after three weeks of fasting (mean ± SEM)

Schweiger *et al.* (1986) conducted a study of two groups of 18 healthy normal-weight young women during decreased calorie intake (1000 kcal/day). One group was on a largely vegetarian diet (low protein and fat content and high carbohydrate content) and the second group on a mixed diet (relatively higher protein and fat content and lower carbohydrate content). During the six-week diet phase, the mood of the women on the low carbohydrate diet (= reduction of the TRP/LNAA quotient) deteriorated. This result also confirms Wurtman's hypothesis concerning serotonin metabolism.

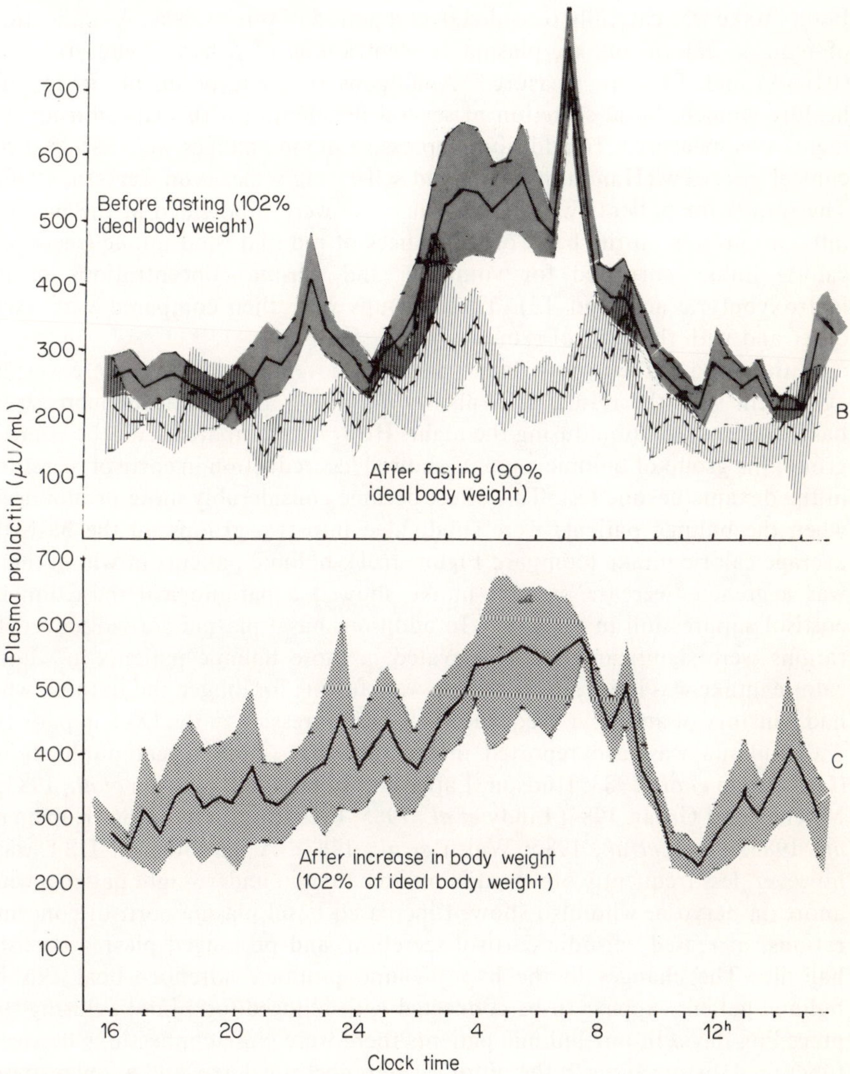

Figure 16.5. Munich fasting experiment. Plasma prolactin concentrations: 24-hour pattern in five healthy females before fasting, after fasting and after return to normal body weight (mean values ± SEM)

Neuroendocrine Observations in Bulimia (Nervosa)

We studied 24 patients with bulimia (diagnosis according to DSM-III criteria, American Psychiatric Association, 1980). The mean age of the patients was 26.7 ± 0.6 (SEM) years and mean body weight amounted to 98 ± 8 (SEM) per cent of average weight for age and sex (Kemsley, 1953, quoted by Crisp, 1980). Food intake was carefully recorded over a period of three weeks. As indicators of reduced calorie intake, plasma concentrations of β-hydroxybutyric acid (BHBA) and T3 were measured. Analogous to the experiments in fasting healthy women, basal secretion of several hormones (in this case during the night) was measured. In addition, depressive mood changes were assessed by clinical interview (Hamilton, 1967) and self-rating scales (von Zerssen, 1976), The results for patients with bulimia nervosa were subdivided at the median into two groups on the basis of the indices of reduced food intake (recorded calorie intake corrected for vomiting, and plasma concentrations of β-hydroxybutyric acid and T3). These groups were then compared with each other and with the control group.

With regard to the hypothalamo–pituitary–adrenocortical axis there was, in agreement with the results of Walsh *et al.* (1987), no significant increase in basal cortisol secretion during the night. However, compared with the control group, the group of bulimic patients showed less reduction in cortisol secretion in the dexamethasone test. This effect became considerably more pronounced when the bulimic patients were subdivided into two groups on the basis of average calorie intake (compare Figure 16.1): bulimic patients in whom there was a greater decrease in food intake showed a pathological reduction in cortisol suppression in the DST. In addition, basal plasma cortisol concentrations were significantly more elevated in those bulimic patients in whom calorie intake was lower, in those who were fasting for longer and in those who had a history of anorexia. Reduced cortisol suppression in the DST in patients with bulimia was also reported in several other, more recent publications (Gwirtsman *et al.*, 1983; Hudson, Laffer and Pope, 1982; Hudson *et al.*, 1983c; Mitchell and Groat, 1984; Lindy *et al.*, 1985; Freedman *et al.*, 1986; Kaplan *et al.*, 1983; Perez *et al.*, 1986; Walsh *et al.*, 1987). A pathological DST was, however, less frequently observed in bulimic than in underweight patients with anorexia nervosa, who also showed increased basal plasma cortisol concentrations, increased episodic cortisol secretion, and prolonged plasma cortisol half-life. The changes in the hypothalamo–pituitary–adrenocortical axis in bulimic patients appear to be connected with reduced food intake during the preceding days. In our bulimic patients there were close connections between functional disturbances in the pituitary–adrenocortical axis and a low proportion of fat in the diet, and with high ß-hydroxybutyric acid and low T3 concentrations in the plasma.

Hypothalmo-pituitary-thyroid axis

Figure 16.3 shows that 30 min after the injection of the releasing factor TRF, the release of TSH was significantly smaller in bulimic patients than in controls. When the bulimic patients were divided into two groups on the basis of their food intake, those with lower food intake showed a smaller response to the TRF injection. This difference was, however, not statistically significant (probably because the food intake was, in fact, lower in both groups than in normal subjects). In both groups of bulimic patients TSH values were significantly lower after stimulation with TRF than in healthy controls with normal food intake, and slightly higher than in healthy, fasting subjects (compare our fasting study). At least in the region between decreased to normal food intake, there appears to be a negative correlation between food intake and TSH secretion in response to stimulation by TRF. In addition, we observed significantly decreased TSH secretion 30 min after TRF injection in those bulimic patients with especially low carbohydrate intake (in comparison with healthy controls as well as with bulimic patients with higher carbohydrate intake). Bulimic patients with high plasma concentrations of β-hydroxybutyric acid (an indication of preceding acute fasting) showed slightly decreased TSH values after stimulation with TSF (statistically not significant). It is, however, known that changes in the thyroid axis (plasma T3 concentrations) occur only after longer periods of hunger or fasting, whereas changes in the plasma concentrations of β-hydroxybutyric acid occur shortly after the start of fasting; thus close parallels between these two parameters cannot be expected. Decreased TSH secretion in response to TRF in bulimic patients has also been reported by Norris, O'Malley and Palmer (1985) and Kiyohara *et al.* (1987).

Furthermore, in our studies we observed a significant decrease in the release of prolactin in response to stimulation with TRF, especially in those bulimic patients with low carbohydrate intake and in those with a history of anorexia. In our bulimic patients there was a high correlation between plasma prolactin concentrations after stimulation with TRF and β-hydroxybutyric acid concentrations indicative of acute fasting. Decrease in TSH secretion in response to TRF and reduction in carbohydrate uptake were also closely correlated.

Growth hormone

Bulimic patients showed a slight tendency towards an increase in nocturnal plasma growth hormone concentrations (not statistically significant). Compared with healthy control subjects, bulimic patients showed a decrease in the release of growth hormone after an injection of clonidine. In female patients this effect was observed only during the ovulation phase in the menstrual cycle, but not during menstruation. The studies of Heufelder *et al.* (1985) of α_2-adrenoreceptors and adenylate cyclase in patients with anorexia nervosa and in bulimic patients suggested decreased sympathetic activity in these patients; this was indicated by increased binding capacity and a decreased affinity of α_2-adrenoreceptors on the blood platelets, as well as increased stimulatory effect of PGE_1 and inhibition of cAMP production by noradrenaline.

As an indication of fasting, patients with bulimia (and patients with anorexia nervosa) showed decreased plasma concentrations of glucose and T3 and increased values for β-hydroxybutyric acid and free fatty acids; patients with bulimia (as well as patients with anorexia nervosa) also showed significantly less elevation of plasma noradrenaline concentrations after orthostatic stress (Pirke *et al.*, 1985). Although none of the above-mentioned parameters is, on its own, proof of a metabolic effect of reduced food intake, the simultaneous alteration of all five parameters can be seen as quite valid. The orthostatic reaction is regarded as a good indicator of noradrenaline turnover (Kopin, Lake and Ziegler, 1978). These changes in noradrenaline turnover in bulimia are involved in a number of changes on the adrenoreceptor and on the postsynaptic receptor (see Heufelder *et al.*, 1985). The lowered noradrenaline and T3 values reflect a decrease in basal metabolism. This may lead to a temporary gain in body weight after ingestion of appropriate amounts of calories.

Glucose tolerance tests

Indications of disturbed glucose tolerance were observed in our bulimic patients. Thirty to 90 minutes after ingestion of a test meal of 500 kcal (63.6 g carbohydrates, 16.8 g proteins and 22.8 g fat), bulimic patients showed a significantly greater increase in plasma insulin concentrations than did the control subjects. After the test meal the bulimic patients also showed significantly higher blood glucose concentrations than the controls. There was a negative correlation between postprandial insulin increase and T3 values, and a positive correlation between increase in plasma glucose concentrations and those of β-hydroxybutyric acid. The postprandial glucose maximum level correlated negatively with carbohydrate intake (Pirke *et al.*, 1987b). It must be assumed that pathological glucose tolerance is a consequence of intermittent fasting and dieting and is also associated with the composition of the food (proportion of carbohydrates). Pathological glucose tolerance with excessive insulin secretion has been observed during low carbohydrate diets (Hales and Randle, 1963) and during starvation (Unger, Eisentraut and Madison, 1963). Russell, Storlion and Beumont (1987) observed on a single case in Australia that 'binge-eating' followed by vomiting caused an especially large increase in insulin secretion in a female bulimic patient after administration of glucose.

Depression as a Nutritional Disorder

Many of the endocrine dysfunctions described in connection with eating abnormalities such as anorexia nervosa and bulimia nervosa and in starving healthy subjects have also been observed in depressed patients. The publications dealing with increased plasma cortisol concentrations and abnormal dexamethasone suppression tests in cases of depression are too numerous to be discussed in detail here. Although body weight has been used in several studies as a 'control variable', the influence of actual food intake has been almost completely neglected. From our results on healthy fasting subjects and on patients with anorexia nervosa (Fichter *et al.*, 1982) and bulimia it seem likely that reduced food intake contributes considerably to neuroendocrine dysfunctions in depression. It should be remembered that lack of appetite and loss of body weight are important symptoms of typical depression (American Psychiatric Association, 1987).

In our study, bulimic patients with high depression scores in clinical interviews and on self-report measures did not show especially large abnormalities in the DST and in the TRF test. These results contradict the 'affective illness hypothesis' of bulimia as a form of affective disorder. Decreased secretion of TSH after injection of TRF has been found in many studies of depressed patients (Extein, Pottash and Gold, 1981; Fleming *et al.*, 1983; Gold *et al.*, 1980, 1981; Kirkegaard *et al.*, 1977; Kirstein *et al.*, 1982; Loosen and Prange, 1980; Loosen, Wilson and Prange, 1980; McGrath *et al.*, 1984; Prange *et al.*, 1972; Schlesser *et al.*, 1983; Winocur *et al.*, 1983). Decreased secretion of prolactin after i.v. administration of clonidine has also been observed in depressive patients (Matussek *et al.*, 1980; Checkley, Slade and Shur, 1981; Charney *et al.*, 1982; Siever *et al.*, 1982; Boyer *et al.*, 1983; Ansseau *et al.*, 1984).

Summary and Conclusions

Multiple endocrine dysfunctions were observed not only in anorexic but also in bulimic eating disorders. They appear to be manifested somewhat less in bulimia (nervosa) than in underweight, anorexic patients. The speed at which various hormonal systems react to changes in food intake varies. Some psychosomatic symptoms in bulimia (nervosa), for example decreased food pressure and orthostatic complaints, headaches, tiredness, tendency to weight increase, can be attributed to changes in thyroid function and in the noradrenergic system. These and all the other endocrine changes which occur under conditions of decreased food intake clearly suggest that in the treatment of bulimia (nervosa) establishment of normal eating habits, sufficient intake of all nutritional constituents (including vitamins and minerals) and normalizing body weight must be central aims. Body weight is idiosyncratic for the individual patient and does not have to agree with the 'ideal weight' as given in body-weight tables. Available results suggest that there is a very close association between reduced food intake and development of neuroendocrine dysfunctions. It can be assumed that the abnormal neuroendocrine findings in bulimia (nervosa) are not permanent. Rather, they are dependent on the phases of fasting and strict dieting, and phases of binge-eating accompanied by increases in body weight which typify this disorder. The critical variable is the reduction in food intake, where the composition of the diet (carbohydrates, proteins, fat) plays an important role. It is of interest that these observations also cast new light on the neuroendocrinology of depression. Depression, too, may be viewed as being partly a nutritional disorder.

References

Alleyne, G. A. O. and V. H. Young (1967). Adrenocortical function with severe protein-calorie malnutrition. *Clinical Science* **33**, 189.

American Psychiatric Association (1980, 1987). *Diagnostic and Statistical Manual for Mental Disorders—Revision (DSM-III-R).* APA, Washington DC.

Ansseau, M., M. Scheyvaerts, A. Doumont, R. Poirrier, J. J. Legros and G. Frank (1984). Current use of REM latency, dexamethasone suppression, clonidine and apomorphine tests as biological markers of endogenous depression: a pilot study. *Psychiatry Research* **12**, 261–272.

Benedict, F. G. (1915). *A Study of Prolonged Fasting*, Vol. 203. Carnegie Institute Publication, Washington.

Benedict, F. G., W. R. Miles, P. Roth and H. M. Smith (1919). *Human Vitality and Efficiency Under Prolonged Restricted Diet*, Vol. 280. Carnegie Institute Publication, Washington.

Boyar, R. M., L. D. Hellmann, H. Roffwarg, J. Katz, B. Zumoff, J. O'Connor, L. Bradlow and K. Fukushima (1977). Cortisol secretion and metabolism in anorexia nervosa. *New England Journal of Medicine* **296**, 190–193.

Boyar, R. M., J. Katz, J. W. Finkelstein, S. Kapen, E. D. Weitzman and L. Hellman (1974). Immaturity of the 24-hour luteinizing hormone secretory pattern. *New England Journal of Medicine* **291**, 861–865.

Boyer, P., C. Schaub, J. D. Guelfi, J. Nassiet and P. Pichot (1983). Growth hormone response to hypothalamic alpha-receptor stimulation in depressive states. Paper presented at the VII World Congress of Psychiatry, Vienna.

Brambilla, F., F. Cavagnini, C. Invitti, F. Poterzio, M. Lampertico, L. Sali *et al.* (1983). Hypothesis on neurotransmitter disturbance in anorexia nervosa. Paper presented at the VII World Congress of Psychiatry, Vienna.

Brambilla, F., D. Cocchi, P. Nabile and E. E. Müller (1981). Anterior pituitary responsiveness to hypothalamic hormones in anorexia nervosa. *Neuropsychiatry* **7**, 225–237.

Brown, G. M., P. Kirwan, P. Garfinkel and H. Moldofsky (1979). Overnight patterning of prolactin and melatonin in anorexia nervosa. Paper presented at the 2nd International Symposium on Clinical Psychoneuroendocrinology in Reproduction, Venice.

Brozek, J., S. Wells and A. Keys (1946). Medical aspects of semi-starvation in Leningrad (siege 1941–1942). *American Review of Soviet Medicine* **4**, 70–86.

Casper, R. C. and L. A. Frohman (1982). Delayed TSH release in anorexia nervosa following injection of thyrotropin-releasing hormone (TRH). *Psychoneuroendocrinology* **7** (1), 59–68.

Charney, D. S., G. R. Heninger, D. E. Sternberg and H. Landis (1982). Abrupt discontinuation of tricyclic antidepressant drugs: evidence for noradrenergic hyperactivity. *British Journal of Psychiatry* **141**, 337–386.

Charney, D. S., G. R. Heninger, D. E. Sternberg, K. M. Hafstad, S. Guinings and H. Landis (1982). Adrenergic receptor sensitivity in depression: effects of clonidine in depressed patients and healthy subjects. *Archives of General Psychiatry* **39**, 290–294.

Checkley, S. A., A. P. Slade and E. Shur (1981). Growth hormone and other responses to clonidine in patients with endogenous depression. *British Journal of Psychiatry* **138**, 51–55.

Chopra, I. J., U. Chopra, S. R. Smith, M. Reza and D. H. Sotomon (1975). Reciprocal changes in serum concentrations of 3, 3, 5-triiodo thyronine (reverse T3) and 3, 3, 5-triiodothyronine (T3) in systemic illness. *Journal of Clinical Endocrinology and Metabolism* **41**, 1043–1049.

Consolazio, C. F., L. O. Matousk, H. L. Johnson, R. A. Nelson and H. J. Krzywicki (1967). Metabolic aspects of acute starvation in normal humans (10 days). *American Journal of Clinical Nutrition* **20**, 672–683.

Cooke, J. N. C., V. H. T. James, J. London and V. Wynn (1964). Adrenocortical function in chronic malnutrition. *British Medical Journal* **1**, 662–666.

Crisp, A. H. (1980). *Anorexia Nervosa: Let Me Be*. Academic Press, London.

Doerr, P., M. M. Fichter, K. M. Pirke and R. Lund (1980). Relationship between weight gain and hypothalamic pituitary adrenal function in patients with anorexia nervosa. *Journal of Steroid Biochemistry* **13**, 529–537.

Extein, I., A. L. C. Pottash and M. S. Gold (1981). Relationship of thyrotropin-releasing hormone test and dexamethasone test abnormalities in unipolar depression. *Psychiatry Research* **4**, 49–53.

Fichter, M. M. (1985). *Magersucht und Bulimia*. Springer Verlag, Berlin, Heidelberg, New York, Tokyo.

Fichter, M. M. and K. M. Pirke (1986a). Effect of experimental and pathological weight loss upon the hypothalamo–pituitary–adrenal axis. *Psychoneuroendocrinology* **11**, 295–305.

Fichter, M. M. and K. M. Pirke (1986b). Effects of experimental starvation on the thyroid axis. In *Disorders of Eating Behavior: A Psychoneuroendocrine Approach*, ed. by E. Ferrari and F. Brambilla, Advances of the Biosciences, Pergamon Press, Oxford.

Fichter, M. M., P. Doerr, K. M. Pirke and P. Lund (1982). Behavior, nutrition and endocrinology in anorexia nervosa. A longitudinal study in 24 patients. *Acta Psychiatrica Scandinavica* **66**, 429–444.

Fichter, M. M., K. M. Pirke and F. Holsboer (1986). Weight loss causes neuroendocrine disturbances: experimental study in healthy starvation subjects. *Psychiatry Research* **17**, 61–72.

Fichter, M. M., K. M. Pirke, J. Poellinger, G. Wolfram and E. Brunner. Disturbances in the hypothalamic, pituitary, adrenal and other neuroendocrine axes in bulimia. *Biological Psychiatry*, in press.

Fleming, J. E., I. Extein, H. A. Sternbach, A. L. C. Pottash and M. S. Gold (1983). The thyrotropin releasing hormone and dexamethasone suppression tests in the familial-classification of depression. *Psychiatry Research* **9**, 53–58.

Freedman, E. J., M. Stolar, R. H. Gerner and M. Kramer (1986). Neuroendocrine aspects of bulimia. Paper presented at the 2nd International Conference on Eating Disorders, New York.

Gold, M. S., A. L. C. Pottash, I. Extein, D. M. Martin, E. Howard, E. A. Mueller and D. R. Sweeney (1981). The TRH-test in the diagnosis of major and minor depression. *Psychoneuroendocrinology* **6**, 159.

Gold, M. S., A. L. C. Pottash, D. R. Sweeney, D. M. Martin and R. K. Davies (1980). TRH-induced TSH-response in unipolar, bipolar and secondary depression. *American Journal of Psychiatry* **137**, 101–102.

Gwirtsman, H. E., P. Roy-Byrne, J. Yager and R. H. Gerner (1983) Neuroendocrine abnormalities in bulimia. *American Journal of Psychiatry* **140** (5), 559–553.

Hales, C. N. and P. J. Randle (1963). Effects of low-carbohydrate diet and diabetes mellitus on plasma concentrations of glucose, nonesterified fatty acid and insulin during oral glucose-tolerance tests. *Lancet* **1**, 790–794.

Halmi, K. A. and B. M. Sherman (1975). Gonadotropin response to LH–RH in anorexia nervosa. *Archives of General Psychiatry* **32**, 875–878.

Hamilton, M. (1967). Development of a rating scale for primary depressive illness. *British Journal of Social and Clinical Psychology* **6**, 278–296.

Hudson, J. I., P. S. Laffer and H. G. Pope (1982). Bulimia related to affective disorder by family history and response to the dexamethasone suppression test. *American Journal of Psychiatry* **139**, 685–697.

Hudson, J. I., H. G. Pope, J. M. Jonas and D. Yurgelun-Tood (1983a). Family history study of anorexia nervosa and bulimia. *British Journal of Psychiatry* **142**, 133–138.

Hudson, J. I., H. G. Pope, J. M. Jonas and D. Yurgelun-Tood (1983b). Phenomenologic relationship of eating disorders to major affective disorder. *Psychiatry Research* **9**, 345–354.

Hudson, J. I., H. G. Pope, J. M. Jonas, P. S. Laffer, M. S. Hudson and J. C. Melby (1983c). Hypothalamic–pituitary–adrenal-axis hyperactivity in bulimia. *Psychiatry Research* **8**, 111–117.

Kalucy, R. C., A. H. Crisp, T. Chard, McNeilly, C. N. Chen and J. H. Lacey (1976). Nocturnal hormonal profiles in massive obesity, anorexia nervosa and normal females. *Journal of Psychosomatic Research* **20**, 595–604.

Kaplan, A. S., P. E. Garfinkel, P. L. Darby and D. M. Garner (1983). Carbamazepine in the treatment of bulimia. *American Journal of Psychiatry* **140**, 1225–1226.

Kemsley, W. F. F. (1953/54) Tables for matched population mean weight. *Annals of Eugenics, London*, cited in Crisp, A. H. (ed.) (1980). *Anorexia Nervosa: Let Me Be*. Academic Press, London.

Keys, A., J. Brozek, A. Henschel, O. Mickelson and H. L. Taylor (1950). *The Biology of Human Starvation*. University of Minneapolis Press.

Kirkegaard, C., N. Bjorum, D. Cohn, J. Farber, U. B. Lauridsen and J. Nerup (1977). *Psychoneuroendocrinology* **2**, 131.

Kirstein, L., M. S. Gold, I. Extein, D. Martin and A. L. C. Pottash (1982). Clinical correlates of the TRH Infusion Test in primary depression. *Journal of Clinical Psychiatry* **43**, 191–194.

Kiyohara, K., H. Tamai, C. Karibe, N. Kobayashi, O. Fujii Fukino, T. Nakagawa, L. F. Kumagai and S. Nagataki (1987). Serum thyrotropin (TSH) responses to thyrotropin-releasing hormone (TRH) in patients with anorexia nervosa and bulimia: influence of changes in body weight and eating disorders. *Psychoneuroendocrinology* **12**, 21–28.

Kling, S. (1978). Einfluss totaler Nahrungskarenz auf klinisch-chemische Befunde bei adipoeser Patienten unter besonderer Berücksichtigung der Serumproteinveränderung. Dissertation, Medical Faculty, University of Munich.

Kollar, E. J., G. R. Slater, J. O. Palmer, R. F. Doctor and A. J. Mandell (1964). Measurement of stress in fasting man. *Archives of General Psychiatry* **11**, 113–125.

Kopin, I. J., R. C. Lake and M. Ziegler (1978). Plasma levels of norepinephrine. *Annals of Internal Medicine* **88**, 671–680.

Lindy, D. C., B. T. Walsh, S. P. Roose, M. Gladis and A. H. Glassman (1985). The dextromethasone suppression test in bulimia. *American Journal of Psychiatry* **142**, 1375–1376.

Loosen, P. T. and A. J. Prange (1980). Thyrotropin-releasing hormone (TRH) a useful tool for psychoneuroendocrine investigation. *Psychoneuroendocrinology* **5**, 63–80.

Loosen, P. T., I. C. Wilson and A. J. Prange (1980). Endocrine and behavioural changes in depression after TRH. *Journal of Affective Disorders* **2**, 267–278.

Marshall, J. C. and T. R. Fraser (1971). Amenorrhea in anorexia nervosa. Assessment and treatment with clomiphene citrate. *British Medical Journal* **4**, 590–592.

Matussek, N., M. Ackenheil, H. Hippius, F. Müller, H. T. Schröder, H. Schultes and J. Wasilewski (1980). Effect of clonidine on growth hormone release in psychiatric patients and controls. *Psychiatry Research* **2**, 25–36.

McGrath, P. J., F. M., Quitkin, J. W. Stewart, G. Asnis, H. Novacenko and J. Puig-Antich (1984). A comparative study of the pituitary TSH response to thyrotropin in outpatient depressives. *Psychiatry Research* **12**, 185–193.

Metropolitan Life Insurance Company (1959). *Statistical Bulletin* **40**, 1.

Mitchell, J. E. and R. Groat (1984). A placebo-controlled, double-blind trial of amitriptyline in bulimia. *Journal of Clinical Psychopharmacology* **4**, 186–193.

Miyai, K., T. Yamamoto, M. Azukizawa, K. Ishibashi and Y. Kumahara (1975). Serum thyroid hormones and thyrotropin in anorexia nervosa. *Journal of Clinical Enocrinology and Metabolism* **40**, 334–338.

Moshang, T., J. S. Parks, L. Baker, V. Vaiday, R. Utiger, A. M. Bongiovanni and P. Snyder (1975). Low serum triiodothyronine in patients with anorexia nervosa. *Journal of Clinical Endocrinology and Metabolism* **40**, 470–473.

Mullen, P. E. von, C. R. Linsell and D. Parker (1987). Der Einfluss von Schlafentzug und Kalorienrestriktion auf Biologische Merkmale der Depression. *Lancet* (*Deutsche Ausgabe*), 1, **2**, 114–118.

Norris, P. D., B. P. O'Malley and R. L. Palmer (1985). The TRH test in bulimia and anorexia nervosa: a controlled study. *Journal of Psychiatric Research* **19**, 215–219.

Owen, O. E., K. A. Reichard, G. Boden *et al.* (1978). Interrelationships among key tissues in the utilization of metabolic substrates. In *Diabetes, Obesity and Vascular Diseases, Metabolic and Molecular Interrelationships. Part 2. Advances in Modern Nutrition*, ed. by H. Katzen and R. J. Mahler. Wiley, New York, pp. 517–550.

Palmblad, L., L. Levi, A. Burger, A. Melander, U. Westgren, H. Von Schenck and G. Skude (1977). Effects of total energy withdrawal (fasting) on the level of growth hormone, thyrotropin, cortisol, adrenaline, noradrenaline, T4, T3 and rT3 in healthy males. *Acta Medica Scandinavica* **201**, 15–22.

Perez, E., J. Blouin, J. Barlow and A. Blouin (1986). The dexamethasone suppression test in bulimia. Paper presented at the 2nd International Conference on Eating Disorders, New York.

Pirke, K. M. and B. Spyra (1981). Influence of starvation on testosterone-luteinizing hormone feedback in the rat. *Acta Endocrinologica* **96**, 1–9.

Pirke, K. M., M. M. Fichter, R. Lund and P. Doerr (1979). Twenty-four hour sleep-wake pattern of plasma LH in patients with anorexia nervosa. *Acta Endocrinologica* **92**, 193–204.

Pirke, K. M., J. Pahl, U. Schweiger and M. Warnhoff (1985). Metabolic and endocrine indices of starvation in bulimia: a comparison with anorexia nervosa. *Psychiatry Research* **15**, 33–39.

Pirke, K. M., U. Schweiger, R. Laessle, B. Dickhaut and M. Waechtler (1986). Dieting influences the menstrual cycle: vegetarian versus non-vegetarian diet. *Fertility and Sterility*. **46**, 1083–1088.

Pirke, K. M., U. Schweiger, M. M. Fichter and G. Wolfram (1987a). Metabolic and endocrine consequences of eating behavior and food composition in bulimia. In *Psychology of Bulimia*, ed. by J. J. Hudson. APA Press, Washington DC.

Pirke, K. M., U. Schweiger, R. Laessle, M. M. Fichter and G. Wolfram (1987b). Altered insulin response to a balanced test meal in bulimic patients. *International Journal of Eating Disorders* **6**, 551–556.

Ploog, D., M. M. Fichter, P. Doerr and K. M. Pirke (1981). Anorexia nervosa. Neurobiologie, Psychosomatik und Verhaltenstherapie. *Internist* **22**, 7–23.

Prange, A. J., I. C. Wilson, P. P. Lara, L. B. Alltop and G. R. Breese (1972). Effects of thyrotropin-releasing hormone in depression. *Lancet* **II**, 999–1002.

Russell, J., L. Storlion and P. Beumont (1987). A proposed model of bulimic behavior: effect on plasma insulin, noradrenalin, and cortisol levels. *International Journal of Eating Disorders* **5**, 609–614.

Schlesser, M. A., A. J. Rush, C. Fairschild, G. Growley and P. Orsulak (1983). The thyrotropin-releasing hormone stimulation test: a methodological study. *Psychiatry Research* **9**, 59–67.

Schweiger, U., R. Laessle, S. Kittl, B. Dickhaut, M. Schweiger and K. M. Pirke (1986). Macronutrient intake, plasma large neutral amino acids and mood during weight-reducing diets. *Journal of Neural Transmission* **67**, 77–86, revised May 6.

Siever, L. S., T. W. Uhde, E. K. Silberman, D. C. Jimmerson, J. A. Aloi, R. M. Post and D. L. Murphy (1982). The growth hormone response to clonidine as a probe of noradrenergic receptor responsiveness in affective disorder patients and controls. *Psychiatry Research* **6**, 171–183.

Simmonds, M. (1916), Über Hypophysenschwund mit tödlichem Ausgang. *Deutsche Medizinische Wochenschrift* **42**, 190.

Smith, S. R., T. Bledsoe and M. K. Chetri (1975). Cortisol metabolism and the pituitary–adrenal axis in adults with protein-calorie malnutrition. *Journal of Clinical Endocrinology and Metabolism* **40**, 43–52.

Spaulding, S. W., I. J. Chopra, R. S. Sherwin and S. S. Lyall (1976). Diversion of peripheral thyroxine metabolism from activating to inactivating pathways during complete fasting. *Journal of Clinical Endocrinology and Metabolism* **42**, 197–200.

Unger, R. H., A. Eisentraut and L. Madison (1963). The effects of total starvation upon the levels of circulating glucagon and insulin in man. *Journal of Clinical Investigation* **42**, 1031–1039.

Vagenakis, A. G., A. Burger, G. I. Portnay, M. Rudolph, J. T. O'Brian, F. Azizi, R. A. Arky and P. Nicod (1975) *Journal of Clinical Enocrinology and Metabolism* **41**, 191–194.

Virgersky, R. A., D. L. Loriaux, A. E. Andersen and M. B. Lipsett (1976a). Anorexia nervosa: behavioral and hypothalamic aspects. *Clinical Endocrinology and Metabolism* **5**, 517–535.

Vigersky, R. A., D. L. Loriaux, A. E. Andersen, R. S. Mecklenburg and J. L. Vaitukaitis (1976b). Delayed pituitary hormone response to LRF and TRF in patients with anorexia nervosa and with secondary amenorrhea associated with simple weight loss. *Journal of Clinical Endocrinology and Metabolism* **43**, 893–900.

Waldhauser, F., K. Toifl, J. Spona, U. Zeitlhuber, M. Waldhauser and H. Frisch (1984). Diminished prolactin response to thyrotropin and insulin in anorexia nervosa. *Journal of Clinical Endocrinology and Metabolism* **59**, 538–541.

Walsh, B. T., J. L. Katz, J. Levin, J. Kream, D. K. Fukushima, L. D. Hellman, H. Weiner and B. Zumoff (1978). Adrenal activity in anorexia nervosa. *Psychosomatic Medicine* **40**, 499–506.

Walsh, B. T., J. L. Katz, J. Levin, J. Kream, D. K. Fukushima, H. Weiner and B. Zumoff (1981). The production rate of cortisol declines during recovery from anorexia nervosa. *Journal of Clinical Endocrinology and Metabolism* **53**, 203–205.

Walsh, B. T., E. S. Lo, T. Cooper, D. Lindy, S. P. Roose, M. Gladis and A. H. Glassman (1987). The DST and plasma dexamethasone levels in bulimia. *Archives of General Psychiatry* **44**, 799–800.

Walsh, B. T., J. W. Stewart, S. P. Roose, M. Gladis and A. H. Glassman (1984). Treatment of bulimia with phenelzine. *Archives of General Psychiatry* **41**, 1105–1109.

Walsh, B. T., S. P. Roose, A. H. Glassman, M. Gladis and C. Sadik (1985). Bulimia and depression. *Psychosomatic Medicine* **47**, 123–131.

Warren, M. and R. L. Van De Wiele (1973). Clinical metabolic features of anorexia nervosa. *American Journal of Obstetrics and Gynaecology* **117**, 435–449.

Winocur, A., J. D. Amsterdam, J. Oler, J. Mendels, P. J. Snyder, S. N. Caroff and D. J. Brunswick (1983). Multiple hormonal responses to protirelin (TRH) in depressed patients. *Archives of General Psychiatry* **40**, 525–531.

Wurtman, R. J. and J. J. Wurtman (1984). Nutritional control of central neurotransmitters. In *The Psychobiology of Anorexia Nervosa*, ed. by K. M. Pirke and D. Ploog. Springer Verlag, Heidelberg, Berlin, pp. 4–11.

Young, J. E. and L. Landsberg (1977). Suppression of sympathetic nervous system during fasting. *Science* **196**, 1473–1475.

Von Zerssen, D. and D. M. Koeller (1976). *Klinische Selbstbeurteilungs-skalen (KSB-S) aus dem Münchener Psychiatrischen Informations system.* Beltz Verlag, Weinheim.

17

Menstrual cycle and neuroendocrine disturbances of the gonadal axis in bulimia (nervosa)

K. M. Pirke
Max-Planck Institute for Psychiatry, Munich

Amenorrhoea is a symptom which is frequently observed in patients with anorexia nervosa. This symptom is caused by a functional disturbance in the hypothalamus, namely, deficient secretion of the gonadotrophin-releasing hormones (GnRH). Although the neuroendocrine mechanisms involved in this functional disorder are not understood in detail, one may assume that undernutrition in anorexic patients is responsible for the suppression of GnRH release. This is outlined in detail by Pirke and Ploog (1986).

Although a large number of studies of the hypothalamo–pituitary–gonadal axis have been conducted in cases of anorexia nervosa, only a few reports are available on disturbances of the menstrual cycle in bulimia nervosa.

In a study of 28 bulimic patients, Russell (1979) found 11 with amenorrhoea and 13 with menstrual cycles. Four took contraceptive hormones. The mean body weight of the patients with menstrual cycles was 13.7 kg higher than that of the amenorrhoeic bulimics. Fairburn and Cooper (1984) found that amongst 35 women with bulimia nervosa (diagnosis according to DSM-III criteria; APA, 1980) 45.7 per cent were taking oral contraceptives, 21.1 per cent reported amenorrhoea and 36.8 per cent very irregular cycles; only one patient reported regular cycles. In a study by Pirke *et al.* (1985a), 50 per cent of the bulimic patients reported amenorrhoea. Leon *et al.* (1986) investigated 45 bulimic women with menstrual cycles; 77.8 per cent of these reported regular cycles, the remainder reported irregular cycles.

In an early endocrinological investigation, Pirke *et al.* (1987) studied 15 women with bulimia. These patients were 20–36 years old (mean: 23.7 years). Their body weight lay between 77 and 119 per cent of the 'ideal body weight' (IBW according to the Metropolitan Life Insurance Company, 1959). The duration of the disorder was 2–14 years (mean: 6.1 years). Seven patients had a history of anorexia nervosa. A control group of 10 healthy women of similar age with regular menstrual cycles and without apparent endocrinological abnormalities was used. All control subjects had preovulatory plasma oestradiol concentrations greater than 120 pg/ml, the luteal phase was longer than eight days and the plasma progesterone concentrations increased to more than 3 ng/ml.

Blood samples were taken from the patients and from the control subjects throughout a full menstrual cycle on Mondays, Wednesdays and Fridays between 8 and 10 am. In patients with amenorrhoea, blood samples were taken over a period of six weeks at the same time intervals as in the menstruating subjects. Oestradiol (E_2) and progesterone (P_4) were estimated in the plasma. The results of the hormone estimations are shown in Figures 17.1, 17.2 and 17.3. The graphs at the bottom of Figure 17.1 show the data which were obtained for patient No. 11; she was the only one of the 15 bulimic patients whose hormone concentrations were similar to those found during a normal cycle. The beginning and end of the cycle are marked by arrows. During the follicular phase, the oestradiol (E_2) values increased gradually and reached a preovulatory maximum of more than 300 pg/ml. This was followed by a transient decrease in the E_2 concentrations followed by a second rise; the oestradiol concentrations fell again to low values before menstruation. The plasma progesterone concentrations started to increase during the time of the preovulatory oestradiol maximum and reached values of more than 10 ng/ml. The luteal phase — from the oestradiol maximum to the end of the cycle — was no longer than eight days.

In patients No. 1 and No. 6 (Figure 17.1), progesterone concentrations reached normal values during the luteal phase ($>$ 3 ng/ml). The duration of the luteal phase was, however, less than eight days and thus pathologically shortened. In the remaining 12 bulimic patients, increases in progesterone concentrations were insufficient ($>$ 3 ng/ml). Seven of these 12 patients can be regarded separately (see Figure 17.3); they differed from the remaining eight patients in that their plasma oestradiol concentrations did not rise to values larger than 120 pg/ml. This indicated that in these patients normal follicles with increasing oestradiol production failed to develop. Of the 15 patients tested, four reported regular menstrual cycles and only 11 reported amenorrhoea (A in Figure 17.3) or oligomenorrhoea (O). This demonstrates that bulimic

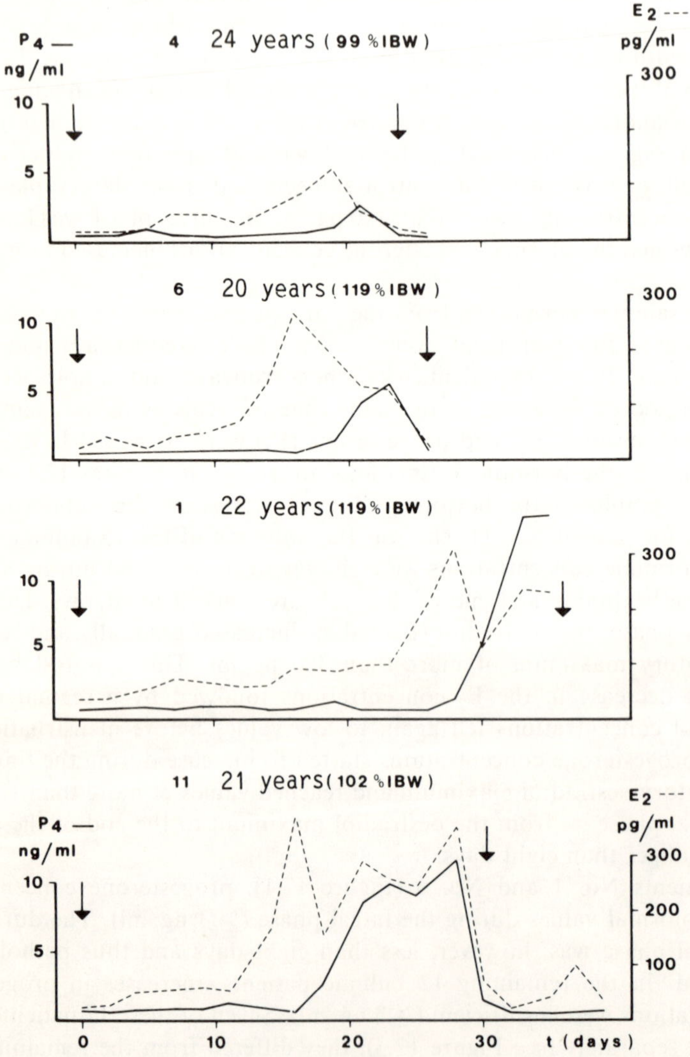

Figure 17.1. Plasma concentrations of progesterone (P_4) and oestradiol (E_2) during the menstrual cycle in four patients with bulimia. Start and end of cycle indicated by arrows. Only patient No. 11 shows a normal cycle during which oestradiol values increase to more than 120 pg/ml. The progesterone values are higher than 3 ng/ml and the luteal phase lasts for more than eight days

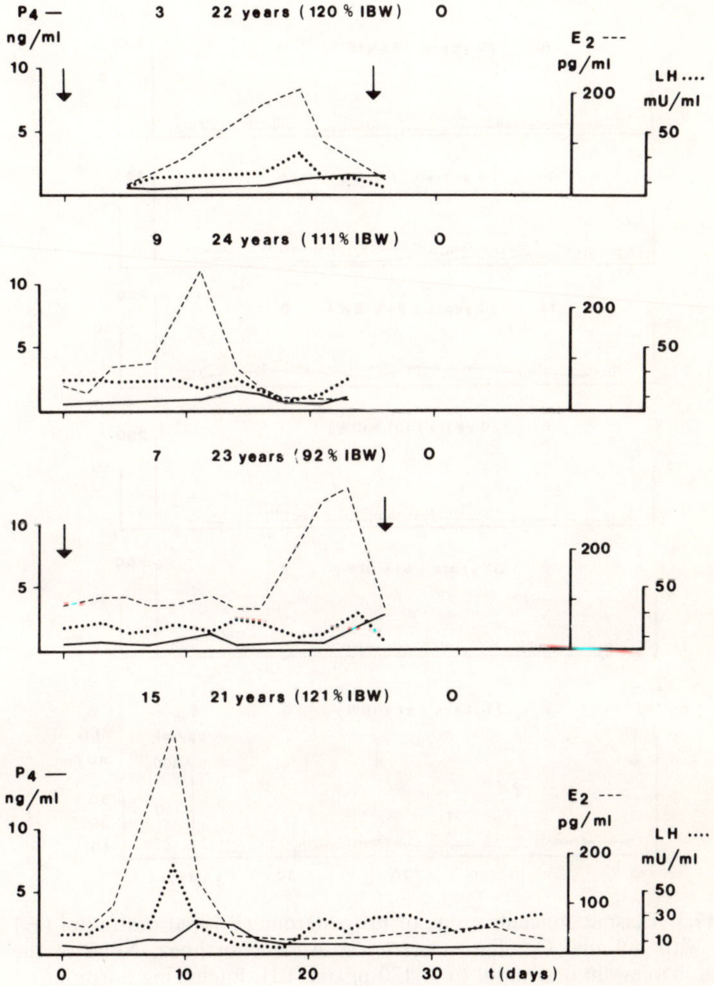

Figure 17.2. Plasma concentrations of progesterone (P_4) and oestradiol (E_2) during the menstrual cycle in four patients with bulimia. O, oligomenorrhoea. All patients show a sufficient increase in oestradiol ($E_2 > 120$ pg/ml). However, a luteal phase occurred in none of the cases. LH, luteinizing hormone

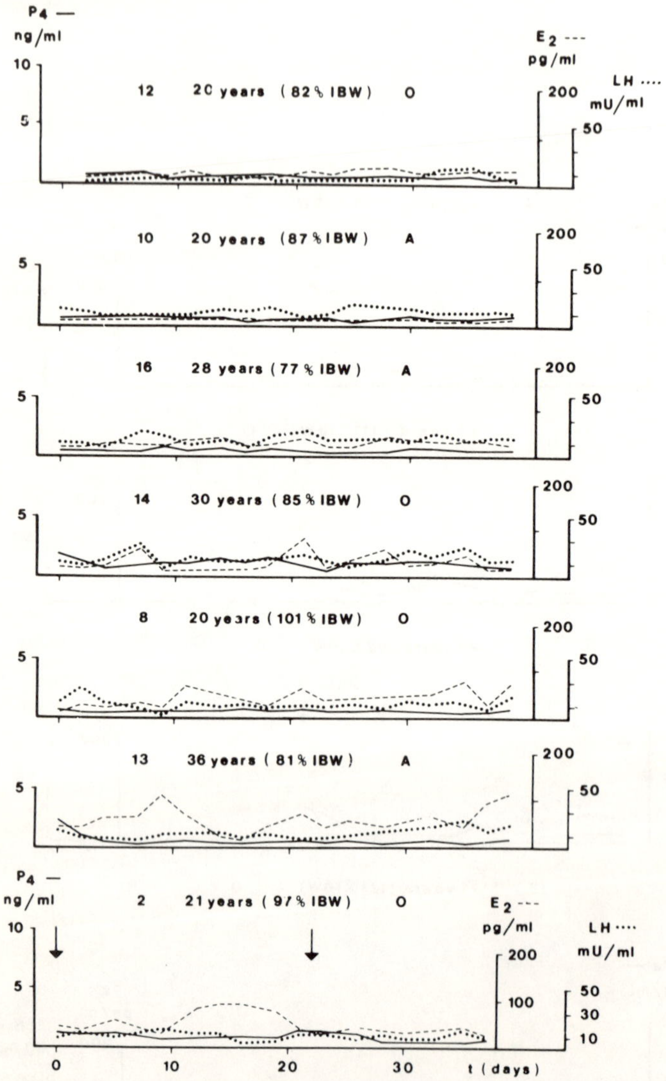

Figure 17.3. Plasma concentrations of progesterone (P_4) and oestradiol (E_2) in seven patients with bulimia. O, oligomenorrhoea; A, amenorrhoea. None of the patients shows an increase in oestradiol to > 120 pg/ml. LH, luteinizing hormone

patients' statements concerning their cycles do not provide an accurate picture of the degree of disturbance of the menstrual cycle as reflected in the results of estimation of blood hormone concentrations. On the basis of measurements of endocrine parameters, disturbances of the cycle can be divided into two groups. The more severe disturbance (group I) is the maturation failure of the follicle, as observed in patients Nos 2, 8, 10, 12, 13, 14 and 15. The less severe disturbance (group II) is disturbance of the luteal phase, with normal oestradiol secretion during the follicular phase (patients Nos 1, 3, 4, 6, 7, 9 and 15). The patients with a history of anorexia nervosa did not differ from those without such a history with regard to the quality of their cycle. Patients with less severe disturbances (II) had a significantly higher body weight than patients with the more severe disturbances (I).

In group I body weight was on average 87.0 ± 8.0 per cent IBW, in group II 110 ± 11.3 per cent. This observation corroborates the findings of Russell (1979), whose amenorrhoeic bulimic patients weighed significantly less than those with menstrual cycles. Body weight is also significant in the development of menstrual dysfunction in the group of normal-weight bulimic patients (mean body weight 99.5 per cent IBW in our study). Body weight alone cannot, however, be the reason for the abnormal production of gonadal hormones, since abnormalities were also observed in the group of patients with 'ideal body weight' and in heavy patients.

Our investigations do not provide information about the endocrine mechanisms responsible for disturbed hormone secretion. First of all, it is not clear whether we are dealing with a primary gonadal disorder or whether the results can be explained by a decreased stimulation of the gonads by the gonadotrophic hormones . Therefore, in a second study, we investigated the following two hypotheses:

(a) Decreased secretion of gonadotrophins during the follicular phase leads to decreased production of oestradiol in the follicular phase and to absence of the preovulatory increase in oestradiol secretion.
(b) A smaller disturbance of gonadotrophin secretion still permits maturation of the follicle but later, during the luteal phase, it causes diminished function of the corpus luteum. This hypothesis was postulated by Di Zerega and Hodgen (1981) on the basis of observations in primates.

Fifteen patients with bulimia were studied. Nine healthy persons of similar age were used as controls. The diagnosis of bulimia was made according to DSM-III criteria. The data for patients and controls are listed in Table 17.1.

Blood samples were taken during one menstrual cycle on Mondays, Wednesdays and Fridays between 8 and 10 am. In cases in which no cycles were reported, blood samples were collected over a period of six weeks. In each case, at the start of the second week of the cycle or of the observation period, blood samples were also taken from a permanent catheter between 1800 and 2400 h at 10-min intervals. Oestradiol and progesterone were estimated in the blood samples collected during the cycle, as described in the first study. In the

Table 17.1 Characteristics of bulimic patients and control subjects

Patient No.	Age (yr)	IBW %	Duration of disease (yr)	Anorexia nervosa in case history
Group I ($N = 8$)	(E_2 max. < 120 pg/ml)			
3	21	83.5	5	+
4	18	86.0	9	+
5	27	95.0	10	+
6	21	87.9	3	–
11	22	107.9	3	–
12	26	82.5	11	+
15	25	100.5	1	–
16	19	93.3	2	+
$\bar{x}$	22.4	91.3	5.6	
SD	3.3	9.1	3.9	
Group II ($N = 7$)	E_2 max. > 120 pg/ml)			
2	25	133.6	4	–
7	21	106.4	7	–
8	26	84.5	8	+
9	21	121.5	6	–
10	21	107.4	6	–
13	26	144.2	3	+
14	31	103.5	—	–
$\bar{x}$	24.4	114.1	5.6	
SD	3.7	20.4	1.7	
Controls (N=9)				
$\bar{x}$	22.8	108.8		
SD	1.4	6.2		

'time-course samples' and in the samples collected over the six-hour periods, luteinizing hormone (LH) and follicle-stimulating hormone (FSH) were measured. The gonadotrophins were estimated with a radioimmunoassay (Mayaclon, Serono). Mean values for LH and for FSH were calculated for the six-hour collection periods. The number and extent of the episodic hormone secretions were calculated as described previously (Pirke *et al.*, 1985b).

In Table 17. 1 the 15 patients of the second study are divided into two groups depending on whether their oestradiol values during the whole observation period reached more than 120 pg/ml (group II) or whether they remained below 120 pg/ml (group I, no follicle maturation). As in the first study, the

Table 17.2 Follicular and luteal phase in bulimic patients and control subjects

	Bulimia group I	Bulimia group II	Controls
E_2 max. (pg/ml)	55.2 ± 24.7*	284.7 ± 176.4	330.3 ± 142.5
Follicular phase			
E_2	26.8 ± 8.0*	88.5 ± 28.5	98.2 ± 36.5
P_4	0.6 ± 0.1**	0.6 ± 0.1***	0.8 ± 0.2
LH	2.2 ± 2.5**	6.4 ± 2.2	7.8 ± 4.0
FSH	5.6 ± 2.0NS	6.3 ± 1.5NS	6.5 ± 1.3
Luteal phase			
E_2	/	102.9 ± 58.4	148.0 ± 46.6
P_4	/	3.6 ± 3.7****	7.2 ± 3.9
LH	/	4.4 ± 2.6***	7.4 ± 4.0
FSH	/	4.6 ± 1.4NS	4.8 ± 1.3

E_2, oestradiol; P_4, progesterone; LH, luteinizing hormone; FSH, follicle-stimulating hormone. Mean values ± SD.

*$p < 0.001$; ** $p < 0.005$;*** $p < 0.01$; **** $p < 0.05$ (Student's t-test).

body weight of the patients with the more severe disturbance (I) was lower than that of the patients in whom follicle maturation occurred (II).

The data (of the time-course) regarding blood concentrations of various hormones during the follicular phase and during the luteal phase are summarized in Table 17.2. The mean values for LH, FSH, oestradiol (E_2) and progesterone (P_4) were calculated in control subjects and in patients.

The follicular phase was defined as the time between the start of the cycle and the E_2 maximum (excluding) and the luteal phase from the E_2 maximum (excluding) to the start of the next cycle. In the patients in group II (E_2 max. > 120 pg/ml), the mean values for the whole observation period were calculated and compared with the mean values of the controls and those of group I. The oestradiol maxima of group I were (in accordance with the division of the groups) significantly lower than in the controls. The E_2 maxima of group II were, however, not significantly different from those of the controls. The mean values for the LH, E_2 and P_4 were significantly lower in the bulimic patients of group I than in the controls. The bulimics of group II did not differ from the controls during the follicular phase (except for the significantly lower mean values for P_4).

During the luteal phase, mean plasma concentrations of LH and P_4 were decreased in the bulimic patients of group II (when compared with the controls). Similar to our first study, the second study demonstrated that in bulimic patients in whom follicle development was apparently normal, hormone production during the luteal phase was nevertheless disturbed.

Table 17.3 shows the results obtained when plasma gonadotrophin concentrations were measured over a period of six hours during the follicular phase. In the bulimic patients in group I the mean LH concentrations and the mean size of the LH 'peaks' were lower than in the controls. Results from the bulimic patients in group II did not differ from those obtained from the controls. The mean plasma FSH concentrations and peak sizes in group I were significantly lower than in group II. They were, however, not significantly different from the values obtained in the healthy controls.

Both studies, incorporating a total of 30 patients with bulimia, revealed menstrual cycle disturbances of varying degrees of severity in the majority of cases. In the more severe dysfunctions the follicles did not develop normally, as evidenced by the persistently lower plasma oestradiol concentrations. This indicated lack of ovulation and infertility in these women. The body weight of this group of patients was significantly lower than that of the group in which plasma hormone values indicated maturation of the follicles (increasing E_2 values). Hypothesis (a), which postulates a decreased stimulation of the gonads by gonadotrophic hormones, is thus confirmed, because patients who did not display the signs typical of follicle maturation had slightly but significantly lower mean values for plasma concentrations of LH and the mean size of the LH peaks was smaller. A definite indication of a decrease in FSH secretion was, however, not obtained. In contrast to the severely underweight patients with anorexia nervosa, who showed an almost total suppression of gonadotropin release (Boyar *et al.*, 1974; Pirke *et al.*, 1979), bulimic patients in whom follicle maturation was impaired showed only a small, although significant, decrease in plasma LH concentrations. Frisch (1979) was able to demonstrate that in anorexia nervosa, after restoration of the body weight to over 87 per cent IBW, cyclic gonadal functions normalized. On the other hand, clinical experience has shown that healthy women whose body weight lies between 80 and 100 per cent IBW can become pregnant. We must therefore assume that in bulimic patients in whom maturation of the follicles does not occur, not only relatively low body weight but also other factors contribute to the impairment of fertility.

A normal increase in blood concentrations of E_2 during the first half of the cycle indicated that in 16 of the bulimic patients in our two studies normal follicle maturation occurred. In the majority of the cases in this group, the luteal phase was, however, disturbed because increase in plasma progesterone concentrations was too small and too short. Disturbances in the luteal phase are often the cause of impaired fertility (Jones, 1976). They are, however, not an absolute obstacle to fertility. In addition, one must take into account that the extent of the disturbances in the luteal phase can vary considerably from cycle to cycle.

In our studies it has not been possible to analyse the endocrine mechanisms which led to disturbance of the luteal phase in bulimia. Measurements of the

Table 17.3 Episodic gonadotrophin secretion

	Bulimia group I (E_2 max. < 120pg/ml)	Bulimia group II (E_2 max. < 120pg/ml)	Healthy controls
Mean LH values over 6 h	1.5 ± 2.6*	2.6 ± 2.1	2.5 ± 1.3
LH: No. of peaks over 6 h	1.9 ± 1.8	2.9 ± 1.6	2.8 ± 1.3
LH: Mean peak size (mU/ml)	1.6 ± 1.3**	2.4 ± 1.3	2.6 ± 0.7
Mean FSH values over 6 h	5.2 ± 1.9**	6.3 ± 1.1	5.6 ± 1.8
FSH: No. of peaks over 6 h	2.0 ± 1.7	2.4 ± 1.3	2.4 ± 1.6
FSH: Mean peak size	2.2 ± 1.5**	3.5 ± 0.6	2.2 ± 1.3

E_2, oestradiol; LH, luteinizing hormone; FSH, follicle-stimulating hormone. Mean values ± SD.
* $p < 0.01$; ** $p < 0.02$ (Student's *t*-test).

episodic gonadotrophin secretions during the follicular phase did not support the hypothesis of Di Zerega (1981), who proposed that decreased gonadotrophin secretion during the follicular phase is the cause of disturbance of the luteal phase. Two results should, however, be considered:

1. Mean LH values in the luteal phase were significantly lower in bulimic patients than in the controls. This may indicate that decreased progesterone production is the consequence of insufficient stimulation of the corpus luteum. This question can be answered by measuring episodic LH secretion during the luteal phase.
2. Progesterone values were significantly decreased not only during the luteal phase but also during the follicular phase (when LH secretion was normal in this group). This may indicate the development of a disturbance of P_4 biosynthesis in bulimia which is independent of LH stimulation.

It is still unclear which aspects of the pathological behaviour of bulimic patients are responsible for disturbances of the menstrual cycle. A possible explanation, which could be tested, lies in the variations in body weight which occur in many patients and are caused by intermittent dieting. As has been shown, disturbances in the menstrual cycle also occur in healthy young women after a loss in body weight of a few kg (Pirke *et al.*, 1985, 1986; Schweiger *et al.*, 1987).

References

Boyar, R. M., J. Katz, J. W. Finkelstein, S. Kapen, H. Weiner, E. D. Weitzman and L. Hellman (1974). Anorexia nervosa immaturity of the 24-hour luteinizing hormone secretory pattern. *New England Journal of Medicine* **291**, 861.

Di Zerega, G. S. and G. D. Hodgen (1981). Luteal phase dysfunction infertility: A sequel to aberrant folliculogenesis. *Fertility and Sterility* **35**, 489.

Fairburn, C. G. and P. J. Cooper (1984) The clinical features of bulimia nervosa. *British Journal of Psychiatry* **144**, 238.

Frisch, R. E. (1979). Fatness and the onset and maintenance of menstrual cycles. In *Psychoneuroendocrinology in Reproduction*, ed. by L. Zichella and P. Pancheri, Elsevier/North Holland Biomedical Press, p. 253.

Jones, G. S. (1976). The luteal phase defect. *Fertility and Sterility*. **27**, 351.

Leon, G. R., P. White Phelan, J. T. Kelly and S. R. Patten (1986). The symptoms of bulimia and the menstrual cycle. *Psychosomatic Medicine* **48**, 415.

Pirke, K. M. and D. Ploog (1986). Psychobiology of anorexia nervosa. In *Nutrition and the Brain*, Vol. 7, ed. by R. J. Wurtman and J. J. Wurtman, Raven Press, New York, 167.

Pirke, K. M., M. M. Fichter, R. Lund and P. Doerr (1979). Twenty-four-hour sleep-wake pattern of plasma LH in patients with anorexia nervosa. *Acta Endocrinologica*. **92**, 193.

Pirke, K. M., J. Pahl, U. Schweiger and M. Warnhoff (1985a). Metabolic and endocrine indices of starvation in bulimia: A comparison with anorexia nervosa. *Psychiatry Research*. **15**, 33.

Pirke, K. M., U. Schweiger, W. Lemmel, J. C. Krieg and M. Berger (1985b). The influence of dieting on the menstrual cycle of healthy young women. *Journal of Clinical Endocrinology and Metabolism* **60**, 1174.

Pirke, K. M., U. Schweiger, R. G. Laessle, B. Dickhaut, M. Schweiger and M. Waechtler (1986). Dieting influences the menstrual cycle: vegetarian versus nonvegetarian diet. *Fertility and Sterility* **46**, 46.

Pirke, K. M., M. M. Fichter, C. Chlond, U. Schweiger, R. G. Laessle, M. Schwingenschloegel and C. Hoehl (1987). Disturbances of the menstrual cycle in bulimia nervosa. *Clinical Endocrinology*. **27**, 245.

Russell, G. (1979). Bulimia nervosa: An ominous variant of anorexia nervosa. *Psychological Medicine*. **9**, 429.

Schweiger, U., R. G. Laessle, H. Pfister, C. Hoehl, M. Schwingenschloegel, M. Schweiger and K. M.. Pirke (1987). Diet-induced menstrual irregularities: Effects of age and weight loss. *Fertility and Sterility*. **48**, 36.

Part IV
Therapy

18

Psychological therapies in bulimia nervosa

M. M. Fichter
University of Munich

A great variety of therapeutic approaches to the treatment of bulimic syndromes have been described. The general conclusion is that there is no simple treatment for bulimia (Russell, 1979; Stunkard, 1980; Fairburn, 1985). There is no rigid, schematic treatment programme applicable to any patient without consideration of her/his special problems. Simple adaptation of the forms of treatment which have been developed for anorexia or obesity is insufficient (Gilbert, 1986). In the *Handbook of Psychotherapy for Anorexia Nervosa and Bulimia* (Garner and Garfinkel, 1985), different approaches to the treatment of these eating disorders are summarized by reputable authors. Other forms of treatment for the bulimic syndrome have been described by Fairburn (1985), Fichter (1985), Mitchell *et al.* (1985) and Vandereycken, Kog and Vanderlinden (1989). The present volume contains chapters by Nutzinger and de Zwaan (Chapter 19) on the recent development of the behavioural treatment of bulimic eating disorders, by Beumont *et al.* (Chapter 20) on the importance of dietary interventions, by Vandereycken (Chapter 21) on the relevance of body-image disturbances for the treatment of bulimia and by Hudson and Pope (Chapter 22) on the psychopharmacological treatment of bulimia. The present contribution is a review of the *psychological* treatments of the bulimic syndrome. Stimulated by psychological research into depression, the importance of cognitive strategies for the modification of irrational thoughts and self-devaluation in bulimia has been especially emphasized by Fairburn (1985). Depending on the approach, the bulimic syndrome may be considered as: (1) an addictive behaviour; (2) a means of avoiding depressive sensations, interpersonal problems or difficult life decisions; (3) an excuse for inadequate performance and mood lability; (4) a passive rebellion; (5) a protection against existing partner relationships; (6) a call for attention; (7) a reaction to a family system which is extremely isolated and interdependent; or (8) an attempt to adjust one's body weight to the 'ideal' in a society in which 'slimness' represents self-esteem, beauty and success (Schwartz, Barrett and Saba, 1985, p. 281). In this chapter special emphasis is laid on the study of deficits in interoceptive and emotional perception, on the establishment of social competence and on the improvement of appropriate emotional expression.

General Guidelines for the Treatment of Bulimic Eating Disorders

Treatment plans, during phases and steps with a predetermined time sequence for certain interventions, can establish order for the therapist in a field which is complex and difficult to control. An experienced and professionally competent therapist will consider the patient's hints and wishes and alter the focus of the treatment accordingly. He will pay attention to apparently unimportant symptoms pointed out by the patient (e.g. migraine headaches) without spending too much time on these. He will persuade the patient at a reasonable point (acceptable to the patient) to discuss the more 'delicate' issues (such as secret eating behaviour or conflicts in the family). In an illness which afflicts mainly women, the question of whether the sex of the therapist is important for therapeutic success frequently arises. In our experience, the sex of the therapist is far less important for the progress of the therapy than is his/her professional competence.

Before the start of the therapy it is important to know the patient's expectations and motivations. If the time is not yet ripe for certain steps (e.g. regulation of eating behaviour, start of clinical treatment), it is better not to force the patient to start treatment immediately. The provision of information and the application of suitable motivational strategies can ensure that, at a later stage, the patient achieves self-imposed aims more easily and directly than if she/he feels forced into the therapy. Examples of suitable motivational strategies are: (1) Removal of external pressure so that patients may understand the nature of their intrinsic motivation. They will then be able to recognize their own expectations, needs and desires and to express these. (2) Informing patients of the consequences and complications of bulimic eating behaviour can activate their healthy instincts. (3) Telling patients about the potential of the therapy and describing the concrete treatment steps will show them the therapeutic prospects and will relieve anxieties. (4) When it becomes apparent that the patient has decided for her/himself to begin treatment, it is important to allow time and opportunity to rethink this (questioning initial aims, emphasizing the usefulness and the function of the symptomatology). The boosting and evaluation of the motivation is a process which continues throughout treatment.

The development of a well-founded therapeutic relationship, based on understanding and confidence, is decisive for therapeutic progress. For all patients, but especially for young ones, the first interactions between patient and therapist are of paramount importance. On this occasion the therapist may make mistakes such as taking decisions 'over the head of the patient', establishing a premature 'understanding' with parents or the partner of the patient, prematurely overloading the therapeutic relationships through excessive therapeutic demands or breaching confidentiality. By contrast, an experienced and skilful therapist will try to inspire motivation and will adopt the role of a therapeutic advisor who leaves the decisions to the patient. He will reduce the patient's fears by clarifying the therapy and will listen to patients in order to discover their real problems (see Köhle and Simons, 1986).

At the onset of treatment the basic principles and concepts of the therapy should be explained to the patient. Once familiar with these, the patient can follow the therapeutic process with open eyes and understanding. During the course of our outpatient and inpatient treatments we familiarize our bulimic patients with the following concepts:

1. *Self-responsibility.* It is the patients who have to make the decisions for themselves and carry the responsibility for these (within the framework that the patient decides upon at the start of the therapy). In the treatment of eating disorders, the therapist must not play the role of policeman, controller or spy. If patients really want to deceive the therapist they can always do so. It can be implied that by taking such steps they can only harm themselves.
2. *Openness and trust.* Therapy is only possible if patients trust the therapist sufficiently to discuss freely even embarrassing and difficult problems. If they have lied to the therapist in a previous session, and thus broken the rule of honesty, it is important that they should feel free to discuss this conflict openly.
3. *Therapy in the 'here and now'.* Patients should experience and express what occupies their minds and what worries and concerns them in the 'here and now'. Even if an event from the distant past worries them at present, it is still 'here and now' that it is important. It must not be permitted for patients whose problem is their own 'overadjustability' to conform with the therapist's expectations or to ratify her/his theories. On the contrary, patients should be able to discover their own needs, thoughts, desires, aims and feelings.

4. *Antidiet models.* Fasting and dieting partly contribute to the development of eating disorders. The observation of a 'restricted diet prescription' is not the solution to an eating disorder. Eating must again become the direct satisfaction of a need and must no longer serve the function of 'stuffing oneself' in situations of increased tension. Obesity is not caused by eating in response to hunger but by eating in order to satisfy other needs.
5. Important parts of the therapy are carried out in *groups* of patients with eating disorders (during clinical treatment in the therapeutic community of the clinic). This creates 'expertise' in dealing with the affliction. Each patient is an autonomous member of this community (see below).
6. The importance of the patient's *active involvement* in the planning of the treatment, rather than passive acceptance of the therapy, is emphasized.

Group therapy and therapeutic community of patients with eating disorders

In the course of the illness, patients with eating disorders usually become socially isolated. The 'withdrawal' into an abnormal eating behaviour reflects suppressed desires and needs, suppressed anger, fear of rejection, demands for perfection and inferiority feelings. Due to shame and guilt feelings or because of social fears, the company of others is increasingly avoided. Thus, important communication with others is absent and patients become increasingly preoccupied with their own problems. In a therapeutic community, individual members have privileges (availability of help). They also have tasks and duties (responsibility for themselves, observation of group rules, e.g. openness). In the therapeutic community of a therapy group all patients can establish for themselves a stable equilibrium in communal activities and contacts with others: they can be of help to others as well as receive help from them. Open discussions with other sufferers lead to feelings of relief. Acceptance into a group of people with similar problems encourages sufferers to admit their problems to themselves and to others. The group can help the patients to recognize (as reflected in the mirror of their cosufferers) their own problems and learn to accept these. In a therapy group, new solutions for ingrained behavioural and thinking patterns may be discovered on the basis of openness, honesty and self-acceptance.

In the treatment of addictions (alcoholism, drug dependency), treatment in groups and the principle of the therapeutic community have taken on an especially important role. Bulimic syndromes also have aspects of addiction (Hatsukami *et al.*, 1982). The 'group' of similarly afflicted patients not only allows economy of treatment but is also an important and decisive means of inducing motivation, of recognizing functional connections and of bringing about behavioural changes within a social context (see also Mitchell *et al.*, 1985). For obese patients, the 'group' also serves a relieving and confronting function. In a group of patients with similar problems, overweight patients lose the feeling of being 'outsiders' in a society dominated by the 'slimness' ideal. They recognize that others have also not achieved lasting success with dietary experiments which, in some cases, have stretched over years. They learn about the precipitants of increased eating. For the typical anorexic patient, the group can be important in overcoming shyness and interpersonal difficulties. Their secret desire to be the centre of attention cannot be achieved through their emaciated appearance in a group of similarly afflicted patients and the symptom thus loses its importance; this may, however, temporarily increase anxieties.

Groups may, on the one hand, be flexible with little structure. Such groups require a very experienced therapist and it is important to take note of the individual needs of the group participants. On the other hand, groups can be strictly structured with predetermined exercises and teaching aims. The advantage of structured groups is that less preparation time is needed (after some developmental work) and less experience is required of the therapist. The type of work planned for the group can be written out and given to the patient as working material. We are, for example, working with structured groups for the training of social skills and for teaching the 'antidiet' model.

Aims of the therapy

The following are appropriate aims for the treatment of bulimic patients: (1) to increase ability to recognize intero- and proprioceptive signals and feelings; (2) to improve social competence and emotional expression; (3) to learn to relax physically and to attain tranquillity; (4) to change depressive thought patterns; (5) to reduce excessive achievement orientation; (6) to take on responsibility; and (7) to organize appropriate leisure activities. The therapist's function is to be an expert advisor, like the mountain guide who accompanies the less experienced mountaineer during a climb to the mountain peak, protecting him from dangers. Patients must, however, learn to walk alone, to decide for themselves what their aims are, and to carry the responsibility for these decisions. Bulimic patients often set their aims too high, even within the therapeutic framework. This predestines failure. The therapist may draw patients' attention to this tendency to demand too much from themselves and may help them to formulate realistic targets in a concrete and positive manner. The patient would like to be 'normal' but may, at the same time, associate normality with boredom, routine and mundaneness and may thus be afraid of it. It is not sufficient to present 'normal eating behaviour' as the aim; aims have to be formulated correctly and precisely. The therapist may point out ambivalence; for example, if patients aim to cease vomiting they will probably feel anxious about becoming too fat.

Functional analysis and behavioural observation

This is a process which continues throughout treatment. Therapeutic interventions may be more target-oriented if precipitating factors and functional connections between external events and patients' specific pathological behaviour are known.

Psychological Treatment Approaches

Table 18.1 summarizes principal approaches to psychological treatment.

Provision of information

A few years ago, a number of bulimic patients still believed themselves to be the only people afflicted by this disorder. Since then, more has become known about bulimia in non-professional circles. Nevertheless, at the start of the treatment most bulimic patients do not know enough about this disorder and its consequences or about the potentials of treatment. In therapeutic discussions, with the help of books and other printed material, lectures, group discussions and video films, patients can be informed about the following: (1) normal physical and psychological reactions to stress; (2) dealing and coping with problems and the development of social competence; (3) healthy eating behaviour, the importance of vitamins, minerals and the intake of sufficient quantities of foods; (4) consequences of bulimic behaviour; (5) possibilities and limitations of therapeutic interventions; (6) possibilities and limitations of self-help and (7) relapse and relapse prevention.

Nutritional counselling, eating behaviour and state of health

Behavioural therapeutic programmes aimed at changing eating patterns incorporate a focus on healthy and regular nutrition (Mitchell *et al.*, 1985; Garner and Bemis, 1985; Andersen, Morse and Santmyer, 1985; Fairburn, 1985). In this volume, the basic principles of advice on nutrition for bulimic patients are systematically outlined by Beumont *et al.* (Chapter 20).

In an eating disorder such as bulimia it is necessary to discuss nutrition in detail, openly and directly, although without regarding this as the only treatment. Patients often seem to be experts at 'counting calories', but actually they have little knowledge of the composition of a healthy diet (Laessle *et al.*, 1988). They are often convinced that eating regular meals or calorie-rich foods leads to obesity and they do not know that the attacks of insatiable hunger are largely reactions to the restricted eating which preceded these attacks. They have lost the ability to recognize interoceptive stimuli for hunger and satiety and to eat accordingly. Healthy nutrition is mixed and balanced with respect to fat, proteins and carbohydrates. It contains 'fibre' to stimulate intestinal activity, sufficient vitamins and minerals *and* sufficient calories.

Table 18.1 Summary of disturbed functions, useful therapeutic aims and special therapeutic measures for the treatment of bulimic syndromes

Disturbed functions or reasons for therapy	Aims and areas for therapy	Special therapeutic measures
Lack of information	Supply of information about:	Stress reactions Nutrition Limitations and potentials of therapy Self-help Relapse prevention Consequences of bulimic behaviour
Pathological eating behaviour	Nutritional advice	Antidiet course Orderly plan for meals Functional analysis between stress and eating behaviour
Disturbance of interoceptive and emotional perception	Perception training	Body-oriented exercises Training of interoceptive perception Training of emotional perception
Disturbance of emotional expression	Training of emotional expression	Adequate expression of emotions Catharsis exercises Training of social competence in role-play exercises
Dysfunctional, irrational thoughts, beliefs and values	Cognitive therapy	Exposure and questioning Reframing
Chronic distress in social environment and inefficient interaction	Inclusion of social environment	Partner therapy Family therapy
Passivity and lack of acceptance of responsibilities and inadequate confidence in own abilities	Activation of own initiative and responsibility	Active participation in self-help groups Self-monitoring
Fear of relapse	Maintenance training	Anticipation of problems Exposure of relevant pressures Planning of further treatments and participation in self-help groups Dealing with medicines

Based on knowledge of physiological effects, a number of rules may help the patient to normalize her/his eating pattern step by step:

1. Eat at regular times (main meals/intermediate meals) and do not miss out on any of these (rather than limiting eating to nocturnal binge-eating episodes following abstention from food during the day).
2. Avoid a restricted diet and aim for a balanced diet which contains, in addition to minerals, vitamins and essential fatty acids, sufficient carbohydrates and fat. Restriction of the spectrum of nutrients consumed is typical for bulimic patients.
3. During meals, relax and concentrate solely on eating.
4. Avoid eating alone; eat, as far as possible, in company.
5. Do not gulp the food; on the other hand, avoid 'picking and poking' at food. Eat at a 'moderate' speed.
6. Vitamin and mineral supplements are not required if the diet is balanced and the eating pattern is normal (no laxatives, no vomiting). Within the framework of a structured 'antidiet course', we teach patients how eating can again become a direct satisfaction of a biological need. On the basis of the 'antidiet model' (Orbach, 1982), patients learn to rely on their own interoceptive hunger and satiety signals and on their own feelings, rather than following a narrow diet schedule and thus becoming slaves to and victims of the fashionable ideal of physical slimness. The patients learn that obesity is not caused by eating in response to hunger but by the 'gorging' of food.

Although bulimia is an eating disorder, it is also a disturbance of the ability to recognize interoceptive stimuli like hunger and satiety and the perception and expression of emotions. It is useful to ask patients to write out eating records. A possible means of establishing connections between eating and emotions is illustrated in Table 18.2

Patients who experience great difficulties in recognizing and expressing feelings are given a list of adjectives (bored, anxious, etc.). They are asked to add to these 'emotional' adjectives certain items of food or drink and also the manner of eating and drinking.

In a further step, patients learn to identify 'precipitating' and 'maintaining' factors which upset them and can lead to bulimic episodes. They also learn to recognize the short- and long-term consequences of this behaviour. Patients keep a written record of eating behaviour, situations which precipitate eating and of their thoughts and feelings. The therapist studies the records; on these occasions further connections are made, consequences discussed and alternative coping behaviour and changes in strategies worked out. Particularly for patients with 'chaotic' eating behaviour, it is very helpful to design eating plans for a whole day and, in this context, discuss intentions, perceptions, feelings and reality. Plans for the day are added to the simple eating record (Table 18.2) and compared with the record of actual eating. When such

Table 18.2 Recording food intake and functional analysis of antecedents and consequences (ABC of 'behaviour')

A Antecedents →	B Reactions Internal (thoughts and feelings)	External (behaviour) →	C Consequences Immediate	Long-term
Attendance at a party with 20 people, some of whom are unknown. Buffet and music. The others seem to be enjoying themselves	Thoughts: They all know each other, only I am on my own. They are watching me because they think I am 'abnormal' Feelings: Sadness, loneliness	Previous, pathological behaviour		
		I shall leave this party as soon as I can ↓ then I will 'gorge' myself and feel better ↓ 'Binge-eating episode'	Positive: Now I feel better; the tension is gone	Negative: I am lonely alone; nobody thinks about me; I am in despair
		Alternative behaviour: I will approach someone in the group and start a conversation. He has a lot of interesting things to say and pays me compliments	Negative: It needed a lot of effort to approach him and I was afraid he would reject me	Positive: I gained confidence in social interactions; I am able to use my own initiative in dealing with others and I feel better and less affraid

records are used it should be ensured, firstly, that the patient is aware of the essential aspects of this procedure, and, secondly, that the development of new obsessions regarding eating is avoided. The essential aspects of the recording of eating and day plans are: recognition of functional connections between eating and emotions, sharpening perceptions of interoceptive stimuli (hunger, satiety, etc.), and laying the foundations for new strategies to overcome the disorder, for example broadening of social skills and conflict resolution.

Perceptual training

Hilde Bruch (1973) was the first to point out the interoceptive and emotional perceptual disturbances in eating-disordered patients. In the present volume, Vandereycken (Chapter 21) discusses the relevance of body-image disturbances to the treatment of bulimic disorders. Garner and Garfinkel (1981) and Fairburn (1985) have chosen a cognitive approach to the consideration of body-image disturbances. As direct feedback has little effect, the patient must (by analogy with colour-blindness) learn to come to terms with the existing disturbance, which is an expression of the eating disorder.

Another focal point for addressing distorted body image and interoceptive perceptual disturbances can be 'perception training' within the framework of a body-oriented therapy. The elaboration of this field is one of the newer developments in the treatment of eating disorders at several institutions. However, at present there are no scientific investigations of the effectiveness of body-oriented methods in bulimia.

Exercises which appear to be effective based on clinical experience have been borrowed from various body-oriented therapies, for example from movement and sport therapy (exercises developed by Feldenkrais, assuming certain positions, jumping on a trampoline, massage — training of active perception by concentration on touch and changes in skin and muscles or, in patients who are afraid of being touched, transmission of direct touch *via* objects, e.g. a ball, relaxation procedures (e.g. autogenic training to enhance perception of cardiac function, respiration, blood flow, heat and gravity) and dance therapy (experience of movement in space, communication by movement, rhythmic exercises) and Gestalt therapy and bioenergetics.

In underweight bulimics, and in restricting anorexics, confrontation with their real body shape as recorded on video can release strong emotional reactions. Various touch exercises sharpen sense perception and also perception of bodily limits, and can induce erotic sensations. Non-verbal body and communication exercises (body sculptures, non-verbal self-confidence training) facilitate experience of the effects on others of their personality and body. Pleasant and unpleasant body postures, movements and contacts can be experienced. 'Pleasure exercises' soon give rise to conflicts regarding this preservation of personal values, for example, 'not being allowed to enjoy oneself'. In athletic exercises which require strength (e.g. playful wrestling) movement, strength and personal effort in interaction with others can be experienced.

Problems of sexual perception can be explored and perceptions in this area can be discussed in the form of 'homework'. Non-verbal physical awareness exercises improve body- and self-perception and physical expression and decrease tension, thus leading to improvements in body image. According to more recent investigations, bulimic patients tend to be suggestible (Pettinatis, Horne and Staats, 1985). Thus far, little therapeutic use has been made of this potential. It seems obvious that it should be employed for the improvement of bodily perception, for example in relaxation exercises or 'journeys into dreamland'.

Training in emotional expression

In some bulimic patients, accurate perception of interoceptive stimuli and their own emotions is a prerequisite for training in physical and emotional expression. Disturbance of emotional expression is present in practically all cases of bulimia nervosa. The bulimic patient has learned to alleviate rising emotions by bulimic eating behaviour, thereby temporarily reducing tension and feelings of anxiety. This means that perception of the real problem situation often becomes diffuse and muddled because emotional differentiation ceases; experiences which evoke emotion become undifferentiated since they are all addressed in bulimic eating behaviour. Social skills, insofar as they were ever developed, also deterioriate during the course of bulimia. Within the framework of the bulimic eating disorder all problems are tackled in a single way. When anxiety- or panic-provoking situations arise, when the feeling of having been tested unfairly prevails, when one feels pushed aside by others, when a task has not been carried out satisfactorily, when there has been a quarrel with a friend or conflict with parents, when one feels hurt or that one has been taken advantage of, the reaction is always the same — namely, to binge eat.

Assuming that patients are aware of precipitating situations and specific events which upset them, it is possible to train emotional expression through so-called 'role-playing exercises'.

1. As a first step, patients feel relieved when they succeed in recognizing potent 'buried' emotions and expressing these in cathartic exercises. For example, an overweight female bulimic patient with a distinct tendency towards self-injury subjectively felt that she was neglected by her parents, that she suppressed her own desires, that she was treated unfairly by her mother and was not helped by her father, and that she had to endure physical and sexual abuse. Through breathing exercises, and whispered suggestions which

stimulated the recall of conflict and emotion-loaded situations, this patient was persuaded by her therapist to express her rage, at first quietly and then screaming, in the therapy group. This has a massive relieving effect which made the patient relaxed and cheerful for days afterwards.

2. In order to be able to deal effectively with past and future problems in everyday life, treatment by training in emotional expression must, however, be considerably extended. Patients must learn how to express their indignation in a socially acceptable way in situations in which they might feel excluded, inhibited, unfairly treated, humiliated or annoyed. They should clarify the situation in a few words, express the nature of their feelings (anger, fury, helplessness, etc.) and state the exact behaviour of others (words, intonation of voice) which triggered these feelings. This can be relatively simple — for example, in a situation where a stranger jumps a queue they can tell him that he or she has to wait at the back. However, in interactions with persons in authority or in dealing with conflicts with partners and within the family, this process can be more difficult and complicated.

In principle, what these tasks have in common is that the patients themselves have to react directly to the action of another person and have to express (with or without words) that this action poses a problem which evokes certain feelings. In role-playing exercises and in different types of 'homework', social skills and assertiveness, stress management and problem-solving techniques can be learned by practical examples. In the case, discussed above, of the patient with self-injuring tendencies, she must, for example, learn to express in future interactions with her father her feelings of having been neglected and let down by him. If this is not done in the form of an accusation but with real feeling on the part of the patient, the father will receive 'feedback information' and understand the consequences of his behaviour. In addition, he will be given the opportunity to clarify any possible misunderstandings, to justify his behaviour or to state that he did not mean to hurt her.

Cognitive therapy: to reduce dysfunctional (irrational) thoughts, beliefs and values

This field has been described in great detail by Fairburn (1985) and Garner, Fairburn and Davis (1987) and is also dealt with in the contribution by Nutzinger and de Zwaan in this volume (Chapter 19). Thus, it will only be summarized here. Bulimic patients tend to make cognitive errors in a manner similar to that described by Beck *et al.* (1979) for (neurotic) depressed patients.

1. *Dichotomous thinking* following the 'all-or-nothing' principle is often apparent ('if I am not able to pass this examination I am a total failure').

This way of thinking is also verbally expressed by the frequent choice of 'extremes', for example 'never', 'ever', 'enormous', 'mad'.

2. *Overgeneralizations* ('The fact that my friend has left me makes me unhappy — all past and future friends will leave me — I will never be able to keep a friend and I will always be unhappy'.)
3. *Personalization.* Neutral events in the environment are taken personally, for example: 'When I entered the restaurant everybody was looking at me. They must have thought that I was a disgusting and uncontrolled person because I gained weight again today'.

The purposes of cognitive therapy are the identification of errors of reasoning, the consideration of alternative strategies and consequences in 'Socratic dialogue', and deciding on realistic judgements and strategies. By examining various dysfunctional thoughts, the therapist will eventually hit on the basic dysfunctional beliefs and values. Typical beliefs of this kind helped by bulimic women are: 'I must always, and in all situations, satisfy the demands made on me by others' or 'only if I am slim will I be successful and accepted by others; if I am not slender or if I am obese then I am useless, unsuccessful and lonely'. The aim of cognitive therapy is to challenge the dysfunctional and irrational dominant beliefs and values, which give rise to a multitude of dysfunctional, self-deprecating, irrational thoughts, and to replace these with realistic values ('I should not evaluate myself solely on the basis of shape and weight; it is more important who I am and what I do').

Inclusion of the social environment (family and partner therapy)

There are no systematic treatment studies assessing the effectiveness of additional family or partner therapy for unselected, individually treated bulimic patients. Based on our own clinical experiences, the inclusion of a significant person to whom reference can be made can help considerably in dealing with emotional processes. It can release tensions and contribute to constructive relapse prevention. Nevertheless, the inclusion of relatives into the therapy should not become dogmatic. Practical considerations play an important role in decisions regarding the inclusion of such persons, for example the distance between their home and the place of treatment, readiness of the person in question to help, and psychotherapeutic reasons (e.g. the existence of a strong symbiotic relationship with a parent or partner; an idealized but distant relationship with the father; a complicated relationship with the partner; indirect conflict-avoiding, interaction patterns within the family). Some important therapeutic concepts in family therapy for anorexic patients (Sargent, Liebman and Silver, 1985) can be transferred to the treatment of bulimic patients with their relations. Therapy which includes the family is especially indicated in those cases where the relatives (and the patient) are strongly opposed to it (Grolnick, 1972).

The diagnostic and therapeutic horizon can be extended by systematic consideration of the whole family system, which reaches beyond the individual (patient) and the dyad (e.g. patient and mother). In this systematic consideration, resolution of guilt becomes irrelevant. As a rule, this is known to the therapist but usually not to the patient or the relatives. At the outset of partner or family therapy it is, therefore, advisable to relieve the patient from any guilt. Thus, the therapist can stress that, with regard to the bulimic disorder, the patient has done his best, even if this did not bring the expected success, and that a family or partner meeting can lead to the discovery of more effective ways of dealing with the situation. Even without explicit inclusion of the social environment into the therapy, effective treatment leads to a change in roles which can precipitate increased arguments and irritation between patients and relatives. It is sensible to prepare the patient and the relatives for this eventually and to tell each of them what can be gained by the change in roles. The key-word for partner and family therapeutic sessions is *understanding* of the position of the other person.

A therapist is not immune to giving preferential treatment to the patient whom he has accompanied through many treatment sessions. It is, therefore, helpful to include a cotherapist in the family and partner therapeutic sessions who acts on behalf of the relatives. A frequent reason for the premature termination of family or partner therapeutic interventions may lie in the therapist's lack of understanding of the anxieties, position, ideas and feelings of the relatives, with whom he or she is less familiar than with the patient. In family and partner therapy sessions, communication and role-playing exercises can be used, so that individuals can learn: (1) to listen to each other and (2) to express negative and positive feelings more directly. If therapy sessions have a time limit, books which explain the above aims should be recommended to the relatives (e.g. Berlin, 1984, *The Open Discourse*).

Activation of personal initiative and responsibility and participation in self-help groups

Frequently, bulimic patients do not rely sufficiently on their own abilities. They are passive and unwilling to accept responsibility for their actions. Initiative and responsibility can be activated in two ways;

1. Active participation in self-help groups. Larocca (1983) regarded self-help as the most important, but frequently neglected, part of the therapy of anorexics. Enright, Butterfield and Berkowitz (1985) have discussed the function and importance of self-help groups and organizations for patients with eating disorders. Therapy and self-help are not contradictory but complement each other. Others have emphasized that stability (continuity) of participation is a *conditio sine qua non* for the success of therapy.

In self-help groups, continuity of structure, and frequently also of attendance, are absent. Self-help groups can, however, fulfil other functions. For example, they provide a place for sharing experiences with other afflicted persons. They can be 'havens' at times of crisis, and can provide a more or less flexible means of social support when the family is losing or has lost this supportive role (Silverman, 1978). Participation in self-help groups can motivate patients to act responsibly and to develop their own initiative.

2. Self-regulation and self-monitoring. The aim can be achieved by encouraging self-control in the patient. An important principle of self-regulation is that the patient is encouraged to be active and to delay temporarily positive reinforcement which may have negative consequences, for example binge-eating. This requires persistence and strength, but in the long run produces positive results. For example, an argument with a friend about an irritating remark can relieve tension and form the basis for reconciliation. Within the framework of the therapy, much is still initiated by the therapist. However, patients have to learn to take their fate actively into their own hands to use the experiences gained during therapy and to become their own therapist. Plans for days, weeks, months or years (which stress long-term perspectives) can contribute to the development of self-control. Furthermore, it is essential that patients not only understand the most important therapeutic principles but also learn to transfer these to everyday life, so that they can become increasingly independent of therapeutic help.

Maintenance training

These considerations lead to the issue of 'relapse prevention'. Towards the end of the therapy it is advisable to prepare for separation from therapist and therapy, to discuss emotional separation from the therapist and the therapeutic institution and to work on the patient's ability to exercise self-control, especially with regard to foreseeable relapses. The following points may be useful in relapse prevention: (1) anticipation of problems and cognitive rehearsal at individual steps towards their resolution; (2) before the end of the therapy patients should subject themselves to relevant stress situations (e.g. a visit to the place of work and resolution of unresolved issues with bosses and colleagues); (3) planning further steps of treatment and participation in self-help groups; (4) preparation of plans for crisis situations (to whom can I go if . . .); (5) for patients who have to take medication, learning to deal constructively with the effects and side-effects.

Indications for Hospitalization

These must be considered in relation to the existing availability of outpatient and inpatient treatment and to the question of payment. Hospital treatment can be far more intensive than outpatient treatment. In an inpatient treatment programme the therapeutic measures discussed above can be used in a far more concentrated manner than is possible for outpatients. In addition, hospitalization puts the patients in an 'out of the ordinary' situation which enables them to be more involved in the consideration of the risks of the therapy, especially with respect to emotional problems. Common, everyday tasks (housework, profession) which demand the patient's constant 'functioning' are eliminated by hospitalization and expected or unexpected crises can be 'caught' by the therapist. Whether outpatient or inpatient therapy is indicated depends on the circumstances and specific aims. Hospital treatment may be indicated if:

1. No satisfactory progress has been achieved in outpatient treatment or if the necessary facilities for outpatient treatment are not available.
2. The eating disorder is so severe that outpatient treatment does not appear to be sufficient (suicide attempts, multiple impulsive reactions).
3. The eating disorder and conflict regarding eating is so ingrained and deeply rooted that it cannot be broken down in the everyday situation.
4. The family or partner relationship is so enmeshed or complex that separation is the only way to bring relief to all concerned and to design and carry out the necessary course of treatment.
5. There is additional dependency on medicines, alcohol or drugs.
6. Additional psychiatric disorders are present which make hospitalization desirable for the treatment of both the eating disorder and the psychiatric disorder (affective disorders, anxiety neurosis, borderline disturbances).

Therapeutic Pitfalls and Recurrent Problems in Therapy

Some examples of pitfalls and recurrent problems in therapy are given below:

1. A severe relapse has already occurred during the treatment. This is usually a devastating experience. However, it can also be regarded in a positive way: the relapse provides an *in vivo* opportunity to study precipitating factors and facilitates the practising of alternative behaviour for similar future situations.
2. The occurrence of self-injurious behaviour, of disguised or obvious suicide threats, abuse of alcohol and disciplinary difficulties including stealing in crisis and tension situations. In such cases, therapeutic experience is required, together with clearly defined structures and immediate consequences. If these events have happened, they should be openly discussed in the group; the group has a steering and regulating function. Distinctly formulated treatment agreements with a clear exposition of the consequences if a transgression should occur clarify the situation for the patient from the very beginning and enable immediate action to be taken, even if a

large team of therapists is involved. Such agreements must not be formulated in a way which forces the therapist into specific actions (e.g. interruption of therapy), but in one which increases flexibility for the therapist if there is a breach of the agreement (e.g. 'the consequences of a breach are to be decided by the therapeutic team'). An increase in contact intensity in crisis situations can help to 'catch' the crisis. In rare cases in which breaches of promises and treatment agreements repeatedly occur, it may be advisable to interrupt or terminate therapy.

3. 'Therapist-killer'. Some bulimic patients are highly intelligent, have more experience of therapy than their therapist and are inclined to use both against their therapy and therapist. Compliments like 'you are my last hope' often open this game. Eventually, these compliments become criticisms ('therapist X would have done this differently') and the therapy becomes stagnant because the patient does not perform certain prescribed tasks, or refuses, with some critical remarks, to accept these. In such cases it is advisable to be outspoken with the patient and with supervisors and to verbalize the state of helplessness which has been induced by the patient's destructive behaviour. If further open confrontation of the patient with his behaviour does not establish a therapeutic basis, it may be best to change the therapist.
4. 'Power struggle'. Some patients with eating disorders show a tendency to initiate power struggles. This can, for example, occur in underweight patients with eating disorders in reaction to normalization of body weight imposed by the therapist. If a power struggle occurs during therapy, it has gone wrong and the therapist needs advice. The therapist's admission of helplessness in the face of certain actions of the patient and attributing responsibility for these actions to the patient, as well as the use of a team of therapists, are ways out of an unnecessary power struggle.
5. Secrets and lies. What is to be done if it emerges that a patient who has apparently adapted to the therapeutic approach has been deceiving the therapist during the previous few weeks by hanging weights on herself before stepping on the scales in order to pretend that she is heavier? What is to be done if breaches of the therapeutic agreement have occurred and the therapist has been told lies when confronting the patient? Secrets and lies are incompatible with the patient–therapist relationship, which must always be built on trust. The resolution of a confidence crisis can establish a feeling of trust in the patient for the first time during therapy. Without confidence, effective therapy cannot be carried out.
6. Control *vs* self-responsibility in the patient. Various treatment programmes deal with this issue. In particular, treatment programmes originating from the orthodox behavioural or internistic tradition of treatment for anorexics are based on the idea that the patient needs continuous supervision and control at the beginning of the therapy. The concept of the self-

responsibility of the patient stands in contrast to this. These two points of view can be reconciled. If restriction of patients' freedom and self-control are required, the whole treatment may be more successful if patients' opinion has first been sought, if they see the necessity and therefore agree to it and if this decision has been made without any coercion (real decision freedom).

7. Stagnation ('nothing is stirring in the therapy, except the emotions of the therapist'). In this case, one has to look for access points which can bring 'movement' into the therapy. It may be useful, in elucidating the 'motivation-situation', to include significant persons who can be referred to in the therapy. Under certain circumstances, hospitalization has to be considered. If justifiable, the therapy may also be interrupted and resumed at a later date. In each case, the problem should be discussed in a team conference.

References

American Psychiatric Association (1980, 1987). *Diagnostic and Statistical Manual of Mental Disorders — Revision (DSM III-R).* APA, Washington DC.

Andersen, A. E., C. L. Morse and K. S. Santmyer (1985). Inpatient treatment for anorexia nervosa. In *Handbook of Psychotherapy for Anorexia Nervosa and Bulimia*, ed. by D. M. Garner and P. E. Garfinkel. Guilford Press, London, New York, pp. 311–343.

Beck, A. T., A. J. Rush, B. F. Shaw and G. Emery (1979). *Cognitive Therapy of Depression.* Guilford Press, New York.

Berlin, J. (1984). *Das Offene Gespräch.* Pfeiffer Verlag, Munich.

Bruch, H. (1973). *Eating Disorders: Obesity, Anorexia Nervosa and the Person Within.* Basic Books, New York.

Enright, A. B., P. Butterfield and B. Berkowitz (1985). Self-help and support groups in the management of eating disorders. In *Handbook of Psychotherapy for Anorexia Nervosa and Bulimia*, ed. by D. M. Garner and P. E. Garfinkel. Guilford Press, London, New York, pp. 491–512.

Fairburn, C. G. (1985). Cognitive-behavioral treatment for bulimia. In *Handbook of Psychotherapy for Anorexia Nervosa and Bulimia,* ed. by D. M. Garner and P. E. Garfinkel. Guilford Press, London, New York, pp. 160–192.

Fichter, M. M. (1985). *Magersucht und Bulimia.* Springer Verlag, Heidelberg, New York.

Foreyt, J. P. (1988). Bulimic syndromes in obesity.

Garner, D. (1988). Predictors of outcome.

Garner, D. M. and K. M. Bemis (1985). Cognitive therapy for anorexia nervosa. In: *Handbook of Psychotherapy for Anorexia Nervosa and Bulimia*, ed. by D. M. Garner and P. E. Garfinkel. Guilford Press, London, New York, pp. 107–146.

Garner, D. M. and P. E. Garfinkel (1981). Body image in anorexia nervosa: measurement, theory and clinical implications. *International Journal of Psychiatry in Medicine* **11**, 263–284.

Garner, D. M. and P. E. Garfinkel (Eds) (1981). *Handbook of Psychotherapy for Anorexia Nervosa and Bulimia.* Guilford Press, London, New York.

Garner, D. M., C. G. Fairburn and R. Davis (1987). Cognitive-behavioral treatment of bulimia nervosa. *Behavior Modification* **II**, 398–431.

Gilbert, S. (1986). *Pathology of Eating. Psychology and Treatment.* Routledge & Kegan Paul, London, New York.

Grolnick, L. (1972). A family perspective of psychosomatic factors in illness: a review of the literature. *Family Process* **11**, 457–486.

Hatsukami, D., P. Owen, R. L. Pyle and J. E. Mitchell (1982). Similarities and differences on the MMPI between women with bulimia and with alcohol or drug abuse problems. *Addictive Behaviors* **7**, 435–439.

Johnson, C. and M. E. Connors (1987). *The Etiology and Treatment of Bulimia Nervosa.* Basic Books, New York.

Köhle, K. and Simons, C. (1986). Anorexia nervosa. In *Psychosmatische Medizin*, ed. by T. von Vexküll. Urban & Schwarzenberg, Munich, Vienna, Baltimore, pp. 600–640.

Laessle, R. G., U. Schweiger, M. M. Fichter and K. M. Pirke (1988). Nutritional knowledge in patients with eating disorders. *International Journal of Eating Disorders* **7**, 63–73.

Larocca, F. E. F. (1983). The relevance of self-help in the management of anorexia and bulimia. *Res Medica* (St John's Mercy Medical Center, St. Louis, MO), 16–19.

Mitchell, J. E., D. Hatsukami, G. Goff, R. L. Pyle, E. D. Eckert and L. E. Davis (1985). Intensive outpatient group treatment for bulimia. In *Handbook of Psychotherapy for Anorexia Nervosa and Bulimia*, ed. by D. M. Garner and P. E. Garfinkel. Guilford Press, London, New York, pp. 240–253.

Nögel, R. (1988). Die Bulimia nervosa bei Zwillingen. Dissertation zum Erwerb des Doktorgrades an der Medizinischen Falkultät der Ludwig-Maximilians-Universität, München.

Orbach, S. (1982). *Fat is a Feminist Issue* II. Berkeley Books, New York.

Orbach, S. (1985). Accepting the symptom: a feminist psychoanalytic treatment of anorexia nervosa. In *Handbook of Psychotherapy for Anorexia Nervosa and Bulimia*, ed. by D. M. Garner and P. E. Garfinkel. Guilford Press, London, New York.

Pettinatis, H. M., R. L. Horne and J. M. Staats (1985). Hypnotizability in patients with anorexia nervosa and bulimia. *Archives of General Psychiatry* **41**, 1014–1016.

Russell, G. F. M. (1979). Bulimia nervosa: an ominous variant of anorexia nervosa. *Psychological Medicine*, **9**, 429–448.

Sargent, J., R. Liebman and M. Silver (1985). Family therapy for anorexia nervosa. *Handbook of Psychotherapy for Anorexia Nervosa and Bulimia.* ed. by D. M. Garner and P. E. Garfinkel. Guilford Press, London, New York, pp. 257–279.

Schwartz, R. C. M. J. Barrett and G. Saba (1985). Family therapy for bulimia. In *Handbook of Psychotherapy for Anorexia Nervosa and Bulimia*, ed. by D. M. Garner and P. E. Garfinkel. Guilford Press, London, New York, pp. 280–307.

Silverman, P. R. (1978). *Mutual Help Groups: A Guide for Mental Health Workers.* National Institute of Mental Health, Rockville, MD.

Stunkard, A. J. (1980). Psychoanalysis and psychotherapy. In *Obesity*, ed. by A. J. Stunkard. W. B. Saunders, Philadelphia, pp. 355–368.

Wooley, O. W., S. C. Wooley and S. R. Dyrenforth (1979). Obesity and women II. A neglected feminist topic. *Women's Studies International Quarterly* **2**, 81–92.

Wooley, O. W. and S. C. Wooley (1982). The Beverly Hills eating disorder: the mass marketing of anorexia nervosa (editorial). *International Journal of Eating Disorders* **1**, 57–69.

Wooley, S. C. and A. Kearney-Cooke (1986). In *Handbook of Eating Disorders. Physiology, Psychology and Treatment of Obesity, Anorexia and Bulimia*, ed. by K. D. Brownell and J. P. Foreyt. Basic Books, New York, pp. 476–502.

19

Behavioural treatment of bulimia (nervosa)

D. O. Nutzinger and **M. de Zwaan**
University of Vienna

The behavioural approach to the treatment of eating disorders has enjoyed a good reputation for many years and behavioural techniques form the backbone of most psychological treatments for bulimia. This leading position of behaviour therapy is largely a consequence of its success in the treatment of obesity. Experience gained from the use of a number of proven interventions in short, focused treatment programmes in obesity has been of benefit in the development of behavioural treatments for bulimia. Since bulimia has been established as a distinct disorder in the third edition of the *Diagnostic and Statistical Manual of Mental Disorders* (American Psychiatric Association, 1980), there has been a growing demand for professional help in its treatment. In the meantime, many publications have appeared describing more or less promising results. However, only a few studies fulfil, at least in part, the methodological requirements of psychotherapeutic research which allow the effectiveness of a particular therapeutic programme to be judged.

In the present article we provide a brief description of the most important behavioural viewpoints on the nature and treatment of bulimia. This is followed by a description of the current status of behavioural research, making reference to some selected studies, and by a discussion of the effectiveness of behavioural interventions in the treatment of bulimia.

First Attempts at Treatment

In 1853 Romberg, in his *Textbook of Nervous Diseases*, had already argued for the use of an 'aversion cure' in patients with insatiable hunger (for reference see Ziolko and Schrader, 1985). Aversion therapy was also the first behavioural approach in the treatment of patients with bulimic symptomatology and was especially employed in overweight patients with binge-eating episodes; the results were described as promising by Wolpe (1958) and later also by others (Foreyt and Kennedy, 1971; Kenny and Solyom, 1971; Wijesinghe, 1973). However, Meyer and Crisp (1964) considered the efficacy of this method to be questionable and its effects to be of only short duration. In attempting to explain the therapeutic success of aversion therapy, Kenny and Solyom (1971) speculated that compulsive vomiting and not the binge-eating episodes provided the primary reinforcement for the maintenance of the eating disorder. They thus anticipated the basic tenet of the 'anxiety-reduction model'. Nowadays, aversion therapy no longer plays a role in the treatment of bulimia of obesity.

Behavioural Models and Treatment Approaches

Four explanatory models for bulimia have thus far been described in the field of behaviour therapy: the anxiety-reduction model, the cognitive model, the eating-habit control model and the interpersonal stress model. Despite markedly differing views on the nature of bulimia, the therapeutic approaches derived from these models overlap in many respects. Furthermore, in practice, the different treatment approaches are integrated in broad treatment programmes which include a great number of individual techniques. As can be seen from Table 19.1, cognitive strategies are used far more frequently in the treatment programmes than is 'exposure and response prevention'. A combination of these two therapeutic approaches has been investigated in only four studies. The most frequently used individual technique is self-monitoring, which is employed in all the treatment programmes listed in Table 19.1. 'Planning of eating', stimulus control, assertiveness training, and relaxation training are also frequently used, whereas relapse prevention is rarely considered.

In the following, these behavioural models and treatment approaches are described together with some selected studies.

The anxiety-reduction model

By analogy with the anxiety-reducing effect of rituals in patients with compulsions, the anxiety-reduction model is based on the idea that in bulimic patients vomiting reduces the fear of gaining weight and is thus a reinforced behaviour. In contrast to other views on the nature of bulimia, in this model

Table 19.1 Summary of characteristics and findings of six psychotherapy studies, Abbreviations used: M = mean value, rem. = remission, red. = reduction, rel. = relapse, sign. = significant, diff. = difference, impr. = improvement, betw. = between, det. = deterioration.

	Yates, Sambrailo (1984)	Ordman, Kirschenbaum (1985)	Kirkley *et al.* (1985)	Ch. Freeman *et al.* (1985)	Fairburn *et al.* (1986)	Wilson *et al.* (1986)
Therapy phase						
Number of Patients at start of therapy	24	20	28	60	26	17
Interrupters of therapy	8	0	6	14	2	4
Age at start of therapy	27.9	19.8	28.3	24.3	22.9	20.5
Duration of disorder in years (M)	7.8	2.7	9–10	6.5	—	—
Diagnostic criteria	Russell	DSM-III	DSM-III	DSM-III	DSM-III Russell	DSM-III Russell
Duration of therapy (weeks)	9–12	4–22	16	15	18	16
Outcome (bulimic attacks)	A B rem. 1 0 red. > 50% 2 2 red. < 50% 4 4 det. 3 2	A B rem. 2 0 red. < 1/w 5 0 no improv. 3 10	sign. impr. A sign. diff. betw. A, B	sign. impr. A B, C no impr. D no sign. diff. A, B, C	sign. impr. A, B no diff. betw. A, B	*A* *B* rem. 5 2 red. > 60% 2 3 red. < 30% 0 1
Follow-up						
Duration of follow-up (months)	1.5	—	3	—	12	12
Interrupters	0	—	0	—	0	2
Outcome (bulimic attacks)	A B rem. 2 0 red. > 50% 2 4 red. < 50% 2 2 det. 1 1 rel. 1 1	—	A B rem. 5 1 red. > 60% 5 7 rel. 3 1 no diff. betw. A, B	—	sign. impr. A, B no diff. betw. A, B	*A* *B* rem. 5 1 rel. 0 4

vomiting is not regarded as a consequence of binge-eating episodes but as the primary maintaining factor of the disorder.

A number of studies have provided some evidence in support of this theoretical account. Thus, Johnson and Larson (1982) showed that vomiting alleviated negative feelings such as anxiety, helplessness and loss of control. Leitenberg *et al.* (1984) observed a massive increase in anxiety when female bulimic patients were told that they were not allowed to vomit and were asked to eat a quantity of food which would, under normal circumstances, give rise to an urge to vomit. The same eating procedure did not cause anxiety if the patients were allowed to plan to vomit after eating. Thus, the authors suggested that bulimic patients permit 'loss of control' to happen only if they plan to vomit afterwards.

On the basis of this anxiety-reduction model a treatment approach has been developed, namely, the 'exposure and response-prevention' method. This method has been propounded especially by Rosen and Leitenberg (1982) and was first tested by them in an experimentally designed, single case study treating a 21-year-old female patient with binges and purges several times per day. The treatment was divided into three phases, each of which consisted of six sessions in which three different types of food were introduced. In each session the patient was asked to eat a quantity of food which would normally lead to vomiting. The authors observed that the anxiety which occurred during the eating episodes decreased during the treatment, despite increased food intake. However, this applied only to the type of food used during the therapy. When the patient was asked to continue this programme at home, she stopped vomiting after 24 weeks of treatment and, without special instructions, the bulimic episodes also ceased. In the course of the follow-up phase (10 months) vomiting occurred on only one occasion.

In a later study, this therapeutic approach was tested in five female bulimic patients (Leitenberg *et al.*, 1984). The treatment consisted of 12–18 sessions. At the end of treatment, two out of five patients were completely free from symptoms, another two showed a reduction in symptoms of more than 50 per cent and one patient showed no improvement, even after an additional treatment attempt at home. This clinical improvement was maintained during a follow-up period of 3–6 months.

Giles, Young and Young (1985) treated 34 female bulimic patients by 'exposure and response prevention'. Twenty patients showed a reduction in binge-eating episodes of between 80 and 100 per cent, two patients showed a reduction of between 50 and 79 per cent, six patients showed no improvement and another six patients terminated treatment prematurely. Treatment gains persisted during the follow-up period (on average 27 weeks).

The cognitive model

In this model the abnormal attitude to body shape and weight and the morbid fear of becoming fat are regarded as the central features of bulimia. These disturbances, which several authors regard as specific to bulimia and anorexia nervosa, have been described under various names (Bruch, 1962, 1973; Crisp, 1967; Fairburn, 1981; Russell, 1979). The extreme and persistent concern about body shape and body weight leads to abnormal behaviour in order to control both, under all circumstances, such as overconcern with food and eating, experimenting with extreme diets, vomiting and abuse of laxatives. In this context binge-eating episodes are a rather paradoxical phenomenon and are considered to be a secondary reaction to the excessive reduction in food intake (Herman and Polivy, 1980). It is therefore of paramount importance that these distorted attitudes and beliefs are changed in treatment. The therapeutic techniques used for these cases were largely derived from treatment programmes developed for overweight patients (Fairburn, 1984; Mahoney and Mahoney, 1976; Meichenbaum, 1977; Stuart, 1978).

Fairburn (1981), who played an essential role in the development of the cognitive approach, reported the use of his programme for the first time in 1981 on 11 female bulimic patients. The programme consists of three therapy phases. The aim of the first phase is to interrupt the disturbed eating behaviour. It consists largely of self-monitoring and 'stimulus control' and of careful 'planning of eating'. The aim of the second phase is to change cognitive distortions regarding body shape and weight by means of cognitive restructuring. The central theme of treatment in the third phase is relapse prevention. After seven months of individual therapy, the binge-eating episodes were reduced to fewer than one per month in nine patients. One patient showed a reduction to two binges per month and in one patient no improvement was achieved. The results were maintained during a follow-up period of 4–12 months.

Schneider and Agras (1985) modified this programme into a group therapy and used it in a study of 13 bulimic patients. After 16 weeks of treatment, seven patients showed remission, five a reduction in binge-eating episodes by more than 50 per cent and one patient a reduction of less than 50 per cent. The treatment was completed by all patients. At a follow-up examination after six months, five patients reported that they had remained free from symptoms but in another five bulimics the frequency of the episodes had again increased.

The eating-habit control model

In this model, described by Johnson and Brief (1983) and by Wardle and Beinart (1981), the main cause of bulimia is viewed as a lack of knowledge and ability to maintain an appropriate body weight through the regulation of food intake and physical activity. Patients attempt to reduce body weight through unrealistic and drastic diets. The occurrence of binge-eating episodes is regarded as a 'counter-regulatory' mechanism which can be experimentally induced in subjects who are on a chronic diet and are, under laboratory conditions, forced to transgress their dietary rules (Herman and Polivy, 1980). Episodes of binge-eating are again followed by drastic dieting. As a further means of reducing body weight, dieting is supplemented by laxative abuse and vomiting. Episodes of binge-eating as a consequence of severely restricted food intake had been previously observed in the Minnesota starvation experiment (published in 1950). After the conclusion of the experiment, binge-eating occurred in some of the volunteers and persisted for several months (Keys *et al.*, 1950). In anorexia nervosa, characterized by long fasting periods, bulimia occurs in 30–50 per cent of cases (Beumont, George and Smart, 1976; Hsu and Holder, 1986). Other authors have found that more than 80 per cent of their bulimic patients had been dieting before the occurrence of the first binge-eating episode (Pyle, Mitchell and Eckert, 1981; Fairburn and Cooper, 1982).

Thus, the main aim of the treatment based on this model is the adoption of healthy eating behaviour and sufficient physical activity. Previously established behavioural treatment strategies from treatment programmes for overweight patients have been adapted for this purpose. In addition, the patient is directly helped to resist episodes of binge-eating (Johnson and Brief, 1983). Johnson *et al.* (1984) compared this 'energy balance' therapeutic approach in six female patients in a crossover design with exposure and response prevention. In this study, 'energy balance' also included 'self-monitoring', 'stimulus control' and 'cognitive restructuring'. The treatment lasted up to 12 weeks with each patient attending one individual session per week. In this pilot study, the two treatment methods were found to be equally effective both with regard to vomiting and to binge-eating episodes. Of the six patients who started the treatment, five completed it. Of these, one achieved complete remission, three were considered to be considerably better and only one patient showed no improvement. No follow-up results were provided.

Cullari and Redmon (1983) treated three patients with a treatment package which was centred on dietary instructions, self-monitoring, goal-setting and reinforcement techniques. The results were surprisingly good. All patients achieved a complete cessation of binge-eating and vomiting after only seven sessions. During the short follow-up period of 4–7 weeks the benefits persisted.

The interpersonal stress model

This is based on the assumption that binge-eating episodes are precipitated by preceding stress situations or negative events. Excessive eating is triggered primarily by negative feelings such as depression, anxiety, anger and interpersonal difficulties such as loss or rejection. In these cases the binge-eating episodes momentarily reduce the immediate tension (Abraham and Beumont, 1982). This model conceptualizes binge-eating episodes as a means of compensating for behavioural deficits in the social sphere and does not regard them as an acquired coping strategy that can develop into an all-powerful controlling mechanism in the battle against negative feelings. Vomiting is not regarded as important, either for the precipitation or for the maintenance of the disorder, but is viewed as a secondary response to ameliorate the guilt feelings and other negative emotions which occur after the binge-eating episodes.

This interpersonal aspect is considered in many therapy programmes where the patient is helped to identify trigger situations. Patients are encouraged to resist binge-eating in these situations and to call into action other stress-reducing behavioural patterns as a substitute for eating.

The Effectiveness of Behaviourally Oriented Treatment Programmes in Controlled Therapy Studies

Among the many studies of behaviourally oriented treatment programmes for bulimics, there are only a few which allow any conclusions as to effectiveness. The six studies which will be described were chosen because they fulfil the following criteria: treatment of at least six patients; definition of bulimia according to DSM-III or Russell (1979); precise description of the therapy programme used; use of a control group; and a sufficiently careful record of, at least, the eating behaviour. Recently, various methodological problems in studies on bulimia have been pointed out by several investigators (Fairburn, 1985; Wilson, 1986; Wilson *et al.*, 1986; Kirkley *et al.*, 1985). Examples are: selection of patients, recording and assessment of the target symptoms, multidimensional recording of the disorder, etc. It is not possible to consider all of these points in detail here. It must, however, be mentioned that it is not sufficient to base on assessment of the success of the treatment of the disorder as a whole on the frequency of binge-eating episodes alone.

Observations of other psychological variables are, however, not consistently recorded and a comparison of relevant data obtained by the use of different measuring instruments is complicated. In order to compare different studies we have therefore also used the frequency of binge-eating episodes as the main criterion of evaluation. The characteristics of the studies described below, together with the results of the active treatment phase and, if available, of the follow-up examination, are given in Table 19.1. The group names used in the text (A, B, C, D) are also used in Figure 19.1 and Table 19.1.

In a controlled treatment study, Freeman *et al.* (1985) compared four groups: cognitive behavioural therapy (group A); behaviour therapy without cognitive intervention consisting mainly of self-control methods, relaxation training and, in some rare cases, exposure and response prevention (group B); group therapy designed to be explorative, supportive and educational (group C); and a waiting list (group D). Sixty female patients were included in

		Self-monitoring	Stimulus control alternative strategies	Goal setting	Self-esteem training	Relaxation training	Exposure	Response prevention	Response retardation	Cognitive restructuring	Problem solving	Relapse prevention	Diet planning	Non-behavioural techniques	Individual therapy	Group therapy
Fairburn	(1981)	*	*	*			*			*	*	*	*		*	
Cullari & Redmon	(1982)	*		*									*	*	*	
Johnson C. *et al.*	(1983)	*	*	*	*	*				*			*			*
Connors *et al.*	(1984)	*	*	*	*	*				*			*	*		*
Fernandez	(1984)	*		*						*		*	*	*		*
Johnson W. *et al.*	(1984)	*					*	*							*	
(Group A, B)		*	*							*			*	*	*	
Leitenberg *et al.*	(1984)	*					*	*							*	
Mitchell *et al.*	(1984)	*	*		*		*	*		*	*	*	*	*		*
Yates & Sambrailo	(1984)	*	*		*	*			*	*			*			*
(Group A, B)		*			*	*				*						*
Freeman *et al.*	(1985)	*			*					*					*	
(Group A, B, C)		*	*	*	*	*	*	*			*		*		*	
		*												*		*
Giles *et al.*	(1985)	*					*	*		*	*	*	*		*	
Huon & Brown	(1985)	*			*	*				*	*					*
Kirkley *et al.*	(1985)	*	*		*	*	*		*	*	*		*			*
(Group A, B)		*												*		*
Ordmann & Kirschenbaum	(1985)	*					*	*		*			*	*	*	
Rossiter & Wilson	(1985)	*					*	*							*	
(Group A, B)		*								*					*	
Schneider & Agras	(1985)	*	*		*	*	*		*	*	*		*			*
Fairburn *et al.*	(1986)	*	*	*			*			*	*	*	*		*	
(Group A, B)		*												*	*	
Hsu & Holder	(1986)	*	*								*		*		*	
Paul & Jacobi	(1986)	*	*		*		*			*			*	*		*
Wilson *et al.*	(1986)	*					*	*		*		*	*			*
(Group A, B)		*								*		*	*			*

Figure 19.1 Various combinations of individual techniques in behaviourally oriented therapy programmes

this study. The number of patients who interrupted treatment, 14 in total, was twice as large in the group therapy, which was not behaviourally oriented, as in the individual therapy, with a behavioural orientation. After treatment for 15 weeks, a significant reduction in bulimic episodes was observed in all the treatments and there were no significant differences between them. The patients on the waiting list did not show improvements with regard to their bulimic behaviour during the 15 weeks' waiting period. Furthermore, all three treatments produced significant improvement with regard to depression but this effect was most pronounced in the cognitive treatment condition. A follow-up examination is planned but results are not yet available.

In a study published by Wilson *et al.* in 1986, a controlled comparison was carried out between a combination of cognitive therapy with exposure and response prevention (group A) and an exclusively cognitive therapy (group B). A treatment programme lasting 16 weeks was started by 17 female bulimic patients; four patients terminated treatment prematurely.

Among the seven patients who were treated with a combination of cognitive and behavioural approaches, five showed a complete cessation of bulimic episodes; in the other two there was a reduction of between 70 and 80 per cent. This success persisted over a follow-up period of one year.

In the group which was treated exclusively by the cognitive approach there was a cessation of bulimic episodes in two patients. In three patients the frequency of episodes was reduced by more than 60 per cent and in one patient by less than 30 per cent. Four of these patients relapsed during the follow-up period. Subsequently, a combination of cognitive therapy with exposure and response prevention was attempted. Two of the four patients who had previously relapsed showed remission of bulimic symptoms. In the other two there was a reduction of vomiting by 33 or 66 per cent. The patients treated with the combined treatment approach also showed greater improvement in their various psychological measures.

In a study by Yates and Sambrailo (1984) on 24 female patients, two broad therapy programmes were compared with each other. Eight patients dropped out, eight were treated with a combination of cognitive behaviour therapy, self-monitoring relaxation training and assertiveness training (group B). The eight patients in the other condition (group A) received additional behavioural instructions such as stimulus control, development of alternative coping strategies and response prevention. The patients were asked to keep a diary during the whole study.

After six weeks of treatment there was no difference between the two therapy groups: three patients in group A and two in group B achieved a reduction in bulimic episodes of more than 50 per cent. The follow-up examination after six weeks showed better results for the group in which the treatment programme included the larger number of behavioural techniques: five patients in this group achieved a significant reduction (two of them a complete cessation) in binge-eating episodes. A similar improvement was seen in only two patients from the other group. All patients showed significant improvement in depression, anxiety and self-esteem; the scores were, however, still significantly above the norm.

Ordmann and Kirschenbaum (1985) compared a combination therapy, consisting of exposure and response prevention, cognitive restructuring and process-oriented psychotherapy (group A), with a 'waiting list' (group B). The treatment was conducted individually; after 4–22 weeks the following results were obtained: of the 10 patients in the therapy group, two showed a complete remission, five a reduction in bulimic episodes to less than one per week, and three patients reported at least one bulimic episode per week after conclusion of the therapy. Furthermore, the patients in the 'index' group showed a significant improvement in depression and on a number of other psychological parameters. Nevertheless, at the end of the treatment the values were still not within the normal range. During the five months, none of the 10 patients on the waiting list showed an improvement in disturbed eating behaviour or a change in psychometric variables. All 20 patients completed the treatment programme. Results of a follow-up examination were not provided.

In a controlled study, Kirkley *et al.* (1985) treated a total of 28 female bulimic patients either by a cognitive therapy (group A) or by a 'non-directive psychotherapy' (group B). In the behaviourally oriented group, stimulus control, cognitive restructuring, exposure and response prevention and relaxation were used. Self-monitoring was used in both groups. After a treatment programme of 16 weeks, the patients in the cognitive therapy group showed significantly better results than the patients in the control group and significant decreases in binge-eating episodes and in vomiting occurred only in the group treated by cognitive therapy. Significantly more patients interrupted the therapy in the 'non-directive' group than in the behaviourally oriented group (five *vs* one). A follow-up examination three months after the end of treatment showed a further improvement of the eating disorder in both groups and there was no longer a statistically significant difference between the two. In the cognitive therapy group five patients showed a remission of binge-eating episodes and another five a reduction of more than 60 per cent. Three patients showed a deterioration from this 'end of treatment' state. In the group treated by 'non-directive psychotherapy' one patient showed a remission, seven a reduction of more than 60 per cent and one a deterioration as compared with the end of treatment. Both forms of treatment resulted in significant improvements in depression, anxiety and cognitive distortions.

Fairburn *et al.* (1988), published the results of a study in which they treated an 'index' group by the cognitive-behavioural treatment programme (group A). The control group was treated by short-term focal psychotherapy (group B). A total of 24 patients were treated for 18 weeks in individual therapy sessions. The treatment programme, described in great detail by Fairburn, consisted of the three therapy phases described above. At the end of treatment, the results revealed a significant improvement in both groups. There was, however, no difference between the patients treated by cognitive behavioural therapy and those treated by focal psychotherapy. The results remained the same at a follow-up examination one year after the end of the treatment phase. In the group which recieved the cognitive therapy, the frequency of binge-eating episodes decreased from an average of 24 per week before treatment to an average of three at the end of treatment and to zero at the end of the follow-up period. The occurrence of vomiting was equally dramatically diminished in this group. In the group treated by focal psychotherapy, the frequency of binge-eating episodes was on average reduced from 20 per week before treatment to four at the end of treatment and to zero after another 12 months. A clear improvement in various psychological measures was achieved in both treatment programmes.

Fairburn *et al.* attributed part of the success of the short-term focal psychotherapy to the self-monitoring and the provision of information about the disorder which was also used in this group. It is quite correct for the authors to consider the possible influence of these behavioural techniques. However, they were used in both therapy programmes and the argument that they are the reason for the equally good results of the treatment in both groups is not convincing.

Summary

Apart from treatment with psychopharmacological agents, behaviour therapy is the most frequently and more carefully investigated treatment approach in the field of bulimia. Furthermore, behavioural techniques such as self-monitoring or control of eating behaviour also play an important role in many treatment approaches which are not specifically behaviourally oriented. In summary, the therapeutic results of behaviourally oriented programmes reveal, at the end of treatment, a cessation of binge-eating in about 40 per cent of the patients; a significant reduction on binge-eating episodes in 30 per cent; and no improvement or deterioration in eating behaviour in another 30 per cent of patients (Johnson and Conners, 1989). In assessing the effectiveness of a specific therapeutic method the value of 'global summaries' of this kind is, however, questionable since, after critical consideration, most of the published results have to be regarded as preliminary.

Treatment research in the field of bulimia suffers from a number of methodological shortcomings which will now be briefly discussed. The episodic course of the disorder and the lack of knowledge of its natural course make it difficult to interpret treatment results. In addition, bulimia is a very complex phenomenon which cannot be adequately assessed merely by consideration of the disturbed eating behaviour. Thus far, the available results only indicate putative predictors for the course of the disorder and for its response to different therapeutic regimes (Lacey, 1984; Freeman *et al.*, 1985; Yates and Sambrailo, 1984; Fernandez, 1984). The phenomenon of the 'bulimic episode' itself is very variable with regard to duration, quality and quantity of the food consumed and its association with vomiting, laxative abuse or emotional disturbances. The extent to which these different disturbances are considered varies from study to study. Thus, several authors demand, quite rightly, that not only the eating behaviour but also psychopathological status and other variables should be recorded by standardize instruments in order to enable a comparison of different research findings (Fairburn, 1984, 1985; Hsu and Holder, 1986; Johnson and Pure, 1986).

Most of the behavioural treatment programmes consist of a combination of several individual techniques which are used either in group or individual therapy. Such multicomponent 'treatment packages' are frequently used in bulimia as in many other disorders, but the assumed 'additive effect' is rarely tested. Some indications in this direction are given by the additional use of relapse prevention, which has been said to improve long-term results (Fairburn, 1984; Wilson *et al.*, 1986). At present, relapse prevention is used only in a few special treatment programmes, despite the fact that bulimia is a disorder with a high relapse rate. A further example is dietary instructions, which have recently been shown as an important component of psychotherapeutic programmes in a meta-analysis (Laessle, Zott and Pirkel, 1989).

On the basis of the available research findings, it is at present not possible to state that any one of the therapeutic approaches discussed above is superior to any other. This is also the case for the recently widely publicized cognitive therapy. This treatment did not achieve any better results when compared with 'exposure and response prevention' (Rossiter and Wilson, 1985). The finding that the combination of cognitive therapy with exposure and response prevention is superior to the use of purely verbal cognitive therapies alone may be of great practical relevance (Wilson *et al.*, 1986). At the same time, this is one of few proven examples of an additive effect for the combination of two therapeutic techniques.

A survey of the development of the behavioural approaches reveals that the first treatment trials on bulimic patients were experimental studies of individual cases which served mainly as a test for a theoretical model regarding the development and maintenance of the disorder. In recent years clinical aspects, such as the practical applicability and the effectiveness of therapy programmes, have come to the fore. The main task of research into behaviour therapy is the transfer of short-term therapeutic effects into long-term benefits. These trends are also reflected in the demand for a treatment-free follow-up period of at least one year (Fairburn, 1986; Hsu and Holder, 1986).

A further development is the integration of non-behavioural therapeutic techniques such as supportive and insight-directed approaches, body-oriented therapies and family therapy. In this way the fact that bulimia is a very complex disorder is increasingly acknowledged. Therefore, treatment has to be flexible and capable of suiting the needs of individual patients. This approach has been used successfully for anorexia nervosa (Andersen, Morse and Santmyer, 1985; Kalucy *et al.*, 1985; Strober and Yager, 1985). In the field of bulimia, the excellent results of Lacey's 'integrated behavioural and psychodynamic approach to bulimia' (1987) argue for the use of a combination of different therapeutic methods. At present, there is no method for deciding which one of the therapeutic methods is best for any given case. Likewise, the question of which patients would profit by the addition of psychopharmacotherapy cannot at present be definitively answered.

Today, behaviour therapy can offer several promising treatment strategies for bulimia; however, some questions of practical relevance cannot yet be answered and these remain the task of future research.

References

Abraham, S. F. and P. J. V. Beumont (1982). How patients describe bulimia or binge eating. *Psychological Medicine* **12**, 625.

American Psychiatric Association (1980). *Diagnostic and Statistical Manual of Mental Disorders*, 3rd edn. APA Washington DC.

Andersen, A. E., C. Morse and K. Santmyer (1985). Inpatient treatment for anorexia nervosa. In *Handbook of Psychotherapy for Anorexia Nervosa and Bulimia*, ed. by D. M. Gardner and P. E. Garfinkel. Guilford Press, New York, London, p. 311.

Beumont, P. J. V., G. C. W. George and D. E. Smart (1976). 'Dieters' and 'vomiters and purgers' in anorexia nervosa. *Psychological Medicine* **6**, 617.

Bruch, H. (1962). Perceptual and conceptual disturbances in anorexia nervosa. *Psychosomatic Medicine* **24**, 187.

Bruch, H. (1973). *Eating Disorders: Obesity, Anorexia Nervosa and the Person Within.* Basic Books, New York.

Connors, M. E., C. L. Johnson and M. K. Stuckey (1984). Treatment of bulimia with brief psychoeducational group therapy. *American Journal of Psychiatry* **141**, 1512.

Crisp, A. H. (1967). The possible significance of some behavioral correlates of weight and carbohydrate intake. *Journal of Psychosomatic Research* **11**, 117.

Cullari, S. and W. K. Redmon (1983). Treatment of bulimarexia through behavior therapy and diet modification. *Behav. Therapist* **6**, 165.

Fairburn, C. G. (1981). A cognitive behavioural approach to the treatment of bulimia. *Psychological Medicine* **11**, 707.

Fairburn, C. G. (1984). Bulimia: its epidemiology and management. In *Eating and its Disorders*, ed. by A. J. Stunkard and E. Stellar. Raven Press, New York, p. 235.

Fairburn, C. G. (1985). The management of bulimia. *Journal of Psychiatric Research* **19**, 465.

Fairburn, C. G. and P. J. Cooper (1982). Self-induced vomiting and bulimia nervosa: an undetected problem. *British Medical Journal* **284**, 1153.

Fairburn, C. G., J Kirik, M. O'Connor and P. J. Cooper (1986). A comparison of two psychological treatments for bulimia nervosa. *Behaviour Research and Therapy* **24**, 629.

Fernandez, R. C. (1984). Group therapy of bulimia. In *Current Treatment of Anorexia Nervosa and Bulimia*, ed. by P. S. Powers and R. C. Fernandez. Karger, Basel, New York, p. 277.

Foreyt, J. P. and W. A. Kennedy (1971). Treatment of overweight by aversion therapy. *Behaviour Research and Therapy* **9**, 29.

Freeman, C., F. Sinclair, J. Turnbull and A. Annandale (1985). Psychotherapy for bulimia: a controlled study. *Journal of Psychiatric Research* **19**, 473.

Freeman, R. J., B. Beach, R. Davis and L. Solyom (1985). The prediction of relapse in bulimia nervosa. *Journal of Psychiatric Research* **19**, 349.

Garfinkel, P. E., H. Moldofsky and D. M. Garner (1980). The heterogeneity of anorexia nervosa: bulimia as a distinct subgroup. *Archives of General Psychiatry* **37**, 1036.

Giles, T. R., R. R. Young and D. E. Young (1985). Behavioural treatment of severe bulimia. *Behavior Therapy* **16**, 393.

Herman, C. P. and J. Polivy (1980). Restrained eating. In *Obesity*, ed. by A. S. Stunkard. Saunders, Philadelphia, p. 208.

Huon, G. F. and L. B. Brown (1985). Evaluating a group treatment for bulimia. *Journal of Psychiatric Research* **19**, 479.

Hsu, L. K. G. and D. Holder (1986). Bulimia nervosa: treatment and short-term outcome. *Psychological Medicine* **16**, 65.

Hsu, L. K. G., A. H. Crisp and B. Harding (1979). Outcome of anorexia nervosa. *Lancet* **1**, 61.

Johnson, C. L. and M. E. Connors (1988). Psychological and psychopharmacological treatment of bulimia, in press.

Johnson, C. and R. Larson (1982). Bulimia: an analysis of mood and behavior. *Psychosomatic Medicine* **44**, 341.

Johnson, C. and D. L. Pure (1986). Assessment of bulimia: a multidimensional model. In *Handbook of Eating Disorders*, ed. by K. D. Brownell and J. P. Foreyt. Basic Books, New York, p. 405.

Johnson, C., M. Connors and M. Stuckey (1983). Short-term group treatment of bulimia. *International Journal of Eating Disorders* **2**, 199.

Johnson, W. G. and D. Brief (1983). Bulimia. *Behavioral Medicine Update* **4**, 16.

Johnson, W. G., D. G. Schlundt, M. L. Kelley and L. Ruggiero (1984). Exposure with response prevention and energy regulation in the treatment of bulimia. *International Journal of Eating Disorders* **3**, 37.

Kalucy, R. S., P. N. Gilchrist, C. M. McFarlane and A. C. McFarlane (1985). The evolution of a multitherapy orientation. In *Handbook of Psychotherapy for Anorexia Nervosa and Bulimia*, ed. by D. M. Garner and P. E. Garfinkel. Guilford Press, New York, London, p. 458.

Kenny, F. and L. Solyom (1971). The treatment of compulsive vomiting through faradic disruption of mental images. *Canadian Medical Association Journal* **1095**, 1071.

Keys, A., J. Brozek, A. Henschel, O. Mickelsen and H. L. Taylor (1980). *The Biology of Human Starvation*. The University of Minnesotta Press, Minneapolis.

Kirkley, B. G., J. A. Schneider, W. S. Agras and J. A. Bachman (1985). Comparison of two group treatments for bulimia. *Journal of Consulting and Clinical Psychology* **53**, 43.

Lacey, J. H. (1983). Bulimia nervosa, binge-eating, and psychogenic vomiting: a controlled treatment study and long term outcome. *British Medical Journal* **286**, 1609.

Lacey, J. H. (1984). Moderation of bulimia. *Journal of Psychosomatic Research* **28**, 397.

Laessle, R. G., C. Zöttland and K. M. Pirke (1989). Meta-analysis of treatment studies for bulimia. *International Journal of Eating Disorders* (in press).

Leitenberg, H., J. Gross, J. Peterson and J. C. Rosen (1984). Analysis of an anxiety model and the process of change during exposure plus response prevention treatment of bulimia nervosa. *Behavior Therapy* **15**, 3.

Mahoney, M. J. and B. K. Mahoney (1976). *Permanent Weight Control: A Total Solution to the Dieter's Dilemma*. W. W. Norton, New York.

Meichenbaum, D. (1977). *Cognitive-Behavior Modification*. Plenum, New York.

Meyer, V. and A. H. Crisp (1964). Aversion therapy in two cases of obesity. *Behaviour Research and Therapy* **2**, 143.

Mitchell, J. E., D. Hatsukami, G. Goff, R. Pyle, E. D. Eckert and L. E. Davis (1985). Intensive outpatient group treatment for bulimia. In *Handbook of Psychotherapy for Anorexia and Bulimia*, ed. by D. M. Garner and P. E. Garfinkel. Guilford Press, New York, London, p. 240.

Mitchell, J. E., R. L. Pyle, E. D. Eckert, C. Pomeroy, D. Hatsukami and R. Zimmerman (1987). Antidepressants versus group therapy in the treatment of bulimia. *Psychopharmacology Bulletin* **23**, 41.

Ordmann, A. M. and D. S. Kirschenbaum (1985). Cognitive-behavioural therapy for bulimia: an initial outcome study. *Journal of Consulting and Clinical Psychology* **53**, 305.

Paul, T. and C. Jacobi (1986). Ein ambulantes verhaltenstherapeutisches Gruppenprogramm bei Bulimia nervosa. *Psychother. Med. Psychol.* **36**, 232.

Pyle, R. L., J. E. Mitchell and E. D. Eckert (1981). Bulimia: a report of 34 cases. *Journal of Clinical Psychiatry* **42**, 60.

Rosen, J. C. and H. Leitenberg (1982). Bulimia nervosa: treatment with exposure and response prevention. *Behavior Therapy* **13**, 117.

Rosen, J. C. and H. Leitenberg (1985). Exposure plus response prevention treatment of bulimia. In *Handbook of Psychotherapy for Anorexia Nervosa and Bulimia*, ed. by D. M. Garner and P. E. Garfinkel. Guilford Press, New York, London, p. 363.

Rossiter, E. M. and G. T. Wilson (1985). Cognitive restructuring and response prevention in the treatment of bulimia nervosa. *Behaviour Research and Therapy* **23**, 349.

Russell, G. F. M. (1979). Bulimia nervosa: an ominous variant of anorexia nervosa. *Psychological Medicine* **9**, 429.

Schneider, J. A. and W. S. Agras (1985). A cognitive behavioural group treatment of bulimia. *British Journal of Psychiatry* **146**, 66.

Strober, M. and J. Yager (1985). A developmental perspective on the treatment of anorexia nervosa in adolescents. In *Handbook of Psychotherapy for Anorexia Nervosa and Bulimia*, ed. by D. M. Garner and P. E. Garfinkel. Guilford Press, New York, London, p. 363.

Stuart, R. B. (1978). *Act Thin. Stay Thin.* Norton, New York.

Wardle, J. and H. Beinart (1981). Binge eating: a theoretical review. *British Journal of Clinical Psychology* **20**, 97.

Wijesinghe, B. (1973). Massed electrical aversion treatment of compulsive eating. *Behavior Therapy and Experimental Psychiatry* **4**, 133.

Wilson, G. T. (1986). Cognitive-behavioral and pharmacological therapies for bulimia. In *Handbook of Eating Disorders*, ed. by K. D. Brownell and J. P. Foreyt. Basic Books, New York.

Wilson, G. T., E. M. Rossiter, E. J. Kleifield and L. Lindholm (1986). Cognitive-behavioral treatment of bulimia nervosa: a controlled evaluation. *Behaviour Research and Therapy* **24**, 277.

Wolpe, J. (1958). *Psychotherapy by Reciprocal Inhibition*. Stanford University Press, Stanford, California.

Yates, A. J. and F. Sambrailo (1984). Bulimia nervosa: a descriptive and therapeutic study. *Behaviour Research and Therapy* **22**, 503.

Ziolko, H. U. and H. C. Schrader (1985). Bulimie. *Forschritte der Neurologie und Psychiatrie* **53**, 231.

20

Nutritional counselling in the treatment of bulimia

P. J. V. Beumont, M. O'Connor, W. Lennerts and S. W. Touyz
Royal Prince Alfred Hospital and The University of Sydney, Camperdown

Bulimia is characterized by disordered eating behaviour and it is this disturbance which distinguishes it from other psychiatric and physical illnesses. Therefore it is surprising that little has been published specifically concerning the nutritional management of these patients. Sometimes it seems to be assumed that, because the abnormal eating behaviour is indicative of underlying emotional difficulties, it will normalize once these problems have been resolved. A more realistic approach is adopted in cognitive behavioural programmes, which include some nutritional instruction and acknowledge the relationship between prior dieting and subsequent binge-eating (Fairburn and Cooper, 1987). However, dietary counselling is presented as only a minor part of the total treatment strategy and few details are given of the advice and supervision which are actually provided for patients.

We believe that nutritional counselling is an important component of the treatment of all bulimic patients, and is usually essential if therapy is to be effective. The purposes of the present chapter are to discuss its rationale and to outline what it entails.

Rationale for Nutritional Counselling

There are several reasons why nutritional counselling is important. First, the chaotic eating behaviour is often so distressing to patients that they need to begin to regain control over it before they can become involved in any other form of psychotherapy. Second, they view their problem as primarily one of overeating and do not understand that the episodic gorging is largely a response to prior restrained eating practices. Third, they have many fears and misconceptions about food and weight control which need to be identified and corrected. Not only are they afraid of becoming obese (so are many other women), but they firmly believe that they will inevitably get fat if they eat regular meals or any high-energy foods. Fourth, their eating has been disordered for so long that they have lost the ability to resume normal eating. They need to relearn the answers to such basic questions as, 'What is hunger? Should I eat only when I am hungry? How much food is enough?' and 'What is normal eating?'.

Nutritional counselling is most beneficial if provided by a trained dietitian experienced in dealing with this disorder. Both qualifications are necessary for optimal effectiveness. Patients are reassured by the fact that the therapist is an expert in nutrition, and they are more likely to accept her advice in these matters than that of another professional who does not have such specialized knowledge. For her part, the dietitian brings a balanced view of healthy eating, backed by a solid scientific training and tempered by her experience in dealing with the nutritional problems of a wide variety of patients. However, it is important that she is aware of the particular problems posed by bulimia, as these are very different to those seen in most of the other illnesses with which she has to deal. Further, she must be aware that these patients need her support and patience before they can gain the necessary confidence to make changes to their eating pattern.

Formulation of the problem of bulimia

Bulimia is a complex condition (Russell, 1979, 1985; American Psychiatric Association, 1979, 1987; Abraham and Beumont, 1982). Its presentation is dysjunctional: not all symptoms occur in every patient, while apparently extraneous features, such as depression or evidence of personality disorder, are sometimes unduly prominent. The syndrome is perhaps better viewed as a common response to the predicament of overconcern with body weight and shape rather than as a distinct illness (Beumont, 1987). Its most important defining criteria are behavioural. They are:

(a) uncontrolled episodes of overeating or binge-eating;
(b) attempts to compensate for the food ingested, usually by purgation (vomiting and laxative abuse) but also by other means such as excessive exercising;
(c) a chronic pattern of severely restricted eating practices.

There have been a number of different models proposed for the treatment of bulimia, which are discussed elsewhere in this volume. What requires emphasis in the current context is that the bulimia patient herself almost invariably views her problem simply as uncontrolled overeating, and expects treatment to be geared towards suppression of the urge to binge. She sees herself as having an 'addiction' to food, particularly to sweetness, and believes that derogatory terms such as 'foodaholic' (Stolz, 1985) are appropriate to her.

The nutritional counsellor should adopt an entirely different approach. She should emphasize the patient's persistent and excessive dietary restraint as the basic problem. Binge-eating is a response to this unrealistic restraint, a reactive hyperphagia, and the bulimic patient is a 'disinhibited dieter' (Herman and Polivy, 1984). If the patient can be persuaded to relinquish her restrictive eating practices and resume normal eating, the urge to binge-eat will gradually dissipate.

The patient's restrained eating has psychological meaning, as do the binge-eating episodes and the purgation. These issues may be approached by cognitive or other psychotherapies. Of course, the nutritionist must be aware of such psychological problems, and make allowance for them in her contact with the patient. But their management is not her direct responsibility. Her role is to understand the eating disorder in relation to the patient's beliefs and attitudes about food and health, to help her correct this disturbance and to encourage her to resume normal eating practices.

The bulimic patient's attitude to food

Rosen (1987) points to the overwhelming importance of cultural factors in human eating behaviour. We are more likely to be correct in predicting the eating preferences of a person from an Indian, Chinese, French or Italian culture than we would be in predicting almost any other aspect of their daily lives. The identity of isolated cultural enclaves in an alien society, such as Jewry in Anglo-Saxon countries, is preserved as much by its particular culinary tradition as by the possession of a distinct language or religion.

In contemporary technologically advanced societies, many young women have preoccupying concerns about weight and appearance. Most normal women diet at some time and lose more than 3 kg in weight; they wish to be thinner than they are, irrespective of their current weight; and a significant minority admit to having abused laxatives or induced vomiting in attempts to achieve a slender figure (Abraham *et al.*, 1983). Such behaviours may relate to aspirations towards adopting a stereotyped feminine role (Worsley, 1981; Squires and Kagan, 1985). Many women equate this role with a slim body, and so successful dieting enhances their self-esteem. In addition, they are subjected to health propaganda condemning the dangers of obesity and extolling the virtues of slenderness. These factors combine to create a subculture of dietary restraint. Almost invariably, patients with bulimia belong to this subculture.

Not only do restrained eaters deliberately try to curtail the absolute amounts of food they eat, but they limit their food choices, avoiding what they consider to be unhealthy or 'junk' foods. These are all foods which have a high energy content. In order to resume normal eating, bulimic patients must broaden their repertoire of foods. They must give up their misperceptions about nutritional values, their misconceived perfectionism about food. Normal eating does not mean eating only 'health' foods. It means taking a mixed and balanced diet containing the essential foodstuffs *and* sufficient calories for the body's needs. It is accepting a 'good enough' diet rather than repeatedly failing in attempts to eat according to an unrealistic, perfectionist 'optimal' diet.

Several studies have shown that the most important factor in food choice is the person's attitude towards various foods (Schwartz, 1975; Perron and Endres, 1985; Shephard and Stockley, 1987). While it is important to educate patients regarding the nutritional aspects of food, this in itself will not be effective in changing their eating behaviours. They need to change their attitudes. This can only really be accomplished if patients can be persuaded to accept the dietitian's advice and follow a meal plan which includes the regular consumption of the high-energy foods that they fear and which they usually consume only during their binge-eating episodes. They will then see for themselves that they are able to maintain weight within a normal range while eating in an unrestrained manner.

Components of Nutritional Counselling

The initial interview

The initial interview is important not only for gathering information related to the patient's bulimic behaviour, but also for eliciting cooperation and establishing a therapeutic contract. Patients must accept that only by refraining from dieting will they be able to successfully control their eating behaviour. If overweight, any reasonable weight loss must be postponed until after normal, unrestrained eating behaviour has been confidently established.

A detailed nutritional history is taken which includes weight changes, attitudes to foods, recent food intake, exercise patterns, binge-eating (including their typical 'binge' foods which are usually high in sugars and/or fats), precipitants to binge-eating and compensatory behaviours. Guidelines are given in Table 20.1.

Based on the information obtained, a suitable meal plan can be formulated consisting of a wide variety of foods. The total energy level (6700–9300 kJ) is determined to maintain weight or, if necessary, to increase it into the healthy weight range, taken as a body mass index (BMI)* of 20–25. The meal plan is

*BMI: Weight in kilograms divided by the square of height in metres.

Table 20.1 Guidelines for eliciting a dietary history from a bulimic patient

Weight and shape

Present weight
Weight history
Recent fluctuations
Highest weight as adult ... When?
Lowest weight as adult ... When?
Past history of anorexia nervosa, When?
Age when began worrying about weight
Premorbid weight
Desired weight
Dissatisfaction with shape? Specify

Binge-eating

Age when commenced
Frequency/duration
Specific day/time/place?
Known precipitants
'Binge' foods/amounts
Successful resistance?

Activity and exercise

Past/present exercise
Main motivation — change shape
— weight control
— fitness
Compulsion to exercise daily?

Eating pattern

(a) At present 'good' and 'bad' days
(b) Prior to onset of disorder
(c) Of others in household
Alcohol intake
Vitamin/other supplements
Avoided ('bad')/preferred ('good') foods

Weight-controlling behaviours

Precipitants(s) of dieting
Method(s) of weight loss
Presently — counts kilojoules/calories?
— limits intake below a set value?
Vomiting/laxatives/diuretics/diet pills
Age when commenced
Frequency (type/quantity)
Periods of abstinence?

Lifestyle

Lifestyle/work pattern
Relationship with others in household/family
Who else is aware of problem —supportive?
Avoids social contact because this may involve eating out?

characterized by three meals and one or more snacks each day, with meals being of average size to help patients become accustomed to a full, satisfied feeling. Spacing of meals and snacks is tailored to suit individuals' needs and to prevent excessive hunger. Keeping to temporally structured regular meals limits decision-making and facilitates relearning of the physiological control mechanisms of appetite and satiety. However, it needs to be stressed to the patient that a flexible approach is required for unavoidable deviations from the recommended regime, such as in social settings.

An individual meal plan is presented in the form of a case illustration — Appendix 20.1. An important feature incorporated into each meal plan is the exchange list. Items in this list are of similar energy levels and include the 'binge' foods. A varied selection from this list is required so that patients are prevented from keeping to a monotonous and 'safe' diet. More importantly, the requirement of regularly having to consume feared foods as part of a weight maintenance regime is helpful in reducing food cravings and feelings of deprivation which would often have led to binge-eating (Garner, Garfinkel and Bemis, 1982).

It is important that patients are made aware of the physical complications of bulimia. As well as being extremely dangerous, laxative abuse should be explained in terms of its ineffectiveness in preventing calorie absorption (Bo-Linn *et al.*, 1985). Also, induced vomiting is less effective than many patients realize since it often fails to remove all food from the stomach.

Patients are asked to keep daily food diaries in which they record quantity of food eating (approximated), the time and place where this occurred, and any bulimic behaviour. Such self-monitoring is useful in increasing awareness of both eating behaviour and precipitants of binge-eating episodes. It is important also to forewarn patients of a possible initial weight gain due to rehydration, especially if diuretics or purgatives were abused. Feeling 'bloated' is a common experience which usually diminishes after the first week.

The place of nutritional education

Simple but sound nutritional education needs to be given throughout treatment, aimed at helping patients understand the role of food in the body and the requirements for normal, healthy eating. It has often been assumed that bulimic patients have a high level of nutrition knowledge, but this knowledge has been found to be specifically channelled to the energy and macronutrient content of foods, not to food as it pertains to health (Laessle *et al.*, 1987). It is important to identify and correct erroneous beliefs related to food and weight control.

One commonly held misconception is that good health can only be achieved by eating an optimal diet — one which includes only those foods high in essential nutrients and low in sugars and fats. All other foods are seen as 'unhealthy' or 'fattening' so that feelings of guilt and panic are aroused by consumption of such foods.

It needs to be explained that a healthy eating pattern must provide:

(a) the daily requirements of vitamins, minerals and protein;
(b) sufficient energy to fuel the body for its daily needs;
(c) sufficient energy to maintain the body weight within the normal healthy weight range.

Since the amount of food needed to meet the daily energy requirements is greater than the amount of food necessary for essential nutrient requirements, good health can be achieved by supplementing a diet of healthy, 'nutritionally' sound foods with a selection of high-energy, less 'nutritious' foods. Such an eating pattern is not only 'good enough' to maintain health but is also socially acceptable, enjoyable, allows for flexibility and is 'normal'.

Particular attention is paid to helping the patient reverse the various eating practices she has previously used to rigidly control weight, such as drinking excessive amounts of water, coffee or diet drinks, accurate measuring of food and eating large amounts of vegetables. Patients are asked to refrain from using dietary or low-fat/low-sugar food substitutes in order to help them overcome the fear of weight gain which they associate with regular use of non-dietary equivalent products. It is explained that vitamin and mineral supplements are not necessary once they are keeping to a varied, regular eating pattern, and any problems with constipation will also be resolved without the needs for laxatives or unprocessed bran products.

Follow-up appointments

Patients should initially see the dietitian on a weekly basis if possible, with sessions of half-hour duration decreasing in frequency to fortnightly and then monthly as self-control is regained. They are not to weigh themselves but are weighed by the dietitian at each counselling session.

Food diaries are carefully reviewed and improvements in eating behaviours identified and positively reinforced. Reassurance and regular support is needed to deal with the fear of becoming fat, which may prevent adherence to the meal plan. Emphasis is placed initially on eating regular meals as prescribed and patients are advised on strategies to help regulate their eating behaviour such as:

- Avoid delaying or missing meals/snacks
- Eat with others when possible
- Sit down and relax when eating
- When at home, eat at the dining-room table (not in the kitchen)
- Serve food onto a plate where appropriate
- Eat at a moderate pace
- Do not pick at food

Once it has been demonstrated that weight can be maintained (and not increased) while eating regular meals and snacks, patients are encouraged to regularly include feared 'binge' foods in the diet. Only by practice in eating a variety of foods on a maintenance diet can patients overcome guilt feelings and eat in a relaxed manner.

When patients report significant difficulties in controlling food intake (such as bingeing, purging or fasting) attention is focused on possible precipitants, thereby helping them develop greater insight into their behaviour. More constructive ways of dealing with similar situations in the future can then be discussed.

It is a common belief amongst bulimic patients that their requirements for food are much lower than those of other people. To counter this misconception, they are advised to cease excessive or daily exercise. It is important that they realize that they, too, require a normal and varied food intake to maintain a healthy weight without the need to 'burn off' calories with exercise.

Patients are told that expectations of an immediate cessation of bulimic behaviour are perhaps unrealistic, but as they resume a normal meal pattern they will gradually gain control over the bulimic episodes. They need to be encouraged not to interpret occasional relapses into gorging behaviour as total failure but merely as part of the process of gaining insight and control. They must not avoid their usual meals after such episodes as the resumption of dietary restriction will precipitate further bulimia.

Advice is given on meal planning, preparation and eating in social settings. Alcohol consumption should be limited as this often leads to a lessening of control and subsequent bulimic behaviour. As patients develop greater confidence and involve themselves in varied social situations, they require a flexible, more relaxed eating pattern. This is encouraged, since it is certainly not normal or socially acceptable to always eat according to a structured meal plan. Patients must learn to cope with the many, varied and often unpredictable eating situations that occur in everyday life, and to develop sensitivity to the usual cues for eating that most people follow, such as appetite, time of day, social situation and visual appeal.

Advising the family

Many patients have difficulty in disclosing to their family or close friends that they are bulimic. This is due either to shame or guilt and perhaps also to the fear that such knowledge would make it more difficult for them to binge in the future. Since it is obviously beneficial for patients to have regular support and understanding, they are encouraged to confide in a close friend or family member(s) and bring them along to a counselling session. Aspects of the disorder can then be explained and helpful strategies discussed, such as portioning out an average serve at meals or involving the patient in distracting activities during stressful periods.

Terminating therapy

It is important that the patient is made aware of the potential for relapse, especially at time of stress or if she embarks once again on a pursuit of thinness. While maintaining a weight within the healthy weight range (BMI of 20–25), she must learn to accept herself as a worthwhile person without having always to diet. Guidelines for relapse need to be given. If and when this happens, patients are advised to return to the structured meal plan, thus limiting decision-making and restoring order to the chaotic behaviour. Recurrence of bulimia is not to be viewed as a total failure but as an indication that they will need to put more effort into applying those strategies acquired during treatment. There should also be ready access for the patient to contact the therapist if she feels the need.

Can Nutritional Counselling Sometimes be the Sole Means of Treatment?

Most authors acknowledge a role for nutritional counselling in bulimia, even if they give few details of what it entails (Garner *et al.*, 1985; Fairburn, 1985; Wilson and Wooley, 1985; Mitchell *et al.*, 1985; Lacey, 1983). They all comment that the patient's habitual restrained eating has to be corrected in order to prevent binge episodes, and Wilson and Wooley (1985) emphasize that hunger is the prime cause of the binge-eating. However, to our knowledge, there has been only one study which has reported the efficacy of nutritional counselling when used as a sole means of treatment (O'Connor, Touyz and Beumont, 1987).

Twenty-eight patients who fulfilled DSM-III criteria for bulimia, but who showed little evidence of underlying psychopathology at psychiatric interview, were referred to a dietitian for sole management. Ten patients fell out of treatment and 18 completed the course. There was no significant change in body weight over its duration. All patients stopped abusing laxatives and 12 ceased all bulimic behaviours. There was a significant reduction in the frequency of binge-eating and of vomiting in the remaining six patients. Unfortunately, follow-up data are not available.

These results suggest that nutritional counselling on its own may be effective in managing at least some bulimic patients. However, usually it should be offered in conjunction with other psychological treatments. It is important that the dietitian providing counselling and the psychotherapist responsible for other aspects of treatment are aware of the particular nutritional problems of the bulimic patient. A clearly defined goal in therapy must be the restoration of normal eating.

References

Abraham, S. F. and P. J. V. Beumont (1982). How patients describe bulimia or binge eating. *Psychological Medicine* **12**, 625–635.

Abraham, S. F., M. Mira, P. J. V. Beumont, T. D. Sowerbutts and D. Llewlyn-Jones (1983). Eating behaviours among young women. *Medical Journal of Australia* **24**, 225–228.

American Psychiatric Association (1979). *Diagnostic and Statistical Manual of Mental Disorders*, 3rd edn. APA, Washington DC, pp. 69–71.

American Psychiatric Association (1987). *Diagnostic and Statistical Manual of Mental Disorders*, 3rd edn revised. APA, Washington DC.

Beumont, P. J. V. (1987). Bulimia: is it an illness entity? *International Journal of Eating Disorders*, in press.

Bo-Linn, G., C. A. Santa Ana, S. G. Morawski and J. S. Fordtran (1985). Purging and calorie absorption in bulimic patients and normal women. *Annals of Internal Medicine* **99**, 14–17.

Fairburn, C. G. (1985). The management of bulimia nervosa. *Journal of Psychiatric Research* **19**, 465–472.

Fairburn, C. G. and Z. Cooper (1987). Behavioural and cognitive approaches to the treatment of anorexia nervosa and bulimia nervosa. In *Handbook of Eating Disorders, Part 1. Anorexia and Bulimia Nervosa*, ed. by P. J. V. Beumont, G. Burrows and R. Casper, Elsevier Biomedical, Amsterdam, pp. 273–300.

Garner, D. M., P. E. Garfinkel and K. M. Bemis (1982). A multi-dimensional psychotherapy for anorexia nervosa. *International Journal of Eating Disorders* **1** (2), 3–46.

Garner, D. M., W. Rockert, M. P. Olmsted, C. Johnson and D. V. Coscina (1985). Psychoeducational principles in the treatment of bulimia and anorexia nervosa. In *Handbook of Psychotherapy for Anorexia Nervosa and Bulimia*, ed. by D. M. Garner and P. E. Garfinkel. Guilford Press, New York, pp. 513–566.

Herman, C. P. and J. Polivy (1984). A boundary model for the regulation of eating. In *Eating and Its Disorders*, ed. by A. J. Stunkard and E. Stellar. Raven Press, New York, pp. 141–156.

Lacey, J. H. (1983). Bulimia nervosa, binge eating and psychogenic vomiting: a controlled treatment study and long term outcome. *British Medical Journal* **286**, 1609–1613.

Laessle, R. G., U. Schweiger, Daute-Herold, M. Schweiger, M. Fichter and K. M. Pirke (1987). Nutrition knowledge in patients with eating disorders. *International Journal of Eating Disorders*, in press.

Mitchell, J. E., D. Hatsukami, G. Goff, R. L. Pyle, E. D. Eckert and L. E. Davis (1985). Intensive out-patient group treatment for bulimia. In *Handbook of Psychotherapy for Anorexia Nervosa and Bulimia*, ed. by D. M. Garner and P. E. Garfinkel. Guilford Press, New York, pp. 240–256.

O'Connor, M. A., S. W. Touyz and P. J. V. Beumont (1987). Nutritional management and dietary counselling in bulimia: some preliminary observations. *International Journal of Eating Disorders*, in press.

Perron, M. and J. Endres (1985). Knowledge, attitudes and dietary practices of female athletes. *Journal of the American Dietetic Association* **85**, 573–576.

Rosen, P. (1987). Cultural determinants of eating. In *Modulation of Neural Function,* ed. by J. Morley.

Russell, G. F. M. (1979). Bulimia nervosa: an ominous variant of anorexia nervosa. *Psychological Medicine* **9**, 429–448.

Russell, G. F. M. (1985). Bulimia revisited. *International Journal of Eating Disorders* **4**, 681–692.

Schwartz, N. E. (1975). Nutritional knowledge, attitudes and practices of high school graduates. *Journal of the American Dietetic Association* **66**, 28–31.

Shephard, R. and L. Stockley (1987). Nutrition knowledge, attitudes and fat consumption. *Journal of the American Dietetic Association* **87**, 615–619.

Squires, R. L. and D. M. Kagan (1985). Sex role and eating behaviours among college women. *International Journal of Eating Disorders* **4**, 539–548.

Stolz, S. G. (1985). Beware of boundary issues. *Transactional Analysis Journal* **15** (1), 37–41.

Wilson, G. T. and O. W. Wooley (1985). Intensive outpatient and residential treatment

for bulimia. In *Handbook of Psychotherapy for Anorexia Nervosa and Bulimia*, ed. by D. M. Garner and P. E. Garfinkel. Guilford Press, New York, pp. 391–430.
Worsley, A. (1981). In the eye of the beholder; social and personal characteristics of teenagers and their impressions of themselves and fat and slim people. *British Journal of Medical Psychology* **54**, 231–242.

Appendix 20.1: Case Illustration (Mrs TG)

Background information

Mrs TG — a 30-year-old married lady with a three-year history of bulimia nervosa. She lives with her husband and 12-year-old son, does not go out to work and has no regular exercise. She has never abused laxatives or diuretics and her weight has gradually increased. BMI = 25.7 on presentation.

Eating pattern

She usually fasts until midafternoon. Thereafter she would gorge for an hour before inducing vomiting. She consumes a large meal in the evening with her family and follows this with another hour of gorging and vomiting. A snack of six chocolate biscuits later is the evening in not regurgitated. Binge foods include chocolates, nuts, cakes, biscuits and potato chips.

Nutritional management

Prescribed meal plan (7150–7980 kJ)

Breakfast

Glass of juice
1 egg or 1 slice cheese
2 toast + butter + topping

Lunch

1 protein-filled sandwich or roll
Fruit
1 glass of juice or milk
} *or* choose 1 exchange

Afternoon

Choose 1 exchange*

Dinner

Average serve of evening meal
(e.g. leg and thigh of chicken, 1 potato, vegetables)
1 bread and butter *or* fruit *or* drink (juice/wine/milk)

Supper

Milk drink
\+ } *or* 1 exchange* *or* dessert at dinner
biscuit

**Exchange list (840–1260 kJ)*

1 slice of cake
Snack bar (including chocolate varieties)
Flavoured yoghurt
2 scoops ice cream (or novelty ice cream)
300 ml carton flavoured milk
2 cream-filled or chocolate biscuits
Fruit/juice + 2 plain/1 chocolate biscuits
4 crackers + butter + topping
2 crackers + butter + cheese
Small packet nuts
Fruit + small packet potato crisps

21

The relevance of body-image disturbances for the treatment of bulimia

Walter Vandereycken
University Psychiatric Center, Kortenberg

The notion of body-image disturbance became basic in the conceptualization of anorexia nervosa after the pioneering writings of Hilde Bruch (1962, 1973). She was the first to draw attention to three reciprocally influencing areas of perceptual and conceptual disturbances which appear to be characteristic in 'primary' anorexia nervosa: (1) disturbances of the body image and the body concept, (2) disturbances in perception and cognitive interpretation of interoceptive stimuli, and (3) an all-embracing, paralyzing feeling of one's own ineffectiveness. According to Bruch, these disturbances result from a process taking place over many years in which the individual psychological development of the anorexic patient is already distorted at the stage of hunger perception in early childhood and becomes misdirected in other functional areas owing to pathological interaction patterns between mother and child in the early socialization process.

Bruch's ideas have led to a whole range of attempts to investigate body-image disturbance in anorexic patients, and more recently in bulimic patients also. These investigations have confirmed what is now considered to be a *diagnostic* criterion for anorexia nervosa, namely that patients overestimate their body size: they 'feel fat' regardless of the degree of emaciation. But it has not yet been conclusively established whether or to what extent this overestimation is a psychologically or socioculturally conditioned factor, a secondary result of the starvation and weight loss, or a psychological compensatory mechanism by which the anorexic patient is trying to avoid a stressful cognitive dissonance (the conflict between 'feeling' good but 'knowing' that her condition is bad). Also still unanswered is the related question of whether body-image disturbance is a predisposing, precipitating or perpetuating factor in the development of the eating disorder (Meermann and Vandereycken, 1987).

Body image itself, however, is a very complex phenomenon, including the integration of a exteroceptive (mainly visual and tactile) information and the perception and interpretation of stimuli from within the body (interoceptive and proprioceptive information), all mixed with subjective experiences of bodily functions (affective emotional components) and personal opinion (cognitive constructs) about one's own body. Regardless of this complexity, most clinicians appear to consider a body-image disturbance as a psychological feature of anorexia nervosa. But the large number of theoretical views and experimental studies concerning body-image disturbance in anorexia nervosa stands in contrast to the few direct attempts to change this aspect therapeutically. This is even more striking in the case of bulimia.

This is not intended as an academic discussion about the delineation of different forms of eating disorders. A static, categorical nosology should be abandoned in favor of a more dimensional and dynamic viewpoint in which eating disorders are situated on a continuum ranging from anorexia nervosa over bulimia to psychosomatic obesity (Meermann and Vandereycken, 1987). What these disorders have in common is not just as eating disturbance but a weak or negative self-concept (low self-esteem), which is crystalized in the urge to keep one's body weight under extreme control. In anorexic and bulimic patients this 'all-consuming' urge is fueled by a constant fear of fatness from, respectively, anticipated or actual loss of control over eating. Bulimia appears to represent the worst fears of an anorexic come true, while the self-discipline and thin body of the starving anorexic represent the Utopian ideal bulimics are constantly trying to attain.

It must be clear now that bulimia is more than a recurrent pattern of unusual overeating connected with stress, frustration or mood fluctuations. Extreme concerns about body shape and weight are a central psychopathological feature, making bulimia a special variant of anorexia nervosa (see also Fairburn and Garner, 1986). As such, and in order to distinguish it from what we may call the 'American' bulimia, it might be better to use the term 'bulimia nervosa' as coined by Russell (1979). In this view, body-image disturbances form an essential element in the clinical picture of bulimia (nervosa).

Assessing Body Image in Bulimics

In the past 15 years, several studies have been published on the measurement of body image in eating disorders. The methods employed range from projective techniques to (semi)experimental procedures (see e.g. Fichter and Meermann, 1981; Fichter, 1985). The problem with projective techniques such as the 'sophistication of body concept' (Strober *et al.*, 1979) is that they rely on theoretical constructs to make inferences about the body experience. Quite popular are the self-reporting questionnaires such as the Eating Disorder Inventory (EDI) of Garner, Olmsted and Polivy (1983), which comprises a subscale for body dissatisfaction. However, the reliability of such an instrument may sometimes be questionable due to the patient's test attitude: anorexics may tend to deny the severity of problems (Vandereycken and Vanderlinden, 1983), whereas bulimics may display varying answer patterns presumably depending on their unstable mood (Ortega *et al.*, 1987).

In recent years, the (semi)experimental methods are more and more preferred though many methodological issues are involved (Meermann, Vandereycken and Napierski, 1986; Slade, 1985). Essentially, these methods try to measure body perception in terms of difference between perceived and actual body width. Since the investigation by Slade and Russell (1973), the visual size estimation apparatus (VSEA) or movable caliper technique has been used quite often in anorexia nervosa patients. With this method, Button, Fransella and Slade (1977) found that anorexic patients who vomit tend to overestimate their size more than do non-vomiters. A comparable result was reported by Strober *et al.* (1979) who used another research instrument, the image-marking procedure (IMP) developed by Askevold (1975). Using the VSEA, Norris (1984) not only confirmed what many others had already found, namely that anorexics overestimate their body size to a greater extent than normal controls, but also established that bulimic patients overestimate to much the same degree as anorexics. With a similar but adapted method, Ruff and Barrios (1986) came to similar conclusions, but Willmuth *et al.* (1985) suggested that body-size distortion might be less extreme in bulimics than in anorexics. Birtchnell *et al.* (Birtchnell, Lacey and Harte, 1985; Birtchnell, Harte and Lacey, 1986), in a study with the VSEA, found that the tendency to overestimation in bulimics is greater when they are above normal body weight, suggesting a link with a greater dissatisfaction with body size in these patients. Though Whitehouse, Freeman and Annadale (1986), using the IMP, also found overestimation in bulimic patients, this was not correlated with the body dissatisfaction subscale of the EDI.

The techniques discussed so far (IMP and VSEA) may be considered as rather simplistic measurements of body image, reducing its perceptual aspect to a simple estimation task. The same applies to the silhouette technique, in which patients have to choose or select drawings of female silhouettes of varying proportions (Buree, Papageorgis and Solyom, 1984; Williamson *et al.*, 1985). The problem with this type of method is its artificiality, which means it has little or no connection at all with the way patients are used to perceiving their bodies in daily-life situations. For this reason, methods employing photographs or videorecordings of the patient's appearance seem more appropriate. Moreover, as we shall see, such an approach has more practical value in the treatment itself.

Inspired by Allebeck *et al.* (1976) Meermann (1983), Freeman *et al.* (1983), Touyz *et al.* (1984) and Fichter, Meister and Koch (1986) used a video distortion method in anorexic patients. Though the technique may vary, the basic idea is the same: by means of a modified videomonitor or camera, subjects can adjust the proportions of their body picture on the screen. Not surprisingly, studies with this method have shown similar results to those described above. Bulimic patients appear to show a strikingly inaccurate body perception: they overestimate their actual body shape and desire to be much thinner (Freeman *et al.*, 1984; Touyz *et al.*, 1985); the degree of overestimation is correlated with the degree of body dissatisfaction (Whitehouse, Freeman and Annandale, 1986); and though patients may acknowledge such a distortion, they claim to feel fatter than they really are (Huon and Brown, 1986).

The problem with this type of assessment is that it overemphasizes the visual aspect while neglecting the affective and cognitive components of one's body image (van der Velde, 1985). The way eating disorder patients 'see' themselves has also much to do with how they 'feel' and 'think' they are. Even without visual information, people may have the conviction that they 'look much too fat', as witnessed for instance by the occurrence of anorexia nervosa in blind girls (Vandereycken, 1986; Yager, Hatton and Ma, 1986). Hence, it might be more appropriate to speak about body *experience* instead of body *image*: the latter notion may be too narrowly linked with visual perception, whereas the former term has by itself a much broader significance. Therefore, the now so often propagated multidimensional approach to the understanding and treatment of eating disorders must also be translated in a multimethod investigation of body experience. Before considering the therapeutic implications of this discussion we would like to mention some other interesting research findings.

Although the aforementioned investigations certainly have their limitations, some of their results may have important clinical value. In view of what has been said up to now, we are struck by the fact that many treatment studies minimize or even completely ignore the significance of the body experience as a therapeutic target and as an outcome variable (e.g. Fairburn *et al.*, 1986; Hsu and Holder, 1986; Lee and Rush, 1986; Merrill, Mines and Starkey, 1987; Mitchell *et al.*, 1986; Norman, Herzog and Chauncey, 1986; Swift *et al.*, 1987; Wilson *et al.*, 1986). Other investigators such as Birtchnell *et al.* (Birtchnell, Lacey and Harte, 1985; Birtchnell, Harte and Lacey, 1986) did not measure body-image distortion before and after treatment and found a decrease in overestimation. They did not take up, however, the fact that many patients at the end of therapy were still overestimating their body shape; what will happen with them at long-term follow-up? This is an important question, since

Freeman *et al.* (1985), assessing body image by means of the video distortion method, found persistent body dissatisfaction to be a risk factor for relapse in bulimic patients. It is, then, interesting to note that these authors used a mixture of psychodynamic and cognitive behavioral techniques, but: 'Although body image was addressed in therapy, it was not the primary focus and the video camera was not employed'! The authors conclude that body dissatisfaction might be the key issue to explain the treatment failure. Other authors (Huon and Brown, 1985) also interested in this subject did focus on 'the body as concept' during their treatment and found significant improvements in the patients' attitude towards their own body (unfortunately, they only used self-reporting questionnaires). Finally, the importance of this issue is demonstrated by Norris (1984), who found that an experimental therapeutic session with mirror confrontation could induce marked improvement of body estimation (assessed with the VSEA), which was correlated with progress in treatment at least in the short run (the author, unfortunately, does not mention long-term outcome). This approach to both research and treatment of eating disorders resembles ours, which we will describe below.

Body-oriented Therapy as an Essential Element of Treatment

For more than 15 years the University Psychiatric Center in Kortenberg has specialized in the inpatient treatment of eating disorders. After several changes during a trial-and-error period (Vandereycken, 1985), the treatment program is now firmly established as a multimodal intensive group approach. We are working with two groups of eight or nine patients who all suffer from anorexia nervosa or bulimia and are hospitalized for an average of four months (practically all patients have a long or complicated illness history and have been treated before unsuccessfully). The major changes in the therapeutic approach over the last five years have to do with the following three components: (1) intensive and directive group treatment, (2) active participation of the patient's family, and (3) emphasis upon the body experience (see Meermann and Vandereycken, 1987). Although it is only one component of a multidimensional treatment program, we will restrict our present discussion to the third therapeutic element.

In the literature on the treatment of eating disorders one can hardly find a publication in which specific attention is paid to the possibility of changing the patient's body image in a direct way. Although many clinicians seem to consider it an important part of treatment, ideas on the subject often remain very vague and so do their therapeutic implications (see Table 21.1).

Over many years we have been searching for and experimenting with different forms of so-called psychomotor therapy in order to help patients with eating disorders (re)build a realistic self-concept and a positive body exper-

Table 21.1 General approaches to the place of body-image disturbance in the treatment of eating disorders

1.	The body-image disturbance is viewed as a *secondary* problem
1.1	It is a cognitive distortion due to malnutrition — restoration of the nutritional status
1.2	It is a symptom of more basic intrapersonal problems — individual (psychodynamic) psychotherapy
1.3	It is a diversion of basically interpersonal problems — interactional (family, marital) therapy
2.	The body-image disturbance is viewed as a *fundamental* problem
2.1	It may be changed in an *indirect* or *non-specific* way with a treatment focusing on self-concept/self-image — all kinds of ego-strengthening therapies, verbal and non-verbal (e.g. art and occupational therapy)
2.2	It may be changed in a *direct* or *specific* way with a treatment focusing on body concept/body experience — verbal, mostly cognitive therapy (influencing special beliefs, attitudes and ideas concerning one's body) — non-verbal, body-oriented (dance-movement or psychomotor) therapy; see Table 21.2

ience (Vandereycken, Depreitere and Probst, 1987). The techniques we used are not necessarily new; we selected them out of a large series of methods ranging from dance-movement therapy to bioenergetic exercises. What is new is the consistent attempt to incorporate those techniques that seem to be the most appropriate for influencing those elements of body experience that most often appear to be underdeveloped or distorted in eating disorders (see Table 21.2). The two basic ingredients of our body-oriented therapy are self-confrontation and self-awareness.

Self-confrontation

In order to bring the self-concept more into agreement with reality, the patient must acknowledge the distortion of her self-perception. For this reason mirror and video confrontation are used throughout treatment. During the first week of admission, an individual videotape of the patient, dressed in a bathing suit, is made according to a standardized procedure: she is requested to pose in certain positions and walk in front of the camera, which records a total body picture from a variety of angles and then zooms in on particular parts of the body. This 'admission' tape will be shown to the patient and her fellow group members in the next group session of the psychomotor therapy (each group has three sessions of one hour a week). She is then encouraged to verbalize her reactions when looking at herself on the screen and afterwards

Table 21.2 Elements of body-oriented therapy in eating disorders

1. *Impression* or body perception
   — confrontation or exteroception (mirror, video)
   — inner awareness or intero/proprioception (posture, massage, relaxation, respiration, trampoline, swimming pool)
   — sensory awareness (especially touch)
2. *Expression* or revealing inner experiences
   — non-verbal expression (body sculpting)
   — free improvisation (dance, pantomine, rhythmic exercises)
3. *Communication* or body in interaction
   — non-verbal assertiveness training
   — partner/group exercises (playing, dancing)
4. *Exertion* or bodily performances
   — sport activities (limiting hyperactivity)
   — power exercises (wrestling for fun)
5. *Sensation* or bodily pleasure
   — enjoying food (with all senses)
   — tactile self-exploration (sexually: in private)

the other group members are asked for their reactions to the video recordings. At the end of hospitalization a similar recording (the 'discharge' tape) is made and compared with the 'admission' tape, and again both the patient and her fellow group members will give their comments.

The standardization of this video-confrontation procedure is part of a research project concerning the possible predictive value of the patient's reactions. It seems to have specific value in breaking through denial in those patients for whom this self-confrontation method appears to produce a clear *dissonance* between conception and perception: the patient reacts emotionally once she realizes that her internal conception of her body is at striking variance with how she perceives it on the TV monitor. In other cases, however, the video playback causes no great surprise: the patient reports little difference between her original self-concept and the actual perception of her body on video (*congruence* between conception and perception). Here the reactions of the other patients as well as the possibility to compare one another's appearance during the group sessions may bring about the necessary correction. Indeed, as well as the standardized video-confrontation procedure, patients can observe themselves during the regular sessions in large mirrors and each session is also videotaped (at the end of the session, excerpts from these recordings are watched and commented on by the group members and the therapist).

Self-awareness

A basic prerequisite for the development of a realistic (and later also positive) body image is getting 'in touch' again with the body, which is a question of reexperiencing and rediscovering it. The body must again belong to oneself, be part of one's own identity and autonomy. Hence, the essence of the treatment is to make patients aware of the feelings and impulses arising in themselves, and of their status as individuals who are able to think, feel and act for themselves. Here we think of any exercises focusing the attention directly on the body: for example breathing exercises, relaxation training, massage (one patient to another), and sensory awareness training (especially exercises of the proprioceptive and kinesthetic senses).

The mere acceptance of one's own body in a normal and healthy shape is certainly an important goal but not enough. We also aim at patients' reinterpretation of their bodies as potentially pleasant instruments. They must learn to enjoy physical sensations again and how the body may be both source and language of emotions. Positive physical experiences may be stimulated by offering patients new possibilities by which physical activity in itself (and not just the result of a physical achievement) becomes a truly pleasurable activity: for example playing in the swimming pool, wrestling for fun, free expression in dance. During the psychomotor therapy sessions there is not much talking, the stress being mainly on acting with the body and on non-verbal means of communication (for this reason, patients are asked to wear comfortable, preferably close-fitting clothes).

In this psychomotor therapy as well as in the other components of our treatment program we only work with homogeneous groups of anorexic and bulimic eating-disorder patients. In our opinion, this adds a lot to the necessary therapeutic balance between support and confrontation. Although many patients are, especially in the beginning, quite tense and anxious when facing these sessions, they are mostly satisfied afterwards and consider this form of psychomotor therapy as an indispensable part of the total treatment program. The group approach also (a) accelerates the motivation process (breaking through denial of the body-image disturbance), (b) allows the patient to correct the discrepancy between her distorted perception and her real physical appearance by means of comparison with the appearance of fellow group members, and (c) facilitates the development of a realistic and positive body image through a process of social learning within the group context.

Conclusion

In few psychophysiological disorders is the complicated interplay between biological and psychological as well as sociocultural factors expressed so strikingly as in the genesis and maintenance of eating disorders like anorexia and bulimia nervosa. In both of them body-image disturbance is considered to be a core problem. A treatment which does not succeed in changing this aspect of the disorder is probably (at least partially) a failure. The disappointing long-term outcome in a considerable number of these patients may be attributed to this shortcoming. Surprisingly, very few therapists appear to focus explicitly (and not just verbally) upon the body experience of bulimic patients. We have therefore developed a specific body-oriented treatment program, including a variety of techniques which are still in a trial-and-error process of testing. Although we do not know the differential therapeutic efficacy of (elements of) this psychomotor therapy, the use of video confrontation seems to have a promising impact. But to our present knowledge, only a multidimensional treatment taking into account the many factors involved appears to be acceptable in the eating-disorder patients we are treating. Hence, the body-oriented therapy we have described here should be considered a tool to be integrated into the rest of the treatment.

References

Askevold, F. (1975). Measuring body image: preliminary report on a new method. *Psychotherapy and Psychosomatics* **26**, 71–77.

Birtchnell, S. A., A. Harte and J. H. Lacey (1986). Body image distortion in bulimia nervosa. In *Proceedings of the 15th European Conference on Psychosomatic Research*, ed. by J. H. Lacey and D. A. Sturgeon. Libbey, London, pp. 148–152.

Birtchnell, S. A., J. H. Lacey and A. Harte (1985). Body image distortion in bulimia nervosa. *British Journal of Psychiatry* **147**, 408–412.

Bruch, H. (1962). Perceptual and conceptual disturbances in anorexia nervosa. *Psychosomatic Medicine* **24**, 187–194.

Bruch, H. (1973). *Eating Disorders. Obesity, Anorexia Nervosa, and the Person Within*. Basic Books, New York.

Buree, B., D. Papageorgis and L. Solyom (1984). Body image perception and preference in anorexia nervosa. *Canadian Journal of Psychiatry* **29**, 557–563.

Button, E. J., F. Fransella and P. D. Slade (1977). A reappraisal of body perception disturbance in anorexia nervosa. *Psychological Medicine* **7**, 235–243.

Counts, C. R. and Adams, H. E. (1985). Body image in bulimic, dieting, and normal females. *Journal of the Psychopathological Behaviour Association* **7**, 289–300.

Fairburn, C. and D. Garner (1986). The diagnosis of bulimia nervosa. *International Journal of Eating Disorders* **5**, 403–419.

Fairburn, C., J. Kirk, M. O'Connor and P. J. Cooper (1986). A comparison of two psychological treatments for bulimia nervosa. *Behaviour Research and Therapy* **24**, 629–643.

Fichter, M. (1985). *Magersucht und Bulimia*. Springer-Verlag, Berlin.

Fichter, M. and R. Meermann (1981). Zur Psychopathometrie der Anorexia nervosa. In *Anorexia Nervosa, Ursachen und Behandlung*, ed. by R. Meermann. Enke, Stuttgart, pp. 17–31.

Fichter, M. M., I. Meister and H. J. Koch (1986). The measurement of body image disturbances in anorexia nervosa. Experimental comparison of different methods. *British Journal of Psychiatry* **148**, 453–461.

Freeman, R., B. Beach, R. Davis and L. Solyom (1985). The prediction of relapse in bulimia nervosa. *Journal of Psychiatric Research* **19**, 349–353.

Freeman, R., C. Thomas, L. Solyom and J. Miles (1983). Body image disturbances in anorexia nervosa. In *Anorexia Nervosa, Recent Developments in Research*, ed by P. Darby, P. Garfinkel, D. Garner and D. Soscina. Alan Liss, New York, pp. 117–127.

Freeman, R., C. Thomas, L. Solyom and M. A. Hunter (1984). A modified video camera for measuring body image distortion. *Psychological Medicine* **14**, 411–416.

Garner, D., M. Olmsted and J. Polivy (1983). Development and validation of a multidimensional eating disorder inventory for anorexia and bulimia. *International Journal of Eating Disorders* **2** (2), 15–34.

Hsu, L. and D. Holder (1986). Bulimia nervosa: treatment and short-term outcome. *Psychological Medicine* **16**, 65–70.

Huon, G. and L. Brown (1985). Evaluating a group treatment for bulimia. *Journal of Psychiatric Research* **19**, 479–483.

Huon, G. and L. Brown (1986). Body images in anorexia nervosa and bulimia. *International Journal of Eating Disorders* **5**, 421–439.

Lee, N. and A. Rush (1986). Cognitive-behavioral group therapy for bulimia. *International Journal of Eating Disorders* **5**, 599–615.

Meermann, R. (1983). Experimental investigations of disturbances in body image estimation in anorexia nervosa patients, and ballet and gymnastic pupils. *International Journal of Eating Disorders* **2**(4), 91–100.

Meermann, R. and W. Vandereycken (1987). *Therapie der Magersucht und Bulima Nervosa*. de Gruyter, Berlin.

Meerman, R., W. Vandereycken and C. Napierski (1986). Methodological problems of body image research in anorexia nervosa patients. *Acta Psychiatrica Belgica* **86**, 42–51.

Merrill, C., R. Mines and R. Starkey (1987). The premature dropout in the group treatment of bulimia. *International Journal of Eating Disorders* **6**, 293–300.

Mitchell, J., L. Davis, G. Goff and R. Pyle (1986). A follow-up study of patients with bulimia. *International Journal of Eating Disorders* **5**, 441–439.

Norman, D., D. Herzog and S. Chauncey (1986). A one-year outcome study of bulimia. *International Journal of Eating Disorders* **5**, 47–57.

Norris, D. L. (1984). The effects of mirror confrontation on self-estimation of body dimensions in anorexia nervosa, bulimia and two control groups. *Psychological Medicine* **14**, 835–842.

Ortega, D., H. Waranch, A. Maldonado and F. Hubbard (1987). A comparative analysis of self-report measures of bulimia. *International Journal of Eating Disorders* **6**, 301–311.

Ruff, G. A. and B. A. Barrios (1986). Realistic assessment of body image. *Behavioral Assessment* **8**, 237–251.

Russell, G. F. M. (1979). Bulimia nervosa: an ominous variant of anorexia nervosa. *Psychological Medicine* **9**, 429–448.

Slade, P. (1985). A review of body image studies in anorexia nervosa and bulimia nervosa. *Journal of Psychiatric Research* **19**, 255–265.

Slade, P. and G. Russell (1973). Awareness of body dimensions in anorexia nervosa. *Psychological Medicine* **3**, 188–199.

Strober, M., I. Goldenberg, J. Green and J. Saxon (1979). Body image disturbances in anorexia nervosa during the acute and recuperative phase. *Psychological Medicine* **9**, 695–701.

Swift, W., M. Ritholz, N. Kalin and N. Kaslow (1987). A follow-up study of thirty hospitalized bulimics. *Psychosomatic Medicine* **49**, 45–55.

Tipton, C. R. and H. E. Adams (1983). The assessment of body image in bulimics and normals. Paper presented at the 17th Annual Meeting of the Association for the

Advancement of Behavior Therapy, Washington DC.

Touyz, S., P. Beumont, J. Collins and I. Cowie (1985). Body shape perception in bulimia and anorexia nervosa. *International Journal of Eating Disorders* **4**, 259–265.

Touyz, S., P. Beumont, J. Collins, M. McCabe and J. Jupp (1984). Body shape perception and its disturbance in anorexia nervosa. *British Journal of Psychiatry* **144**, 167–171.

Vandereycken, W. (1985). Inpatient treatment of anorexia nervosa: some research-guided changes. *Journal of Psychiatric Research* **19**, 413–422.

Vandereycken, W. (1986). Anorexia nervosa and visual impairment. *Comprehensive Psychiatry* **27**, 545–548.

Vandereycken, W. and J. Vanderlinden (1983). Denial of illness and the use of self-reporting measures in anorexia nervosa patients. *International Journal of Eating Disorders* **2**(4), 101–107.

Vandereycken, W., L. Depreitere and M. Probst (1987). Body-oriented therapy for anorexia nervosa patients. *American Journal of Psychotherapy* **61**, 252–259.

van der Velde, C. D. (1985). Body images of one's self and of others. *American Journal of Psychiatry* **142**, 527–537.

Whitehouse, A., C. Freeman and A. Annandale (1986). Body size estimation in bulimia. *British Journal of Psychiatry* **149**, 98–103.

Williamson, D., M. Kelly, C. Davis, L. Ruggiero and D. Blouin (1985). Psychopathology of eating disorders. *Journal of Consulting and Clinical Psychology* **53**, 161–166.

Willmuth, M., H. Leitenberg, J. Rosen, K. Fondacaro and J. Gross (1985). Body size distortion in bulimia nervosa. *International Journal of Eating Disorders* **4**, 71–78.

Wilson, G., E. Rossiter, E. Kleifield and L. Lindholm (1986). Cognitive-behavioral treatment of bulimia nervosa: a controlled evaluation. *Behaviour Research and Therapy* **24**, 277–288.

Yager, J., C. Hatton and L. Ma (1986). Anorexia nervosa in a woman totally blind since the age of two. *British Journal of Psychiatry* **149**, 506–509.

22

Psychopharmacological treatment of bulimia

James I. Hudson and **Harrison G. Pope, Jr**
McLean Hospital, Belmont and Harvard Medical School, Boston

During the last five years, a rapidly expanding literature has indicated that a wide range of medications, most of them thymoleptics, are effective in the treatment of bulimia (Hudson and Pope, 1987; Pope and Hudson, 1986). This literature has now grown to the point where it is not possible to summarize each of the individual studies in a brief chapter. Accordingly, we present here a short overview of the studies published to date, together with a detailed reference list for the reader who is interested in examining individual studies in detail. Following this we address several of the practical and theoretical questions raised by these findings.

Controlled Studies

At least 19 controlled studies have tested various pharmacological agents in the treatment of bulimia (see Table 22.1). Ten studies used antidepressant agents (Agras *et al.*, 1987; Blouin *et al.*, 1987; Horne *et al.*, 1989; Hughes *et al.*, 1986; Kaplan, Garfinkel and Garner, 1987; Kennedy, Piran and Garfinkel, 1985; Mitchell and Groat, 1984; Pope *et al.*, 1983; Sabine *et al.*, 1983; Walsh *et al.*, 1987, 1984); all but two of those (Mitchell and Groat, 1984; Sabine *et al.*, 1983) found antidepressants significantly superior to placebo in treatment of bulimic symptoms. However, the one negative study (using mianserin) (Sabine *et al.*, 1983) and the one equivocal study (using amitriptyline) (Mitchell and Groat,

Table 22.1 Controlled drug studies in bulimia

Study	Drug; maximum dose	No. of subjects[a]	Duration of trial[b]	Design[c]	Findings: drugs *vs* placebo[d] Bulimic symptoms	Depressive symptoms
Tricyclics						
Pope *et al.* (1983)	Imipramine 200 mg	19	6 wk	Rand DB	+	+
Mitchell and Groat (1984)	Amitriptyline 150 mg	32	8 wk	Rand DB	+/–	+
Hughes *et al.* (1986)	Desipramine 200 mg	22	6 wk	Rand DB	+	+
Blouin *et al.* (1987)	Desipramine 150 mg	9	6 wk	Xover	+	0
Agras *et al.* (1987)	Imipramine 300 mg	20	16 wk	Rand DB	+	+/–
Kaplan, Garfinkel and Garner (1987)	Imipramine[e]	11	6 wk	Xover	+	+/–
Monoamine oxidase inhibitors						
Walsh *et al.* (1984, 1987)	Phenelzine 90 mg	50	8 wk	Rand DB	+	+
Kennedy, Piran and Garfinkel (1986)	Isocarboxazid 60 mg	18	6 wk	Xover	+	+
Other antidepressants						
Sabine *et al.* (1983)	Mianserin 60 mg	36	8 wk	Rand DB	0	0
Horne *et al.* (1989)	Bupropion 450 mg	81	8 wk	Rand DB	+	+
Anticonvulsants						
Wermuth *et al.* (1977)	Phenytoin[e]	19	6 wk	Xover	+/–	NA[f]
Kaplan *et al.* (1983); Kaplan, Garfinkel and Garner (1987); Kaplan (1987)	Carbamazepine[e]	16	6 wk	Xover	+/–[g]	+/–[g]

Sympathomimetic/anorexiants						
Ong, Checkley and Russell (1983)	Methylamphetamine 0.2 mg/kg i.v.	8	1 dose[h]	Xover	+	NA
Robinson, Checkley and Russell (1985)	Fenfluramine 60 mg	15	1 dose[h]	Xover	+	NA
Blouin *et al.* (1987)	Fenfluramine 60 mg	11	6 wk	Xover	+	+
Other drugs						
Mitchell *et al.* (1986)	Naloxone 18 mg	5	1 dose[h]	Xover	+/–	NA
	Cholecystokinin 140 ng	5	1 dose[h]	Xover	0	NA
Krahn and Mitchell (1985)	L-tryptophan 3 kg	13	4 wk	Rand DB	0	0
Hsu *et al.* (1987)	Lithium carbonate[e]	13	8 wk	Rand DB	0	+/–

[a] Number of subjects who completed the trial or enough of the trial to be included in data analysis by the authors.
[b] Period of time that subjects received active drug rather than total duration of the study.
[c] Rand DB, randomized double blind; Xover, drug–placebo crossover.
[d] + drug significantly superior to placebo on most or all outcome measures; +/– some evidence that drug superior to placebo but not clearly significant; 0 little or no difference between drug and placebo.
[e] Dose not specified, but plasma levels adjusted to therapeutic range.
[f] NA, not formally assessed.
[g] One subject had a remission of, and another had a marked decrease in, bulimic and affective symptoms; three subjects improved on drug compared to baseline, but showed no change on drug compared to placebo.
[h] Drug given as a single administration.

1984) both used doses of medication which were probably below the therapeutic range for the drugs employed (Braithwaite *et al.*, 1972; Hudson and Pope, 1987; Kupfer *et al.*, 1977; McGrath *et al.*, 1981; Pope and Hudson, 1986; Zeigler, Clayton and Biggs, 1977).

Most of these same studies reported significant improvement in depressive as well as bulimic symptoms in the subjects studied. Of the four studies which failed to show a significant antidepressant effect, two had very small sample sizes (Blouin *et al.*, 1987; Kaplan, Garfinkel and Garner, 1987) (with the consequent risk of a type II error), and one (Sabine *et al.*, 1983), as mentioned above, may well have used inadequate doses of medication.

Results with other categories of medication, however, are less impressive. Two controlled studies with anticonvulsants have produced weak results (Kaplan, 1987; Kaplan, Garfinkel and Garner, 1987; Kaplan *et al.*, 1983; Wermuth *et al.*, 1977), although the investigators reported striking improvement under double-blind conditions in a few individual patients. Sympathomimetic and anorexiant drugs appear more promising, but two (Ong, Checkley and Russell, 1983; Robinson, Checkley and Russell, 1985) of the three available studies involved only a single dose of active drug. Naloxone, cholecystokinin, and L-tryptophan have not proven effective in double-blind studies (Krahn and Mitchell, 1985; Mitchell *et al.*, 1986), despite previous evidence for efficacy of these and similar agents in uncontrolled trials (Cole and Lapierre, 1986; Jonas and Gold, 1986, 1987). However, the available controlled studies with these latter agents have involved very small samples, and hence must be regarded as extremely tentative.

Uncontrolled Studies

Many additional uncontrolled reports have described improvement in bulimic symptoms with a variety of agents, including tricyclic antidepressants (Brotman, Herzog and Woods, 1984; Mendels, 1983; Moore, 1977; Pope and Hudson, 1982; Pope, Hudson and Jonas, 1983; Rich, 1978; Roy-Byrne *et al.*, 1983), monoamine oxidase inhibitors (Brotman, Herzog and Woods, 1984; Kennedy, Piran and Garfinkel, 1985; Pope, Hudson and Jonas, 1983; Roy-Byrne *et al.*, 1983; Shader and Greenblatt, 1982; Stewart *et al.*, 1984; Walsh *et al.*, 1982), trazodone (Brotman, Herzog and Woods 1984; Damlouji and Ferguson, 1984 a, b; Pope, Hudson and Jonas, 1983; Wold, 1983); lithium carbonate (Chevlen, 1984; Hsu, 1984; Pope and Hudson, 1982; Pope, Hudson and Jonas, 1983), bupropion (Horne, 1984), nomifensine (Crane *et al.*, 1987; Nassr, 1986; Pope *et al.*, 1986), and fluoxetine (Ferguson, 1987; Freeman, 1986). More limited uncontrolled evidence (in most instances restricted to only one or a few case reports) exists for L-tryptophan (Cole and Lapierre, 1986), magnesium pemoline (Pope, Hudson and Jonas, 1983), alprazolam (Opler and Hickley, 1986), phenytoin (Green and Rau, 1974, 1977; Greenway,

Dahms and Brag, 1977; Rau and Green, 1978, Rau, Struve and Green, 1979), carbamazepine (Pope, Hudson and Jonas, 1983), valproate (Herridge and Pope, 1985; McElroy *et al.*, 1987), and naltrexone (Jones and Gold, 1986, 1987). These results — especially those with the latter agents — must be regarded with caution, especially when it is considered that investigations are more likely to report positive results than negative ones.

In summary, the results of the uncontrolled studies, like those of the controlled studies, suggest that a wide range of thymoleptic medications — indeed virtually the entire range of medications commonly used in the treatment of major affective disorder — are probably effective in the treatment of bulimia. In addition, several other medications not generally considered to be thymoleptics, including alprazolam (Opler and Hickley, 1986), anticonvulsants (Green and Rau, 1974, 1977; Greenway, Dahms and Brag, 1977; Herridge and Pope, 1985; Kaplan, 1987; Kaplan, Garfinkel and Garner, 1987; Kaplan *et al.*, 1983, McElroy, Keck and Pope, 1987; Pope, Hudson and Jonas, 1983; Rau and Green, 1978; Rau, Struve and Green, 1979; Robinson, Checkley and Russell, 1985), sympathomimetic and anorexiant drugs (Blouin *et al.*, 1987; Ong, Checkley and Russell, 1983; Pope, Hudson and Jonas, 1983; Robinson, Checkley and Russell, 1985), and opiate antagonists (Jonas and Gold, 1986, 1987; Mitchell *et al.*, 1986), tentatively appear effective in at least some cases of bulimia. However, it should be noted that all of those latter types of agents have been shown in controlled studies to possess thymoleptic properties themselves (Bogoch and Dreyfus, 1975; Costu and Garratini, 1970; Feighner *et al.*, 1983; Judd *et al.*, 1980; Klein *et al.*, 1980; Lechin *et al.*, 1983; McElroy, Keck and Pope, 1987; Okuma *et al.*, 1979; Stephen and Shaffer, 1973). Thus, if they are indeed effective in bulimia, one cannot exclude the possibility that their efficacy is related to their thymoleptic properties.

Practical Considerations

Given the wide variety of apparently useful agents available for treatment of bulimia, several practical questions arise. First, how effective are these agents, particularly when compared to non-pharmacological treatments? Second, which agent should be selected for a given patient? Third, what special considerations are required in managing bulimic patients with these drugs? Fourth, what is the outcome of such patients on long-term follow-up? Some data, albeit preliminary, are available in answer to these questions.

Efficacy

The efficacy of antidepressant medications in bulimia appears to be at least as good as that of these same agents in the treatment of ordinary major depression (Klein *et al.*, 1980; Pope and Hudson, 1983). However, the response rate of bulimic patients to a given individual agent is of only academic interest since, in practice, a physician will normally try subsequent agents if an initial trial fails. It is of note in this connection that preliminary results of the one available study comparing drug and group therapy for bulimia found approximately equal improvements (Mitchell *et al.*, 1987); however, because of the necessary constraints of the double-blind study design, subjects were offered only a single drug (imipramine) and were not offered trials of different agents (such as monoamine oxidase inhibitors or fluoxetine) if imipramine proved unsatisfactory. Hence, the findings of this study seem very likely to underestimate the efficacy of drug treatment as it is actually practiced in clinical settings. At present, to our knowledge, only one study has systematically assessed response rates in an ordinary clinical setting, in which patients refractory to an initial trial were offered one or more additional trials with drugs from other families (Pope, Hudson and Jonas, 1983). In this study, 73 per cent of 65 patients achieved either a marked reduction (greater than 75 per cent) or a remission of their bulimic symptoms on the drug ultimately chosen for treatment. However, this figure may also be an underestimate of efficacy since our group was using almost exclusively 'first-generation' antidepressants (primarily tricyclics and monoamine oxidase inhibitors) and did not have available 'second-generation' drugs (Hudson and Pope, 1987). With the addition of fluoxetine to the therapeutic armamentarium, we have achieved marked improvement or remission in a majority of those patients who were refractory to trials of 'first-generation' agents.

Choice of agents

The choice of agents remains empirical. Currently in our center, we start with fluoxetine, raising the dose to 60–80 mg per day, in most bulimic patients. This drug appears to be particularly efficacious in bulimic patients (Ferguson, 1987; Freeman, 1986) and has a low incidence of side-effects. In patients with only a partial response to fluoxetine, the addition of lithium carbonate, at levels of 0.8–1.0 mEq per liter, may yield an improved effect. In patients refractory to these trials, we typically will try one of the following agents (after a 14-day washout of fluoxetine): (a) the monoamine oxidase inhibitor tranylcypromine, up to 60 mg or even 80 mg per day; (b) trazodone, up to 400–600 mg per day (often administered in conjunction with tranylcypromine); or (c) the tricyclic antidepressants desipramine (3.5 mg/kg daily dose, or adjusting dose to achieve a plasma level of greater than 160 ng/ml) or nortriptyline (1.8 mg/kg daily dose, or adjusting dose to achieve a plasma level of 50–140 ng/ml). The occasional patients unresponsive to trials of all of the above agents will often respond to the sympathomimetic agent magnesium pemoline, given as a single dose of 75–225 mg in the early morning. It should be emphasized, however, that these recommendations are based on uncontrolled observations.

Management

Management of bulimic patients on medications is little different from that of patients in treatment with the same drugs for major depression. It should be noted, however, that bulimic patients are usually younger, and hence may metabolize drugs quickly. Self-induced vomiting or laxative abuse may further compromise available plasma drug levels. Hence, large doses of antidepressants are often necessary to achieve an optimal effect. Evidence of this phenomenon has been provided by Hughes *et al.* (1986), who found that 200 mg per day of desipramine — a robust dose — produced subtherapeutic plasma levels in 10 of 20 bulimic patients tested.

Long-term follow-up

Long-term follow-up data are limited. One study from our center provided follow-up of up to two years on 20 patients who had initially been treated in a double-blind study with imipramine (Pope *et al.*, 1985). At time of last follow-up, 19 (95 per cent) of these patients reported at least 50 per cent decrease in their frequency of eating binges and 10 (50 per cent) reported a remission of bulimic symptoms with either imipramine or a subsequently administered agent. None of the remitted patients was receiving psychotherapy or other non-pharmacological treatment.

Theoretical Considerations

Why are thymoleptic drugs effective in bulimia? Two general hypotheses have been proposed: (a) bulimia may be related to major affective disorder, and hence thymoleptics ameliorate bulimic symptoms *via* the same mechanism by which they benefit major affective disorder (Pope and Hudson, 1984, 1986); or (b) thymoleptics may benefit bulimia and major affective disorder *via* independent mechanisms (Blouin *et al.*, 1987; Brotman, Herzog and Woods, 1984).

In favor of the latter hypothesis, various investigators have pointed out that the antidepressant and antibulimic effects of the various drugs do not always parallel one another; depression may improve while bulimia does not, or *vice versa* (Blouin *et al.*, 1987; Brotman, Herzog and Woods, 1984). However, although this undoubtedly occurs in certain cases, it appears in a majority of studies that most bulimic patients tended to improve in both their eating disorder and their depression if they responded to the drug.

In favor of the former hypothesis, it should be noted that not one, but a wide range of thymoleptic agents appear to benefit bulimia. These agents come from many different drug families and have little in common other than the fact that they are all known to be thymoleptics. Therefore it would seem odd if these various drugs also happened to share an antibulimic property, independent of their mutual thymoleptic property. The more parsimonious explanation would seem to be that the drugs' thymoleptic effect and antibulimic effect are mediated by a single mechanism rather than by two independent mechanisms (Pope and Hudson, 1986).

In further support of this hypothesis are several other observations: (1) the dose and plasma levels of antidepressants required to treat bulimia appear similar to those required to treat depression (Hughes *et al.*, 1986; Pope and Hudson, 1986); (2) the time course of antibulimic and antidepressant effects appears generally similar (Pope and Hudson, 1986); and (3) in the one study which calculated the correlation between improvement in depression and in bulimia, a significant correlation was found (Pope *et al.*, 1983). To these observations must be added the evidence suggesting a relationship between bulimia and major affective disorder on the basis of phenomenologic (Hudson *et al.*, 1983, 1989b; Walsh *et al.*, 1985) and family (Hudson *et al.*, 1989a) studies.

At present, then, the most economical explanation for the above observations would seem to be that bulimia is in some way related to major affective disorder, and that thymoleptic agents benefit bulimia *via* the same mechanism (albeit presently unknown) by which they benefit major affective symptoms.

Granting the above as a tentative working hypothesis, it follows that newer agents for the treatment of major affective disorder, as they become available, may well represent promising treatments for bulimia as well. With the addition of such agents to the therapeutic armamentarium, it should become possible to offer successful pharmacological treatment to a large majority of the bulimic population.

References

Agras, W. S., B. Dorian, B. G. Kirkley, B. Arnow and J. Bachman (1987). Imipramine in the treatment of bulimia: a double-blind controlled study. *International Journal of Eating Disorders* **6**, 29–38.

Blouin, A. G., J. H. Blouin, E. L. Perez, T. Bushnik, E. Mulder and C. Zuro (1987). Bulimia treated with desipramine and fenfluramine. Paper presented at the American Psychiatric Association Annual Meeting, Chicago, 13 May 1987.

Bogoch, S. and J. Dreyfus (1975). *The Broad Range of Use of Diphenylhydantoin: Bibliography and Review*, Vol. I. Dreyfus Medical Foundation, New York.

Braithwaite, R. A., R. Goulding, G. Theano, J. Bailey and A. Coppen (1972). Plasma concentration of amitriptyline and clinical response. *Lancet* **1**, 1297–1300.

Brotman, A. W., D. B. Herzog and S. W. Woods (1984). Antidepressant treatment of bulimia: the relationship between bingeing and depressive symptomatology. *Journal of Clinical Psychiatry* **45**, 7–9.

Chevlen, E. M. (1984). The adjunctive use of lithium carbonate in the management of bulimia resistant to antidepressant therapy. Paper presented at the First International Conference on Eating Disorders, New York, 8 April 1984.

Cole, W. and Y. D. Lapierre (1986). The use of tryptophan in normal-weight bulimia. *Canadian Journal of Psychiatry* **31**, 755–756.

Costa, E. and S. Garattini (Eds) (1970). *International Symposium on Amphetamines and Related Compounds*. Raven Press, New York.

Crane, R. A., V. Raskin, M. Weiler, J. Perri, T. H. Jobe, J. Anderson and B. Burg (1987). Nomifensine treatment of bulimia: results of an open trial. *International Journal of Eating Disorders* **6**, 427–430.

Damlouji, N. F. and J. M. Ferguson (1984a). Trazodone-induced delirium in bulimic patients. *American Journal of Psychiatry* **141**, 434–435.

Damlouji, N. F. and J. M. Ferguson (1984b). Trazodone in the treatment of bulimic patients. Paper presented at the First International Conference on Eating Disorders, New York, April 1984.

Feighner, J., G. Aden, L. F. Fabre, K. Rickels and R. T. Smith (1983). Comparison of alprazolam, imipramine, and placebo in the treatment of depression. *Journal of the American Medical Association* **249**, 3057–3064.

Ferguson, J. M. (1987). Treatment of an anorexia nervosa patient with fluoxetine. *American Journal of Psychiatry* **144**, 1239.

Freeman, C. P. L. (1986). Fluoxetine treatment for bulimia. Paper presented at the Second International Conference on Eating Disorders, New York, 19 April 1986.

Green, R. S. and J. H. Rau (1974). Treatment of compulsive eating disturbances with anticonvulsant medication. *American Journal of Psychiatry* **131**, 428–432.

Green, R. S. and J. H. Rau (1977). The use of diphenylhydantoin in compulsive eating disorders: further studies. In *Anorexia Nervosa*, ed. by R. A. Vigersky. Raven Press, New York.

Greenway, F. L., W. T. Dahms and D. A. Brag (1977). Phenytoin as a treatment of obesity associated with compulsive eating. *Current Therapeutic Research* **21**, 338–342.

Herridge, P. L. and H. G. Pope Jr (1985). Treatment of bulimia and rapid-cycling bipolar disorder with sodium valproate. *Journal of Clinical Psychopharmacology* **5**, 229–230.

Horne, R. L. (1984). Bupropion in the treatment of bulimia. Paper presented at the First International Conference on Eating Disorders, New York, 8 April 1984.

Horne, R. L., J. M. Ferguson, H. G. Pope Jr, J. I. Hudson, C. G. Lineberry, J. Ascher and A. Cato (1989). Treatment of bulimia with bupropion: a multi-center controlled trial. *Journal of Clinical Psychiatry*, in press.

Hsu, L. K. G. (1984). Treatment of bulimia with lithium. *American Journal of Psychiatry* **141**, 1260–1262.

Hudson, J. I. and H. G. Pope Jr (1987). Newer antidepressants in the treatment of bulimia nervosa. *Psychopharmacology Bulletin* **23**, 52–57.

Hudson, J. I., H. G. Pope Jr, J. M. Jonas and D. Yurgelun-Todd (1983). Phenomenologic relationship of eating disorders to major affective disorder. *Psychiatry Research* **9**, 345–354.

Hudson, J. I., H. G. Pope Jr, J. M. Jonas, D. Yurgelun-Todd and F. R. Frankenburg (1989a). A controlled family history study of bulimia. *Psychological Medicine*, in press.

Hudson, J. I., H. G. Pope, Jr, D. Yurgelun-Todd, J. M. Jonas and F. R. Frankenburg (1989b). A controlled study of lifetime prevalence of affective and other psychiatric disorders in bulimic outpatients. *American Journal of Psychiatry*, in press.

Hughes, P. L., L. A. Wells, C. J. Cunningham and D. M. Ilstrup (1986). Treating bulimia with desipramine: a placebo-controlled double-blind study. *Archives of General Psychiatry* **43**, 182–186.

Jonas, J. M. and M. S. Gold (1986). Naltrexone reverses bulimic symptoms. *Lancet* **1**, 807.

Jonas, J. M. and M. S. Gold (1987). Treatment of antidepressant-resistant bulimia with naltrexone. *International Journal of Psychiatry in Medicine* **16**, 305–309.

Jonas, J. M., H. G. Pope Jr and J. I. Hudson (1983). Eating disorders and antidepressants. *Journal of Clinical Psychopharmacology* **3**, 59–60.

Judd, L. L., D. S. Janowsky, D. S. Segal and L. Y. Huey (1980). Naloxone-induced behavioral and physiological effects in normal and manic subjects. *Archives of General Psychiatry* **37**, 583–586.

Kaplan, A. S. (1987). Anticonvulsant treatment of eating disorders. In *The Role of Drug Treatments for Eating Disorders*, ed. by P. E. Garfinkel and D. M. Garner. Brunner/Mazel, New York, pp. 96–123.

Kaplan, A. S., P. E. Garfinkel and D. M. Garner (1987). Bulimia treated with carbamazepine and imipramine. Paper presented at American Psychiatric Association Annual Meeting, Chicago, 13 May 1987.

Kaplan, A. S., P. E. Garfinkel, P. L. Darby and D. M. Garner (1983). Carbamazepine in the treatment of bulimia. *American Journal of Psychiatry* **140**, 1225–1226.

Kennedy, S. H., N. Piran and P. E. Garfinkel (1985). Monoamine oxidase inhibitor therapy for anorexia nervosa and bulimia: a preliminary trial of isocarboxazid. *Journal of Clinical Psychopharmacology* **5**, 279–285.

Kennedy, S. H., N. Piran and P. E. Garfinkel (1986). Isocarboxazid in the treatment of bulimia. *American Journal of Psychiatry* **143**, 1495–1496.

Klein, D. F., R. Gittleman, F. Quitkin and A. Rifkin (1980). *Diagnosis and Drug Treatment of Psychiatric Disorders: Adults and Children*, 2nd edn. Williams and Wilkins, Baltimore.

Krahn, D. and J. Mitchell (1985). Use of L-tryptophan in treating bulimia. *American Journal of Psychiatry* **142**, 1130.

Kupfer, D. J., I. Hanin, D. G. Spiker, T. Grau and P. Coble (1977). Amitriptyline plasma levels and clinical response in primary depression. *Clinical Pharmacology and Therapeutics* **22**, 904–911.

Lechin, F., B. Vander Dijs, F. Gomez, L. Arocha, E. Acosta and E. Lechin (1983). Distal colon motility as a predictor of antidepressant response to fenfluramine, imipramine and chlorimipramine. *Journal of Affective Disorders* **5**, 27–35.

McElroy, S. L., P. E. Keck Jr and H. G. Pope Jr (1987). Sodium valproate: its use in primary psychiatric disorders. *Journal of Clinical Psychopharmacology* **7**, 16–24.

McGrath, P. J., E. M. Quitkin, J. E. Stewart, M. Liebowitz, A. Fyer and S. Davies (1981). An open clinical trial of mainserin. *American Journal of Psychiatry* **138**, 530–532.

Mendels, J. (1983). Eating disorders and antidepressants. *Journal of Clinical Psychopharmacology* **3**, 59.

Mitchell, J. E. and R. Groat (1984). A placebo-controlled, double-blind trial of amitriptyline in bulimia. *Journal of Clinical Psychopharmacology* **4**, 186–193.

Mitchell, J. E., D. E. Laine, J. E. Morley and A. S. Levine (1986). Naloxone but not CCK-8 may attenuate binge-eating behavior in patients with the bulimia syndrome. *Biological Psychiatry* **21**, 1399–1406.

Mitchell, J. E., R. L. Pyle, E. D. Eckert, C. Pomeroy, D. Hatsukami and R. Zimmerman (1987). Antidepressants vs group therapy in the treatment of bulimia. *Psychopharmacology Bulletin* **23**, 41–44.

Moore, D. C. (1977). Amitriptyline therapy in anorexia nervosa. *American Journal of Psychiatry* **134**, 1303–1304.

Moore, S. L. and S. M. Rakes (1982). Binge-eating — therapeutic response to *diphenylhydantoin: case report. Journal of Clinical Psychiatry* **43**, 385–386.

Nassr, D. G. (1986). Successful treatment of bulimia with nomifensine. *American Journal of Psychiatry* **143**, 373–374.

Okuma, T., K. Inanaga, S. Otsuki, K. Sarai, R. Takahashi, H. Hazama, A. Mori and M. Watanabe (1979). Comparison of the antimanic efficacy of carbamazepine and chlorpromazine: a double-blind study. *Psychopharmacology* **66**, 211–217.

Ong, Y. L., S. A. Checkley and G. F. M. Russell (1983). Suppression of bulimic symptoms with methylamphetamine. *British Journal of Psychiatry* **143**, 288–293.

Opler, L. A. and D. Hickley (1986). Alprazolam in the treatment of bulimia. *Journal of Clinical Psychiatry* **47**, 49.

Pope, H. G. Jr and J. I. Hudson (1982). Treatment of bulimia with antidepressants. *Psychopharmacology* **78**, 167–179.

Pope, H. G. Jr and J. I. Hudson (1984). *New Hope for Binge Eaters: Advances in the Understanding and Treatment of Bulimia.* Harper and Row, New York.

Pope, H. G. Jr and J. I. Hudson (1986). Antidepressant drug therapy of bulimia: current status. *Journal of Clinical Psychiatry* **47**, 339–345.

Pope, H. G. Jr, P. L. Herridge, J. I. Hudson and R. Fontaine (1986). Treatment of bulimia with nomifensine. *American Journal of Psychiatry* **143**, 371–373.

Pope, H. G. Jr, J. I. Hudson and J. M. Jonas (1983). Antidepressant treatment of bulimia: preliminary experience and practical recommendations. *Journal of Clinical Psychopharmacology* **3**, 274–281.

Pope, H. G. Jr, J. I. Hudson, J. M. Jonas and D. Yurgelun-Todd (1983). Bulimia treated with imipramine: a placebo-controlled, double-blind study. *American Journal of Psychiatry* **140**, 554–558.

Pope, H. G. Jr, J. I. Hudson, J. M. Jonas and D. Yurgelun-Todd (1985). Antidepressant treatment of bulimia: a two-year follow-up study. *Journal of Clinical Psychopharmacology* **5**, 320–327.

Rau, J. H. and R. S. Green (1978). Soft neurological correlates of compulsive eating. *Journal of Nervous and Mental Disease* **166**, 435–437.

Rau, J. H., F. A. Struve and R. S. Green (1979). Electroencephalographic correlates of compulsive eating. *Clinical Electroencephalography* **10**, 180–188.

Rich, C. L. (1978). Self-induced vomiting: psychiatric considerations. *Journal of the American Medical Association* **239**, 2688–2689.

Robinson, P. H., S. A. Checkley and G. P. M. Russell (1985). Suppression of eating by fenfluramine in patients with bulimia nervosa. *British Journal of Psychiatry* **146**, 169–176.

Roy-Byrne, P., H. Gwirtsman, C. K. Edelstein, J. Yager and R. H. Geruer (1983). Eating disorders and antidepressants. *Journal of Clinical Psychopharmacology* **3**, 60–61.

Sabine, E. J., A. Yonance, A. J. Farrington, K. E. Barratt and E. Wakeling (1983). Bulimia nervosa: a placebo-controlled double-blind therapeutic trial of mianserin. *British Journal of Clinical Pharmacology* **15**, 195S–202S.

Shader, R. I. and D. J. Greenblatt (1982). The psychiatrist as mind sweeper. *Journal of Clinical Psychopharmacology* **2**, 233–234.

Stephen, J. H. and J. W. Shaffer (1973). A controlled replication of the effectiveness of diphenylhydantoin in reducing irritability and anxiety in selected neurotic outpatients. *Journal of Clinical Pharmacology* **13**, 351–356.

Stewart, J. W., B. T. Walsh, L. Wright, S. P. Roose and A. H. Glassman (1984). An open trial of MAO inhibitors in bulimia. *Journal of Clinical Psychiatry* **45**, 217–219.

Walsh, B. T., M. Gladis, S. P. Roose, J. W. Stewart and A. H. Glassman (1987). A controlled trial of phenelzine in bulimia. *Psychopharmacology Bulletin* **23**, 49–51.

Walsh, B. T., S. P. Roose, A. H. Glassman, M. Gladis and C. Sadik (1985). Bulimia and depression. *Psychosomatic Medicine* **47**, 123–131.

Walsh, B. T., J. W. Stewart, S. P. Roose, M. Gladis and A. H. Glassman (1984). Treatment of bulimia with phenelzine: a double-blind, placebo-controlled study. *Archives of General Psychiatry* **41**, 1105–1109.

Walsh, B. T., J. W. Stewart, L. Wright *et al.* (1982). Treatment of bulimia with monoamine oxidase inhibitors. *American Journal of Psychiatry* **139**, 1629–1630.

Wermuth, B. M., K. L. Davis, L. E. Hollister and A. J. Stunkard (1977). Phenytoin treatment of the binge-eating syndrome. *American Journal of Psychiatry* **134**, 1249–1253.

Wold, P. (1983). Trazodone in the treatment of bulimia. (Letter). *Journal of Clinical Psychiatry* **44**, 275–276.

Zeigler, V. E., P. J. Clayton and J. T. Biggs (1977). A comparison study of amitriptyline and nortriptyline with plasma levels. *Archives of General Psychiatry* **34**, 607–612.

Part V

Appendices

Appendix 1
Diagnostic criteria

Diagnostic Criteria for Eating Disorders According to the Draft of the International Classification of Disorders (ICD 10) World Health Organization, 1987, 8896–8898 (shortened)

F 50 Eating Disorders

F 50.0 Anorexia Nervosa

Diagnostic guidelines

The disturbances 1–5 listed below are all necessary for the diagnosis.

1. There is a significant weight loss (Quetelet's body mass index, BMI, of 16 or less). Prepubertal patients may show failure to make the expected weight gain during the period of growth.
2. The weight loss is self-induced by (a) avoidance of 'fattening foods'; and one or more of the following: (b) self-induced vomiting; (c) self-induced purging; (d) excessive exercise; (e) use of appetite suppressants and/or diuretics.
3. A specific psychopathology whereby a dread of fatness and/or flabbiness of body contour persists as an intrusive overvalued idea, and the patient imposes a low weight threshold on herself.
4. A widespread endocrine disorder involving the hypothalamic–pituitary–gonadal axis, manifest in the female as amenorrhoea and in the male as a loss of sexual interest and potency (an apparent exception is the persistence

of vaginal bleeds in anorexic women who are on replacement hormonal therapy, most commonly taken as a contraceptive pill). Usually there are also other endocrine disturbances.

5. If onset is prepubertal, the sequence of pubertal events is delayed or even arrested (growth ceases; in girls the breasts do not develop and there is a primary amenorrhoea; in boys the genitals remain juvenile). With recovery, puberty is often completed normally, but the menarche is late.

F 50.1 Bulimia nervosa

Bulimia nervosa is a syndrome characterized by repeated bouts of overeating and an excessive preoccupation with the control of body weight, leading the patient to adopt extreme measures so as to mitigate the 'fattening' effects of ingested food. The term should be restricted to the form of the disorder that is related to anorexia nervosa by virtue of sharing the same psychopathology. The age and sex distribution is similar to that of anorexia nervosa but the age of presentation tends to be slightly later.

The disorder may be viewed as a sequel to persistent anorexia nervosa (although the reverse sequence may also occur). A previously anorexic patient may first appear to improve as a result of a gain in weight and possibly a return of menstruation, but a pernicious pattern of overeating and vomiting then becomes established. Repeated vomiting is likely to give rise to disturbances of body electrolytes and physical complications (tetany, epileptic seizures, cardiac arrhythmias, muscular weakness).

Diagnostic guidelines

The following four disturbances are all necessary for the diagnosis of bulimia nervosa:

1. There is a persistent preoccupation with eating, irresistible craving for food, and the patient succumbs to episodes of overeating in which large amounts of food are consumed in short periods of time.
2. The patient attempts to counteract the fattening effects of food by one or more of the following: self-induced vomiting, purgative abuse, alternative periods of starvation, use of drugs such as appetite suppressants, thyroid preparations or diuretics. When bulimia occurs in diabetic patients they may choose to neglect their insulin treatment.
3. The psychopathology consists of a morbid dread of fatness and the patient sets herself a sharply defined weight threshold, well below her premorbid weight, which she then considers her optimum of 'healthy' weight.
4. There is often, but not always, a history of an earlier episode of anorexia nervosa, the interval ranging from a few months to several years.

Differential diagnosis

(i) upper gastrointestinal disorders;
(ii) a more general abnormality of personality as the eating disorder may coexist with alcohol abuse and petty offences (e.g. shoplifting);
(iii) depressive disorder.

F 50.4 Normal-weight bulimia

Normal-weight bulimia is a frequent but less specific and less severe disorder than bulimia nervosa, and constitutes a more heterogeneous group. The patients are more likely to be of normal or even excessive weight. The psychopathology is less clear-cut and there is no previous history of anorexia nervosa. The disorder occurs predominantly in females.

Diagnostic guidelines

1. The patient reports recurrent bouts of overeating which cause her distress.
2. Various attempts are made to counteract the fattening effects of food by self-induced vomiting, purgative abuse, alternating starvation, or the use of drugs calculated to reduce body weight.
3. The patient explains her behaviour as a loss of self-control, leading to loss of control over her body weight. Depressive symptoms may coexist.

Differential diagnosis

As for bulimia nervosa.

F 50.5 Obesity associated with other psychological disturbance

(i) Obesity as a reaction to distressing events.
(ii) Obesity as a cause of psychological disturbance.
(iii) Obesity as an undesirable effect of long-term treatment with neuroleptic or antidepressant drugs.

F 50.6 Vomiting associated with other psychological disturbances such as

(i) dissociative disorders (F 44);
(ii) hypochondriasis (F 45.2), where vomiting may be one of several bodily symptoms;
(iii) pregnancy, where emotional factors may contribute to recurrent nausea and vomiting.

F 50.8 Other eating disorders

F 50.0 Unspecified eating disorders

Diagnostic Criteria for Eating Disorders According to the Diagnostic and Statistical Manual for Mental Disorders — Revision (DSM-III-R) of the American Psychiatric Association (1987) (Shortened)

Anorexia Nervosa

Associated features

Some people with this disorder cannot exert continuous control over their intended voluntary restriction of food intake and have bulimic episodes (eating binges), often followed by vomiting. Many of these people also have bulimia nervosa.

Other peculiar behaviors concerning food are common. For example, people with anorexia nervosa often prepare elaborate meals for others but tend to limit themselves to a narrow selection of low-calorie foods. In addition, they may hoard, conceal, crumble, or throw away food.

Most people with this disorder steadfastly deny or minimize the severity of their illness and are uninterested in, or resistant to, therapy. Many of the adolescents have delayed psychosexual development, and adults have a markedly decreased interest in sex. Compulsive behavior, such as hand-washing, may be present during the illness and may justify the additional diagnosis of obsessive compulsive disorders.

Differential diagnosis

In depressive disorders and certain physical disorders weight loss can occur, but there is no disturbance of body image or intense fear of obesity.

In schizophrenia there may be bizarre eating patterns. However, the full syndrome of anorexia nervosa is rarely present; when it is, both diagnoses should be given.

In bulimia nervosa (without associated anorexia nervosa) there may be a fear of fatness, and weight loss may be substantial, but the weight does not fall below a minimal normal weight. In some instances anorexia nervosa occurs in a person with bulimia nervosa, in which case both diagnoses are given.

Diagnostic criteria

1. Refusal to maintain body weight over a minimal weight for age and height, for example, weight loss leading to maintenance of body weight 15 per cent

below that expected, or failure to make expected weight gain during period of growth, leading to body weight 15 per cent below that expected.
2. Intense fear of gaining weight or becoming fat, even though underweight.
3. Disturbance in the way in which one's body weight, size, or shape is experienced, for example, the person claims to 'feel fat' even when emaciated, believes that one area of the body is 'too fat' even when obviously underweight.
4. In females, absence of at least three consecutive menstrual cycles when otherwise expected to occur (primary or secondary amenorrhea). A woman is considered to have amenorrhea if her periods occur only following hormone, e.g. estrogen, administration.

Bulimia nervosa

The essential features of this disorder are: recurrent episodes of binge-eating (rapid consumption of a large amount of food in a discrete period of time); a feeling of lack of control over eating behavior during the eating binges; self-induced vomiting, use of laxatives or diuretics, strict dieting or fasting, or vigorous exercise in order to prevent weight gain; and persistent overconcern with body shape and weight. In order to qualify for the diagnosis, the person must have had, on average, a minimum of two binge-eating episodes a week for at least three months.

Eating binges may be planned. The food consumed during a binge often has a high caloric content, a sweet taste, and a texture that facilitates rapid eating. The food is usually eaten as inconspicuously as possible, or secretly. It is usually gobbled down quite rapidly, with little chewing. Once eating has begun, additional food may be sought to continue the binge. A binge is usually terminated by abdominal discomfort, sleep, social interruption, or induced vomiting. Vomiting decreases the physical pain of abdominal distension, allowing either continued eating or termination of the binge, and often reduces postbinge anguish. In some cases vomiting may itself be desired, so that the person will binge in order to vomit, or will vomit after eating a small amount of food. Although eating binges may be pleasurable, disparaging self-criticism and a depressed mood often follow.

People with bulimia nervosa invariably exhibit great concern about their weight and make repeated attempts to control it by dieting, vomiting, or the use of cathartics or diuretics. Frequent weight fluctuations due to alternating binges and fasts are common. Often these people feel that their life is dominated by conflicts about eating.

Associated features

Although most people with bulimia nervosa are within a normal weight range, some may be slightly underweight, and others may be overweight. A depressed mood that may be part of a depressive disorder is commonly observed. Some people with this disorder are subject to psychoactive substance abuse or dependence, most frequently involving sedatives, amphetamines, cocaine, or alcohol.

Differential diagnosis

In anorexia nervosa there is severe weight loss, but in bulimia nervosa (without associated anorexia nervosa) the weight fluctuations are rarely so extreme as to be life-threatening. In some instances anorexia nervosa occurs in a person with bulimia nervosa, in which case both diagnoses are given.

In schizophrenia there may be unusual eating behavior, but the full syndrome of bulimia nervosa is rarely present; when it is, both diagnoses should be given. In certain neurologic diseases, such as epileptic equivalent seizures, central nervous system tumors, Klüver–Bucy-like syndromes, and Kleine–Levin syndrome, there are abnormal eating patterns, but the diagnosis of bulimia nervosa is rarely warranted; when it is, both diagnoses should be given. Binge-eating is often a feature of borderline personality disorder in females. If the full criteria for bulimia nervosa are met, both diagnoses should be given.

Diagnostic criteria

A Recurrent episodes of binge-eating (rapid consumption of a large amount of food in a discrete period of time).
B A feeling of lack of control over eating behavior during the eating binges.
C The person regularly engages in either self-induced vomiting, use of laxatives or diuretics, strict dieting or fasting, or vigorous exercise in order to prevent weight gain.
D A minimum average of two binge-eating episodes a week for at least three months.
E Persistent overconcern with body shape and weight.

Rumination disorder of infancy

Diagnostic criteria

A Repeated regurgitation, without nausea or associated gastrointestinal illness, for at least one month following a period of normal functioning.
B Weight loss or failure to make expected weight gain.

Eating disorder not otherwise specified

Disorders of eating that do not meet the criteria for a specific eating disorder.

Examples:

1. A person of average weight who does not have binge-eating episodes, but frequently engages in self-induced vomiting for fear of gaining weight.
2. All of the features of anorexia nervosa in a female except absence of menses.
3. All of the features of bulimia nervosa except the frequency of binge-eating episodes.

Appendix 2
Self-report instruments for the assessment of relevant symptoms in eating disorders

The Anorexia Nervosa Inventory for Selftraining (ANIS)*

ANIS 32

*A*norexia *N*ervosa *I*nventory for *S*elf-rating

	FACTORS						
	I	II	III	IV	V	VI	TOT
	FIG	INS	ANA	NAE	SX	BUL	

To be filled out by patient:

Family name: ____________________ Height: ____________________ (cm)
First name: ____________________ Weight: ____________________ (kg)
Date of birth: ____________________ Today's date: ________________

Please read the following statements carefully. Decide to what extent each statement applies to you by making an X in one of the six columns on the right (applies not at all, ... applies very much). Make your judgements according to your current (today's) state. Please fill out the questionnaire carefully, quickly and on your own. Don't forget any items.

*Copyrights with the author (Fichter and Keeser, 1989).

	Applies not at all	Applies a little	Applies moderately	Applies considerably	Applies pretty much	Applies very much
1. I cannot stand boredom at all	0	1	2	3	4	5
2. Many demands are put on me which I can hardly cope with	0	1	2	3	4	5
3. I am afraid of becoming too fat	0	1	2	3	4	5
4. Deep inside I feel inferior and helpless	0	1	2	3	4	5
5. Thinking of sexual contacts makes me feel very anxious	0	1	2	3	4	5
6. I tend to terminate a meal not when I am sated but rather when I have reached the limit I regard appropriate for my figure	0	1	2	3	4	5
7. When I have eaten I feel sick	0	1	2	3	4	5
8. I have rituals, obsessions or obsessive acts concerning eating	0	1	2	3	4	5
9. I often feel hungry but try to overcome and control this feeling	0	1	2	3	4	5
10. When I start eating it can happen that I experience an irresistible impulse to eat till I burst	0	1	2	3	4	5
11. Compared to others I am quite conscientious and exact in whatever I do	0	1	2	3	4	5
12. Having a good figure is very important to me and I often check myself in a mirror	0	1	2	3	4	5
13. It is hard for me just to sit around and do nothing	0	1	2	3	4	5
14. I feel pressured by the expectations others have of me	0	1	2	3	4	5

	Applies not at all	Applies a little	Applies moderately	Applies considerably	Applies pretty much	Applies very much
15. I try to keep up a diet and eat as little fat and carbohydrates as possible (potatoes, sweets, etc.)	0	1	2	3	4	5
16. I feel bloated and empty	0	1	2	3	4	5
17. After eating I feel stuffed	0	1	2	3	4	5
18. It embarrasses me to see other people sexually aroused	0	1	2	3	4	5
19. I am not totally honest about my actual eating habits	0	1	2	3	4	5
20. I feel there is no sense in striving for achievement in life, since all my efforts will not change anything	0	1	2	3	4	5
21. Every time I succeed in fasting for a certain length of time I am proud of it	0	1	2	3	4	5
22. I feel less well after meals than before	0	1	2	3	4	5
23. Occasionally I negotiate or bargain about the things I eat (e.g. I'm gonna eat this, if I don't have to eat that)	0	1	2	3	4	5
24. There is a point in eating at which I can hardly stop	0	1	2	3	4	5
25. Because of the many demands and expectations that others have of me, I feel that I am not the master of my life	0	1	2	3	4	5
26. Kissing makes me anxious	0	1	2	3	4	5
27. I often hesitate and procrastinate before I start eating	0	1	2	3	4	5
28. After the meal I feel so sick that I would like to throw up	0	1	2	3	4	5

	Applies not at all	Applies a little	Applies moder-ately	Applies consider-ably	Applies pretty much	Applies very much
29. After eating I worry about gaining too much weight	0	1	2	3	4	5
30. Whenever I start to do something I feel compelled to do it exactly and perfectly	0	1	2	3	4	5
31. I am tense and restless	0	1	2	3	4	5
32. I think that I have answered all questions truthfully	0	1	2	3	4	5

Scoring of the ANIS: Add the scores as marked by the patient for each factor:

		Item
Factor I	Figure consciousness Maximal value 50 pts	3, 6, 9, 12, 15, 19, 21, 23, 27, 29
Factor II	Insufficiency Maximal value 35 pts	2, 4, 14, 16, 20, 25, 31
Factor III	Anankasm Maximal value 25 pts	1, 8, 11, 13, 30
Factor IV	Negative effect of meals Maximal value 20 pts	7, 17, 22, 28
Factor V	Sexual anxieties Maximal value 15 pts	5, 18, 26
Factor VI	Binge-eating Maximal value 10 pts	10, 24
Total ANIS scale	Maximal value 155 pts	Sum of items 1–31

For scoring, the additional item 32 is disregarded. For calculation of the score for each subscale, add the item scores and divide by the number of items in the subscale.

References

Fichter, M. M. and W. Keeser (1980). Das Anorexia-Nervosa Inventar zur Selbstbeurteilung (ANIS). *Archiv für Psychiatrie und Nervenkrankheiten* (= *Europ. Arch. Psychiat. Neurol. Sci.*) **228**, 228–239.

Fichter, M. M., M. Elton, L. Sourdi, S. Weyerer and G. Koptagel-Ilal (1988). Anorexia nervosa in Greek and Turkish adolescents. *Europ. Arch. Psychiat. Neurol. Sci.* **336**, 200–212.

Body-image Screening Scale (BISS)
by Fichter

Name ....Today's date ....

Please imagine a photo of yourself on which your size corresponds to the length of the arrow below. Please indicate the width of certain body parts (head, waist, ...) with a mark as shown in the upper right picture. Make the marks so that the estimated width corresponds to your inner estimation and feeling about your body and its parts.

Head
widest part

Shoulder
widest part

Waist
narrowest part

Hip
widest part

Upper Thigh
at beginning of beginning of leg
(inner side)

Calf
widest part

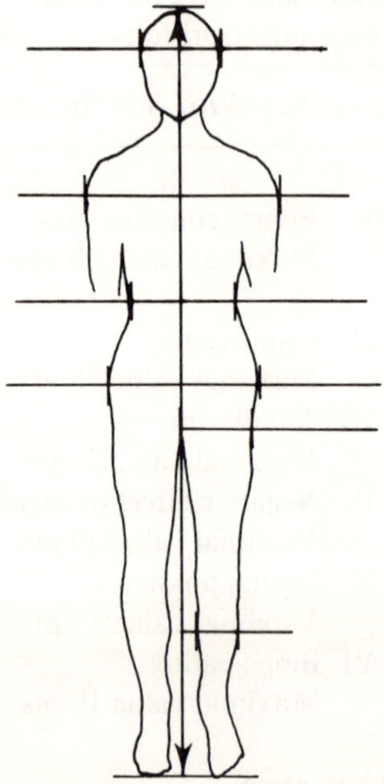

Index

ABC of behaviour 281
Abdominal fullness 73
Acetoacetate 239
Achievement orientation 63, 65, 277
Acid--base abnormality 74
Addiction 276
Adipsia 151, 152
Adolescence 22, 84–98
Adrenal gland 236
α-Adrenoreceptors 224
Aetiological factors 9
Affective disorders 26, 28, 76, 94, 100, 112–25, 131, 134, 137, 138, 335
Affective illness 22, 27, 135
Affective illness hypothesis 238, 251
Alcohol abuse 19, 27, 64, 91, 116, 133, 276, 288
Amenorrhoea 20, 25, 77, 88, 96, 215, 258, 259, 262, 349
American Psychiatric Association 34, 38, 126
Amitryptiline 200, 331
Amphetamine 24, 196, 199
Animal model of controllability 214
Anorexia nervosa 5, 17, 18, 24–6, 31–4, 85, 87, 92, 95, 99, 114, 135, 139, 169–72, 208, 210, 240, 244, 248, 251, 263, 266, 297, 304, 320, 346, 348
Anorexia Nervosa Inventory for Self-assessment (ANIS) 96
Anorexia Nervosa Inventory for Self-rating (ANIS) 62, 66, 67
Anorexia Nervosa Inventory for Self-training (ANIS) 352–5
Anorexic agents 195
Antecedent anorexia nervosa 29
Antecedents 21–2, 34
Anthropological perspective 6
Anthropological theory 211
Anticonvulsant drugs 203, 333, 335
Antidepressant drugs 86, 122, 131, 195, 331, 336, 337
Antidiet model 7, 276, 277
Anxiety 37, 64, 133, 283, 301
Anxiety-reduction model 293–5
Anxiety theory 211
Aphagia 146, 151, 152
Appetite 149, 189, 193, 195, 197, 312
Appetite control 188, 192, 202
Appetite disorder 548
Appetite regulation 203
Appetite suppressants 24, 47, 72, 101, 109, 345, 346
Arousal dysfunctions 152–3
Assertiveness training 293
Assessment 17–56
Attrition 27
Autogenic training 282
Autonomic nervous system 148

Beck Depression Inventory 135
Behavioural models 293–8
Behavioural observation 277–8
Behavioural treatment 292–307
Benzodiazepines 203
Bereavement 208, 214
Binge Eating Scale 44
Binge Scale 44
Bioenergetics 282, 325
Biological factors 10
Biological markers 117, 238, 245
Bipolar disorders 113
Bisexuality 104
Blood–brain barrier 238
Blood pressure 225
BMI (body mass index) 224, 311, 345

Body dissatisfaction 102, 121
Body experience 323, 325
Body image 6, 63, 68, 102
Body image disturbances 60, 63, 282, 320–30
  all-pervasive feeling of 8
Body Image Screening Scale (BISS) 356
Body mass index (BMI) 224, 311, 345
Body-oriented therapies 279, 282, 304, 324–7, 325
Body Shape Questionnaire (BSQ) 51
Body size distortion 322
Body size estimation techniques 52–3
Body weight 88, 90, 121, 135, 151, 189, 241, 247, 251, 259, 263, 348
  regulation 145–59, 190
  see also Ideal body weight
Bombesin 197
Boredom 211
Brain mechanisms 145–59
Brain stimulation 156
Breathing exercises 327
BROCA formula 90
Broken homes 90
Bulimanorexia 3, 87, 93, 94, 189, 211
Bulimia Test (BULIT) 44
Bulimic Investigatory Test (BITE) 44
Bulivomia 3
Butorphanol tartrate 200

Cachectin (tumor necrosis factor) 215
Caffeine 189, 203
Carbohydrates 23, 74, 120, 184, 195, 225, 227, 231, 238, 249
Cardiac arrhythmias 25
Cardiac functioning 79
Catharsis exercises 279
Cephalic phase reflexes 194
Cerebrospinal fluid (CSF) 157, 226
Chewing and spitting out of food 72
Childhood 106, 320
Chlorophenylpiperazine 231
Chlorphentermine 196
Cholecystokinin (CCK) 160–4, 171, 197, 198
Clinical assessment 17–36
Clinical Eating Disorder Rating Instrument (CEDRI) 39–40, 58
Clomiphen 237
Clonidine 249
  test 241, 244
CNS lesions 78
Coagulation 78
Cognitive approach 120
Cognitive behavioural techniques 130, 324
Cognitive model 295–6
Cognitive restructuring 297
Cognitive strategies 273, 293
Cognitive therapy 284–5
Communication exercises 282
Confidentiality 275
Consequences of bulimic behaviour 278
Constipation 25
Contraceptive pill 346
Controlled therapy studies 298–302
Coping 278
Corpus luteum 263
Corticotropin-releasing factor (CRF) 209, 213, 215–18
Cortisol 91, 241, 243, 248, 251
Course of illness 18, 112, 115, 126–41, 303
  in men 108–9
Craving for food 346
Cyclic AMP 224
Cyproheptadine 200

Dance therapy 282
Denial of hunger 183
Denial of symptoms 39–41, 64
Dental problems 73
Depression 37, 62, 63, 68, 76, 94, 100, 112–18, 122, 133, 135, 184, 210, 214, 224, 251, 273, 301, 336, 337
Depressive mood 93, 119
Depressive symptoms 26, 120–2
Depressive syndromes 116
Depressive thoughts 60, 63, 277
Desipramine 336, 337
Dexamethasone 212
Dexamethasone suppression test (DST) 76, 88, 90, 91, 117, 236, 241, 242, 244, 251
Diabetes mellitus 77
Diagnostic and Statistical Manual of Mental Disorders (DSM-III) 4, 118, 127, 134, 136
Diagnostic and Statistical Manual of Mental Disorders — Revised (DSM-III-R) 27–31, 34, 38–41, 58, 69, 84–6, 103, 132, 292, 348

Diagnostic criteria 17, 345–51
Diagnostic Interview Schedule (DIS) 58, 135
Diagnostic status 17–36
Dichotomous thinking 120, 284
Diet 120
  palatability of 146, 182
Dietary chaos syndrome 3, 189
Dietary restraint 45, 46
Diethylpropion 196
Dieting 7, 102, 203, 311
  intermittent 268
Disinhibited dieter 310
Dissatisfaction with body 322
Diuretics 24, 47, 72, 74, 101, 345, 346, 350
Dominance among parents 60
Dopamine 152, 213
Dopaminergic agonists 147
Dorsolateral hypothalamus (DLH) 146
Drinking 155
Drive for thinness 121
Duration of disease 100
Dutch Eating Behaviour Questionnaire (DEBQ) 45
Dynorphin 213
Dysfunctional beliefs and values 285
Dysfunctional cognitive schemata 60
Dysfunctional (irrational) thoughts 284–5

Eating attitudes 133
Eating Attitudes Test (EAT) 51, 102
Eating behaviours 130–4, 136, 277–82
Eating diaries 41
Eating Disorder Examination (EDE) 39–41, 50, 58, 62, 66–8
Eating Disorder Inventory (EDI) 51, 102, 121, 135
Eating disorders 348
  not otherwise specified 351
Eating-habit control model 293
Eclectic treatment 130
Educational standard 100
Electrical stimulation 146, 147, 151, 155
Electroencephalographic (EEG) abnormalities 78
Electrolyte disturbances 25
Electrolytic lesions 146
Emotional expression 277, 283–4
Emotional perception 279
Enamel erosion 72
Endocrine dysfunctions 235–57
Endogenous depression 244
Endogenous opioid activation 213
Energy balance 297
Enmeshment 65, 66
Epidemiology 3, 86
Epileptic seizures 25
Epinephrine 152
Erosion of dental enamel 25
Errors of reasoning 285
Erysichton 3
Esophageal perforation 74
Esophageal rupture 75
Estradiol 77, 259–62
Exercise 20, 208, 282–3
  excessive 24, 47, 215, 345
Expectations 274
Exposure and response prevention 279, 295
External validity 66
Extrapyramidal motor system 152

Family conflict resolution 65
Family environment 22
Family Environment Scale (FES) 139
Family influences 34
Family isolation 65
Family pathology 59
Family system 274
Family therapy 136, 279, 285, 304, 315
Fasting 7, 63, 72, 79, 147, 239, 244, 249, 251
Fear of gaining weight 349
Feeding 161, 210
Feelings of insufficiency 63, 66, 68
Feighner's criteria 87, 90
Fenfluramine 27, 164–9, 195, 196, 198, 199, 202
Figure consciousness 68
Finger calluses 73
First-generation antidepressants 336
Fitness ideal 107
Fluoxetine 195, 336
Fluvoxamine 195
Focal psychotherapy 302
Folate deficiency 78
Follicle-stimulating hormone (FSH) 241, 264
Follicular phase 263, 265

Follow-up 115, 127, 132–4, 137, 296, 301, 303, 314–15
Food consumption 192
Food deprivation 147
Food intake 145–79, 181, 202, 235, 296, 311
  reduced 9, 238, 239, 244, 250
Foodaholic 310
Free fatty acids 250
Frontal cortex 148
Fullness 183, 185
Functional analysis 277–8

Gag reflex 23
Gamma-amino-butyric acid (GABA) 147
Gastric control 160–79
Gastric dilatation 169
Gastric emptying 151, 162, 167, 169–72, 175
Gastric inhibition hypothesis 162
Gastric perforation 74
Gastric rupture 75
Gastro-oesophageal reflux 172, 176
Gastronintestinal bleeding 75
Gastrointestinal disorders 347
Genetic transmission 117
Gestalt therapy 282
Global Assessment Scale (GAS) 135
Gluconeogenesis 239
Glucoreceptors 147
Glucose and glucose tolerance 77, 147, 169, 250
Glucostatic theory of hunger 147
Glycogen deposits 239
Goal-setting 297
Gonadal axis 258–69
Gonadal hormones 263
Gonadotrophin-releasing hormones (GnRH) 258
Gonadotrophine 237
Gonadotrophins 263, 266, 268
Group therapy 136, 276–7, 336
Growth hormone 150, 237, 240, 241, 246, 249–50
Guilt feelings 314

Hamilton Depression Scale (HAMD) 90–1, 93
Haute cuisine 149
Headache 73
Hedonic disinhibition hypothesis 149, 181
Hedonic factors 148–51
Here and now 275
Heterosexual behaviour 105
Hiatal hernia 75
High-density foods 211
Hoarding 155
Homework 283
Homosexuality 101–2, 104, 105, 107, 108
Hopkins Symptom Checklist (HSCL) 133
Hospitalization 287–8
Human starvation 240
Hunger 145, 148, 173, 176, 183, 188–207, 211, 223, 280
  role of hypothalamus in 151–3
β-Hydroxybutyric acid (BHBA) 118, 239, 248–50
5-Hydroxyindolylacetic acid (5-HIAA) 231
Hyperactivity 95, 96, 155, 214
Hyperaldosteronism 74
Hyperamylasemia 74
Hyperemesis gravidarum 75
Hyperinsulinema 151
Hyperlipidemic pancreatitis 74
Hyperorexia nervosa 3
Hyperphagia 5, 8, 146, 148, 150–1, 208, 216, 310
Hypochloremia 74
Hypoglycemia 77
Hypokalemia 74, 78
Hypokalemic neuropathy 78
Hyponatremia 74
Hypothalamic tumours 78
Hypothalamo–hypophyseal–adrenocortical axis 224, 240
Hypothalamo–hypophyseal–gonadal axis 223–4
Hypothalamo–hypophyseal–thyroid axis 224
Hypothalamo–pituitary–adrenocortical axis 241–4
Hypothalamo–pituitary–gonadal axis 258, 345
Hypothalamo–pituitary–thyroid axis 249
Hypothalamocentric theory 145–8, 157
Hypothalamus 145, 147, 216, 235

role in hunger 151–3
role in satiety 148–51
specific mechanism of 153–7
ventromedial 149, 157

ICD-10 4, 26–31, 34, 58, 69
Ideal body weight (Metropolitan Life Insurance Company) 241, 259
see also Body weight
Ideal of slimness 10, 63, 239, 277
Imipramine 336, 337
Impairment 136
Impulsivity 22
Individual deficiencies, perception of 10
Individual therapy 131, 300
Ineffectiveness 8, 320
Infertility 266
Ingestive behaviours 208–22
Insight-directed approaches 304
Insight-oriented short-term focal psychotherapy 130
Insufficiency 63, 66, 68
Insulin 24, 77, 146–8, 150, 157, 232, 238
Intercourse 105, 106
Interleukin-1 215
Intermittent dieting 268
Interoceptive perception 8
disturbances of 282
Interoceptive signals 277
Interpersonal relationships 22
Interpersonal stress model 293, 297–8
Interview techniques 39–41, 47, 49–50
Intrafamilial environmental conditions 117
Intragastric intubation 146
Ipecac 76
Irrational assumptions 120

Joint family activities 65
Junk foods 311

Lack of appetite 251
Lack of control over eating behaviour 350
Large neutral amino acids (LNAA) 120, 231, 238
Laxative abuse 23, 25, 62–4, 74, 75, 96, 101, 169, 214, 296, 310
Leisure activities 277
Lesch–Nyhan syndrome 211
Leukopenia 79
Life events and chronic difficulties 10
Lifetime rates 116
Lithium carbonate 336
Liver function 79
Long-term course 96
Longitudinal Interval Follow-up Evaluation — Baseline version (LIFE Base) 135
Loss of body weight 251
Loss of control 295
Loss of libido 63, 115
Loss of self-control 38
Low calorie diet 245
Luteal phase 259, 263, 265, 268
Luteinizing hormone (LH) 77, 241, 264
secretory pattern 237

Magnesium pemoline 336
Maintenance training 287
Major affective disorder 113, 335
Major depression 113, 114, 116, 214, 337
Male 99–111
Malnutrition 9, 11, 74, 215, 230, 242
Marital dissatisfaction 65
Masculinity 105
Massage 327
Masturbation 104
Mazindol 196
Medical complications 71–83
Medical problems 136
Melancholia 115
Menarche 346
Menstrual cycle 88, 258–69, 349
Menstrual dysfunction 263
Metabolic disturbances 150
Metergoline 200
MHPG (3-methoxy-4-hydroxy-phenylglycol sulphate) 224
Mianserin 331
Millon Clinical Multiaxial Inventory 139
Minerals 313
Minnesota Multiphasic Personality Inventory (MMPI) 240
Minor dysthymia 135
Mitral valve prolapse 76
Monitoring sheets 41, 43
Monoamine oxidase inhibitors 333, 336

Morbid dread of fatness 24, 31, 346
Motivation 19, 27, 192, 274
Moveable caliper technique 322
Munich fasting experiments 241–4, 247
Muscular paralysis 25
Myopathies 76

Naloxone 197, 199, 212, 213
Naltrexone 199
Natural course 134
Nausea 73, 173
Negative perception 120
Negative self-concept 321
Neuroendocrine abnormalities 95, 239
Neuroendocrine functions 117
Neurological functioning 77
Neurotransmitters 147, 195, 223–34
Nicotine 189, 194, 203
Noradrenaline 223–30, 250
Norepinephrine 147, 152, 216
Norepinephrine-induced feeding 217
Normal-weight bulimia 347
Nortriptyline 336
Nutrition 117, 201, 278, 279
Nutrition hypothesis 238, 239
Nutritional counselling 278–82, 308–19
  as sole means of treatment 316
  components of 311–16
Nutritional state 239

Obesity 6, 8, 22, 45, 146, 148, 150–1, 188, 211, 310, 347
Objective bulimic episodes 41
Objective measures 52
Objective overeating 41
Oligomenorrhoea 77, 259, 262
Onset of illness 88, 100
Opiate agonist 197
Opiate antagonists 335
Orthopaedic damage 101
Orthostatic challenge 119
Osteoporosis 79
Outcome of illness 115, 126–41
Overadjustability 275
Overconcern with body shape and weight 103, 350
Overeaters Anonymous 136
Overeating 23, 208, 211, 346
Overgeneralizations 120, 285
Overvalued ideas concerning shape and weight 49–53
Ovulation 266

Palatability of diet 146, 182
Partner therapy 279, 285–6
Pathological pursuit of weight loss 24
Peer integration 63
Peptides 197–8
Perceived Family Interaction Scale 139
Perception 180–7
  of interoceptive stimuli 283, 320
  of satiety 185
Perceptual training 282–3
Perfectionism 121
Performance expectancy 65
Periodic overeating 22
Peripheral myopathy 78
Persistent overconcern with food and eating 63
Personality disorder 26–8, 131
Personality profile 108
Personalization 285
Phenmetrazine 196
Phentermine 196, 199
Phenylalanine 200
Phenylethylamines 195, 196
Phenylpropanolamine 199
Physiological mechanisms 166
Pleasure and pleasure exercises 282–3, 326
Pneumomediastinum 75
Ponderostat 146
Positive reinforcement 287
Postprandial glucose maximum 250
Potassium 25
Power struggle 289
Precipitating factors 278
Predictors 303
Predisposing factors 230
Pregnancy 266
Present State Examination 58, 59
Procioceptive perception 8
Procioceptive signals 277
Progesterone 259–62
Prolactin 231, 237, 241, 244, 247, 249
Prostaglandin E_1 224
Protein-deficient diet 244
Protein-losing gastroenteropathy 75
Psychodynamic group treatment 132
Psychodynamic psychotherapy 131

Psychodynamic theories 211
Psychological symptoms 133–4
Psychological therapies 273–91
Psychomotor therapy 327
Psychopathology, specific 24, 37–56
Psychopharmacological treatment 331–42
Psychopharmacology of hunger 188
Psychosexual development 103–8, 348
Psychosocial functioning 127, 134, 135
Psychosomatic illness 115
Psychotropic drugs 189, 194
Puberty 6, 346
Purgative abuse 47, 346, 347
Pursuit of thinness 11
Pyloric sphincter 162

Recovery rate 137, 138
Reduced food intake 9, 238, 239, 244, 250
Refeeding 147
Reframing 279
Regulation of appetite 203
Reinforcement techniques 149, 287, 297
Rejection by father 65
Rejection by mother 65
Relapse and its prevention 133, 136, 278, 279, 287, 288, 293, 296
Relaxation 282, 293, 327
REM latencies 245
Remissions 137
Renal impairment 25
Research diagnostic criteria (RDC) 133, 135, 162
Responsibility 286–7, 289
Restrained eating 182, 211, 310
Retrospective studies 131
Rhythmic exercises 282
Rigidity 65, 66
Rituals 293
Role-play 279, 283
Rumination disorder 23, 39, 64, 350

Saccharine 193
Salivary gland hypertrophy 74
Salivary gland swelling 25, 73
Satiety 145, 147, 148, 163, 169, 171, 173, 176, 180–207, 223, 280, 312
  cascade 191–4
  role of hypothalamus in 148–51
Satiety peptides 163
Schedule for Affective Disorders and Schizophrenia — Lifetime version (SADS-L) 135
Schedule of reinforcement 149, 297
Schizophrenia 116, 348
Self-awareness 326–7
Self-confrontation 325–6
Self-control 287
Self-esteem 10, 37, 63, 301, 321
Self-help groups 131, 279, 286–7
Self-induced vomiting 23, 47, 96, 101
Self-injurious behaviour 288
Self-monitoring 41–2, 48, 50–1, 293, 296, 297, 301, 302
Self-Rating Depression Scale (SDS) 90
Self-report instruments 42–6, 48, 51–2, 352–6
Self-responsibility 275
Semantic differential 107, 108
Sensitivity to weight gain 24
Sensory feedback 153
Sensory perception 185
Separation 108
Serotonergic activity 119
Serotonergic agonists 213
Serotonergic drugs 195, 203
Serotonin 166, 195, 216, 223, 230–3, 238
  inhibition of feeding 217
Sertraline 195
Serum bicarbonate 74
Serum salivary amylase levels 25
Set-point theory 31
Sex-role identification 103–8
Sexual anxieties 63
Sexual behaviour 63
Sexuality 68, 104–8
Sham feeding 163
Shoplifting 347
Sleep EEG 117
Slimness ideal 10, 63, 239, 277
Smoking 189
Social adjustment 134
Social Adjustment Scale (SAS) 134
Social class 6, 100
Social competence 277–9
Social eating 40
Social environment 285–6
Social skills 277, 282, 283
Social withdrawal 63

Sociocultural factors 9, 10
Socratic dialogue 285
Somatization 133
Somatomedin 215
Somatostatin 213
Specific psychopathology 24, 37–56
Standard test meals 46
Starvation 6, 23, 77, 79, 118, 119, 146, 147, 164, 171, 203, 214, 216, 235, 244, 346, 347
State-dependency 239
Stealing 133, 288
Steatorrhea 75
Stereotyped feminine role 310
Stimulus control 296, 297
Stress 208–22, 278
Stress-induced anorexia 214–15
Stress-induced eating 209–13
Stress-induced hyperphagia 210
Stroop technique 52
Structured Clinical Interview for DSM-III-R Diagnosis (SCID) 58
Structured Interview for Anorexia and Bulimia Nervosa (SIAB) 57–70, 103–4
Structured Interview for DSM-III Personality Disorders (SIDP) 139
Subjective bulimic episodes 41
Subjective overeating 41
Suboptimal body weight 31, 239
Substance P 213
Suicide attempts 115, 133, 288
Supportive psychotherapy 19
Sweetness 185
Sympathetic nervous system 227
Systolic blood pressure 229

Tail-pinch model 213
Test meals 46–8, 201
Tetany 25
Therapeutic community 276–7
Therapeutic pitfalls 288–90
Therapist-killer 289
Thin-fat people 3, 8
Thinness ideal 8, 102, 107
Thoughts of food and eating 193
Three-factor Eating Questionnaire 45
Thymoleptics 335, 337
Thyroid gland 236
Thyroid preparations 24
Thyroid-stimulating hormone (TSH) 76, 240, 249
Thyropin-releasing hormone (TRH) 76
Thyrotrophin-releasing factor (TRF) 244, 249
Total food abstinence 239, 241
Training of social skills 277
Tranylcypromine 336
TRF test 241
TRH test 117
Tricyclics 200, 333
Triiodothyronin (T3) 239, 240, 248, 250
Tryptophan 119, 120, 200, 231, 232
Tryptophan/LNAA quotient 238
Twins 9

Unipolar depression 115
Urge to eat 38, 166, 173, 175
Urinary infection 25

Vagotomy 150, 162
Vegetarian diet 246
Venn diagram 31
Ventromedial hypothalamus (VMH) 146
  lesions of 148–51
Ventromedial nucleus 148
Video confrontation procedure 326
Video distortion method 323, 324
Video recordings 323
Visual perception 323
Vitamin K 78
Vitamins 280, 313
Vomiting 19, 23, 26, 47, 64, 72, 75, 77, 96, 101, 296, 297, 310, 345–7, 350
Vulnerability 34

Weight control methods 47–9
Weight gain 93, 171, 313
Weight loss 24, 117, 311, 345
  pathological pursuit of 24
Weight-reducing diet 22, 120
World Health Organization 36